The Art of Opposition

Edited by Scott Prasser and David Clune

THE ART OF OPPOSITION

EDITORS

SCOTT PRASSER & DAVID CLUNE

connorcourt
PUBLISHING

The Art of Opposition

Edited by Scott Prasser and David Clune

Published in 2024 by Connor Court Publishing Pty Ltd

Connor Court Publishing Pty Ltd
PO Box 7257
Redland Bay QLD 4165
sales@connorcourt.com
www.connorcourt.com

Printed in Australia

ISBN: 9781922815903

Front Cover Ian James

CONTENTS

Foreword

How effective is parliamentary opposition? As Professor Joad would say, "it all depends on what you mean by parliamentary opposition". It also depends on what you mean by effectiveness.

There is opposition outside Parliament – extra-parliamentary opposition – and there can be opposition by Parliament to the executive which is, like some extra-parliamentary opposition, opposed to the system of government. This has been seen in the history of Britain, neatly detailed by Graham Maddox in this volume. *Parliamentary opposition* is opposition that works within an accepted constitutional framework. It is an opposition that accepts the legitimacy of the system and in which the system accepts the legitimacy of the opposition to operate as an opposition. As Graham Maddox shows, there was a transition from one to the other in Britain in the 18th Century.

Parliamentary opposition comes in multiple forms. One can offer a simple definition of opposition which is relational – responding to a proposition by rejecting it – but the problem is identifying the bodies engaging in that activity. The discussion is further complicated by the need to distinguish, primarily within a parliament that falls within the 'Westminster' family of legislatures, between opposition and the Opposition. The distinction is between behaviour and structure. There may be an overlap, the Opposition opposing, but the Opposition may not necessarily oppose instead supporting what the Government brings forward. There may be occasions when opposition comes from those who ostensibly are supporters of the body, here typically the Government, bringing forward the proposal, or from political parties that do not form the Government, that is, opposition parties, none of which is designated as the Opposition. One can have a situation where Government brings forward a proposal that is supported by the Opposition, but opposed by members of the governing party or parties or, indeed, by members drawn from all parts of the legislature.

One can identify objectively the behaviour as well as subjective views of the behaviour. One view of Opposition is simply that it exists to oppose. Thus, it is immediate and reactive. There is a separate but related view that one adheres unquestionably to the stance taken by one's party: "my party right or wrong". A different view permits of constructive opposition, where alternatives may be expressed, be it by the Opposition or by members of any party. Again, constructive opposition may be immediate, directed at a particular proposal, or more long term, advancing an alternative set of policies to those put forward by the incumbent administration.

In terms of effectiveness, it depends on what opposition is trying to achieve. There is opposition that has the goal of changing a particular outcome. That focuses on winning the vote. There is the Opposition which may ideally wish to change a particular outcome, but is concerned with the reality of winning the next election. The purpose of opposing is therefore to win the argument. One is immediate, appealing to those within the chamber, the other more long-term, appealing to voters outside the chamber. As David Docherty notes in this volume, not all opposition parties are power-seeking. The Opposition seeks to form the next Government.

There is also a systemic value, in essence contributing to the effectiveness of the political system, in ensuring that government cannot simply get its way without being challenged, be it by voice and vote. The Opposition ensures there is consistent critical scrutiny of whatever is brought forward; it may not result in opposing what is proposed, but the key point is that it may and that it is in the interest of the Opposition to see if there are flaws in the government's argument. The government has to anticipate that the Opposition is vigilant and therefore be prepared to argue its case in the full glare of the parliamentary arena.

Westminster parliaments tend to be plenary oriented and open, the parties engaging in public debate. The government may enjoy agenda control, but the Opposition has the oxygen of publicity. And the fact that opposition may come from elsewhere than the Opposition also ensures that Government has to be ready for friendly fire that may cause as much damage as that inflicted by the Opposition. Splits within the ranks of the Government's supporters are newsworthy in a way that 'the Opposition opposes the Government' is not.

In short, parliamentary opposition is neither simple nor unimportant. It matters, and matters greatly, for the health of the polity. Yet given its importance, what is remarkable is how little it is studied as opposition. There are studies of parliamentary voting behaviour, both in terms of aggregate data and specific instances, but little discussion of opposition, especially as structure. The fact that party cohesion tends to be the norm and that the Opposition, by virtue of being the Opposition, is not likely to defeat the Government may deter interest in the subject, but the dearth of scholarly studies is noteworthy. As Simone Wegmann notes in the conclusion, it is only recently that legislative scholars have started to pay more attention to oppositions in democracies

That dearth of material makes this volume especially welcome. It contributes significantly to our understanding, not only by focusing on Opposition *qua* Opposition, but also doing so through a breadth of scholarship. The work avoids the danger of being Westminster-centric, that is, looking at the subject from the perspective of the UK Parliament. Australia, like Canada, provides not only a Westminster parliament that has developed its own distinctive form of Opposition, but through its component states has experience of a range of Government-Opposition relations. This magisterial study helps establish two key points, both made by Wegmann, namely that the way in which Opposition operates has consequences, both legislative and extra-legislative, and that there is no one size fits all form of Opposition. It is a distinctive mode of executive-legislative relations, prevalent in nations of the

Commonwealth, with key features that distinguish it from other forms of parliamentary government, not least consensus systems, but each nation has developed its own system of Opposition.

This volume constitutes a major contribution to the literature on Opposition and is characterised by a stellar line-up of contributors, their analyses and insights enabling the reader to appreciate both how Opposition has developed in different polities and the nuances of each system. It is an essential work for understanding how legislatures go about fulfilling their key role in democratic polities.

Philip Norton

[Lord Norton of Louth]

Preface and

Acknowledgements

A formal, legitimate opposition able to criticise freely the government of the day is essential for the well-being of any democracy. It has long been a distinctive feature of the Westminster system, but other countries also have oppositions if not necessarily in the same form. In the United States with its presidential system and separation of powers there is no "government in waiting" as such but there is intensive, unfettered debate in Congress about a President's proposals. In many European nations, with their proportional voting systems and mixture of presidential and parliamentary structures, there are not only multi-party governments but also complex cross-partisan alliances that make up oppositions.

Despite the importance of oppositions in their various forms, opposition is a largely neglected area of study. This volume seeks to fill some of that gap.

Some recent trends make this an opportune time to study oppositions both in Australia and internationally.

One is that several long-term incumbent governments have moved to the opposition benches or seem to be about to. How they cope in this new role in holding government to account is as important as how well the new governments transition to office and manage the business of governing. At stake is the robustness of our democracy and the quality of the policies and administration that enrich our lives.

Another trend is that the movement of government to opposition, and opposition to government, has quickened. Electorates seem increasingly restless and less wedded to major political party allegiances, more easily frustrated with the way they are governed and less accepting of the status quo.

This is partly reflected in the declining proportion of votes now attracted by most of the major established parties across many western democracies. It has been accompanied by the growth of independents and minor and micro parties which, combined with the growth of extra-parliamentary movements, has the potential to shift the locus of opposition in political systems and, indeed, the very meaning of opposition itself and how it operates.

It is such developments which this volume has sought to identify, assess, and provide the background to. Hence the coverage across all Australian jurisdictions – federal and state – and several key international ones as well.

Of course, to achieve this we acknowledge, first and foremost, our over twenty different contributors from Australia and around the world. It was their support and enthusiasm that has allowed this volume to be so comprehensive and at the same time to probe some newly emerging issues. Our interactions with contributors were positive, our learnings from them great, and the final product as now compiled for all to read, we believe is distinctly worthwhile.

All this effort would be for nought without Anthony Cappello of Connor Court Publishing. It was Anthony who urged us to revive this project that had languished for a decade. And it is Connor Court Publishing investing its time and resources that not only allowed this topic to be covered, but also resulted in the volume's high production quality.

Lastly, we hope this volume is the beginning of further study and teaching about how the important institution of opposition can work better to make our democracies stronger.

Scott Prasser and David Clune

March 2024

Introduction

"Conflict Become Discussion": The Importance of Opposition

David Clune

The Opposition is a fundamental part of a traditional Westminster-type polity such as operates in Britain, Canada, New Zealand and Australia. It is the alternative government and, in time, usually becomes the actual government. In the interim, it holds the government to account as a by-product of trying to displace it. This system essentially emerged in Britain in the eighteenth century.

Graham Maddox in his outline in Chapter One of the philosophical and historical development of the concept of opposition from ancient Athens to the present concludes:

> Precious though it is to live in a free society, opposition signifies yet more than this. It marks the capacity of each person living in a society to think independently and to express opinion freely about how the community should be governed. In this light, opposition sets the seal on a democratic community, whose ideal surely is to acknowledge the innate capacity of all adult persons not legally disqualified to govern themselves.

He further observes:

> Since a community requires collective decision-making, it is acknowledged that individual persons cannot simply do as they please regardless of the consequences to others; but democracy gives as much latitude as possible while at the same time encouraging citizens to take part in the collective running of the community. Just as those with power tolerate opposing views, so a society becomes a tolerant one.

What a radical concept this is! Instead of the rulers hunting down and destroying opponents, as was the case for most of human history, they are invited (in a circumscribed way) to criticise legitimately as this is assumed to be in the long-term interests of the polity. GM Trevelyan has said that critics of autocratic monarchs in Europe envied the freedom of the House of Commons of James I where "some country gentleman, who had ridden up a few days before from his home beyond the Dorset Downs, rose in his seat to attack the highest minister of state, and was suffered to walk back unmolested through the darkening streets to his lodging in Holborn" (Trevelyan 1925: 104). This tolerance of opposition allows society to function "politically", as defined by Bernard Crick: "Politics is a bold prudence, a diverse unity, an armed conciliation, a natural artifice, a creative compromise ... it is conflict become discussion" (Crick 1992: 161).

The Opposition at Westminster has historically and significantly been known as His Majesty's Loyal Opposition. The word "loyal" implies that, if the opposition is not quite in the tent, it is not completely out of it either. A loyal opposition accepts the constitutional framework but not the policies of the incumbent government. It is a typically British pragmatic constitutional compromise. As Nigel Fletcher expresses it in Chapter 17:

> The name connotes an institution which combines insurgency with responsibility, dissent with respect. A body of people whose sole objective is to tear down and replace the government of the day is given official sanction for its endeavours, on the tacit understanding that they remain loyal to the Crown as the embodiment of the constitution. It is a curious and seemingly contradictory idea, but one which lies at the heart of the Westminster system, and on which the democratic settlement of the UK now rests.

Although the opposition thus plays a vital role in the political process - as important in its own way as the performance of the government it faces – it has been little studied. The aim of this book is to rectify some of that neglect.

Issues about opposition

John Howard in Chapter Five gives an insightful perspective on the role of an opposition leader from his experience of a total of almost five years in the job:

> I did not take the view that the Coalition should oppose just for the sake of being different. In my view, each policy initiative of the Hawke Government should be addressed on its merits. If it made sense and was in accord with the attitudes of the Coalition, the policy should be supported. Examples of such policies included deregulation of the financial system and reduction in levels of tariff protection.

In Howard's view, an effective opposition is one that "spends the minimum possible amount of time on the wrong side of the Speaker. This means that it must constantly have a policy agenda fit for the circumstances of the nation. It goes without saying that an opposition should approach elections with detailed policies, yet present them in a way which does not leave it vulnerable to attack". He stresses that internal unity "is essential if the transition from opposition to government is to occur".

Scott Prasser in Chapter Three analyses the challenges oppositions face in formulating credible and appealing policies:

> There are increasing expectations of oppositions in relation to the development and presentation of policy. They need to be more than critics of governments. To win office they need to do more than just rely on government mistakes. To be truly seen as 'governments in waiting', they need to have real policy options ready to implement. A more sophisticated electorate, the growing expertise of interest groups that are challenging governments as well as political parties in policy analysis, the complexity of modern policies, and the demands for improved rationality and 'evidence' in policies, all require oppositions to improve their policy efforts.

Rodney Tiffen examines the interaction of the media and oppositions in Chapter Four and concludes that audiences for the mainstream media are becoming more fragmented, in addition to declining audiences for some of the most important media of the past. Although the role of social media and local campaigning are increasing, the news media are still the central arena in which the inter-party conflict is pursued, but at the least it no longer has the unchallenged dominance it once did. These trends do not necessarily favour either government or opposition. They probably make governing more difficult, but the more fragmented politics and media make it more difficult for oppositions to mobilise majority size coalitions of support. So many conflicting forces are at work that the only safe prediction is that the future will not be a simple extrapolation from the past.

He adds: "As politics has become more professional, the trend towards negative campaigning has contributed to growing public cynicism about and distaste for both the major parties. What may be best for advancing immediate party interests may not be best for contributing to long-term democratic efficacy".

Upper house opposition

The nature of opposition in Australia has changed over the years. The lower house was usually rigidly controlled by the government to the opposition's disadvantage. However, traditionally, it was the forum in which the opposition leader went head-to-head with their governmental counterpart, particularly at Question Time. It was a gladiatorial contest that gave a talented opposition leader the chance to humble their opponent.

Although performance in the lower house remains important, it has, to an extent, been eclipsed in the digital age by the influence of media management and social media. Parliament has, nonetheless, become a source of opposition in a different way, with the rise in recent decades of upper houses where the crossbenches have the balance of power. This trend looks set to continue as independents and minor parties eat into the vote of the major parties. The use of a proportional representation voting system in most Australian upper houses strengthens the likelihood of lack of government control.

If those holding the upper house balance of power formulate an approach that rises beyond favours for votes, are constructive not destructive, and do not indulge in egotism or extremism, they can effectively scrutinise and improve government performance and legislation. They have powerful tools at their disposal, such as strong committee systems, the ability to amend bills, and motions to force the government to table official documents. Crossbenchers can also reform the procedures of the house to enhance their power. The upper house can thus become a permanent opposition, although a diverse one consisting of a constantly changing combination of forces.

Steffen Ganghof has provided a useful conceptual framework for such a system, calling it semi-parliamentarianism. He gives the following operational definition:

1. There is no direct (or popular) election of the chief executive or head of state.

2. The assembly [parliament] has two directly elected chambers.

3. Only the first chamber can dismiss the cabinet in a no confidence vote.

4. The second chamber has veto power over ordinary legislation that is not merely suspensory and/or cannot be overridden by a simple or absolute majority in the first chamber.

The advantage of such a system is that the lower house retains its traditional role under responsible government of making and breaking governments; responsible government in its other sense of scrutinising the executive on behalf of the electors becomes largely an upper house role. Ganghof concludes that "the empirical cases of semi-parliamentary government are the Australian Commonwealth and Japan, as well as the following five Australian states: New South Wales, South Australia, Tasmania, Victoria, and Western Australia" (Ganghof 2021: 36-7).

Nicholas Aroney and Ben Saunders in Chapter Two examine the way in which the framers of the Australian Constitution understood the role and nature of opposition within contemporary Westminster parliamentary systems. They observe that some of the framers of the Australian Constitution presciently "recognised that the Senate itself could constitute a form of opposition to the government". Aroney and Saunders further conclude that

> a certain idealism about the roles of opposition and parties went with those who supported the traditional picture of Westminster responsible government focussed on the lower house of Parliament, while the realists were those who feared a concentration of power in the prime minister, cabinet and lower house, and who called for a powerful Senate, representative of the peoples of the States, as a means of strengthening the capacity of the Parliament as a whole to be an effective check on the powers of the government. If the mix of parties operating within the Australian Senate today constitutes an even more effective form of opposition than those based in the lower house, it is due in part to the balance of power between the House of Representatives and the Senate that the framers more or less intended.

In Chapter Six, Scott Prasser gives a modern perspective on the role of the Senate as a source of opposition through a series of case studies of the passage of government legislation. He concludes:

> These case studies highlight that managing the Senate no longer means solely dealing with the formal opposition. Rather, to have legislation passed requires multiple negotiations across a wide range of players – minor parties like the now persistent Greens, micro parties whose existence is often ephemeral and whose views are diverse, mercurial Senators who are often in conflict with each other even if in the same party. These developments have challenged many once settled aspects of Australian government – executive government dominance over parliament, the acceptance of a government mandate (always a bit thin), the hegemony of the two major party system, and the very role of the traditional opposition as it operates in the Senate (Chalmers and David 2000-01).

Opposition in Australia

Part Two examines opposition in the Australian Commonwealth and State parliaments.

Although all basically adhere to the fundamentals of the Westminster system, it is interesting to note that state variants of opposition have emerged due to regional, cultural and economic differences.

Brendan McCaffrie analyses the Federal Labor Opposition's recovery from defeat in 2019 and subsequent victory in 2022, in spite of the challenges posed by the COVID pandemic. He concludes that the result largely supported

> the conventional wisdom about the battle between Australian governments and oppositions. When in a two-party contest, being more appealing than the alternative is frequently enough. However, the biggest electoral surprise in 2022 was the emergence of the "Teal" independents and the surge of the Greens. Should minor parties and independents continue to grow in strength, the conventional approach of being more appealing than the other major party may well not be enough. A politics in which both major parties' traditional supporters have palatable alternatives to vote for is one in which the major parties will need to work harder to appeal to those supporters.

Liz Dowd and Scott Prasser provide a detailed history of the resourcing of the Commonwealth government and opposition from Federation to the present. They conclude that if full discussion of all matters is a central task of parliament, "it is fundamental that both sides of the discussion are equipped to be able to have it". However, "while resources for governments have always been greater than for oppositions, the level of support for the executive government has increased dramatically in the last fifty years". The main cause of this deleterious disparity is that "decisions about resourcing for parliamentarians and oppositions remain firmly in the hands of executive government with little real parliamentary oversight, let alone wider public consultation and discussion". Concerns about the lack of resources for oppositions are echoed in several other chapters highlighting the importance of this issue.

Kevin Martin, from his perspective as Chief of Staff to three Queensland Opposition Leaders, highlights the adverse results of unicameralism on opposition and democracy in that State:

> In the absence of the brake of a second chamber on the powers of executive government, Queensland needs to explore enhancing the role of the opposition through providing it with resources that are independent of the intense oversight and control of the government of the day and which the opposition can utilise in whatever way it believes to be politically effective in holding government to account. Unless this occurs, one party domination of parliament and thus executive government will continue to be the rule. This is not good for the maintenance of democracy in Queensland.

Paul Williams echoes Martin's view about the damaging effect on democracy in Queensland of the lack of an upper house. He argues that Queensland politics are different owing to "a separate political culture itself shaped by a unique geography, economy and demography". This has led to long periods of government hegemony. However, on the rare occasions when governments have been defeated, this has usually been as a result of "major economic or political earthquakes". Williams concludes that

> government crisis alone is insufficient to induce defeat; mediocre administrations often win successive elections because voters have little confidence in lacklustre oppositions. The key to a transition to government in Queensland therefore rests with the quality of oppositions - party unity (and unity between parties in coalitions), the appeal of policy platforms, and accessible 'strong' leadership – as a measure of readiness for government.

This is a significant observation that other contributors have supported. The old cliché that "oppositions don't win elections, governments lose them" should be well and truly buried on the evidence contained in this book. As Rodney Tiffen comments in Chapter Four: "The central flaw in such conventional wisdom is that elections involve a preferential rather than an absolute decision. If an opposition is not seen as a viable alternative, then an unpopular incumbent may survive, the lesser of two evils, or the most palatable among a limited menu".

Clem Macintyre, John Williams and Rob Mainwaring conclude about South Australia:

> Over the past 50 years, the Parliament of South Australia has seen a fairly stable pattern of government and opposition. Most oppositions in that time have been close to government in terms of bare numbers on the floor of the House of Assembly. Yet despite this, since 1970 only two governments lost office after a single term and most have lasted for long enough to leave a considerable policy legacy in South Australia. Through this time, oppositions have struggled to be heard. There are only a few examples of an opposition attack making a significant mark upon the government of the day.

Significantly, they add:

> It is true that oppositions have been limited in their role by the way in which the parliamentary processes are determined by the government. At the same time, it is also true (especially over most of the past 50 years) that several (Liberal) oppositions in South Australia have allowed internal disagreements and a lack of discipline to distract them from the valuable contribution a strong opposition should make.

In his chapter on the Victorian Coalition Opposition, Terry Barnes reaches a similar conclusion about the slough of long-term opposition:

> For members of parliament, and aspiring MPs, opposition is a soul-destroying place. On both sides of politics, the careers of talented and committed people have been wasted as their expertise and careers are shunted aside by voters. If not defeated in a general election, experienced MPs, including former ministers, are often quick to make their exit rather than stay for the long haul back to government. As the days of real power recede into the past, the only thing helping opposition MPs in maintaining their commitment and morale is that each new day in opposition is one day closer to returning to government. In short, giving some hope that the wilderness years ultimately will be worth it.

He comments on the future prospects for the Coalition, particularly the Liberal Party:

> In some jurisdictions, there is little hope. The political scene has become so weighted in favour of one party of government, winning election after election, that the other is left in a state of near-permanent opposition, its frustration and powerlessness leading it to feed on itself and putting a return to government even more out of reach.

Rodney Smith, contrastingly, argues that in New South Wales the traditional disadvantages of opposition are now largely counter-balanced by a bicameral system in which the government lacks a majority in the upper house and strong extra-parliamentary scrutiny mechanisms such as the Independent Commission Against Corruption. He concludes that there is

> no necessary contradiction for an opposition between pursuing electoral victory and enhancing the contribution of parliament to democracy while still in opposition. The scrutiny and legislative successes of Labor (in combination with the crossbench) when in opposition between 1988 and 1995, followed by Labor's 1995 narrow election victory, is probably the best example of this; however, most subsequent oppositions have combined playing to the electorate and engaging with parliamentary processes to produce better legislation and more transparent government.

Unlike Queensland, South Australia and Victoria which have experienced long periods of one party hegemony, Narelle Miragliotta and Finley Watson find that since the consolidation of the party system in Western Australia, there has been "strong electoral competition with frequent government alternation. Of the 23 elections held since 1947, Labor has held office in ten instances, and the Coalition on 13 occasions. On average, state governments served 2.25 terms, suggesting that Western Australian oppositions are perceived by voters as credible alternative governments".

However, the 2021 election resulted in the smallest Opposition in the Western Australian Assembly since 1911, with the incumbent Labor Government winning 53 of the 59 seats. Miragliotta and Watson find this a concerning development:

> While opposition is central to parliamentary politics in the state, the average size of the opposition is shrinking, with governments eclipsing the opposition to a much greater extent in recent times. While this is not ideal, regular alternation in office between the main parties continues and so the systemic benefits of opposition are generally realised. However, the significantly reduced size of the Opposition affects its access to the resources needed to influence public opinion and debate. Across a range of different dimensions, the opposition's depleted legislative strength constrains its competitiveness in ways that are not likely beneficial for it, the government or ultimately voters.

Richard Herr provides a case study of the negative effect of reducing the size of an already small parliament: in 1998, the Tasmanian Legislative Assembly was reduced from 35 to 25 and the Council from 19 to 15. The motivation was the "resolve of the two major parties to eliminate the crossbench 'threat'." He concludes that the major parties "recognised, belatedly, that the 1998 reduction was a mistake and that it had seriously compromised the parliament in every direction, but nowhere more importantly than in its roles of oversighting and checking the government of the day". In 2022, the Liberal Government restored the lower house to 35. While populist criticism that there are "too many politicians" abounds, the Tasmanian example indicates that a certain "critical mass" of MPs is necessary for an effective parliament. Interestingly, David Docherty, in his examination of Canadian provincial legislatures in Part Three, reaches a similar conclusion.

A comparative perspective

In Part Three we look beyond Australia to give a comparative perspective on opposition. Nigel Fletcher says of the role of the Opposition in the House of Commons:

> Getting the balance right between kneejerk opposition and deep thinking about policy is one of the perennial challenges of strategy for any opposition seeking power. On the one hand they

wish to score political points and be seen to hold the government to account, whilst on the other they need to develop a clear and coherent agenda of their own that will appeal to the electorate. The two are by no means mutually exclusive, but they are frequently in tension. Particularly in the modern era, shadow ministers are expected to have a view on everything, and the temptation to denounce everything the government is doing is very strong. But they also face persistent questions about what they would do differently in office, how their alternative policy would work, and how they would pay for it.

He adds that although the opposition performs "a vital democratic role in holding the government to account and providing a credible alternative government to give the electorate a meaningful choice at elections … it still has nothing like the resources that are truly required to fulfil its fundamental roles of scrutiny and policy development".

Louise Thompson examines how minor parties have fared in that traditional bastion of the two-party system, the House of Commons. Nine minor parties were represented in the Commons after the 2019 election. She concludes that they have carved out a role for themselves by "strong collegiality and cross-party work" which "ensures some uniformity of information resources and which aids visibility on the parliamentary stage". This is an intriguing development, as some other houses (upper and lower) have experienced a centrifugal rather than centralising effect as the crossbench increases.

David Docherty surveys the role of oppositions in Canada at both federal and provincial levels. He argues that despite the obstacles facing them "opposition parties have managed to effectively challenge the government and force cabinets to be accountable for their actions". However, the downside is that

> the lack of resources and institutional rules that favour government have meant that the level of critical analysis offered by opposition parties is often reduced to negative attacks and attempts to embarrass the government. As a result, opposition parties rarely spend time developing and explaining their own policies and squander their chances to present voters with a viable positive alternative to the party in power. In this way, when a party in

opposition eventually unseats a government, they come into power
with a greater capacity to oppose than a capacity to govern.

Kenneth Kitts points out that the US political system has not
"institutionalised opposition to the same extent as the parliamentary
democracies with which the country otherwise has much in common.
There is no real equivalent to the loyal opposition tradition in the US – no
shadow government, opposition days, or fixed opportunities to question
the head of government". He attributes much of this to the separation of
powers doctrine James Madison inserted in the US Constitution: "Simply
put, the concept of opposition politics makes greatest sense when there
is a party that is demonstrably out of power – and that assumes there is
another party no less demonstrably in power. These assumptions do not
work, or at least work less well, in the US given the unique structure of
the Madisonian system".

In spite of this, Kitts argues that there is still a degree of unity despite
the diversity: "The [US] governmental system, characterised as it is by
a strong separation of powers and two-party dominance, lacks the clear
accountability and logic of its parliamentary counterparts. Similarly, the
concept of loyal opposition remains largely alien to most Americans
and difficult to effect in practice". Nonetheless, the American system
has managed to "capture the spirit of opposition politics, even if that
term is rarely invoked. Ironically, the same Madisonian structure that has
discouraged the rise of a defined loyal opposition tradition in the US has
also made it possible for the system to vent political steam and allow for
minority interests to be heard".

Simone Wegmann provides a comparative analysis of opposition in
Australia, Canada, Denmark, Finland, Germany, New Zealand, Norway,
Sweden and the United Kingdom. She concludes that a properly
functioning legislature and opposition are vital elements of a healthy
democracy, either old or new:

> Opposition behaviour in legislative chambers has both legislative
> and extra-legislative consequences. Implications for the function-
> ing of democracy are significant. Even though the crucial role of the

legislature for the consolidation of democracies has been highlighted in some [research] contributions, the legislature – and especially the opposition – has not figured prominently in this research tradition. The influence of the strong policy-making power of opposition players on public opinion, especially in more established democracies, clearly shows that the opposition is not only vital during the first years of democratic consolidation, but legislative organisation and the behaviour of opposition players remain crucial for the stability of established democracies.

The nature of Australian opposition

The title "opposition" raises a basic issue. Should it mean a total, unrelenting opposition to everything a government proposes? Or should it be more responsible: support the government if it is in the national interest and save the aggressive attacks for its failings? An opposition that is relentlessly negative can wound a government but incur popular displeasure for having nothing constructive to propose. On the other hand, a consensus-type opposition leader can be criticised for lacking the "killer instinct"; however, they can earn public approval for civility in political discourse. Perhaps the successful opposition leader needs to have a bit of the mongrel and a bit of the statesman.

Another challenge for an opposition is policy. Should it take to an election a collection of policies, driven by polling, that exploit every government weakness, but with little regard to their practicality and positivity? Irresponsibility is a temptation for an opposition – vigorously attacking unpopular government actions while privately admitting they are good policy. Or should an election program be a well-thought-out, well-researched body of reforms? Should a platform be based on appeals to sectional interests or those of the nation as a whole? Should anodyne, "small target" policies be publicly promoted to mask a more radical agenda in government? The danger of the "whatever it takes" attitude is that electorally expedient but impractical policies will have to be abandoned in office, damaging a government's credibility. Alternatively, the government committed to a program often has to stick with unpopular policies to its detriment. Another consideration for an opposition is that the bigger the platform, the bigger the target it presents at election time. An opposition leader operates between the twin polarities of popularity and principle.

The general socio-economic climate can be an influence on the type of platform best calculated to bring an opposition to power. There are times, particularly after long eras of unadventurous government, where the electorate is hungry for "big picture" change. At other times, hesitation and anxiety about change prevail and the voters prefer mundane, comforting promises.

The political cycle is an important factor in determining how well an opposition performs. A party that is thrust into opposition after a long term in government is often disoriented, struggling to come to terms with what has happened. There is also a more physical readjustment as former government MPs are suddenly bereft of the considerable resources they enjoyed in office. A new opposition may struggle to find a leader who is more than a stopgap. It has often lost many of its most capable MPs and may not have the "critical mass" of members needed to be effective. Time and experience are needed to hone the skills (often hard-won) that make an opposition effective and credible.

Conversely, a long-term opposition can be marginalised by the disinclination of major interest groups and stakeholders to back what seems to be an obvious loser. They increasingly accept the government's apparent stranglehold on power and cooperate with it rather than risk being permanently "out in the cold". This tendency further strengthens a long-lived government's hold on office and makes talk of its hegemony, to some extent, a self-fulfilling prophecy. A party perceived as a permanent opposition also has difficulty attracting strong, credible candidates who are not inclined to forsake lucrative careers for long, cold years in the wilderness.

In spite of all these handicaps, oppositions do win elections. The electoral pendulum still swings, if at times slowly. Long-term incumbency can be detrimental to a government if it is widely perceived as sclerotic and unable to handle effectively the basics of government and administration. Opposition attacks and alternatives then start to become more credible to the voters. An astute opposition can successfully begin to sheet home responsibility for almost any problem to a faltering government, with a good chance of being believed by the voters. A government's high media profile then becomes a disadvantage as it ensures that the government's failings (real and alleged) are prominently displayed before the electorate. A government in this situation becomes a highly visible, slow-moving target. The claim that it is "time for a change" can be a powerful weapon for an opposition when it is coupled with palpable evidence that a government is failing and the opposition is widely perceived as an attractive alternative.

In opposition, success or failure, hinges very much on the leader. Some opposition leaders are visionaries, motivated to seek office to implement a program they believe will transform society. Others are more *ad hoc* – not averse to reform, but in a controlled, targeted way. Some are cynical opportunists who will promise anything to win power. An effective opposition leader needs to exploit the government's weaknesses aggressively, work the media successfully, create a viable alternative vision, and persuade the voters that they will deliver a better future. They have to discipline, rally and inspire their team – if such it is. It is usually the mentally and physically tough, relentlessly driven opposition leader who eventually succeeds.

An opposition leader faces multiple challenges. Personal popularity and public performance are more critical for opposition leaders than for leaders of government, as opposition is even more a "one man band". Few opposition leaders have more than a handful of able and energetic colleagues. As well as possessing greatly superior media, staffing and budgetary resources, governments can dispense patronage to many groups in the community to buy support. At the most blatant level, governments can manipulate the electoral system to minimise opposition representation in parliament.

As party leaders, opposition leaders have to be constantly wary of disgruntled, jealous or ambitious colleagues. Even the most unimpressive MP has to be courted. Opposition leaders lack the ability to shore up support by dispensing jobs and perquisites as those in office can. Parliamentary parties can become fractious and unmotivated in opposition; long-term oppositions often fall prey to chronic infighting. Relations between opposition leaders and the party machine can be strained, with both thinking they know best about how to win government. In office, the leader often has the prestige to get their own way; in opposition, the machine is more inclined to exert its authority.

Rodney Tiffen in Chapter Four identifies another disadvantage opposition leaders labour under as premiers and prime ministers are

> the custodians of the administrative and ceremonial roles of the state. They may embody national unity on occasions of both national tragedy and triumph. The publicity given to prime ministers at sporting events is much greater than to opposition leaders. Their capacity to show concern and leadership during and after national tragedies is another occasion where oppositions are reduced to irrelevance.

Opposition is an unrewarding business. An opposition leader is largely impotent in terms of implementing policy; their influence is indirect at best, for example, by exposing maladministration under parliamentary privilege. A persistent problem is the standard criticism that an opposition leader has no policies; yet when they launch policies, the media often decide it is not a story and don't cover it.

Being in opposition is usually a long period of frustration, enlivened by the occasional boost of a successful assault on the government to sustain motivation. It is only in those periods when a government is self-destructing that an opposition leader can maintain an adrenaline high. Bob Carr (Leader of the New South Wales Labor Opposition 1988-1995, Premier 1995-2005) has provided a good summary of the highs and lows of opposition. In the bad times: "Your personality is corroded by the frustrations of opposition leadership. You're failing to sell yourself against a mood of public dislike. You find the whole political process unpalatable. You even doubt the viability of your own party". However, there are also times when an opposition leader can be "predatory and opportunistic": "You've got to bring down the minister. Staple his scalp to your belt. Your best days are when you rise in parliament and, taking them by surprise, press questions that leave a minister or a premier struggling, eyes swivelling, sounding indignant and muddle-headed" (Carr 2018: 71-2).

Conclusion

The conventional Westminster system is based on a democratically elected government having the right to govern and implement its policies. The loyal opposition has the legitimate right to criticise the government's program and propose alternative policies. This system has, on the whole, worked advantageously. As British Prime Minister Harold Wilson said in 1974 when introducing increased resources for the Opposition: "No Government has anything to gain, and certainly the country has nothing to gain, from opposition parties lacking the necessary facilities, financial and otherwise, for doing their job in the House" (quoted by Nigel Fletcher in Chapter 17).

However, this traditional model can be subverted by governments. They can abuse their power by depriving oppositions of the resources needed to function, creating a very unlevel playing field. Drawing on the case studies in this book, this seems to be a growing and disturbing tendency. It strikes at the heart of functional parliamentary government; it is also a short-sighted strategy as sooner or later the government becomes the opposition.

A successful opposition has to overcome external and internal challenges. The external challenges relate to the fact that an opposition is outgunned by the government in terms of resources, staff, finance and media exposure. Governments can also manipulate the electoral and parliamentary rules to their advantage. The internal challenges relate to maintaining discipline, morale, unity and focus, particularly over a long period. As well, an opposition has to create viable policies, recruit capable personnel and skilfully exploit government weaknesses.

A key factor in the operation of the Australian system of loyal opposition is that most members of society believe that, even if their party does not win on a particular occasion, the chance will come. The system is anchored by the popular assumption that, on the whole, parties contending for office will govern in the interests of all citizens and have a core of commonality about the national interest. If the supporters of a party that loses an election believe that there will be no place for them in the new order, social dislocation follows. As Rodney Tiffen observes: "In most elections 47 per cent or more of the electorate effectively give their vote to the losing side. Rarely do all the public react one way or the other".

Thankfully, to use a sporting analogy, in Australia the adherents of the party that loses are like the supporters of a team that loses the big match on Saturday, ruefully saying, "Oh well, we will get there next time". Another basic assumption is that both government and opposition, no matter how hard they play the game, ultimately respect the written and unwritten rules, the mutually agreed proprieties and boundaries that underpin democracy. In this respect, the fundamental principle is that a defeated government unhesitatingly departs and allows the victor to assume office. Again fortunately, this principle is deeply and unquestioningly rooted in Australian society. However, this is no reason for complacency as recent events in the US have shown.

References

Carr, B., *Run for your life*, Carlton: Melbourne University Press, 2018

Crick, B., *In Defence of Politics*, London: Weidenfeld and Nicholson, 4th ed, 1992

Ganghof, S., *Beyond Presidentialism and Parliamentarism*, Oxford: Oxford University Press, 2021

Trevelyan, G.M., *England Under the Stuarts*, London: Routledge, 2nd ed, 1925, reprinted 2021

1

The Dialectic of Democracy:

The Emergence of Political Opposition

Graham Maddox

At least by the mid-nineteenth century, the existence of a constituted and recognised opposition was regarded as "the most salient characteristic of a free society" (Foord 1964: 4). It meant that a free society was constituted by freedom of speech and assembly, and, in contrast to despotisms, by a willingness on the part of rulers to tolerate criticism and for opposing parties to tolerate one another (Williams 1961: 111). Of importance are not merely views contrary to government: "…a great variety of opinion is a certain sign of free government" (Toland in Kramnick 1968: 154).

Precious though it is to live in a free society, opposition signifies yet more than this. It marks the capacity of each person living in a society to think independently and to express opinion freely about how the community should be governed. In this light, opposition sets the seal on a democratic community, whose ideal surely is to acknowledge the innate capacity of all adult persons not legally disqualified to govern themselves. Since a community requires collective decision-making, it is acknowledged that individual persons cannot simply do as they please regardless of the consequences to others; but democracy gives as much latitude as possible while at the same time encouraging citizens to take part in the collective running of the community. Just as those with power tolerate opposing views, so a society becomes a tolerant one. A truly open society "breeds" tolerance (Krygier 2005: 53).

Before long we encounter the conundrum of opposition: if a government is morally convinced it is in the right, would it not be selling out its own integrity by tolerating opinion that it believes to be wrong? Why should an opposition remain loyal to a government it believes to be in the wrong? To this conundrum D'Agostino offers a resolution from ethical pluralism, under which no proposition can be regarded as *complete*: varied approaches *complement* each other, various ideals are *incommensurable*, and each person holds a perspective which renders the grounds of other people's ideals *inaccessible*. He quotes Hampshire to the point: human beings "...find themselves trying to reconcile, or to assign priorities to, widely different and diverging and changing concerns and interests, both within the single life of an individual and within a single society..." (D'Agostino 1990: 449).

This chapter seeks to amplify the philosophical perspective with the historical. Toleration of different points of view arose because modern political opposition emerged under a worldview that might be characterized as "Christendom" (Maddox 2011). John Milton gave a resounding endorsement of toleration and free speech during the censorship controversy of the Independents with the Presbyterians during the English Civil War, praising assent "to the force of reason and convincement" (Milton 1951: 45). Opposition was distinctively European, the exemplar being supplied by the Parliament of Westminster. This is not to say that other forms of opposition did not occur elsewhere; they did not evolve into the European conception of *constitutional* and *responsible* opposition.

What D'Agostino attributes to a limited perspective on society's intricacies was widely held in the Augustinian tradition to be inherent fallibility deriving from the human condition. There is a strong Platonism behind this perspective, since only in thought can things be conceived as perfect, or even 'right'. Augustinianism, and the pervasive Calvinism that came in its wake, held that all human institutions were fallible, and that the pretension to rule others was tainted by the worst of sins, pride.

It was a short step to say that it was therefore a more moral thing to do to oppose a government than to be in one. Democracy implicitly adopts this attitude; no government is good enough to rule us absolutely, and even the "best" governments in some eyes are "bad" governments to others, so the system of parliamentary democracy has evolved to allow for a dialectical process that lets us move on from one unsatisfactory situation to another that is, it is hoped, a little less unsatisfactory.

If ancient Athens is taken as the "prototype" democracy, it was never structured to accommodate formal opposition. The ruling assembly was open to all male citizens who often had to be coerced into raising a quorum of about six thousand members as measured by filling the designated arena. The composition of an assembly could shift radically from one meeting to another. Yet clearly there were contrary opinions, often fiercely expressed. Policy formation was the work of leaders, probably mostly from the elites who had to organise support for their position among the "lower orders" on whose equal votes they relied. Some modern writers have sought to detect the embryos of political parties among such loose organisation. Political leaders often formed temporary coalitions among groups of friends known as *hetaireiai.*[1] Josiah Ober has defended the stability of the Athenian democracy by showing how the elite leaders could balance their work with support among the many (Ober 1989: 85). But clearly there was no lasting organisation resembling political parties (Hansen 1991). The remarkable demonstration of this "model" democracy was that for two hundred years it maintained social stability within an open society that was meet home to all kinds of opinion ranging from Socrates to Diogenes. Within it Plato could explore to its depths the notion of justice.

Classical democracy

As Lindsay (1935: 32-3) once wrote during the heyday of "classical" thinking about democracy:

> I am not sure that we always realize how much of the essence of democracy is contained in this insistence of tolerated and official opposition. It implies the business of representative government is to make articulate and get expressed different not consentaneous points of view – that democratic equality is not an equality of sameness but of difference – that we want everyone to have political rights, not because and in so far as they agree with other people, but because and in so far as they each have their peculiar contribution to make. But democracy is based on the assumption that men [and women] can agree on common action which yet leaves each to live his [or her] own life – that if we really respect one another's personality we can find a common framework or system of rights within which a free moral life of the individual is possible.

A collectivity can hardly work if all voices shout at once, except perhaps under extreme provocation arousing public demonstration, so representative institutions "refine and focus public voices onto the centres of power; the system of opposition and government means that quite differing opinions can be gathered together and pitted against each other. This situation is arguably best served by the two-party system of government. It was long ago held that political issues resolve themselves into whether to do something or not to do it – in crude binary form the progressive and the conservative positions. Two-party systems generally resolve themselves into progressive and conservative sides. But this was not Rousseau's view.

Rousseau and the common good

It was Jean-Jacques Rousseau's impossible dream that a society should live in absolute harmony according to the unified will of the people. His *volonte generale* has perplexed many, even to the point of incurring the calumny that Rousseau was a totalitarian (Talmon 1952). He believed that a community could be unified with a clear perception of the common good:

> So long as a number of men assembled together regard themselves
> as forming a single body, they have but one will, which is con-
> cerned with their common preservation and with the well-being of
> all.   When this is so, the springs of the State are vigorous and
> simple, its principles plain and clear-cut. It is not encumbered with
> confused or conflicting interests. The common good is everywhere
> plainly in evidence and needs only good sense to be perceived.
> (Rousseau 1971: 269).

The simple fact of human experience, however, is that people do not have a unified will. They are separately instructed by education, religion, and social mores to think for themselves, and human nature, characterized by the very freedom Rousseau extols, guides them individually in different directions. The philosophical and social pluralism inherent in humankind leads to the problem of establishing government over people of un-like minds, and therein lies the impossibility of Rousseau's dream. Rousseau himself was cognizant of the fallibility of human governments; he seriously explored the possibility of political opposition, locating its origins in the Roman republican institution of the tribunate. Yet his opposition was contained within the unitary structure overseen by the "general will".

To the tribunate as a foundation of opposition we shall return shortly. In view of Rousseau's insistence that individual rights be "alienated" to the common body, however, the charge of authoritarianism is understandable. Yet this charge can scarcely be sustained against the impassioned prophet of freedom (Rousseau: 1. 1).

Hobbes

A little more than one hundred years earlier there was something of a precedent for Rousseau's approach, set at the beginning of modern political theory by Thomas Hobbes (to whom Rousseau himself attributes a political theory akin to the nihilist rule of the emperor Caligula) (Rousseau 1. 2). In Hobbes's version of the contract, a person's individual powers are surrendered to the Leviathan, the ultimately unanswerable state power, an authority constituted to clarify the terms of social engagement. In 1651 Hobbes was living through the English Civil War, a horrendous time of internecine carnage in which a king lost not only his crown but also his head. The political turbulence of the time, according to Hobbes, derived from the fact that there was no authority to define meanings, and everyone did as he or she pleased:

> For if men be to learn their duty from the sentence which other men shall give concerning the meaning of the Scriptures, and not from their own interpretation, I understand not to what end they were translated into English, and every man not only permitted, but also exhorted, to read them. For what could that produce, but diversity of opinion, and consequently, as man's nature is, disputation, breach of charity, disobedience, and at last rebellion. (Hobbes 1679: Dialogue 1)

To Hobbes this was tantamount to a war of all against all since all exercised their own powers against everyone else. England had reverted to a state of nature.[2] In this condition, Hobbes taught, each person had an absolute freedom, and "every man hath a right to every thing; even to one anothers body". This state of affairs quite undermined each person's security; hence the need for an overriding authority (Hobbes 1651: 1. 4).

In all this, Hobbes locates the political condition beneath the rubric of the sovereign individual person. It is to secure one's own safety that each person surrenders liberty to the state. His state power is not so much an aggregation or consolidation of the will of all to one general will, but rather a prudential submission to an authority that is independently representative of all subjects (Pitkin 1967). At bottom, each person has a right to self-government, even though that right is willingly surrendered. Rousseau's consolidation of the wills is more akin to Plato's wish for solidarity based on adherence to the Form of the Good; his belief that the general will is the will of all when each is thinking rightly is more like

Socrates's dictum that no one does wrong willingly (Maddox 2011).

Unlike John Locke, whose religious "fundamentalism" apparently disqualifies him, Hobbes retains the favour of modern liberals on account of his apparently clear separation of political affairs from private lives (Haakonssen 1988; Kraynak 1982). Hobbes was raised a Calvinist and accepted the omnipotence of the creator God and the doctrine of predestination; as Calvin had taught, no person can achieve salvation by their "good works", but only by the pre-ordained grace of God. This teaching for Hobbes quite removed religion from the realm of politics; his *Leviathan* was designed to contain the almost unlimited tendency to human evil that Calvin had taught (Gillespie 2009: 220). Moreover, it was a necessary remedy for the "second fall" of humankind that occurred when the Israelites rejected the direct rule of God and pined for kingly rulers. The second coming of Christ would end the interregnum begun with King Saul; Jesus would reign over civil society directly in the name of God (Pocock 1973).

Calvinism

At the time of their constitutional Founding, the American colonists were deeply influenced by Hobbes, along with Machiavelli, Harrington, Locke, Montesquieu, Rousseau and classical scholarship, and the Calvinism which was a first cause of the founding of the New England colonies. They held the run of humankind in low esteem, believing that people were capable of endless vice and unrestrained self-interest. The Founders "did not believe in man, but they did believe in the power of a good political constitution to control him". They therefore devised a constitution whose essential purpose was "cribbing and confining the popular spirit..."; a constitution meant to deprive "the people" of every opportunity of influencing the course of policy (Hofstadter 1977: 73-4). A rigid constitution meant weak government as far as implementing policy for the good of the people was concerned, since much legislation aimed at improving social and economic conditions was vetoed by its provisions.

The corollary of suspect government and virtually outlawed collective action was a strong emphasis on the individual person, and his or her opportunities to make economic and social progress through individual endeavour. It is therefore ironic that America should have contributed to the awareness of opposition studies by focusing on the individual person against the state.

Despite the generally low opinion of depraved humanity, it was also part of the Calvinist outlook that injustice should be rooted out. Here we find the stem of the adversary system; as Calvin adjured his followers, "search out matters to the very bottom" (Calvin 1968: 60). To deal with the rampant individualism that their Constitution, and their emerging national ethos, encouraged, the Americans deployed the "adversary method": "It seemed clear that no stubborn search for singular truths or monolithic standards or agreed upon powers could wring from the economic and social heterogeneity of America substantive consensus on anything … Only where there were two sides could there be a reasonable outcome; only where contraries were aired could unity be anticipated". If there were to be an American version of truth, it would "have to be hammered out on the anvil of debate" (Barber 1977: 26-7). The institutions of American government, however, scarcely allowed for organised debate between a governing party and an opposition party within a parliamentary context, and its protagonists had to find other explanations to discover opposition within their governmental system to justify it as a constituent of democracy, as will be considered shortly.

Opposition and divine right

The parliamentary system of organised government and opposition emerged in Britain in the eighteenth century. Yet the prehistory of adversarial political relations is essential ancestry to its birth. In an otherwise useful survey of emerging opposition, Thomas Hocking, having considered the status of the "Old Tory model" of opposition under Elizabeth I and James I, dismisses the English Revolution and

Restoration as a period offering new forms of political organisation that were "varied and transitory" (Hocking 1971:57). On the other hand, Thomas Cartwright's contribution to the Admonition Controversy helped to establish parliament as a more equal partner in ruling with the Queen, opening the way to expressions of contrary opinion (Chavura 2015: 319). Hobbes indeed ascribed total chaos to the subsequent Civil War in the time of the Stuarts, yet it is in this period that the first modern demonstrations of something akin to political opposition may be discerned. More important, we find precise articulation of the follies of concentrated and illegitimate power, ideas that were to persist into the eighteenth century. While opposing viewpoints were expressed in violent fashion, the term "political opposition" is not appropriately applied to the collisions of the Civil War and the Interregnum, because it has acquired a technical sense that implies the formal airing of different political opinions, and the contradiction of different political actions, under peaceful conditions of settled procedures. These did not manifestly emerge, under the supervision of parliamentary government, for more than a century after Hobbes's time. Yet it should be recalled that the Civil War was essentially a conflict between King and Parliament. Moreover, the literature of the conflict provided the basis of legitimate contradiction in political affairs that was to send down the roots of parliamentary adversarial politics for the future. Those in the eighteenth century who followed the logic of parliamentary sovereignty of the seventeenth century were called "Commonwealthmen" (Robbins 1968).

At issue first of all, was the so-called Divine Right of Kings, and the alleged tyranny of the Crown. Underlying all was a passionate controversy about the "true" practice of the Christian religion and its impact on the politics of the day. Hobbes himself spent much of his energies in *Leviathan* adumbrating a true Christian "commonwealth" (and it is interesting that he chose the same translation of the ancient *res publica* as adopted by Oliver Cromwell). Cromwell has recently enjoyed a very bad press, but there is still a case, such as that promoted by Geoffrey Robertson (2005), that he stands at the foundation of the modern cause of liberty and the confrontation of tyranny. "God drunk" as he was, he trusted the ear attentive to God's will: decisions could be made by groups of people open to divine guidance. He therefore opposed pre-set positions, and confessed that when he entered a deliberative meeting, he did not have any idea what the outcome would be. This was the basis of his objection to the Agreement of the People, "on the grounds that predetermined propositions could not be debated as befitted a 'company of men that really would be guided by God'". The search for God's guidance was "an effort to humble individual will to the good of the public, and extraordinary fasts and humiliations were frequent during political crises" (Kishlansky 1977: 628).

King Charles I's tyranny involved many secular issues, particularly the raising of irregular taxes to fight unauthorised wars and, above all, to rule for long periods without Parliament. Yet the Civil War was saturated in religious controversy. The alleged tyranny of the Stuart kings was based on the doctrine of "the divine right of kings" espoused by King James and acted upon more purposefully by his son, Charles. The Puritan parliamentarians who opposed the King were devout adherents to scriptural authority, upon which ground they sought to purify the Church of England of its ritualistic practices such as the use of distinguishing vestments for the clergy, statuary, making the sign of the cross, kneeling for prayers and following prescribed prayers. Moreover, James enacted what was anathema to Puritans: officially sanctioned sports on Sundays. Above all, the Puritans, both Presbyterian and Independent, rejected the rule of bishops and resented their participation in the secular administration of the realm. The former preferred rule by presbyteries, the latter by congregational meetings.

The parliamentarians were well equipped with recent anti-authoritarian literature from the persecuted Huguenots of France (Franklin: 1969; Cottret 1991). More directly, however, they had the resource of scripture, which they scoured for precedent and instruction, as well as for spiritual guidance. Therein lay ample precedent for opposition to kingly rule. Hobbes asserted that the need for authoritative human government entered the world when the ancient Jews turned their back on the direct rule of God and asked the prophet Samuel to supply them with an earthly king to defend them against the Philistines. The prophet replied with a tirade against the innate rapacity of kings,[3] but the Israelites persisted in their wish, and the reign of kingship was introduced, in most instances with disastrous consequences. Hobbes called this event the Second Fall. The second coming of Christ would end the interregnum begun with King Saul; Jesus would reign over civil society directly in the name of God (Pocock 1973).

Despite Hobbes's insistence that the Civil War carnage occurred because of the arrogant belief of Calvinist preachers in their own righteousness, those Calvinists, Presbyterians, and Independents alike, had serious and legitimate grievances against the Crown, which they held to be a tyranny. There were precedents aplenty for the type of tyranny they feared in the "fallen" Israel of the Israelite monarchy. It was all laid out for them in the scriptures they searched so avidly for instruction. The prehistory of the idea of political opposition may perhaps be located in the ancient Jewish prophecy.[4]

The prehistory of opposition: the role of prophecy

A few examples may suffice. King David, in Israelite lore far from a bad king, sent a neighbour to his death to steal the man's beautiful wife. The court prophet, Nathan, confronted the King with a parable of a rich man who stole his poor neighbour's single pet sheep. Outraged, the King demanded that the thief be punished, to which the fearless prophet, no doubt in dread of his life, declaimed "Thou art the man!"[5] Elijah's legendary confrontation with the rapacious King Ahab is beyond the reach of history, but supplies a colourful myth illustrating the fallibility of the office of kingship, and the beginnings of a tradition of holding power to account.[6]

In the historical realm, however, the classical or writing prophets[7] demonstrate a powerful alternative to the dominant ideology of kingship, supporting, as it did, a hubristic aristocracy. The first writing prophet, Amos, was the champion of the oppressed against the luxury and extravagance of the 'establishment': "Let justice roll down like a river, and righteousness a never failing torrent".[8] Over a century later, one of the authors of the book of Jeremiah railed against the extravagance of King Zedekiah, who had built himself a preposterous palace at the expense of the poor. Jeremiah roars: your lavish palace signifies nothing, even if "it will be panelled with cedar and painted with vermilion. Though your cedar is so splendid, does that prove you a king? Think of your father: he ate and drank, dealt justly and fairly: all went well with him. He upheld the cause of the lowly and poor; then all was well." [9]

Prophetic opposition was not confined to the king alone. Around each king was a large group of hangers-on, a kind of ruling institution. In the late eighth century BC Isaiah denounced the rulers of Judaea: for they "make unjust laws and draft oppressive edicts, depriving the poor of justice ... plundering the widow and despoiling the fatherless." In their opposition to the rich and famous, the prophets became, as it were, representatives of the underclass, their repeated formula, "the widow and the fatherless" standing for all who were destitute, since security generally meant dependence upon a provident male.

For Amos it was axiomatic that the existence of an upper class meant the oppression of the many: "You loll on beds inlaid with ivory and lounge on your couches....you drink wine by the bowlful and anoint yourselves with the richest of oils, but at the ruin of Joseph you feel no grief".[10] The rich systematically exploit the poor, cornering the grain markets, exacting exorbitant rents, and enslaving defaulters, wielding extortionate loan terms to acquire the meagre property of the weak for themselves. At the same time Hosea was denouncing large landholders for stealing their neighbours' land, and merchants who use "false scales" and "love to cheat".[11] Such exploitation was rife, as the rapacious sought to 'add house to house and join field to field, until everyone else is displaced, and you are left sole inhabitants of the countryside'.[12] The first Isaiah thundered: "....in your houses are the spoils of the poor. Is it nothing to you that you crush my people and grind the faces of the poor?"[13]

The examples of prophetic challenges to the ruling classes, and especially to corrupt rulers, can be repeated many times over, bitter complaints also coming from such as Ezekiel. That the action of the prophets was political as well as religious cannot be doubted, and yet, as religious leaders, the prophets were decisively non-political in their designs: there was no pretension to power, and no ambition to replace in office those they criticised (Maddox 2008). To some, that would set them up as the paradigm of opposition, but the position is far from as simple as that, as will be outlined shortly.

Puritanism and prophecy

It might likewise be thought that the execution of a king in early modern England could be the ultimate expression of political opposition, but it bears no more resemblance to the modern institution of opposition than to be a powerful foundation myth in its prehistory. The Independents, who carried out the execution, were saturated in knowledge of the scriptures, and found therein ample precedent for opposing tyrannical kings. There is nowadays a great deal of scepticism about the role of religion in the deliberations of the Puritans, their reference to biblical theology often brushed aside as "rationalisations". This scepticism was long ago anticipated, and forcefully refuted, by one of the leading scholars of puritan literature, Woodhouse: "…if these are rationalizations they involve the terms in which the Puritan viewed his world (sic) and they rest upon the convictions with which he was prepared to face not only his fellows, but his Maker. We shall gain nothing by brushing those terms and convictions aside…" As for the Puritans,

> Israel was ever before their eyes. Forget that and the policy of the Presbyterians becomes in part at least unintelligible. Had not God given the Jews kings, and, whenever they could do so with impunity, had not that model knocked them about? … Puritan religion in the various phases of the struggle with Charles, and beyond it, was

a mighty revolutionary agent. Nothing indeed could withstand the divinity that hedged a king save the divinity of religion itself when it was ranged against him. (Woodhouse 1938: 2)

Despite the widespread fashion to discount such an interpretation, it has had some impressive recent advocates. Jacqueline Eales, for example, has argued "[t]hat religion was a mainspring to opposition to Charles I during the English Civil War was fully apparent to contemporaries caught in the unfolding events of the conflict in the early 1640s", while "[r]ecent scholarship into the progress of the Civil War in the localities has also consistently demonstrated the links between religious belief and parliamentarianism in the 1640s" (Eales 1996: 207).

Although there was support in the sixteenth century for using the law to limit the powers of government, and to reject the rule of one person, from none other than a puritan antagonist, Richard Hooker (who follows Aristotle and the Schoolmen) (Hooker 1593: 345ff), the particular cast of puritan theology was Calvinist. Jean Calvin himself, generally following biblical injunctions to obey "the powers that be", was cautious in exhortation to disobedience in the face of ungodly rule, yet it is there in his *Institutes,* nevertheless. The very last section recommends opposition and downright disobedience to impious rulers:

…in that obedience which we hold to be due to the commands of rulers, we must always make the exception, nay, must be particularly careful that it is not incompatible with obedience to Him to whose will the wishes of all kings should be subject, to whose decrees their commands must yield, to whose majesty their sceptres must bow…

We are subject to the men who rule over us, but subject only in the Lord…

But since Peter, one of heaven's heralds, has published the edict, 'We ought to obey God rather than men' (Acts 5. 29), let us console ourselves with the thought, that we are rendering the obedience which the Lord requires, when we endure anything rather than turn aside from piety…

> Paul stimulates us by the additional consideration (I Cor. 7. 23),
> that we were redeemed by Christ at the great price which our re-
> demption cost him, in order that we might not yield to a slavish
> obedience to the depraved wishes of men, far less do homage to
> their impiety. (Calvin 1989: 675-6)

Calvin reveals a "sharp dislike of kingship" as a consequence of original
sin and leaves the "iron gate" open to later ideas of resistance to tyrants
(McNeill 1949: 161-2). For Scottish and English followers, the idea of
the King's occupation of the "headship" of the English Church could be
nothing but usurpation. Calvinist "resistance" literature reaching England
was deeply influential. In 1648 an anonymous translator published an
English version of the Huguenot anti-monarchist tract, *Vindiciae Contra
Tyrannos*, itself anonymously published in France in 1579 in the wake
of the St Bartholomew's Day massacre. In a detailed analysis of the
Vindiciae, McLaren shows how the Calvinist antithesis of tyranny was
a "democratic patriarchy, in which the people rule in partnership with
God" (McLaren 1996: 23-52).

One of the intellectual protagonists of the English Civil War, the Scottish
Presbyterian Samuel Rutherford, did much to undermine the claims of
earthly kingship, particularly in his *Lex, Rex* (Rutherford 1649). John
Coffey identifies three Puritan contributions to proto-liberal thought
which subsequently developed under the nurture of John Locke: popular
sovereignty, resistance theory, and the rule of law (Coffey 1997: 146-8,
187). Rutherford says that the "Law hath a supremacy of constitution
above the King" (Rutherford: 230), and places limits on royal power.
Both the people and the Parliament are understood to be above the King,
and the Parliament is obliged to act "if the King turn Tyrant" (Rutherford:
210). Rutherford begins with the sociability of humans and the idea
that "there is no reason in Nature, why one Man should be King and
Lord it over another"; the "power of creating a man a King, is from the
people"; and so the "power of Government, by the light of nature must
be *radically* and *originally*, in a Communitie". Kings are not divine, and
kingship itself is scarcely essential (Rutherford: 3, 10, 94, 413). Even

more famously, John Milton found ample precedent in the scriptures for the deposition of the tyrannical king (Milton 2001).

The first adumbrations of the role of Parliament in formulating oppositional politics actually began during the Civil War. As Kishlansky pointed out some time ago, the regular Parliament inherited from Queen Elizabeth first operated on consensual lines. Royal legislation took precedence and was managed through Parliament in order finally to secure unanimous support. There was nothing resembling political parties, although factions and tendencies, both religious and secular, abounded in amorphous and ephemeral formations (Kishlansky: 619-200).

In truth, the exigencies of parliamentary procedure supplied the first adumbrations of an adversary process. The consensual endeavour "with its practice speeches and persuasive debates, was entirely too cumbersome when confronted by the need for rapid policy formation..." By 1646 factions were being moulded into 'parties' whose "emergence as ideological bodies stressed, for the first time, permanent contrariety, leaving disputes to be resolved not by debate but by divisions of the House of Commons into majority and minority opinions" (Kishlansky: 629).[14]

Regardless of the fact that the established interplay between government and opposition forces was to wait another century in the making, the Civil War had legitimated polarized opinion and "the organic political nation had become pluralistic". The systematised adversary politics emerging in the eighteenth century was a distant, but unmistakable, legacy of the English Revolution (Kishlansky 640).

Parliamentary opposition

Setting the monarchy on a constitutional basis after the Glorious Revolution of 1688 and the promulgation of the Bill of Rights reduced individual kings and queens as objects of political hatred, when attention was increasingly directed at the king's ministry. Political opposition became a matter of challenging the king's ministry for its action in the king's name. It is only then that we begin to see the operation of political opposition as it is understood in the modern world. It also demonstrates that it is closely associated with parliamentary government.

Ministries continued to survive at the monarch's pleasure under William and Mary, Queen Anne and George I and George II. No one questioned the king or queen's right to choose the ministers he or she wished; and no one could remove a ministry which the monarch continued to favour Swift (see Swift in Foord: 19).[15] Nevertheless, opposition to official policy was fully, and often scurrilously, expressed. When Queen Anne died, George I threw out her ministry in favour of a group unconnected with the Stuarts, casting the former ministry into a formidable opposition role.

The term "opposition", however, came into its own in political usage during the long term of Robert Walpole's ascendancy in the ministry under the first two Georges – an ascendancy so complete that he is often held informally to have carved out the first effective position of a "prime minister", although the term did not come into general use until the next century. During this period opposition was transformed from a word denoting the act of opposing and became attached to a more or less stable body of people consistently antagonistic to the government (Foord: 155). We are not yet in the era of two-party politics, however. The names Whig and Tory were much in circulation, but these were vague and fluid terms, and certainly did not denote any party in the modern sense. Several opposition factions could group or regroup around certain issues, but generally a loose coalition could be discerned, having only in common an aversion to the king's ministry.

Bolingbroke

Most consistently central to the opposition to Walpole was Viscount Bolingbroke. There had been an irreconcilable enmity between Bolingbroke and Walpole since the time of Queen Anne. The original cause of their dispute was Bolingbroke's attempt to have Walpole impeached for corruption, and Bolingbroke's subsequently suffering an act of attainder at Walpole's hands, going into exile in France. The question of government corruption continued to simmer with Bolingbroke, who campaigned to turn opposition to the government into a righteous cause, however suspect his private motives may have been. Bolingbroke's opposition coalesced around his October Club, political pamphleteering galvanizing support. His journal, *The Craftsman*, a name chosen to calumniate the craftiness of scheming politicians, maintained a constant stream of criticism against "maladministration, corruption, weakness, and tyranny" (Foord 143). Eminent writers took up the fray. In the popular *Beggars' Opera* John Gay lampooned Walpole; Samuel Johnson, Henry Fielding, Jonathan Swift and Alexander Pope all joined in the criticism (Gerrard 1994; Uhr 2004).

The terms "Court" and "Country" had emerged during the decades leading up to the English Civil War to emphasize the contrast between the Stuart kings' administrations and the widespread opposition out in the country. Bolingbroke played these terms anew for all they were worth. These were the days of the South Sea Bubble and Bolingbroke tainted the Court with a symbol of corruption at its core (though Walpole himself was not involved). Bolingbroke went much further. He tapped into the long Augustinian tradition of condemning all earthly government as infected with the original sin of all human institutions: "Absolute stability is not to be expected in anything human" (Bolingbroke 1967 vol 3: 397). He was also influenced by the neo-Stoicism of his age, quoting Seneca for instruction (Bolingbroke vol 2: 376); Bolingbroke's Stoicism was suspicious of "ambition" and tended toward the Cynicism from which ancient Stoicism grew, namely, to regard all power-seeking as an irrelevance to true human life.

Long before John Stuart Mill and Lord Acton, Bolingbroke was denouncing government as an ever-present danger to liberty (Bolingbroke vol 1: 296). The problem was to contain the excesses of government which inevitably tend to corruption. Montesquieu took up Bolingbroke's complaints and, after his encounter with Bolingbroke, proposed the theory of the separation of powers (Maddox 1996: 171-2; Vile 1967: 72-3). Bolingbroke's own conservatism is patent. On governments: "Every hour they live is an hour less they have to live. All that can be done, therefore, to prolong the duration of a good government, is to draw it back on every favourable occasion, to the first good principles on which it was founded" (Bolingbroke vol 2: 397).

Bolingbroke's own approach was to organize a broad-based opposition "party" that would coalesce around a 'patriot king' to unite the country and stamp out corruption. He contrasted Country – the purity of fresh air and the simplicity of country folk – to the sleaziness of the city and the backroom deals of the Court. Bolingbroke had a candidate for a patriot king: the disaffected son of George II, Frederick, the Prince of Wales, around whom groups alienated from the Crown gathered. The patriot king would be the Stoic good man, who would rule not for himself but for his people. While the Country ideology began in praise of the rural life as opposed to the sins of the city, it was expanded by Bolingbroke to mean the nation itself as alienated from its government. Country ideology therefore became patriotic – it existed to save the whole country. The argument was dignified by an appeal to constitutional propriety in the face of government corruption: opposition was a righteous cause in defence of the constitution against governments who would undermine it (Uhr 2006).

For its part, Walpole's ministry denigrated all opposition as traitors, since "Whig vindictiveness had goaded them into Jacobitism". All opposition to the Crown became Jacobitical, and the Court party aimed "to have all malcontents excluded under a cloud of treason" (Foord: 65). In turn, those so rejected built their own martyrology (Foord: 124). Foord discerns the beginning of what we might call the 'dialectic' of modern democracy in the interplay between government and opposition forces. For the opposition, the "principles of action derived from the contemporary scene at Westminster" (Foord: 146).

As Foord sees it, Bolingbroke's conception of an opposition party was *eschatological*, its program ending in self-extinction. It came into being to achieve its purpose and then, having done so, would go out of existence in favour of a new order that would render all faction and party irrelevant. Its aim was not merely to expunge corruption from the public scene, but even to restore the deranged constitution, from which talented men were, they complained, totally excluded. One formidable interpretation sees Bolingbroke's parties as corresponding to the ancient divisions of the human soul: the government party, dealing constantly with power and dispositioning material wealth, corresponded to the baser part of the soul, while the opposition party corresponded to the finer elements of the soul, seeking wisdom and purity (Kramnick 156-7).[16] Walpole's experience had yet more to contribute to the emerging concept of political opposition, and in this one might say no contribution in office became him so well as the leaving of it.

Towards the end of Walpole's ascendancy, a "broad-bottomed" coalition of opposition forces, containing disaffected Tories and Country party members as well as alienated Whigs, had accumulated considerable debating skill and force in Parliament. For the first time the legislature came to the fore as the determinant of the ministry rather than simply the King's wish. This also meant that the opposition had to contemplate office, to formulate realistic policies which could be implemented in office, and to avoid mere criticism which offered no solution and no alternative. Foord sees this coalition, under Pulteney and Carteret, as the very beginning of *responsible opposition*, a concept absolutely central to the idea of a free, democratic society. Prime responsibility for government was shifting away from the monarch towards Parliament and the ministry responsible to it. We are still not yet, however, in the era of party politics, which was also necessary for the development of a regulated transfer of power from one group, and one set of principles, to the alternative (Kramnick: 151).

Burke and the emergence of modern political opposition

During the following decades of the eighteenth century, opposition was in the air, much of it emanating from Dissenters, such as Richard Price and Joseph Priestley, Trenchard and Gordon, James Burgh and Isaac Watts, all excluded by the *Test Act* from offices of state (Robbins 1968). Their complaints against aristocratic government took a distinctly democratic turn. Price, who crossed swords vigorously with Edmund Burke over the French assertion of liberties, declared that "government is conceived to be an agency for executing the will of the people" (Price 1991:109). Advocating reference of constitutional issues to the people, Priestley differed sharply from Burke's view of a political constitution and, as with Thomas Jefferson, argued: "Were the best formed state in the world to be fixed to its present condition, I make no doubt but that, in a course of time, it would be the worst" (Priestley 1993: 109).

Burke's association with the Rockingham Whigs adds point to the story of the emergence of opposition. Much historical controversy swirls over the role of the "Rockingham Connexion", whose ambiguous opposition under George III to the British war against the American independence movement (Christie 1977: 214-17) is sometimes pinpointed as the real beginnings of party government (O'Gorman 1975; O'Gorman 1982). They were to all intents and purposes a political party in embryo.

They were pioneers in the art of party discipline, even to the point of issuing summons for attendance at Parliament. They were most distinguished, however, by the attempt of their chief thinker, Edmund Burke, to establish a rationale for party. Though at odds with his predecessor, Bolingbroke, on many issues, preferring a "patriot parliament" to a patriot king, Burke shared with him a sense of the moral superiority of opposition over government, since, left unchecked, all government would tend to tyranny. His idea of party was also "eschatological", since it only needed to exist in order to remove the offending policies of an offending government (O'Gorman 1971: 115). Yet he inspired subsequent generations (Foord: 321) with his transforming a general distaste for 'faction' into respect for party united on some principle "for promoting by their joint endeavours the national interest" (Burke 1889 vol 1: 375). Connexions avoided becoming 'factions' by keeping in touch with the "sentiments and opinions of the people" (Burke vol 1: 311). Like Madison in America, Burke heartily disapproved direct reference to the people, but approved their temper, so different from that of the French rabble, because residing within them was a "native religiosity" that emptied them of "lust and self-will" (Burke vol 5: 236). The perennial puzzle with Burke is that he opposed the war against the Americans in favour of the colonists' aspirations while execrating the French revolutionaries for destroying the ties of constitutional probity.[17] The usual explanation is that he upheld the liberties of the Americans *as English citizens* allegedly being poorly treated by their own government, but there is also an argument that he feared the novel American ideas about their new governmental arrangements and the possible impact they might have on Britain itself (Spinner 1991: 401). Burke was never a friend of revolution.

Throughout his reign, King George III struggled to regain an unfettered prerogative over the selection of his ministers; the regency crisis of 1788 all but finished the opposition's chance of taking the Treasury benches. It was at this time that opposition forces began to take up a functional position of constitutional opposition — that is, to contribute constructively to the formation of public policy: "It acquired the function of an institution through which grievances could be ventilated and solved, not with the merely factional purpose of fomenting discontent, but with the genuine purpose of seeking a remedy; and it undertook the task of amending legislation with a view to improving it" (Ionescu and de Madariaga: 56). An esteemed student of Democracy, Dorothy Pickles, averred that opposition should always be constructive (Pickles 1971: 16-30).

During Lord North's long administration of the American war, his opponents built up enough strength and coherence within the Parliament to assume the role of government when the ministry failed. We may date from this time, 1782, the first genuine case of alternation in office, so complete was the transition, 'thus providing an external sign of the recognition of the opposition's right *to be regarded as the alternative government'* (Ionescu and de Madariaga: 394) [18] By the end of the eighteenth century opposition had become a well-accepted and regular feature of British government; in the nineteenth it sharpened into an indispensable component of parliamentary and governmental institutions. The rivalry between Gladstone and Disraeli from the middle of the nineteenth century dramatised the conversation of opposite sides in a highly public manner. The polarisation of politics led to strengthening of internal party ties which tended towards a permanent duality (Hanham 1971: 132).

In 1855 the *Edinburgh Review* contrasted British freedom with European despotism:

> ...the distinctive mark of a free government is, not so much the mildness, moderation and equity of its administration (although it in general avoids the measures of harshness and cruelty which occur from time to time in despotic states), as its permission of a free discussion of its measures – of its toleration of adverse criticism in Parliament, at public meetings, in newspapers, pamphlets and books. It is the legal and acknowledged existence of an organized opposition to the Government which is, in these times, the most salient characteristic of a free country and its principal distinction from despotism... (Foord 4)

The story so far has necessarily concentrated on two-party politics. Traditionally, government and opposition operate *par excellence* within two-party systems (Duverger 1964: 207-8). And the viability of the system rests on the probability that opposing parties would alternate in office. Of course, electorates cannot be instructed or accustomed to changing government for its own sake, but the lack of alternation carries its own dangers. According to Pickles, parties locked into seemingly interminable opposition fall into the "temptation to indulge in irresponsible criticisms and promises" (Pickles: 167). And the viability of the system rests on the probability that opposing parties would alternate in office. Classic two-party systems are increasingly difficult to find, especially when Britain has succumbed to coalition government, so vehemently execrated by Tory ideologues in the past, and Australian governments often cling to office by a thread of independent support. The point was that the personnel, and the stated policies, of potential governments were most clearly evident when identified with a single party with an established, and well-known record. To cobble governments together after inconclusive elections was to invite compromise in published policies, the breaking of promises, the elevation to high office of untested persons, and the making of back-room deals out of sight of the public. This is a potential dissipation of much of the good that constituted opposition stands for, which at the least is open dialogue within a democratic setting. Nevertheless, even multi-party systems with established traditions still operate on broad if not rigid lines of government and opposition. Coalition governments eventually stamp their identity and have opposition forces identifiably ranged up against them. Multi-party systems do not produce the ideal of government and opposition, but they are certainly in advance of some other suggestions for opposition.

Structural opposition?

There have been notable suggestions that political opposition should be a full-time function devoid of the distractions of party politics. One might say that the removal of opposition from the party system would provide an example of "irresponsible government" (Maddox 1982). The French author, Bertrand de Jouvenel, apparently found the multi-party system of his own country too messy to comprehend party opposition and declared "...the party of opposition [to be] simply an element of superstructure". He proposed separate organs, possibly like a constitutional court, to be "'social advocates', public officials who are ready to respond to the appeal of citizens, either in groups or as individuals to whom violence is being done by governmental act" (De Jouvenel 1966: 173).

Inventive though it is, De Jouvenel's vision is restrictive and does nothing to advance the claims of opposition as the prime guarantor of a free society. He envisages only official abuse of citizens and some quasi-judicial redress of their grievances. The courts are part of the structure of democracy under two-party systems, but they leave much scope for the political representatives to act as advocates for their constituents. Moreover, De Jouvenel's proposition tends to bypass the reality that rights and liberties are politically constituted. Worst of all, he permanently denies to opposition the potential power to make structural changes within a society to eliminate the deep-seated causes of the abuse.

The model for De Jouvenel's idea is remote, transmitted through Rousseau's admiration for much that was Roman. Rousseau (288-9) himself proposes a kind of modern revival of the Roman Tribunate of the People:

> This body, which I shall call the *Tribunate*, is the guardian of the laws and of the Legislative Power. It serves sometimes to protect the Sovereign against the Government — as the Tribunes of the People did in Rome; sometimes to support the Government against the People, as the Council of Ten in Venice does...

> [The Tribunate] lapses into tyranny whenever it usurps the Executive Power whose moderator it is and tries to make laws instead of confining itself to its proper function of protecting them.

To support his contentions, De Jouvenel quotes the first-century Roman jurist, Labeo, to say that "the tribunes were not set up to exercise any jurisdiction, but solely to oppose the violence and abuses of the other magistrates and to give help and aid to plaintiffs who were unjustly treated and to imprison those who would not defer to the opposition" (De Jouvenel: 160). For him, "...a power should exist that checks power, without replacing it..." (De Jouvenel: 158) From the Romans he gleans that "...the essential value of the Tribunate was that the people were defended by those who did not aspire to become masters" (De Jouvenel: 161).

Unfortunately, on the tribunes De Jouvenel is in blatant error, even if Labeo whom he quotes is strictly correct about the way the tribunes were "set up". The Roman tribunate was never strictly what might be termed an official office of the Roman state. Cicero called it an office "born in, and for the purposes of, sedition" (Cicero 3. 19). It emerged during the long struggle of the orders, as an "office" representing the disprivileged plebeian caste against the patrician magistrates, who were prone to abusing plebeians, particularly when drafting them to military service. Their original function was the *ius auxilii*, the right of bringing aid to citizens. For this the *plebs* as a body had sworn a curse that any magistrate who violated the henceforth 'inviolable' person of a tribune would be torn to pieces by the mob. From this developed their sacrosanctity, and their *intercessio*, their right of intercession — literally, of "stepping in between" a magistrate and an abused citizen, in order to protect the latter with an inviolable person.

Yet the disabilities of the *plebs* were structural and could only be addressed by changing the constitution. For this the tribunes did indeed require a legislative competence, which the *plebs* wrested from the patricians by a revolutionary secession from the city at time of military threat. The patricians conceded with a law, the famous *lex Hortensia* of 287 BC, that equated all resolutions of the plebeian assembly, hitherto purely informal, with laws of the republic. The legal discrimination against the *plebs* was thus removed by plebeian self-help, even though there remained a social discrimination between the castes. It became regular practice for laws of the republic to be carried by the plebeian assembly, and the ten tribunes were its presiding officers.

It is quite untrue to suggest that the tribunes did not aspire to power.

It *is* true that they sometimes complained that they lacked the official *imperium* — magisterial authority — of the higher magistrates (Livy 6. 37. 4), but as presiding officers of the people's assembly, they wielded considerable power (*tribunicia potestas*) within the Roman state, with legislation necessary to redress structural grievances.

This example is adduced not so much for consideration of a new possible model of opposition, but to demonstrate the importance of party government to the concepts of government and opposition. The Romans never achieved a peaceful transfer of power between the orders of society, and one of the chief impediments was the denial of access to real power on the part of the lower orders. The tribunes sought and won the power of legislation, but they effectively remained under the control of the aristocracy, who ordered affairs largely for their own benefit. No doubt *arcana imperii* — hidden means of wielding power — operate also under party systems of government. No doubt there are obstacles to reform set up by power structures outside the party system. Nevertheless, as far as history teaches so far, party systems offer the best hope of open government, and the best prospects of genuine social change, as witness, for example, the Beveridge Report of 1942, or the introduction of Medibank in Australia in 1973-1974.

The United States

A more immediate object of structural opposition, and one of immense international significance, is the Constitution of the United States. Barack Obama at last introduced a sweeping social reform with his health care system, but against enormous odds (Balz 2010) – never overcome by previous attempts to introduce similar reforms (apart from in the early, extraordinary, Roosevelt era, which conservative forces have done all they can almost to expunge from the historical record (Folsom 2008). The United States does, indeed, have a party system, easily identifiable in the Republican and Democrat parties. Yet America might be called a one-hundred-and-two party system, since the Republican and Democrat party in each State constitutes an entity sufficient unto itself, and with little control over the federal parties, except for participation in the choice of presidential and vice-presidential nominations. The system hardly makes for coherent policy formation, still less for discipline in the carriage of legislation. The Constitution itself has been characterised as "a constitution against party" (Hofstadter 1969: 40-73). Designed by people strongly convinced of Calvinist teachings about the human propensity to sin, the Constitution was shot through with checks-and-balances, as propounded by Montesquieu in his reflections on the propaganda of Bolingbroke. Government might be necessary, but it is a necessary evil, and its immense power in the hands of malefactors, who would inevitably take charge unless prevented, would be destructive of the liberties of all. The Constitution, with its legendary separation of powers and checks and balances, sets up inertia against coherent policy formation which is designed to avoid the use of government power in any concerted way. This may seem strange to say about the 'most powerful government the world has ever seen' in terms of its military might and diplomatic prominence, but it holds good for the scant opportunity would-be reformers can win to carry out their plans vis-à-vis the internal society. All this is overlaid with a heavy ideology of individualism: "Ask not what your country can do for you...", where people are frequently told that "government is not the solution, it is the problem".

In the 1960s Robert Dahl virtually canonised the international study of opposition with his edited collection *Political Opposition in Western Democracies*, even though a persuasive case for institutional opposition could scarcely be found within the American polity (Dahl 1966). American theorists are wont to idealise this situation as the essential preservation of individual liberties, and when the topic of opposition comes into focus, it is seen to be located in the structures of political impediment. Carl Friedrich, for example, argued that the layers of the federal system create a "pattern of opposition" that "increases the opportunities for dissenting minorities to make their views known to other citizens and policymakers" (Friedrich 1966; 287).

As with De Jouvenel, this does not envisage the possibility of an opposition wresting the power of government in order to make reformatory changes to the society. The opportunity for minority groups to pop up in protest at various decisions does not identify any coherent opposition and does not improve upon the possibility of neighbourhood groups and protest movements in more orthodox two-party systems. It may, however, increase the opportunity of small minority groups to thwart the will of majorities, which the system inherently holds in suspicion. The diffuse nature of the immense American federal system disperses opposition and blurs the focus on truly objectionable government activity. Despite a strong claim on the part of various American academics that it favours opposition, it is difficult to locate the phenomenon within their system.

The crisis of democracy

In light of a growing pessimism about the international state of democracy and a turn to some level of absolutism in countries claiming to be democracies, much of the above discussion might appear to refer to a utopian past, at least in terms of the dialectical image. The key to much of the pessimism is what we have seen as the United States experience. It was founded on a constitution specifically designed to neuter the influence of the unwashed commoner. Much more important, however, is the crushing dominance of the market ideology, which advocates the free economic choice of individual persons and relegates government activity to protecting the system. In the United States the power of corporations overwhelms public opinion on all fronts. This 'protection' has sometimes incurred the mammoth outlay of public funds to private enterprises that are "too big to fail", even though their private dealings have failed themselves and the public.

Some distinguished American writers have lamented the situation, among them Noam Chomsky and Benjamin Barber (Chomsky 2006; Barber 2001; Barber 2008). The revered student of the history of political ideas, Sheldon Wolin (2008), eventually evinced an enormous shudder of despair in his final testament, *Democracy Incorporated. Managed Democracy and the Specter of Inverted Totalitarianism*. Unions, churches, guilds and associations are all subsumed under the reigning culture of commercialism, while the major political parties, far from representing truly diverse interests, are varieties of boards under the whole commercial empire. Totalitarianism was always a fearful word in American political expression, and its adoption by such an outstanding thinker was truly a cry of despair. Democracy had disappeared.

The decline of democratic commitment around the world has become widely noticed. There have been recent signs of erosion in Venezuela, Hungary, Brazil, Turkey, Israel, and Poland. Going so far as to pronounce the "twilight" of democracy, Anne Applebaum (2020; 56) exposes the "eternal" appeal of spreading authoritarianism and the rise of demagoguery in many countries. The New York political scientist, Adam Przeworski, as is fitting for someone working from the United States, adopts a severely minimalist definition of democracy: "simply a system in which incumbents lose elections and leave when they lose" (Przeworski 2019: 5). Democracy is in decline where rulers refuse to leave after losing the ballot. It is in crisis when fists, stones, or bullets replace ballots (Przeworski 13). He notes, there are, "Two structural conditions, I think, deserve special attention. The first is that political equality, which democracy is supposed to be based on, coexists uneasily with capitalism, a system of economic inequality. The second is the sheer quest for political power, whether or not based on economic interests" (Przeworski: 16). There are distinct signs of the decline of commitment even to the idea of democracy in the United States.

The British evolution of party opposition was admired from the continent by such as Duverger, Kluxen and Sartori, but its recent politics have been severely criticized from within. In a more-or-less populist outburst, A.C. Grayling has denounced the recent crop of British politicians for having departed from the high ideals that the nation's unwritten constitution required for its survival. The Parliament, he argues, no longer carries sovereign authority since power has devolved onto the executive government with the Crown prerogative. It rules effectively without Parliament through "orders in council" (Grayling 2017: 134-6). The Commons has lost prestige through the lack of personal authority in its members. Often, he argues, their behaviour would be illegal in any other workplace:

> This picture of a vigorous democratic debate summoning the en-
> franchised to make a choice is of course idealized. In practice the
> process involves spin and dirty tricks, half truths and untruths, dis-
> tortion, propaganda, *ad hominem* attacks on individuals rather than

their ideas, all aimed at inflating the positives of one party and undermining the credibility of the other. (Grayling: 141-2)

Conclusion

For all the evidence of a declining commitment to democracy in much of the world, the ideal of self-determination for responsible adults remains. Political opposition is the outcome of the desire of human beings to govern their own affairs, to think their own thoughts, and to experience freedom within an organized civil setting. It has taken different forms, but few of them resemble "constitutional, responsible opposition" whereby the political system is upheld regardless of whether one wins or loses the immediate battle, and where one opposes *responsibly* in the expectation that one might soon have to answer for one's actions and opinions within the responsibility of government. What is preferred in this chapter is the possibility of strong government, capable of reform, matched by strong, focused opposition, that can concentrate on reviewing a government's action, and replace it with preferable reform, or consolidation, as far as it is able to persuade the electorate. There is furthermore a practical effect of the balance between government and opposition. As one astute British politician proclaimed, even when *he* was in office, a condition of good government was a vibrant opposition, and one that nearly balanced the government in numbers. This same Lord Simon also declared that opposition was a means of upholding the comity of good government: "Our parliamentary system will work as long as the responsible people in different parties accept the view that it is better that the other side should win than that the constitution should be broken" (Simon 1947: 31-20. Simon would no doubt be horrified at Grayling's more recent conclusions. His lesson is lost on some Australian politicians, but that is another story (Warhurst 2010).

References

Amery, L.S., *Thoughts on the Constitution*, Oxford: Oxford University Press, 1947

Applebaum, A., *Twilight of Democracy*, London: Allen Lane, 2020

Balz D., et al (the Staff of the Washington Post), *Landmark. America's New Health-Care Law and What it Means for Us All*, New York: Public Affairs, 2010

D'Agostino, F., 'Ethical Pluralism and the Role of Opposition in Democratic Politics", *The Monist*, 73(3), 1990, 437-63

Barber, B.R., "The Compromised Republic: Public Purposelessness in America", in Horwitz, R.H., (ed), *The Moral Foundations of the American Republic*, Charlottesville: University Press of Virginia, 2nd ed, 1977, 19-38

Barber, B.R., *Jihad vs McWorld: Terrorism's Challenge to Democracy*, New York: Ballantine Books, 2001

Barber, B.R., *Consumed. How Markets Corrupt Children, Infantilize Adults and Swallow Citizens Whole,* New York: Norton, 2008

Barker, R., (ed), *Studies in Opposition*, London, Macmillan, 1971

Bolingbroke. Henry St John, Viscount Bolingbroke, *The Works of Lord Bolingbroke* [1844], London, Frank Cass reprint. 1967

Burke, E., "Thoughts on the Cause of Present Discontents", [1770] in *The Works of Edmund Burke,* London: George Bell and Son, 1889, 6 vols

Calvin, J., *Institutes of the Christian Religion* [1559] IV. 20. 32 (trans. Henry Beveridge) Grand Rapids: Eerdmans, 1989

Chavura, S.A., "Mixed Constitutionalism and Parliamentarism in Elizabethan England: The Case of Thomas Cartwright", *History of European Ideas*, 41(3), 2015, 318-37

Chomsky, N., *Failed States: The Abuse of Power and the Assault on Democracy,* New York: Metropolitan Books, 2006

Christie, I.R., "British Politics and the American Revolution", *Albion*, 9(3) Autumn 1977, 214-17

Christie, I.R., *The End of North's Ministry*, New York: St Martin's Press, 1958

Cicero, M.T., *De legibus* (On the Laws)

Clements, R.E., *Prophecy and Tradition*, Oxford: Blackwell, 1962

Coffey, J., *Politics, Religion and the British Revolutions – The Mind of Samuel Rutherford,* Cambridge: Cambridge University Press, 1997

Cottret, B., *The Huguenots in England. Immigration and Settlement c. 1550-1700.* (trans. P. and A. Stevenson) Cambridge: Cambridge University Press, 1991

Duverger, M., *Political Parties*, (trans. B and R. North), London: Methuen, 3rd ed 1964

Eales, J., "A Road to Revolution: The Continuity of Puritanism, 1559-1642", in Durston C., and Eales, J., (eds), *The Culture of English Puritanism, 1560-1700*, Basingstoke: Bloomsbury, 1996, 184-209

Elazar D., and Kincaid, J., (eds), *The Covenant Connection: From Federal Theology to Modern Federalism*, Lanham MD: Lexington Books, 2000

Foord, A.S., *His Majesty's Opposition 1714-1830*, Oxford: Clarendon Press, 1964

Franklin, J.H., (ed), *Constitutionalism and Resistance in the Sixteenth Century: Three Treatises by Hotman, Beza & Mornay*, New York: Pegasus, 1969

Friedrich, C.J., "Federalism as Opposition", *Government and Opposition*, 1(3), April 1966, 286-96

Gerrard, C., *The Patriot Opposition to Walpole 1725-1742*, Oxford: Oxford University Press, 1994

Gillespie, M.A., *The Theological Origins of Modernity*, Chicago: University of Chicago Press, 2009

Grayling, A.C., *Democracy and Its Crisis,* London: Oneworld, 2017

Gunn, J.A.W., "'Interest Will Not Lie': A Seventeenth-Century Political Maxim", *Journal of the History of Ideas*, 29(4), October-December 1968, 551-64

Gunn, J.A.W., *Factions No More. Attitudes to Party Government and Opposition in Eighteenth-Century England*, London: Frank Cass, 1972

Haakonssen K., (ed), *Traditions of Liberalism. Essays on John Locke, Adam Smith and John Stuart Mill,* St Leonards: Centre for Independent Studies, 1988

Hampsher-Monk, I., "Edmund Burke's Changing Justification for Intervention", *The Historical Journal*, 48(1), March 2005, 65-100

Hancock, R.C., *Calvin and the Foundations of Modern Politics*, Ithaca: Cornell University Press, 1989

Hanham, H.J., "Opposition Techniques in British Politics, 1867-1914", in Barker, R., (ed), *Studies in Opposition*, 1971: 131-45

Hansen, M.H., *The Athenian Democracy in the Age of Demosthenes,* Oxford: Blackwell, 1991

Hobbes, T., *Behemoth, or the Epitome of the Civil Wars of England, 1640-1660*, London, 1679

Hofstadter, R., "The Founding Fathers: An Age of Realism", in Horwitz, *The Moral Foundations of the American Republic*, 73-85

Hooker, R., *Laws of Ecclesiastical Polity*, London, 1593, I. 10. 5

Hocking, T.A., "The Roles of Loyal Opposition in Britain's House of Commons: Three Historical Paradigms", *Parliamentary Affairs*, 5(1), 1971, 50-68

Ionescu, G., and de Madariaga, I., *Opposition*, Harmondsworth: Penguin, 1972

De Jouvenel, B., "The Means of Contestation", *Government and Opposition*, 1(2), January 1966, 155-74

Kishlansky, M., "The Emergence of Adversary Politics in the Long Parliament", *Journal of Modern History*, 49(4), December 1977, 617-40

Kluxen, K., *Das Problem der Politischen Opposition: Entwicklung u. Wesen d. engl. Zweiparteien im 18 Jh.*, Freiburg and Munich: Alber, 1956

Kluxen, K., *Parlamentarismus*, Cologne: Kiepenheuer and Witsch, 1967

Kraynak, R.P., "Hobbes's *Behemoth* and the Argument for Absolutism", *American Political Science Review*, 76(4), 1982, 621-33

Krygier, M., *Civil Passions. Selected Writings*, Melbourne: Black Inc., 2005

Lindsay, A.D., *The Essentials of Democracy*, Oxford: Oxford University Press, 2 ed 1935

Maddox, G., "Responsible and Irresponsible Opposition: The Case of the Roman Tribunes", *Government and Opposition*, 17(2), Spring 1982, 212-20

Maddox, G., *Religion and the Rise of Democracy*, London: Routledge, 1996

Maddox, G., "Hebrew Prophecy and the Foundations of Political Opposition", *Australian Religion Studies Review*, 21(1), 2008, 69-82

Maddox, G., "The Religious Background to Modern Political Opposition", *Australian Religion Studies Review*, 24(3), 2011, 37-58

Maddox, G., "The Spell of Parmenides and the Paradox of the Commonwealth", *History of Political Thought*, 22(2), Summer 2011, 253-79

McLaren, A., "Rethinking Republicanism: *Vindiciae Contra Tyrannos* in Context", *The Historical Journal*, 49(1), 2006, 23-52

McNeill, J.T., "The Democratic Element in Calvin's Thought", *Church History*, 18(3), September 1949, 161-2

Milton, J., *Areopagitica* and *Of Education*, (George H. Sabine ed), New York: Crofts Classics, 1951

Milton, J., "The Tenure of Kings and Magistrates", [1649] in Dzelzainis M., (ed), *Milton. Political Writings*, Cambridge: Cambridge University Press, 2001, 3-48

Moore, T., "Recycling Aristotle. The Sovereignty Theory of Richard Hooker", *History of Political Thought*, 19, 1993, 345-59

Ober, J., *Mass and Elite in Democratic Athens. Rhetoric, Ideology and the Power of the People*, Princeton: Princeton University Press, 1989

O'Gorman, F., *The Rise of Party in England. The Rockingham Whigs, 1760-1782*, London: Allen and Unwin, 1975

O'Gorman, F., *The Emergence of the British Two-Party System, 1760-1782*, New York: Holmes and Meier, 1982

Pickles, D., *Democracy,* London: Methuen, 1971

Pitkin, H.F., *The Concept of Representation*, Berkeley and Los Angeles: University of California Press, 1967

Pocock, J.G.A., *Politics, Language and Time. Essays on Political Thought and History*, New York: Atheneum, 1973

Przeworski, A., *Crises of Democracy*, Cambridge: Cambridge University Press, 2019

Price, R., in "Introduction" in Thomas D.O., (ed), *Political Writings*, Cambridge: Cambridge University Press, 1991, x

Priestley, J., "Essay on the First Principles", in Miller, P., (ed). *Political Writings*, Cambridge: University Press, Cambridge, 1993.

Robbins, C., *The Eighteenth Century Commonwealthman*, New York: Athenaeum, 1968

Robertson, G., *The Tyrannicide Brief,* London: Chatto and Windus, 2005

Rousseau, J., *The Social Contract* 4. 1 (trans. G. Hopkins), in Ernest Barker (ed), *Social Contract: Essays by Locke, Hume, Rousseau*, Oxford: Oxford University Press, 1971

Rutherford, S., *Lex, Rex, or the Law and the Prince*, London: John Field, 1644

de Sanctis, A., *The 'Puritan' Democracy of Thomas Hill Green*, Exeter: Imprint Academic, 2005

Sartori, G., *Parties and Party Systems. A framework for analysis*, Cambridge: Cambridge University Press, 1976

Spinner, J., "Constructing Communities: Edmund Burke on Revolution", *Polity*, 23(3), Spring 1991, 395-421

Swift, J., *Some Reasons to Prove that no Person is Obliged by his Principles as a Whig to Oppose Her Majesty or her Present Ministry*, London: 1712

Talmon, J.L., *The Rise of Totalitarian Democracy*, Boston: Beacon Press, 1952

Uhr, J., "Inequality and Inequity in Political Leadership: Henry Fielding's Satire in Jonathan Wild", Paper presented to the American Political Science Association Annual Meeting, Chicago, 2004

Uhr, J., "The Power of Opposition: Reconsidering Bolingbroke's Political Theory of Opposition", Paper presented to the American Political Science Association Annual Meeting, Philadelphia, 2006

Walzer, M., *The Revolution of the Saints: A Study in the Origins of Radical Politics*, New York: Athenaeum, 1968

Warhurst, J., "Political opposition need not be nasty", *Eureka Street*, 20(21), 3 November 2010

Winship, M. P., *Godly Republicanism: Puritans, Pilgrims, and a City on a Hill*, Cambridge, MA: Harvard University Press, 2012

Woodhouse, A.S.P., *Puritanism and Liberty*, London: Dent, 2nd ed, 1974

Woodhouse, A.S.P, "Puritanism and Democracy", *Canadian Journal of Economics and Political Science*, 4(1), February 1938, 1-21

Endnotes

1   *Hetaireia*= 'association', 'brotherhood', 'political club'.

2   A parallel account came from the French Huguenot writer, the Duc de Rohan, who wrote in the tradition of the "mirror of princes". Expecting England to be "the balancer of Europe", he exhorted the English to unity under their Protestant King. He had great influence on subsequent English writers. See Gunn, "'Interest Will Not Lie'", 554.

3   1 Samuel 8.

4   Contra the fashion, following Rousseau, to locate the origins of political opposition in the Roman institution of the tribunate. See De Jouvenel, "The Means of Contestation"; and Ionescu and de Madariaga, *Opposition*.

5   2 Samuel 12. 7.

6   1 Kings 18 & 21.

7   Prophets began writing to ensure that their message had been delivered to rulers who were prone to taking little notice of them. See Clements, *Prophecy and Tradition*, 309.

8   Amos 5. 21-24. (Scriptural quotations are from the New English Bible.)

9   Jeremiah 22. 13-17.

10 Amos 6. 4-6.

11 Hosea 5. 10.

12 Isaiah 5. 8.

13 Isaiah 3. 14-25.

14 For a detailed survey of attitudes to parties before the time of Edmund Burke, see Gunn, *Factions No More*.

15 Swift, *Some Reasons to Prove*, as cited in Foord, *His Majesty's Opposition*, 9.

16 Kramnick, *Bolingbroke and his Circle*, 156-157, and citing Kluxen, *Das Problem der politischen Opposition*.

17 Burke eventually came to advocate intervention in revolutionary France, arguing that France was integral to a 'Diplomatick Republick of Europe'; see Hampsher-Monk, "Edmund Burke's Changing Justification for Intervention", 86.

18 Ionescu and de Madariaga, *Opposition*, 5-56, at n. 47, and citing Kurt Kluxen, *Parlamentarismus*, 1967, 394 (emphasis added); cf. Christie, *The End of North's Ministry*.

2

An "Organised Living Representation" of the Government's Opponents: The Views of the Framers of the Australian Constitution on Governments, Oppositions and Party Government

Nicholas Aroney and Benjamin B. Saunders

Introduction

This chapter examines the way in which the framers of the Constitution of Australia understood the role and nature of "the opposition" within Westminster parliamentary systems of government. It traces how their understandings, hopes and expectations for such a system of government influenced the terms and structure of the Constitution. The debates at the various conventions and the related literature of the time are examined with a view to identifying relevant statements of principle, categorising the key themes that emerge, and drawing inferences about the framers' underlying assumptions, beliefs and principles about politics, democracy and the design implications for the federal Constitution.

The framers did not articulate their views of the role of oppositions in detail but tended to presuppose the general understanding of that role that prevailed in the Australian colonies. Accordingly, writings of the federation period are important in illuminating contemporary beliefs and understandings. This article therefore examines such writings with a focus on the views that were articulated by the framers that materially influenced the drafting of the Constitution.

The framers expected the Commonwealth to operate in accordance with the conventional practices of Westminster parliamentary government and ministerial responsibility, where the ministry was responsible to the parliament for performance of its functions, and parliament retained a measure of control over and independence from the ministry.[1] Political parties were considered essential to provide stability and effective government under this system. This system was, however, soon to undergo a profound change early in the 20th century with the advent of disciplined party government. The framers did not predict the precise form in which party government would function, but they nevertheless understood that parties would exist in the Commonwealth and were well aware of the problems that parties could create. During the federation debates there was an unease about cabinet government and political parties and their tendency to undermine ministerial responsibility and other features of the traditional conception of parliamentary responsible government. It was in this context that the framers understood the role of the opposition.

The Framers on opposition

With the introduction of responsible government to the Australian colonies in the mid-1850s[2] came the necessity for ministers to be appointed and governments to be formed, led by a member of parliament able to command the support of a majority of members of the lower house (McMinn 1979: 40-91). But prior to the 1890s there were no formal political parties and so governments were formed on the basis of loose, semi-permanent political agreements among like-minded members of parliament. These parliamentary factions formed temporary governing coalitions which lacked a coherent political program and the structure and discipline of modern parties (Loveday and Martin 1966). "Oppositions" were likewise improvised and informal.

Organised parties and party discipline began to emerge from the 1890s, and in 1909 the modern two party system was born when the non-labour parties fused to form the Liberal Party (Moore et al 1998: 17; Miller 1953: 3; Strangio and Dyrenfurth 2009). This fundamental change to the patterns of Australian politics was a welcome development for many given the instability of factional politics (Loveday et al 1977: 14; Loveday and Martin 1966: 1-5). The formality and permanence of the opposition tracked the developments in the nature of parties: it was only as political parties began to take the form of permanent organisations with rules, procedures, platforms and discipline that the office of "leader of the opposition" was formally recognised in colonial legislatures (Loveday and Martin: ch 6).

The framers of the Australian Constitution did not articulate a detailed philosophy of opposition, for its nature and role was not a central topic of debate at the Constitutional Conventions. Their views about oppositions can be reconstructed, however, from comments scattered throughout the debates and accompanying writings. The evidence suggests a shared common understanding formed in the context of similar experiences in the several colonies, combined with nonetheless significant differences over matters of detail. Where such disagreement existed, it was often heated because it was related to fundamental matters in dispute concerning the nature of democratic representation and the proper place of parliamentary responsible government within a federal system. The framers' understanding of the role and nature of the opposition within a Westminster system was thus a focal point for more fundamental disagreements about the nature of the polity that the framers wished to establish.

Oppositions were seen as an inevitable and necessary feature of parliamentary government, reflecting differences of opinion which were considered to be entirely legitimate; they were therefore an essential part of a healthy functioning parliamentary system. As Duncan Gillies put it:

> it must be self-evident to everybody that as soon as ever a govern-
> ment might be formed, no matter what it might represent, an oppo-
> sition to it would be forthcoming immediately . . . It is impossible
> to find gentlemen who will agree upon every point. I am taking the

facts as I find them. The universal experience is that there never has
been a government in this or any other country which has not had a
very fair amount of opposition.[3]

As the pendulum of public opinion swung to and fro, governments
and oppositions would hold office in turn. Robert Garran, for example,
referred to what he called the "comfortable see-saw of government
and opposition"; another influential contemporary observed that
"Governments are but the creatures of a day and that those on the left
of the Speaker usually in time are entrusted with the responsibilities of
office" (Garran 1933: 440; Kirwan 1936: 255).

The importance of opposition

Notwithstanding their differences, the framers were clearly of the opinion
that opposition was indispensable in a parliamentary system, primarily
for holding government accountable through parliamentary scrutiny and
criticism, and also for the capacity to represent a greater diversity of
views in Parliament in the form of an alternative government. William
McMillan reflected the views of many when he expressed the hope that
there would "always be an opposition, sturdy, critical, and independent,
so that the ministry may always feel the breath of the people and be
turned out as soon as they cease to represent the people" (Convention
Debates, Thursday 12 March 1891: 273). One anonymous pamphleteer
adopted colourful biblical imagery to describe the contrast between
government and opposition: "the fact is that the life of religion, like that
of parliamentary or party government, depends upon the existence of an
opposition – the dualism of God and Satan" (Anonymous 1898: 272).

For Richard O'Connor, this was elevated into a crucial element of the
workings of parliament. He expressed strong faith in the ability of the
press and the opposition to maintain the purity of parliament in preference
to entrenching safeguards in the Constitution which would unduly fetter
the legislative powers of the parliament:

The main consideration is surely the public interest, and considering the large trust which we are placing in the federal parliament, and the enormous powers which we have given them in every direction, we may fairly allow them to administer these matters subject to the criticism of an opposition, and under the eyes of the press and public. It is to this criticism that we must look for the maintenance of the purity of parliament (Convention Debates, Tuesday 21 September 1897: 1033).

O'Connor's position, which was accepted by the majority of the framers, was that "we should trust the federal parliament, and leave it to the ordinary operations of the criticism of the opposition and of the press to see that purity is observed" (Convention Debates, Tuesday 21 September 1897: 1033). The framers thus expected the opposition to closely examine the exercise of power by the ministry (Clark 1901: 252-3). It has often been noted that the framers trusted the workings of parliament and responsible government to protect rights, but the crucial role of opposition in this conception has not always been recognised (La Nauze 1972: 227-32; Galligan 1993: 100, 106; Irving 1997: 162). By not adopting a bill of rights the framers evidenced a faith in the ordinary workings of parliament and responsible government,[4] but O'Connor's statement suggests an important additional detail, namely, that an active opposition was seen as one of the most crucial elements in providing this scrutiny.

In terms reminiscent of John Stuart Mill,[5] Henry Parkes added a second important function, namely that of giving voice to opposing views in the formation of policy, thus sharpening the deliberations of parliament and making good decisions more likely in the long run:

Every question of sufficient magnitude to enter into the policy of a government, which means the active governing power of the country, must have two sides. By the moral and intellectual contentions as to which is the true side, light is thrown even upon the opposite forces, public opinion is informed and strengthened, and all classes of the community are better enabled to discern and appreciate the nature of the interests at stake. The wrong side – the side most detrimental to the country – may for a time prevail, but it has the least chance of prevailing under honest and open debate by opposing sides; and the right in most cases is sure to come uppermost in the long run (Parkes 1892: 401).

For Parkes, the opposition thus fulfilled an important representative and corrective function. A similar view was expressed in debate in the Queensland Legislative Assembly in 1898. The Queensland Government had urged the Labor Party to formally assume the position of "Her Majesty's constitutional opposition" (Parliament Queensland 1898: 79, 252), the Home Secretary, James Dickson, arguing that a well-functioning government

> . . . can best be attained by the constant criticisms of an intelligent opposition . . . But that opposition should not be of a pragmatic or accidental character. It should be an organised living representation of those who are opposed in politics to the existing government. In that light I believe a good opposition is as essential to the maintenance of the true parliamentary and political life of the country as the very best government that ever existed (Queensland 1898: 79, 252).

In response the leader of the Labor Party was cautious but positive: "the party have, after very careful consideration and a good deal of thought, decided to assume the position of an opposition, with all the contingent responsibilities", a statement that was greeted with approval by the government (Queensland 1898: vol 79, 365). By accepting these responsibilities, the Labor Party was not only affirming its willingness to hold the government to account but also to remain loyal to the constitutional system as a whole. The terms in which the government and the then leader of the Labor Party approached the issue show a recognition of the importance of the role. Accepting the office of His or Her Majesty's Loyal Opposition – a phrase often found in the contemporary literature – was a deliberate step, understood to involve serious obligations, and not to be taken lightly but with due recognition of its importance within the system of government (Parliament Queensland 1898: 79, 365). In fulfilling this important role the opposition played a crucial constitutional function; Parkes maintained that remaining in opposition and failing to win government was accordingly not to be considered a failure, "so long as the principles of a sound policy are faithfully maintained".[6]

Characteristics of a successful and effective opposition

To the framers, both vigour and unity were considered essential for an opposition to be effective. Alfred Deakin, reflecting on English experience at the end of the 19th century, observed that although the (Liberal) Opposition had consisted of highly capable individuals – in his view, perhaps even more capable than the Government – they were nevertheless "disunited, repressed and distrustful to such a degree that they scarcely counted in politics and appeared to have no future before them".[7] For Deakin (1944: 132-3), a weak opposition allowed a government to exercise enormous unrestrained power:

> Chamberlain . . . [in 1900] was practically the master of the House of Commons. The opposition benches contained no peer of his after Harcourt withdrew. The dispirited and divided Liberals fairly cowered before their old colleague . . . The overwhelming Tory majority, the ascendancy of Chamberlain in debate, the patent fact that in maintaining the war the country was behind them, added to their own jealousies, had reduced the Commons to a chamber of registration for Ministerial proposals and of apparently unanswerable expositions of the soundness of Ministerial policy. The opposition existed, but was powerless to oppose with either force or effect, and therefore merely preserved the forms of debate without its reality.

Absent a strong opposition, the government will be able to function with little scrutiny or resistance, Deakin believed, a point that is particularly important when the opposition was considered to be the primary constitutional actor responsible for maintaining the purity of the political process.

A related issue concerned the appropriate conduct of an opposition. The leader of the opposition should be "a man of great political capability" and prepared to devote the time and effort to discharging his duties faithfully" (Wise 1913: 173). The ideal was that an opposition should act for the public good, and not to further its own ambitions. Parkes considered that political actors should be able to transcend party when required by the public interest: "Party action in parliament", he said, "is to give way to perfect harmony, where the best men on all sides are to unite in doing the best work" (Parkes 1892: 313). The opposition, as well as the government, therefore ought to act "responsibly" when criticising the other side. This was one benefit of the increasing institutionalisation of the opposition, for it effectively formalised the position of the opposition as the alternative government within the constitutional structure. This ought to impose a sense of responsibility, for when criticising the government and putting forward alternative policies the opposition may have the burden of implementing those policies if it subsequently won government. Oppositions could therefore be responsible or irresponsible.[8]

While they considered oppositions to be legitimate and necessary to the functioning of parliamentary democracy, the framers were clearly aware of their shortcomings in the usual course of events. The framers recognised that oppositions are constantly subjected to the temptation to act to further partisan goals or other sectional or personal interests. Indeed, this was an inherent feature of the parliamentary system. Earl Grey wrote in 1864 that "[p]arliamentary government derives its whole force and power of action from the exercise of an influence which is at least very much akin to corruption" (Grey 1864: 41, 43). The need for the ministry to maintain the confidence of the lower house of parliament distorted the incentives of MPs, who could not regard measures dispassionately but were constantly forced to consider their political impact on their party.[9] Under the Westminster system, "the character and conduct of the members of the Government, [were] habitually and professionally judged by their declared personal rivals" (Cecil 1855: 1, 4).

Accordingly, the framers recognised that an opposition might oppose virtually everything a Government does, for political or personal reasons. Deakin described the behaviour of George Dibbs in the following terms:

> Decorous as were the proceedings of the 1891 Convention as a
> whole, there was by no means perfect harmony within its several

delegations. There was in the first place an open antagonism between Parkes and Dibbs which gave smouldering evidences of activity even in the public debates. While ostentatiously admitting the President's right to the Chair, Dibbs could not throw off his familiar role of leader of the opposition sufficiently to allow him to regard the propositions submitted by his rival dispassionately. They emanated from Parkes and as such it was his duty to defeat or at least to mutilate them as much as possible. (Deakin 1944: 41).

Parkes expressed strong views about the propriety of opposition behaviour, much of it no doubt coloured by several decades of experience as one of the leading politicians in New South Wales,[10] criticising the opposition for its "irresponsible" manoeuvrings designed to waste the time of parliament and prevent it from accomplishing anything, purely for party ends, and referred to the "transient fury of opposition" which he said had worked harm to the interests of New South Wales (Parkes 1892: 41-2, 236-7). In the course of a discussion regarding jurisdiction over internal waters, Premier George Reid made the following statement which, in a rare instance of statesmanship, is revealing as to the usual course of colonial politics:

> I can assure honourable members that the ardour and earnestness with which I am fighting this matter are entirely above the tricks of local politics. Surely if there are two men in New South Wales who may be supposed to have a very fair idea of the opinion of the people, it is the two men who happen to be the Premier of the colony and the leader of the opposition. And when gentlemen, accustomed as we are to differ perpetually and to fight constantly, agree and tell you what the public opinion of New South Wales is on this point, instead of being a proof of some trick or of a desire of the one to overpass the other in our own colony, I think the more candid-minded members of this Convention will regard it as a proof that both of us are representing what we believe to be the feelings of the people of our colony. (Convention Debates, Friday 4 February 1898: 577).

At one point in the Convention debates in 1898, John Forrest[11] made his views on the behaviour of the opposition clear: "I feel sure that upon our return to our respective colonies we shall be confronted with questions, not only by the supporters of the government in the house, but also by the opposition, who, on all subjects, even upon those which commend themselves generally, take an opposite side to that taken by the government" (Convention Debates, Tuesday 10 March 1891: 220). Given that Forrest was Premier of Western Australia there may be an element of hyperbole in this comment, but it illustrates the attitude of those in power towards the opposition. Not infrequently, colonial rivalries between governments and oppositions were manifested at the federal conventions.[12]

The anonymous tract, *Is Federation Our True Policy?* (published in 1898), contained the following passage, describing what it regarded as the demise of parliamentary government, in a way that also set forth an important set of normative expectations:

> 1. All the glorious institutions of parliament as conducted in the old country, and after which our own parliament is supposed to be modelled, are being neglected and falling to decay.
>
> 2. It was commonly understood that a parliament should comprise a government and an opposition.
>
> 3. Instead of this desirable and legitimate system prevailing here, rival factions were bidding fair to make good government impossible.
>
> 4. There was no recognised or properly organised opposition in the house; there was no person amongst the different factions opposing the government who could take the premier's place should a crisis arise.
>
> 5. At most, all these factions could do was to carry on a sort of guerrilla warfare; none of them were prepared or able to take any responsibility for his action or vote.
>
> 6. The members of the opposition, being utterly irresponsible, took every opportunity to talk upon every conceivable subject.[13]

Selfish ambition was recognised as lying behind much oppositional behaviour. Andrew Inglis Clark approvingly quoted the following extract from a speech of Chief Justice Higinbotham:

> it ought to be observed, that there are many persons now in this country who have even begun to question the foundations of our Constitution – to ask, 'What is the use of responsible government; what good can possibly come out of this House?' These feelings of distrust and disapproval are, if I do not mistake, almost entirely occasioned and generated by the accursed system under which the party on this side of the House are always striving to murder the reputations of the party on the other side, in order to leap over the dead bodies of their reputations on to the seats in the Treasury bench.[14]

Opposition and parties

These perceived weaknesses anticipate another aspect of political propriety that was strongly emphasised at the time of federation. Parkes argued that the weaknesses of parliamentary government do not stem from the existence of parties *per se*, but from parties formed for reasons of ambition and self-interest, rather than a common commitment to a particular political principle:[15]

> It is not party in any true sense, but party so-called, brought together by other means than attachment to and promulgation of openly avowed principles, which works the mischief at the ballot-box or in the parliamentary arena . . . Instead of the abolition of party, we want an intelligent and a conscientious adherence to party lines, the strongest cast of which is quite consistent with personal respect and courtesy in political intercourse (Parkes 1892: 314-5).

Such a view echoed Edmund Burke's famous definition of party as "a body of men united for promoting by their joint endeavours the national interest upon some particular principle in which they are all agreed" (Burke 1852:170). For Parkes, parties formed on this basis are legitimate and honourable. The conditions necessary for producing this are often lacking, however: in Bagehot's words, "[w]here great questions end, little parties begin" (Bagehot 1867: 45). Charles Gavan Duffy and Howard Willoughby, although not participants in the federation debates, both expressed the view that a lack of political passions leads to uninspiring politics. According to Duffy (1898: pt 4(2), 161), when great issues are at stake in the political arena, politicians are inspired to great statesmanship but otherwise politics degenerates into factional struggles:

> It was plain to an experienced eye that there was no party organi-
> sation among the opposition ... there was no secretary to summon
> the party, and no Whip to secure their punctual attendance. When
> there are not great political passions at work the political activity of
> a new country is like the movements of an anthill, and the absence
> of permanent relations in public or private life robs it of one of the
> centres round which party combinations gradually form.

Willoughby (1891: 70) expressed a similar view:

> When a great principle is at stake a division into parties is inevi-
> table, but in ordinary times and in ordinary countries there will be
> no such great principles to persistently fight about; and then party
> government is liable to degenerate into the struggle of factions. The
> opposition will resort to unworthy practices to bring their party into
> power, and the ministry will be tempted to resort to countermining
> in order to retain possession. When matters are at their very worst,
> the one party will bitterly vilify the other so as to expose it to public
> opprobrium, and the worse the faction the lower it is in intelligence,
> and the less lofty it is in principle and aim, the more readily will
> it use such weapons and the greater for the moment its chance of
> success with the multitude. The cure comes later on, but not until
> mistakes have been made and excesses committed. The frequent
> formation of coalition governments in the Australian colonies is ev-
> idence in itself that the party system is by no means an unqualified
> success here.

This suggests the view that although parties are an inevitable feature of politics in a democracy, in the usual course they will not reach the lofty standards idealised by the likes of Burke and Parkes. Parties will rise to the occasion only when "great principles" are at stake, and this is not usually the case; the unfortunate fact is that all too often parties are formed, and their activities carried on, to further sectional and self-interest.

Those who opposed the system of responsible government challenged political parties on a more fundamental level, extending to a critique of the lack of a truly "representative" character of those in opposition, which was considered one of their most important functions (Reid 1917: 42). Clark (1901: 383), in particular, argued that parties are not necessarily representative of the views of the people:

> In England a ministerial or opposition majority is frequently obtained by the inclusion of a number of secondary questions in the electoral programme which secure the adherence of various sections of the community who are perfectly indifferent or very lukewarm in regard to the principal plank in the party platform. But if the majority obtained by that process is sufficiently large, it is taken to be an acceptance by the people of the entire platform, and legislation immediately follows to give effect to it.

Critics of parties such as Clark were also critics of parliamentary responsible government, especially as it operated within the Australian colonies. Not only were they critical of their arguably unrepresentative character, but it was argued that the whole apparatus of responsible government was simply inconsistent with federalism.

Parties, federalism and responsible government

Parliamentary government, political parties and the institutions of government and opposition were understood to be inextricably linked. Parkes wrote in 1892 that "parliamentary government can only be carried on by political parties" (Parkes 1892: 401). Three years later, Deakin defined the key features of the British system as one that includes a leader of government, an opposition, and political parties with established programs (Deakin 1895: 154, 155). In 1896 Samuel Walker Griffith observed that the system of responsible government "is in practice so intimately connected with parliamentary government and party government that the terms are often used as convertible".[16] John Quick and Robert Garran quoted Griffith to this effect in their magisterial commentary on the Australian Constitution (Quick and Garran 1901: 704).

When the framers referred to parties, however, they did not envisage the parties of today, which have been aptly described as "machines for providing access to power" (Jupp 1964: 181). Rather, the early view was that parties are "movements striving after ideals," formed on the basis of common ideological conviction in the Burkean sense (Jupp 1964: 181). But such a conception rested on the view that governments ought to be formed on the basis of the lower, representative house of parliament, whereas late 19th century federal theory dictated that power should be more or less equally distributed between both houses of a legislature in which the constituent states of the federation are especially represented in the second or upper chamber (Aroney 2009: chs 7, 8). The framers were well accustomed to the practices of Westminster parliamentary government as it operated in the Australian colonies, but a federation of the colonies meant introducing a somewhat different political system, patterned on the examples of the United States, Canada and Switzerland (Quick 1896; Williams 2005: 65-79; Hunt 1930). This presented choices to be made among a range of possible institutional designs, and far-reaching divisions about these matters emerged in the debates.[17] Those framers who most wished to see the formation of a strong national government tended to reject the American and Swiss models of a Senate or states' house that would be representative of the constituent states and co-equal in power with the House of Representatives. They generally preferred what they understood to be the British model as it prevailed at the time of federation, where the government would be responsible primarily to the House of Commons and the House of Lords would be, in practice, the weaker house, particularly in relation to money bills (La Nauze 1965:154-5, 168-9, 182).

On the other hand, those who wished to see the States retain substantial powers of local self-government generally favoured a Senate in which each of the original States was equally represented and which had powers virtually equal to those of the House of Representatives, including powers over taxation and appropriation bills (La Nauze 1972: 40, 139-44). Against this latter position, proponents of a strong national government argued that in practice the Senate would not actually represent the interests of the States but would rather tend to divide along party lines, with the government on one side and the opposition on the other (Crisp 1983: 327). Those on the other side advanced several responses to this line of argument, one of which strongly attacked the existence of political parties and, by implication, emerging two-party systems with their strict party discipline and rigid divisions between government and opposition.[18] Several exchanges during debates at the conventions reflected this tension of views. At the Constitutional Convention of 1891, for example, Thomas Playford had argued that in order to prevent the larger colonies from dominating the smaller ones under a highly nationalised system, the federal government ought to be composed of representatives from all the States.[19] Premier Duncan Gillies of Victoria responded that the government would divide along party, not State lines, even if all the States were represented in the government:

> I look around this hall, and I can see gentlemen who would be in opposition instantly, whether you represented New South Wales or not. There is my hon. friend, Mr. Dibbs. Do you think that he would submit to such a government? It would be impossible. There are a number of other hon. members of the New South Wales Parliament as well as Mr. Dibbs who would as naturally go into opposition as they would take their breakfasts if they were hungry (Convention Debates, Wednesday 11 March 1891: 240–1).

Underlying Gillies' taunt was the belief that divisions along party lines and distinctions between government and opposition are inevitable features of parliamentary politics. Those who disagreed with Gillies, however, questioned not only the strongly nationalist model that he favoured, but also with key aspects of the model of parliamentary responsible government that he took for granted. According to this alternative view, parliamentary government had too much of a tendency to polarise politics into a contest between two parties, formalised in the institutions of government and opposition (Bennett 1971: 156-7). Their preference was to avoid party contests and they hoped this would be advanced by constructing a Senate in which each of the States would be equally represented and which would have substantial powers over money bills – in order to make the government responsible not only to the House of Representatives but also the Senate.[20] In this vein, Henry Dobson railed against the "evils" of both "party government" and "responsible government," asserting that the two were "inseparably connected."[21] John Bray expressed a similar view when he asked:

> Is it necessary to have men on the one side proposing what they believe to be best for the state, and men on the other side who advocate an opposite course, and who can only carry out their views by removing those who compose the government? It does not appear to me to be absolutely necessary to have a responsible government and an opposition. (Convention Debates, Wednesday 11 March 1891: 259)

Various 19th century authors and commentators had warned against the dangers of both opposition and political parties,[22] and some of these warnings were articulated by several framers. Most of these critiques were from the standpoint of a conventional understanding of the constitution and so were within the Westminster tradition. Parkes, for example, said that "[t]he evils of party government, of which we hear much in the colonies as elsewhere, may be admitted, and they cannot be denied; but then every good thing is susceptible of abuse" (Parkes 1892: 314). John Cockburn argued that a distinction needed to be made between party government on one hand and responsible government on the other: "We should not desire to have party government but at the same time we ought not to do away with responsible government".[23] In drawing this distinction, Cockburn was not only objecting to the existence of political parties, he was also seeking to articulate a particular understanding of responsible government, which differed from the conventional wisdom that parties were necessary for the proper functioning of parliamentary systems.

Partly for reasons connected with concerns with party, partly for federal reasons, some framers suggested alternative ways of structuring the national government to be established by the Constitution. In this Richard

Baker assumed the role of an intellectual leader, supported by Frederick Holder, Henry Dobson, John Downer, Andrew Inglis Clark, John Gordon, Wiliam Trenwith and John Cockburn.[24] All of these individuals were highly critical of responsible government and, in particular, the "predominating power of one Chamber" (Convention Debates, Adelaide 1897: 28.) Several framers at the 1891 conventions alternatively suggested a federal executive modelled on the Swiss system, including Downer[25] (Crommelin 1987: 138-141). Later, at Sydney in 1897, Baker again proposed a federal executive modelled on the Swiss system.[26] Willoughby urged the framers to adopt a federal executive which lessened the influence of party:

> We are bound to proceed on British lines, and yet it may be submit-
> ted that not even from the first should the party system be pushed
> to any extreme, but, on the contrary, a real or genuine effort should
> be made to give the Federal Executive an Australian rather than a
> sectional character. Is it desirable to create party issues here; is it
> advisable to split the newly-founded Australia – or try to split it –
> into two camps, each party or each camp raging against the other
> and endeavouring to make it appear that the hostile faction would
> subvert Australia? Such questions have only to be put to obtain the
> one answer . . . Reflection shows that there is every reason why we
> should endeavour to diminish the party character of the Australian
> Executive; and, certainly, a great opportunity would be missed if
> the effort were not made (Willoughby 1891:73-74).

In the upshot, none of these proposals were successful.

In wrestling with the competing demands of parties, federalism and responsible government, the framers did not have a homogenous view of responsible government, but rather held competing conceptions.[27] At the commencement of debate in 1891 Parkes had proposed three resolutions which were to serve as the foundational principles for the structure of the federal government, one of which required the government to retain the support of the lower house to remain in office.[28] This resolution would have effectively entrenched party or responsible government as part of the Constitution.[29] Griffith and others challenged this, arguing that the convention that the government must possess the confidence of the lower house of parliament was not of the essence of responsible government but merely the stage of development as at Federation, and responsible government would continue to evolve and adapt as circumstances changed.[30] Critics of Parkes questioned his characterisation of the British Constitution,[31] claiming (as accurately summarised by Willoughby):

> that the principle that the Ministry proceeds from a party and is responsible to that party is no fixed part of the British Constitution, nor is it mentioned or legislated for in any of the constitutions granted by Great Britain to her dependencies . . . The essence of the British Constitution, it was pointed out, is not an Executive responsible to a party, but is elasticity and freedom. If this generation has a right to appoint and to remove Ministers in one way, another generation should be at liberty to appoint and to remove them in another (Willoughby 1891: 110-1).

This position was accepted by the majority, with the draft Constitution providing only that there was to be "an executive, consisting of a governor-general and such persons as may from time to time be appointed as his advisers" (Convention Debates, Wednesday 18 March 1891: 464-73). According to Willoughby, the 1891 Convention agreed that the Commonwealth Parliament must be given freedom to constitute the executive (Convention Debates, Wednesday 18 March 1891: 464-73). The broad elements of responsible government were agreed, but with a flexibility which allowed the political system to evolve and adapt.[32] Although there was a stronger focus on responsible government in the 1897–8 Convention, this position was not materially altered, other than to include a requirement that ministers must hold a seat in either house of parliament. Harrison Moore wrote that the provisions of the Constitution did "not preclude very extensive modifications" to the cabinet system: "[a]ll that has been done is to establish a parliamentary executive; the rest is left, as in England and the colonies generally, to custom and convention".[33] Griffith considered that although the 1898 Bill required ministers to sit in parliament, it did not specify how they were to be selected, and there remained "ample power in the Constitution" to make any alterations thought necessary "without undue friction or difficulty" (Griffith 1899: 16). The British system was seen as not being fixed or rigid in all its particulars, even in important matters, but as involving an element of flexibility to enable it to adapt to changing circumstances.

An Oppositional Senate

A majority of the framers affirmed that they wished to create a constitution on the basis of what was understood to be the British model of responsible government and expected that the familiar institutions of government and opposition would emerge. In many ways, therefore, the framers' views of "the Opposition" reflected widely held views about the role of "the Opposition" within Westminster systems of government. However, there were also significant differences. Under the British model of the Constitution, the lower house was the representative house and the house in which government was formed. The upper house was the weaker house, and ultimately did not have strength to resist the lower house (Bagehot 1867: 128-135, 145). Accordingly, responsibility for holding the government to account rested primarily on the opposition within the representative chamber. Federal considerations embodied in the co-ordinate legislative power of the Senate entailed a significant departure from traditional conceptions of responsible government. Some of the framers hoped that they had forged a middle way between the British and American systems, in which the polarities of parliamentary responsible government would be moderated by the existence of the Senate.[34] Others recognised that the Senate itself could constitute a form of opposition to the government.

The Constitution approved at the 1897-8 Convention provided that the senators would be directly chosen by the people;[35] as a result, the Senate would be representative of the people.[36] The Senate was entitled, in appropriate cases, to oppose the House. This was not because the Senate was intended to be conservative and a check on the people, but rather to more accurately give effect to the wishes of the people.[37] Given that it could be difficult to determine the people's will,[38] the lower house did not have a monopoly on that will and "may not faithfully represent the wishes of their constituents" (Convention Debates, Sydney 1897: 580 [Kingston], 544 [Carruthers]). In the Federal Parliament disputes between the two houses were expected to occur where "one party is in possession of a majority in the one chamber, and the other in the possession of a majority in the other chamber".[39] The framers recognised that the party which held government may not hold a majority in the upper house, but notwithstanding this created the Senate as a co-equal partner in the legislature with power, if it wished, to bring a government to its knees by refusing supply (Winterton 1983: 5-7). The Senate thus had a duty to ensure that the House of Representatives gave effect to the will of the people, including in appropriate cases by rejecting measures proposed by the lower house (Convention Debates, Sydney 1897: 830 [Symon]).

If the framers considered that the Westminster system was sufficient to guard against the dangers of party government, it was largely due to the role of both the formal opposition in the House and other forms of opposition based in the Senate. And what the framers said about "opposition" needs to be understood in this context. While they supported the retention of responsible government, the framers remained cautious about its precise nature and practical operation and sought to design a constitution in which governments would be accountable and responsible. In such a system, the institutional powers of both houses of parliament would be necessary in order to enable effective opposition within the context of a federal system of government.

Conclusion

The debates at the Constitutional Conventions were conducted assuming that the established paradigms of Westminster democracy would operate in the new federal government, but these paradigms were soon to be altered in important ways by the strengthening of party government (Anson 1897: II, xviii-xxx; Low 1914: ch 7; Jupp 1964: ch 10). Some framers who articulated a vision of the Australian system which diverged from the British theories reflected a growing unease with the dominance of cabinet and party in the Australian political system.[40] The framers considered various proposals for implementing a system of government that were significantly different from the traditional Westminster conceptions of responsible government, and concerns about parties and the roles of the opposition were central to these developments. As a system of "government versus opposition" was considered an essential part of parliamentary government, these critiques represent a different vision of how the Australian federation should be constructed. One key source of these concerns was unease with the party system.

Nonetheless, certain conceptions of the role and purpose of an opposition within such a system were generally agreed. It was widely believed that some form of opposition was needed in order to ensure that governments remain popularly accountable. Indeed, the decision not to include a bill of rights in the Constitution stemmed very centrally from a view of the role of an opposition within the parliament as a vital – and effective – check on government power. An opposition was also valued for its capacity to represent interests other than those represented by the government, as well as to improve the quality of democratic deliberation by giving voice to alternative views on the floor of the house. And yet it was recognised that an opposition, like a government, would be liable to be captured by sectional interests and subverted by personal ambitions. Moreover, the temptation for oppositions to adopt oppositional and obstructionist stances was well understood. Idealistic conceptions of the role of opposition thus accompanied idealistic conceptions of the role of political parties, while sceptical realism about parties necessarily suggested a similar sceptical realism about oppositions.

On the account presented in this chapter, a certain idealism about the roles of opposition and parties went with those who supported the traditional picture of Westminster responsible government focussed on the lower house of parliament, while the realists were those who feared a concentration of power in the prime minister, cabinet and lower house, and who called for a powerful Senate, representative of the peoples of the States, as a means of strengthening the capacity of the parliament as a whole to be an effective check on the powers of the government. If the mix of parties operating within the Australian Senate today constitute an even more effective form of opposition than those based in the lower house, it is due in part to the balance of power between the House of Representatives and the Senate that the framers more or less intended.

References

Anonymous, *Is Federation Our True Policy? The Politician Revealed to Himself*, George Robertson and Company, 1898

Anonymous, "Party Government", *Westminster Review*, 125, 1886, 429-61

Anson, W.R., *The Law and Custom of the Constitution*, 3rd ed, Oxford: Clarendon Press, 1897

Aroney, N., *The Constitution of a Federal Commonwealth*, Cambridge: Cambridge University Press, 2009

Bagehot, W., *The English Constitution*, London: Chapman and Hall, 1867

Bennett, S., *The Making of the Commonwealth*, Melbourne: Cassell Australia, 1971

Brassey, T., "Australian Federation", *Nineteenth Century*, 1899, 548-57

Bryce, J., *The American Commonwealth*, 2nd ed, London: Macmillan, 1889

Burke, E., "Thoughts on the Cause of the Present Discontents", in *The Works and Correspondence of the Right Honourable Edmund Burke*, London: F and J Rivington, new ed, vol 3, 1852, 109-74

Cecil, R., "Parliamentary Opposition", 1855, *Edinburgh Review*, 101, 1-22

Clark, A. I., "*Memorandum to Delegates*", in Williams, J., *The Australian Constitution: A Documentary History*, Carlton: Melbourne University Press, 1891, 65-79

Clark, A. I., *Studies in Australian Constitutional Law*, Melbourne: Charles F Maxwell, 1901

Clark, M., *A History of Australia, Volume 5: The People Make Laws 1888-1915*, Carlton: Melbourne University Press, 1981

Cochrane, P., *Colonial Ambition: Foundations of Australian Democracy*, Carlton: Melbourne University Press, 2006

Cockburn, J.A., *Australian Federation*, London: Horace Marshall, 1901

Crisp, L.F., *Australian National Government*, 5th ed, Croydon: Longman Cheshire, 1983

Crommelin, M., "The Executive", in Craven, G., (ed), *The Convention Debates 1891-1898: Commentaries, Indices and Guide*, Sydney: Legal Books, 1987, 127-48

Crowley, F., *Big John Forrest 1847-1918: A Founding Father of the Commonwealth of Australia*, Nedlands: University of Western Australia Press, 2000

Deakin, A., "Federal Council of Australasia", *Review of Reviews*, 1895, 154-59

Deakin, A., *The Federal Story: The Inner History of the Federal Cause*, Melbourne: Robertson and Mullens, 1944

Dicey, A V., *Introduction to the Study of the Law of the Constitution*, 6th ed, London: MacMillan, 1902

Duffy, C. G., *My Life in Two Hemispheres*, London: Fisher Unwin, 1898

Galligan, B., *A Federal Republic: Australia's Constitutional System of Government*, Cambridge: Cambridge University Press, 1995

Galligan, B., "Parliamentary Responsible Government and the Protection of Rights", *Public Law Review*, 4, June 1993, 100-12

Garran, R., "The Federation Movement and the Founding of the Commonwealth", in Rose, J.H., Newton, A.P., Benians, E.A., (eds), *Cambridge History of the British Empire*, Cambridge: Cambridge University Press, 7(I), 1933, 425-53.

Goldsworthy, J., "Australia: Devotion to Legalism", in Goldsworthy, J., (ed), *Interpreting Constitutions: A Comparative Study*, New York: Oxford University Press, 2006, 106-60

Goldsworthy, J., "The Constitutional Protection of Rights in Australia", in Craven, G., (ed), *Australian Federation: Towards the Second Century*, Carlton: Melbourne University Press, 1992, 151-176

Grey, E., *Parliamentary Government Considered with Reference to Reform*, 2nd ed, London: John Murray, 1864

Griffith, S.W., *Australian Federation and the Draft Commonwealth Bill*, Brisbane: Government Printer, 1899

Griffith, S.W., *Notes on Australian Federation: Its Nature and Probable Effects*, Brisbane: Government Printer, 1896

Hearn, W.E., *The Government of England: Its Structure, and Its Development*, Melbourne: George Robertson, 1867

Hunt, Erling M., *American Precedents in Australian Federation*, New York: Columbia University Press, 1930

Irving, H., *To Constitute a Nation: A Cultural History of Australia's Constitution*, Cambridge: Cambridge University Press, 1997

Jupp, J., *Australian Party Politics*, Carlton: Melbourne University Press, 1964

Kirwan, J., *My Life's Adventure,* London: Eyre and Spottiswoode, 1936

La Nauze, J.A., *Alfred Deakin: A Biography*, Carlton: Melbourne University Press, 1965

La Nauze, J.A., *The Making of the Australian Constitution*, Carlton: Melbourne University Press, 1972

Loveday, and P., Martin, A W., *Parliament Factions and Parties: The First Thirty Years of Responsible Government in New South Wales, 1856-1889*, Carlton: Melbourne University Press, 1966

Loveday, P., Bourke, S., and Maddox, G., *The Emergence of the Australian Party System*, Sydney: Hale and Iremonger, 1977

Low, S., *The Governance of England*, London: Fisher Unwin, 1914

Maine, H. S., *Popular Government*, New York: Henry Holt & Co, 1886

Marchant, S., *The Historical Traditions of the Australian Senate: The Upper House we Had to Have,* PhD Thesis, Research School of the Humanities, Australian National University, 2009

Martin, A W., *Henry Parkes: A Biography*, Carlton: Melbourne University Press, 1980

McMinn, W., *A Constitutional History of Australia*, Melbourne: Oxford University Press, 1979

Mill, J. S., "Of the Liberty of Thought and Discussion", in *On Liberty*, London: Longman, Roberts and Green, 1859

Miller, J.D.B., "An Historical Survey: Party Discipline in Australia (I)", *Political Science,* 5(1), 1953, 3-15

Moore, T., Bourke, S., and Maddox, G., "Australia and the Emergence of the Modern Two-Party System", *Australian Journal of Politics and History,* 44(1), 1998, 17-31

Moore, W.H., *The Constitution of the Commonwealth of Australia*, 2nd ed, Melbourne: Maxwell, 1910

Nairn, N.B., "The Political Mastery of Sir Henry Parkes: New South Wales Politics 1871-1891", *Journal of the Royal Australian Historical Society* 53(1), 1967, 1-51

Norris, R., *The Emergent Commonwealth: Australian Federation, Expectations and Fulfilment 1889–1910,* Carlton: Melbourne University Press, 1975

Official Records of the Debates of the Legislative Assembly, Brisbane, Queensland, 1898

Official Report of the National Australasian Convention Debates, Sydney, 2 March to 9 April 1891 (Acting Government Printer, 1891)

Parkes, H., *Fifty Years in the Making of Australian History,* London: Longmans, Green, and Co., 1892

Quick, J., *A Digest of Federal Constitutions,* Bendigo: JB Young, 1896

Quick, J., *The Annotated Constitution of the Australian Commonwealth,* Sydney: Angus and Robertson, 1901

Reid, G.H., *My Reminiscences,* London; Melbourne: Cassell, 1917

Reid, R L., "South Australian Politicians and the Proposals for Federation", *Melbourne Studies in Education,* 1960, 4:1, 204-219

Strangio, P., Dyrenfurth, N., (eds), *Confusion: The Making of the Australian Two–Party System,* Carlton: Melbourne University Press, 2009

Syme, D., *Representative Government in England: Its Faults and Failures,* London: K Paul, Trench and Co, 1881

Todd, A., *On Parliamentary Government in England: Its Origin, Development, and Practical Operation,* 2nd ed, London: Longmans, 1887

Todd, A., *Parliamentary Government in the British Colonies,* 2nd ed, London: Longmans, Green, 1894

Travers, R., *The Grand Old Man of Australian Politics: The Life and Times of Sir Henry Parkes,* Kenthurst, New South Wales: Kangaroo Press, 1992

Williams, J., "The Emergence of the Commonwealth Constitution" in Lee, H.P., and Winterton, G., (eds), *Australian Constitutional Landmarks,* Cambridge: Cambridge University Press, 2003, 1-33

Williams, J.M., *The Australian Constitution: A Documentary History,* Carlton: Melbourne University Press, 2005

Willoughby, H., *Australian Federation: Its Aims and its Possibilities,* Melbourne: Sands and McDougall, 1891

Winterton, G., *Parliament, the Executive and the Governor-General: A Constitutional Analysis,* Carlton: Melbourne University Press, 1983

Wise, B., *The Making of the Australian Commonwealth, 1889-1900: A Stage in the Growth of the Empire,* London: Longmans Green, 1913

Endnotes

1   The classic works examining parliamentary government were Todd 1887, Todd 1894, Hearn 1867, Bagehot 1867, Garran, R.R., Dicey 1902, Grey 1864.

2   Responsible government was introduced to New South Wales, Victoria, South Australia and Tasmania in 1856. Queensland was established as a separate colony with responsible government in 1859, while Western Australia had to wait until 1890 before it was given the same rights of local self-government. On the attainment of democracy and responsible government see Cochrane 2006.

3   *Official Report of the National Australasian Convention Debates,* Sydney, 2 March to 9 April, 1891 (Acting Government Printer, 1891), 11 March, 1891, 241 ('Convention Debates').

4   Goldsworthy 1992: 152-4; Goldsworthy 2006: 109; Williams 2003: 22-5.

5   See Mill 1859: ch 2.

6   "Letter to the Electors of East Sydney", in Parkes 1892, 270:

"It is to be fervently hoped that this appeal to the people will result in the return of a body of men who will be prepared at all hazards to stem the torrent of chicanery and corruption which has set in upon our free institutions,— who, from an enlightened conviction, and by a firm example, will teach that political triumph does not always accompany the possession of power, but that victory is to be achieved by remaining in Opposition or by retiring from office, so long as the principles of a sound policy are faithfully maintained."

7   Deakin 1944: 130. See also at 168: "The Liberal party was a chaos, a few unpopular factions contending intermittently and unsuccessfully within it for its control. Without a leader and with but few capable lieutenants its condition was hopeless."

8   Eg Deakin, 1944: 42, 71.

9   Syme 1881: 62; Anonymous, 1886: 429, 447-8.

10   On Parkes, see Martin 1980, Travers 1992, Nairn 1967

11   On Forrest see Crowley 2000.

12   For example, *Convention Debates*, Tuesday 30 March, 1897, 323: "The hon. member cannot divest himself of the idea that he is leader of the Opposition" (Gordon); *Convention Debates*, Tuesday, 15 February, 1898, 981: "As leader of the Opposition you are usually in conflict with him" (Peacock); *Convention Debates*, Monday 20 September, 1897, 850: "From the opposition point of view they [i.e. the government] are always unscrupulous!" (Holder).

13   Anonymous 1898: 140-1. The quotations are cryptically referred to as "Tozer's 'dying swan song' of parliamentary government, the psalm of death". Each numbered point is presented as a separate quotation.

14   *Convention Debates*, Wednesday 11 March, 1891, 245, Clark noting that this extract "was so full of high thought and eloquence that it impressed itself permanently" on his mind.

15   Parkes 1892: 401: "The mischief in party warfare is done by the pretenders, by those men who, with false notions of public distinction, seek election to the Legislature by professing a belief which is repugnant to their consciences".

16   Griffith 1896: 17-18. Note, however, Griffith's statement in the convention debates of 1891 on Tuesday 17 March: *Convention Debates*, 431.

17   A description of the controversy in contained in Wise 1913: 120-8.

18   Note the discussion in Norris 1975: 36-8.

19   "[I]n drafting a constitution we should take up this point for the protection of the other colonies: that they should have some representatives, at all events, in whatever government is formed, and that the government of the country shall not be formed out of one state alone": *Convention Debates*, Thursday 5 March, 1891, 59.

20   Aroney 2009: 198. See, eg *Convention Debates, Sydney* (1897), 185 (Dobson), 584, 677–8 (Cockburn).

21   Cockburn attributed this to him: "The Hon. member, Mr. Dobson, declaimed against the evils of party government as inseparably connected with responsible government"(*Convention Debates*, Tuesday 30 March, 1897, 345), referring to a speech of Dobson's made on Friday March 26, 1897: *Convention Debates*, 190.

22   For example, Cecil 1855: Grey 1864: 47; Bryce 1889: vol 1, 70, vol 2, 20-4; Maine 1886: 94–9.

23   "Speech on propositions submitted by the Honourable Edmund Barton" delivered at the National Australian Convention in Adelaide, 1897, in Cockburn 1901: 188-9.

24   Crommelin 1987: 139.

25   *Convention Debates*, Sydney 1891, 102: "The method adopted in Switzerland might be resorted to. The two houses might meet as one - the senate and the house of representatives - and appoint their ministry, who should retain office - there it is for three years - for a time to be determined. That would be a government which would have the confidence of the house, not responsible in the ordinary sense, and it would impinge upon our English notions to that extent".

26   *Convention Debates*, Sydney 1897, 782-3: "There shall be a council of six to aid and advise the governor-general in the government of the commonwealth, and such council shall be styled the federal executive council, and the persons who are members of the council shall be chosen at the commencement of each parliament to hold office for three years, unless the two houses of parliament sitting together as one house should otherwise determine. The senate and house of representatives shall each choose three members".

27   See also the important discussion by A.I. Clark, in his *Memorandum to Delegates*, 6 February 1891, in Williams 2005: 70–1.

28   "I have the honor to move: That in order to establish and secure an enduring foundation for the structure of a federal government, the principles embodied in the resolutions following be agreed to: - . . . (3) An executive, consisting of a governor-general and such persons as may from time to time be appointed as his advisers, such persons sitting in Parliament, and whose term of office shall depend upon their possessing the confidence of the house of representatives, expressed by the support of the majority" (*Convention Debates*, Wednesday 4 March, 1891, 23).

29   Willoughby 1891: 110. See also *Convention Debates* (1891), 23, 26-7, 447, cf 46 (Munro).

30   *Convention Debates* (1891), 34-5, 37, 767. See also 298 (Douglas), Griffith 1896.

31 Such as Griffith: *Convention Debates*, Wednesday 4 March, 1891, 34.

32 See also *Convention Debates*, Thursday 25 March, 1897, 96 (Higgins).

33 Moore 1910: 168–9. See also Brassey: 1899, 550-1.

34 See also the discussions in Galligan 1995: ch 3 and Winterton 1983: 5-13.

35 See Aroney, 2009: 208–9, 217–8.

36 *Convention Debates*, Adelaide (1897), 386 (Barton); *Convention Debates*, Sydney (1897), 537, 680 (Cockburn), 736 (Kingston), 819–23 (Deakin), 868 (Kingston), 883 (O'Connor), 890 (Higgins), 905 (Barton), 939–40 (Carruthers); *Convention Debates* (1898), 2060 (Barton).

37 Eg Clark 1981: ch 5; Marchant 2009: 270, 275; Crisp 1983: 18, 349; Reid 1960: 207.

38 *Convention Debates*, Adelaide (1897), 333; *Convention Debates*, Sydney (1897), 518, 636 (Dobson), 549–50 (McMillan), 562 (Holder), 580 (Kingston), 666 (Isaacs), 729 (Glynn), 826 (Deakin), 838–9 (Reid).

39 *Convention Debates*, Sydney (1897), 584 (Deakin), 813 (McMillan), 819 (Deakin), 870 (Kingston); (1898), 723 (Isaacs), 725-6 (Downer). Cf 947 (Trenwith).

40 Note also Irving 1997: 74.

3

Opposition One Day, Government the Next: Can Oppositions Make Policy and be Ready for Office?[1]

Scott Prasser

Introduction

This chapter examines whether oppositions can not only be effective critics of governments, particularly given their relatively fewer resources, but more importantly, can they be ready to take office in terms of the policies they propose? That this issue of resources is given prominence in several chapters in this volume, including one chapter devoted specifically to this topic (Chapter 7), highlights its importance.[2] What makes this such as special issue in Westminster systems is that an opposition, if it wins the election, moves within a very short time – usually a day to two – to being the government. This is unlike in the United States (US) where after the presidential election in November, there is a transition period of several months before the newly elected administration takes office. This gives the new president time to select the cabinet and to make appointments across several thousand positions.

Oppositions in Westminster democracies serve a variety of roles. First and foremost, they are expected to criticise the government, to hold it to account, to scrutinise its proposals and assess its actions and to ensure, as Bagehot (1971: 72) observed in the 19th Century that "the nation is forced to hear two sides, all the sides perhaps, that which most concerns it."

The fundamental role of oppositions is to oppose. This is what they are expected to do. And there are all sorts of means within parliament that oppositions can use to perform this basic function, ranging from questions to ministers, debates on legislation and budgets, participation in committees and, where numbers and constitutional practice allow, the use of upper houses to block or delay government proposals or even to force governments out of office. Activities to harass governments outside of parliament include seeking to change public opinion against proposed government actions through media commentary, highlighting government 'scandals' and ongoing debate with government members in a variety of public forums.

Oppositions complain, usually accurately, that they are often unable to fulfil these roles as effectively as they might because government parties dominate lower house parliamentary processes and use their majority to camouflage their mistakes, to protect their ministers, and to deflect criticism on key government projects. This control by executive dominance is well documented and discussed in this volume in relation to different jurisdictions.

Despite these limitations, criticising government presents opportunities for oppositions at one level. Governments and their large bureaucracies, budgets, and the complex programs they now administer inevitably result in some mistakes for even the most inept oppositions and lazy shadow ministers to use. There are always insider "leaks", media investigations, information garnered through normal parliamentary processes of question time and committees, reports from auditors-general and other review bodies, and interest group reactions to government policy initiatives. Criticising government is also relatively cheap in terms of resources. Rarely have an opposition's forensic efforts been responsible for exposing government vulnerabilities. More usually, oppositions rely on other sources and often get their cue from the media, reports from external review or integrity agencies, and sometimes even from the government itself in the form of leaks.

'Government in waiting' roles and responsibilities

The issue that arises from being a "government in waiting" is that criticising the government and exposing examples of maladministration is not the only role for oppositions. Criticism is just part of the wider function of seeking to highlight a government's deficiencies so that voter support will change. The real challenge is for oppositions to pose an alternative to the government of the day and to convince voters that they would be better than the incumbents.

Because an opposition in Westminster systems is the alternative government it has to be more than just critical. While there are other critics of government – numerous statutory review agencies, interest groups, academics, think tanks, the media, and citizens both as individuals and through public opinion – none seek office. Minority parties and independents may be influential, but they are not the alternative government which partly explains their often extravagant polices and extreme stances. Their target is not the government benches but appealing to their core supporters. It is this role of being the alternative government that distinguishes oppositions in Westminster systems from other critics, and importantly imposes heavier requirements and responsibilities on them in relation to 'policy' not experienced in many other political systems (see the chapter 20 on the US in this volume).

Oppositions that just criticise without an alternative policy framework are easily portrayed as being negative, complaining, and lacking capacity to tackle current public policy problems. Policies distinguish oppositions from governments in the ongoing electoral battle. Policies are the prime incentive for voters to change allegiances. Policy differences reflect the competition of ideas that are necessary for healthy political debate in a democracy which improves policy outcomes.

As already highlighted, opposition policies count more in Westminster systems because they must be ready to take over the reins of office immediately after an election or some other political event like a government falling on the floor of parliament for want of confidence. In

Westminster systems it is opposition one day, government the next. The very speed of this transition, and its occasional unexpectedness, imposes real demands on oppositions concerning their policy "readiness". Sometimes in cans be handled well, at other times it takes the new administration time to handle their new roles (see Richards 2009 for United Kingdom case studies).

So, policy is important, but doing policy is hard for oppositions for a variety of reasons and they are often accused of doing this least effectively. Governments often accuse oppositions of being a "policy free zone", of failing to produce an immediate policy in response to their just announced statement. At the same time, the media and interest groups condemn opposition policies for being too hastily assembled, contrived, political, impractical, ideological, lacking detail and poorly costed. Oppositions thus tread a difficult path.

Challenges facing oppositions in developing policy to be ready for office

This raises the issue as to whether the electorate, the media and others involved in the policy process expect too much from oppositions in terms of being "policy ready" given a whole range of issues. Also, it ignores the realities of the political environment in which oppositions (and the political parties that constitute them) operate and the multiple roles they have to serve simultaneously. Oppositions are not just there to do policy. They are also there to win office, represent certain parts of society – particularly their base – and be a lightning rod for complaints about government.

Political constraints

Foremost in the constraints on oppositions is that while they want to develop, and be seen to develop, policies that are based on "evidence" and rational, they are at the same time seeking to win office by proposing policies that are popular with voters and certain interest groups.

A further related constraint is that oppositions must try to be consistent with previous party stances or their earlier times in office and the long held ideological beliefs, even though these might be the antithesis of "good policy" or even "good politics" in attracting voter support. The other problem is that previous stances in office or those made in earlier times may have been examples of misjudgement and driven by the political context of the time.

Another issue is that oppositions may be tempted to opt for policies that they know they will not have to implement and thus be more "populist" or extreme, appealing to narrow segments of the political market at the expense of the wider public interest, which is more the focus of government. This is, however, more of a problem for minority parties than those that constitute the official opposition where the expectations of their policy proposals will be much higher in terms of practicality and costing.

Resources – and the advantages of incumbency

A key challenge for any opposition is the lack of resources it has compared to an incumbent government backed as it is by a large public bureaucracy, expanded ministerial staff and funds for hiring consultants. This is an important issue given special attention in Chapter 7 concerning current arrangements at the federal level and is covered in several other chapters covering oppositions across the states. Clearly, despite improvements in staffing and support for oppositions in recent years, the disparity concerning the availability of resources compared to government remains great. Incumbency also gives governments considerable resources to market their policies through taxpayer funded advertising campaigns – an issue of some continuing controversy regardless of who is in office (Wood and Stobart 2022). Oppositions have to pay for their own promotional efforts.

Incumbency becomes even more important the longer a government is in power, as tends to be more the case at the state level. It allows governments to consolidate further their hold over existing institutions such as the public service, the many statutory boards of government business enterprises, regulatory bodies, a host of other advisory committees and even the judiciary. Such bodies become, it is often argued, if not "politicised" then more sympathetic to the goals of the long running incumbent government. And if impending elections suggest little change in the existing status quo, the public service and other bodies will be less willing to co-operate or assist an opposition in its search for information or advice. As well, the longer a party is in opposition the less ability it has to attract new recruits to its parliamentary ranks let alone high calibre staff, and financial assistance from would be supporters.

Finally, long periods out of office mean oppositions lack of ministerial and governing experience. This is another resource constraint. Consequently, there is sometimes a "bedding in" period for new governments during which mistakes occur which if not quickly resolved may affect its longevity.

Executive dominance of parliamentary procedures

Executive governments in Westminster democracies through their dominance of parliament, can and do prevent oppositions from gaining information. Mechanisms introduced to make governments more transparent and accountable, like freedom of information laws have not always been as successful as originally hoped (see Solomon 2008 for Queensland examples).

The saving grace for this in Australia in terms of giving oppositions greater opportunities to gain information is the existence of elected upper houses across five of the six States[3] and at the federal level where governments often do not command a majority.[4] Consequently, oppositions, in conjunction with minority parties and independents can often hold governments more to account, to gain information not usually released and to be highly critical of the incumbent government (Evans 2008). This can be seen in the dominance of oppositions and minority parties of upper house parliamentary committees as occurs with Senate committees. In recent years, Labor Party opposition in the Senate has been enhanced because the other minority party members and independents have been generally supportive of its critical approaches on government legislation and other issues.[5] By contrast, the Coalition in opposition since 2022, will have less effectiveness in the Senate because it lacks the same rapport with these minority parties and most independents compared to the Labor Party.

Policy complexity and the demand for details

Another constraint on oppositions is the increasing complexity of modern public policy issues requiring more research, more data, more analysis and longer lead times for implementation. How can an opposition match the resources and policy knowledge of government departments? Moreover, governments also are increasingly assisted by many specially employed external consultants (ANAO 2017) further augmented by government appointed public inquiries (Prasser 2021). In addition, there are the direct, usually confidential interest group inputs into government policy development which oppositions do not have access to in developing policy.

Of course, there has also been debate about not just whether oppositions can develop   detailed policies on increasingly complex issues, but whether they should. The focus, it has been suggested, should be on broad principles of policy and overall directions rather than the detail of policies which they are patently unfit to develop. British Prime Minister Harold Macmillan (quoted in Rose 1976: 282) quipped about his opposite number, Hugh Gaitskell, who developed detailed policies covering every policy area:

> The trouble with Mr Gaitskell is that he is going through all the mo-
> tions of being a government when he isn't a government. It is bad

enough having to behave like a government when one is in power. The whole point of being in opposition is that one can have fun and lend colour to what one says and does.

Macmillan's point is that being in opposition should be a time for political parties to range more freely over policy debates, to engage in more discussions and to propose a wider range of options than if in government. Being in government requires a focus on what is 'doable,' on costs and on working with a wider range of constraints.

However, avoiding detailed policy statements is increasingly difficult for oppositions for several reasons. As mentioned, one is that in Westminster democracies oppositions have got to be ready to govern immediately they have won the elections. This is often reflected in proclamations by oppositions poised to win the election that they will "hit the ground running" – a claim certainly made by the incoming Albanese Labor Government in 2022 (Chambers 2022) like many of its predecessors. Sometimes, this is given further emphasis by oppositions appointing in preparation for government, "expert" committees often eminent business and academic leaders and former senior public servants.[6]

An additional development in Westminster democracies has been the tendency for political parties to develop bigger and more detailed programmatic election platforms. These were seen as a means to both attract voter support and, especially for left of centre "reformist" or "visionary" parties, an important means to keep the parliamentary party on track both in ideological and policy terms once it gained office. The concern was that once in office the party platform would be resisted by other institutions, such as the bureaucracy, or seduced by day-to-day crises and pressures from key interests (Rose: 378). This program of action also becomes tied up with an incoming government's mandate and thus justification for certain policy actions once in power (Beer 1973; Emy 1978: 227-30).

Certainly, in Australia such trends have been clearly observable for both sides of politics to develop ever more detailed policy statements before and during an election campaign. Oppositions that try to produce less detailed policies are often attacked by the government, the media and interest groups. The epitome of this detail was the program outlined by the Whitlam Labor Party in the 1972 federal elections. While it contributed to Labor's electoral success that year, in office over-adherence to the election promises regardless of changing economic circumstances and the impracticality of many of the ideas became one of the causes of the Whitlam Government's perceived failure (Kelly 1992).

Time and again governments will chide oppositions for the lack of details of their policies, for too simplistic solutions to complex technical issues, and the slowness of their responses. Adding to this pressure is that oppositions are now expected to submit costings of their proposed new policies for public scrutiny. Despite these pressures, oppositions sometimes still have a reluctance to release detailed policies prior to an election. They fear their policies might be "stolen" and adopted as the government's own. The other issue is too early release of policies allow the government with resources of the public service to analyse and criticise them with great success. This occurred to the Coalition's large, detailed and complex *Fightback!* policy package developed by opposition leader John Hewson in the run-up to the 1993 election. The Keating Government attacked it relentlessly in terms of its inaccuracies, gaps and complexity and potential impacts on the cost of living. Consequently, the Coalition lost the "unlosable election" (Robb 2017).

Realities of developing and implementing policy – can oppositions connect?

The other aspect of developing policy rarely touched upon is the very realities of how policies emerge within government and societies. The view that politicians make policy and public servants just administer these is too simplistic. The policy vs administration dichotomy has long been disproved. Policy emerges by ongoing interaction between politician and official through day-to-day grappling with problems including how a particular policy is actually operating. Although governments might start with some specific policy they inevitably have to develop policies incrementally, constantly changing and modifying direction in response to feedback from their public servants, and interest group and client responses (Colebatch 1998). How well they do this often determines the "success" or "failure" of the policy, both in terms of whether it delivered what was envisaged or, more importantly, if it was in the public interest as well as being politically accepted and popular.

The challenge for oppositions is that they are often marginalised in the policy network and cannot appreciate completely the information and feedback being generated by the ongoing development and implementation of a policy. They can talk to some of the players, interest groups and even the public servants within certain limitations, such as through parliamentary committee hearings, approved briefings and transition to government arrangements. However, certain information will always be necessarily withheld, the interactions will be sporadic and the real nuances of the policy as it working and how it is needing to be changed are not fully understood. Hence, oppositions often express surprise about what they did not know about a policy area once they gain office and take time to initiate changes as they learn about these new developments (Weller 1983). This can also be used as an excuse by a new government for reneging on election promises – they did not know how bad things were, such as the often discovered post-election budget "black hole" necessitating corrective action like making extensive cuts in the administration's first budget. This is what happened when the Howard Government came to office in 1996 and it was executed more effectively than the incoming Abbott Coalition Government in 2014 (McKibbin 2017; Kelly 2017: 171-2).

Policies as political weapons

Another obstacle that makes developing coherent policies difficult for oppositions is the adversarial nature of Westminster politics. This means that policies are as much a means to criticise the government and gain electoral support as they are about developing solutions to problems. It is a competitive exercise. Taking certain policy stances will reflect political opportunism often in contradiction to views/policies previously held by the opposition in government (and by governments in opposition). Federal Labor when in opposition opposed the GST at the 1998 election, although in office, Treasurer Keating supported (unsuccessfully) this proposal.

Policy will also be driven by attempts to gain first mover advantage, to capitalise on changing circumstances and to ride certain popular views or trends about issues to gain votes. Similarly, the Howard Coalition in government supported an emissions trading scheme, but in opposition opposed it partly for reasons of political expediency and partly to reflect its rediscovery of its "principles". As Lees and Kimber (1972: 178) observed of the United Kingdom, despite all the effort that parties seem to put into policy development and programs they "often seem little more than vote-catching devices". And if this is what they really are, can they be effective guides to political parties' performance once in office or reliable guides to the electorate upon which to make voting decisions?

Avoiding policy 'me-tooism'

Given the importance of policy as a political weapon, and as a means to distinguish one side from the other, a challenge for oppositions is to avoid policy "me-tooism" – following too closely the incumbent government's policy line. This problem is particularly pronounced when an opposition is new after being in government for a long time, and a new administration has been swept to office on an apparent popular and very successful policy platform. Complicating a new opposition's situation is that often many of the successor government's policy initiatives will in fact be policies already in the pipeline from the previous administration which have been largely relabelled to suit the new government's style and rhetoric. It is hard for an opposition to criticise these. At best it might claim some ownership of these policies but that is hardly a vote winner. Also, as a new government after a big victory has both an obvious electoral mandate and is enjoying a "honeymoon" period of popularity, an opposition finds it is initially hard to criticise for fear of being perceived as a "sore loser" and denying the electoral mandate – concerns that the new government will exploit.

Nevertheless, as Robert Menzies observed, oppositions must resist the temptation to follow the government line as this surrenders all initiative to government. Oppositions, warned Menzies, must strive to be, "as different as possible" from the government of the day (Menzies 1972: 15-20). It was policy "me-tooism" that was seen to undo Billy Snedden as leader of the Coalition Opposition in 1975, when he sought too steer a middle course with his initiated revision of the Liberal Party's platform (Jaensch 1994: 63-6; Tiver 1978: 46-51). It was what many saw as the cause of Malcolm Turnbull's initial downfall as leader of the parliamentary Liberal Party and Opposition in December 2009. Turnbull's approach to policy on the aforementioned emissions trading scheme was, it can be argued, too accommodating to the Rudd Labor Government, too bipartisan (Tiffen 2017: 50-69). The same challenges face the current federal Coalition Opposition since it lost office in 2022 as it copes with being in opposition after almost nine years in office. Adding to the opposition's difficulties is a new government finding and exploiting considerable flaws in the previous administration concerning Prime Minister Morrison's assuming responsibility for several portfolio (Bell 2022) and the Coalition's mismanagement of the Robodebt program now exposed by a royal commission (Prasser 2023).

Oppositions need to be careful of calls for bipartisanship from governments. While seeking to develop consensus or "bipartisanship" on important policy issues is initially and superficially popular with the media and the electorate, such support is often short-lived and politically unsustainable. It amounts to giving up too much policy ground and initiative to the government. While there are some areas and issues where bipartisanship can occur, oppositions need to tread warily. Too much bipartisanship makes the opposition irrelevant. For this reason, then Coalition Opposition leader Tony Abbott rejected Prime Minister Rudd's call for a bipartisan agreement on homelessness. Similarly, current opposition leader, Peter Dutton has been unwilling to support the Albanese Government's 2023 Constitutional referendum on the Aboriginal Voice issue. At the same time, oppositions must be careful not to be seen as too negative. Such negativity often expressed in strong attacks and obstruction may gain strong party partisan support, but the general voter is less convinced, often preferring to see evidence of co-operation, or at least some recognition that not all the government's policies are wrong. All in all, these matters require considerable political judgement of the part of any opposition.

Managing ideological tensions – avoiding "extreme" policies

All political parties – big and small – face dilemmas as to how closely they should adhere to their ideology and their core supporters' views and when they should stray from ideological purity to deal with the realities of gaining wider electoral support. Party members views tend to be narrower and more extreme than the broader community. In government, parties necessarily move away from their ideological base as they confront the realities of office, resource constraints and the need to compromise if they have to get legislation through a hostile upper house like the Senate, Also, policies drafted in opposition become out of date or are found to be just wrong. However, in opposition, the party leadership, cut off from the support of the public bureaucracy, necessarily turns to partisan supporters for advice and the funding now needed to sustain it in opposition. The temptation for opposition parties is to return to their roots, to sip again at their ideological well as a means of redefining their political and policy stands, to restore depleted partisan support, and to distinguish themselves from government.[7] Labor parties in opposition tend to turn to trade unions and place greater emphasis on social equity and increased government intervention as their policy concerns, rather than more practical matters like managing the economy.[8] Non-Labor parties look to business and right wing think tanks (Hagland 2023) and in the usual post-election surveys rediscover small government, deregulation, federalism and fiscal restraint. Ideological purity in policy is what partisans preach. The danger is that subsequent policies may please the party faithful but are too "ideological" and thus alienate the more moderate and larger parts of the electorate.

Developing new policies and directions

Adding to all these woes is that oppositions entering their new role initially find the policy cupboard bare. The new government is in the process of taking over many of the policies of the former government. Meanwhile some of the policies that the former government was strongly advocating, especially during its last term and recent election campaign, are now seen as electoral losers and are quickly disowned and dumped. The Coalition after its 2007 federal election loss was quick to dump the Howard Government's *Workchoices* industrial relations policy. Similarly, Labor after its surprising 2019 federal election loss dropped several key planks of its platform concerning superannuation and taxation policies (Manwaring 2020). This might provide a clean policy slate, but it also leaves the opposition in a policy vacuum and directionless for some time. Also, a new opposition must wait for the incoming government's new policies to be implemented before they can be legitimately criticised. This takes time. In the meantime, all oppositions can do at best is to criticise other aspects of policy – such as its processes of development (such as lack of consultation, poor cost-benefit analysis prior to their introduction and possibly poor implementation). Such criticisms can come across at "nit-picking" and missing the "big picture" which only the new government is in a position to understand. At the same time the understandable reluctance of an opposition to attack immediately a newly elected government's initial policy initiatives will be challenged by its rank and file supporters and some within the parliamentary wing with leadership aspirations, as avoiding taking clear unambiguous stands based on "principle" – which is not always clearly articulated or even agreed.

Conclusion

There are increasing expectations of oppositions in relation to the development and presentation of policy. They need to be more than just critics of governments. To win office they need to do more than just rely on government mistakes. To be truly seen as "governments in waiting" oppositions are required to have real policy options ready to implement once in office. A more sophisticated electorate, the growing expertise of interest groups that are challenging governments as well as political parties in policy analysis, the complexity of modern policies, and the demands for improved rationality and 'evidence' in policies, all require oppositions to improve their policy efforts.

Institutionally, given the "winner takes all" approach of Westminster systems and the increasing dominance of executive government, oppositions find it increasingly hard to be competitive in the policy game. However, the future of any opposition lies in developing distinctive alternative policies that have both good content and the right political appeal. Coalition Opposition Leader and then Prime Minister, Tony Abbott, acknowledged this: "knowing what you are against is important for oppositions, but it's not a recipe for effective government" (Abbott 2010).

References

Abbott, T., "The Choice will be clear cut", *The Australian*, 1 March 2010

Australian National Audit Office (ANAO), *Australian Government Procurement Contract Reporting*, Report No 19 2017-18, Canberra; Commonwealth of Australia, 2017

Aroney, N., Prasser, S., and Nethercote, J.R., *Restraining Elective Dictatorship: The Upper House Solution?*, Perth: University of Western Australia Press, 2008

Bagehot, W., *The English Constitution*, Harmondsworth: Penguin, 1971

Bateman, J., *In the Shadows: The Shadow Cabinet in Australia*, Canberra: Commonwealth Parliamentary Library, 2009

Beer, S., and Ulam, A.B., (eds), *Patterns of Government: The Major Political Systems of Europe*, 3rd ed, New York: Random House, 1973

Bell, V., (Chair), Inquiry into the Appointment of the Former Prime Minister to Administer Multiple Departments, *Report*, Canberra: Commonwealth Government of Australia, 2022

Chambers, G., "We won't waste a single day in office" Anthony Albanese", *The Australian*, 1 June 2022

Colebatch, H.K., *Policy*, Bristol: Open University Press, 1998

Dahl, R., *Political Opposition in Western Democracies,* New Haven, Connecticut: Yale University Press, 1965

EARC, *Report on Review of Information and Resource Needs of Non-Government Members of the Legislative Assembly*, Brisbane: Queensland Government, December 1991

Emy, H.V., *The Politics of Australian Democracy*, Melbourne: Macmillan, 1978

Evans, H., "The case for bicameralism", in Aroney, N., et al, *Restraining Elective Dictatorship*, 67-80

Hagland, T., *Think Tanks in Australia: Policy Contributions and Influence*, London: Palgrave Macmillan, 2023

Jaensch, D., *The Liberals*, Sydney: Allen and Unwin, 1994

Kelly, P., *The End of Certainty*, St Leonards: Allen and Unwin, 1992

Kelly, P., "The foundational year", in Frame, T., (ed), *The Ascent to Power, 1996: The Howard Government Volume 1*, Sydney: UNSW Press, 2017, 166-78

Lees, J.D., and Kimber, R., *Political Parties in Modern Britain*, London: Routledge and Kegan Paul, 1972

Manwaring, R., "The Australian Labor Party", in Gauja, A., Sawer, M., and Simms, M., (eds), *Morrison Miracle: The 2019 Australian Federal Election*, Canberra: ANU Press, 2020, 277-94; see also other chapters in this volume.

McKibbin, W., "Economic management", in Frame, T., (ed), *The Ascent to Power, 1996: The Howard Government Volume 1*, Sydney: UNSW Press, 2017, 141-54

Menzies, R.G., *Measure of the Years*, Melbourne: Cassell, 1972

Prasser, S., *Royal Commissions and Public Inquiries in Australia*, 2nd ed., Chatswood: LexisNexis, 2021

Prasser, S., "Issues go well beyond Coalition and robodebt. Can reform win?", *Canberra Times*, 13 March 2023

Richard, D., "Sustaining the Westminster Model: A Case Study of the Transition in Power between Political Parties in British Government", *Parliamentary Affairs,* 62(1), June 2009, 108-28

Robb, A., "Learning from Campaigns", in Frame, T., (ed), *The Ascent to Power 1996, Volume I*, Sydney: UNSW Press, 2017, 71-9

Rose, R., *Party Government*, Harmondsworth: Penguin, 1976

Solomon, D., (Chair), "The Right to Information: Reviewing Queensland's Freedom of Information Act," *Report of the FOI Independent Review Panel*, June, Brisbane: Queensland Government, 2008

Tiffen, R., *Disposal Leaders: Media and Leadership Coups from Menzies to Abbott*, Sydney: NewSouth Publishing, 2017

Tiver, P., *The Liberal Party: Principles and Performance,* Milton: The Jacaranda Press, 1978

Valder, J., (Chair), Report of the Committee of Review, *Facing the Facts,* Federal Executive, Liberal Party of Australia, September 1985

Weller, P., "Transition: Taking Power in 1983", *Australian Journal of Public Administration*, XLII(3), September 1983, 303-19

Wood, D., and Stobart, A., "Politicised government ads: costly and anti-democratic, *Sydney Morning Herald*, 10 October 2022

Endnotes

1   This chapter is based on an article published by the author under the same title in *Australasian Parliamentary Review*, 5(1), Autumn, 2010, 151-61 but has been revised and updated. The author acknowledges the contributions to the original article by the late Dr Graeme Starr.

2   See chapters 7, 10, 11, 17, and 19.

3   Queensland abolished its upper house in 1922 and the ACT and Northern Territory governments have unicameral assemblies.

4   After the 2004 election when the Howard Coalition Government secured a Senate majority from 2005 till its demise in 2007.

5   The 2022 Senate COVID committee monitoring the Morrison Government's response to the pandemic was dominated by Labor Opposition and Green senators, with its chair, Labor Senator Katy Gallagher. The Committee's report, released on the eve of the May 2022 election, was highly critically of

all aspects of the Morrison Coalition Government's handling of the pandemic. Senator Gallagher subsequently became Finance Minister in the new Albanese Labor Government.

6   The Coalition in the lead up to the 2013 federal election appointed a three person committee comprising of: former senior public servant, Peter Shergold, economist Geoff Carmody and former Queensland Auditor-General, Len Scanlan to overview its polices so the Coalition would be ready for office.

7   See the Liberal Party's Valder Report conducted after the 1983 election defeat for these concerns.

8   This was one of the criticisms of the Hawke-Keating Labor Government from some supporters – see Kelly 1992.

4

Oppositions and Elections: The Media and Pathways to Office

Rodney Tiffen

Publicity interests of incumbents and oppositions

Governments are inherently more newsworthy than oppositions. Governments enact decisions and their actions have consequences and public relevance; oppositions only criticize or ask questions, usually in predictable ways. Governments by their activity show concern and so help focus the news agenda into particular areas. Their capacity to do this is far from total, but neither is it insignificant. In contrast, oppositions are often reduced in news coverage to reactive and secondary roles.

Governments have further publicity advantages as the custodians of the administrative and ceremonial roles of the state. They may embody national unity on occasions of both national tragedy and triumph. The publicity given to prime ministers at sporting events is much greater than to opposition leaders. Their capacity to show concern and leadership during and after national tragedies is another occasion where oppositions are reduced to irrelevance.

A prime minister who gets this wrong, however, can suffer lasting consequences. Gough Whitlam flew back to Australia from his diplomatic visit to Europe after Cyclone Tracy hit Darwin in December 1974, but then flew back to resume his European travels, occasioning much criticism including from such Labor colleagues as Bob Hawke (Hawke 1994: 66). The most damaging example was Scott Morrison having a Hawaiian holiday during terrible east coast bushfires, and then seeking to dismiss criticisms with his offhand quip in the aftermath of the 2019-20 bushfires, that "I don't hold a hose mate", a phrase which haunted him for the rest of his tenure.

On the other hand, oppositions are not completely powerless in gaining news coverage. Their greatest opportunities lie in embarrassing the government on scandals and policy failures and fiascoes, posing questions that they say the government is unwilling or unable to answer. So, the principal way they appear in the news is as a negative and critical presence. This stems partly from the priorities of the news media and their sense of newsworthiness, but more basically from the publicity interests and strategies flowing from the nature of party competition.

The two-sided competition between the major parties to form government is a unique type of conflict – zero-sum, winner-take-all with the result determined by the public. The nature of a zero-sum game does not allow mutual advancement or compromise and accommodation. One side improves its prospects only at the expense of the other. In a winner-take-all game, for the parties there is an absolute chasm between winning and losing, the perks and opportunities of government or the frustrations and irrelevance of opposition. Competitions of this kind – winner take all and zero-sum - are not conducive to a strong sense of fair play. Winning in whatever way is preferable to losing nobly.

This essential logic of party competition drives the eternal vigour of party conflict. Antagonistic interests exist irrespective of the degree of policy agreement or difference. The appearance of polarization is constant and the pursuit of inter-party competition often leads to an exaggeration of policy differences.

It is not in an opposition's interest to stress the constraints on all governments, or the intractability of the problems facing them. Rather their strategy is to promote a simple equation: the blame for all existing problems is attributed to the government, and the solution lies simply in changing governments. As presidential candidate Richard Nixon said in 1968, in a theme often echoed by opposition leaders: "There is nothing wrong with this country that a good election wouldn't fix".

While the publicity interests for oppositions are constant, their pursuit is dynamic. The parties have become increasingly professional, and the main effect of this has been to increase ruthlessness and cynicism. The professionals seem to have decided that attack is more potent than exposition. So, there is much more emphasis on not offering "hostages to fortune" which the other side can attack and/or misrepresent, and more emphasis on negative campaigning on the disastrous nature of their opponents.

Election campaigns as opportunities for oppositions?

Given that governments have so many more opportunities to influence news coverage in normal political times, it might be thought that election campaigns when the news coverage tends to be much more evenly split, are an opportunity for oppositions to have more impact. But, as Wallace proposes, in reality, "every season is open season on oppositions" (Wallace 2020: 3).

This section looks at where oppositions stood when the election was called and then at the subsequent election outcome for the twenty federal elections held in the half century between 1972 and 2022. In the following table (Table1), the state of the parties at the beginning of the campaign is the author's judgement based on a mix of poll watching and pundits' forecasts. Other judgements may differ.

Table 1: Oppositions and Federal Election Campaigns 1972-2022

Started Ahead and Won (7)	1972 (Whitlam ALP); 1975 (Fraser LNP); 1983 (Hawke ALP); 1996 (Howard LNP); 2007 (Rudd ALP); 2013 (Abbott 2013); 2022 (Albanese ALP)
Started Behind, Lost, but Gained Ground (6)	1974 (Snedden LNP); 1984 (Peacock LNP); 1998 (Beazley ALP); 2001 (Beazley ALP); 2010 (Abbott LNP); 2016 (Shorten ALP)
Started and Finished Way Behind (1)	1977 (Whitlam ALP)
Started Equal and Lost (4)	1980 (Hayden ALP); 1987 (Howard LNP); 1990 (Peacock LNP); 2004 (Latham ALP)
Started Ahead but Lost (2)	1993 (Hewson LNP); 2019 (Shorten ALP)

Victorious oppositions: Seven of the 20 elections over the 50 years resulted in a change of government. This shows more volatility than the preceding period when incumbents won nine of the previous ten elections, covering the long conservative hegemony between 1949 and 1972. Nevertheless, incumbents retained government about two thirds of the time.

What do these seven opposition successes have in common? And to what extent do they differ?

The most striking feature of Table 1 is that all winning oppositions started the campaign already ahead. Probably in all these seven elections, barring some extraordinary development, the government's fate was sealed before the campaign began. In the memorable phrase of Wayne Goss, speaking of the Keating Government in 1996, voters were sitting on their verandahs waiting with baseball bats (Kenny 2023: 2). The degree of anger varies but in nearly every case, the incumbent was facing, what Peter Hartcher (2007) referring to John Howard in 2007, called opinion 'polls of chilling steadiness and deadly intent.' In these campaigns it was less important for the opposition to gain the advantage and more important for it not to lose the lead it already had.

In each case the result was decisive – all victors had a two-party preferred share of 52 per cent or more, and all involved a two-party preferred swing of three per cent or higher (except Whitlam in 1972 achieving 2.5 per cent but this built on the very large 7.4 per cent swing Labor achieved in 1969). So, changes of government in Australia in this period have tended to reflect a long-term and decisive shift of support.

The oppositions' roads to success, however, were varied. What will work in any particular campaign requires sensing and accommodating to the mood of the public, or at least to that segment of it whose support is not yet determined. All party political campaigning is a mix of positive and negative, of what parties want to present as attractive about their side and terrible about the other side. For oppositions, the positive involves laying out what they would do as an alternative government, while the negative involves attacking the record and policies of the incumbents. But the mix and emphasis of these is hugely variable, and the seeds of success are far from constant.

The archetype of a campaign laying out promises for an alternative government was Gough Whitlam in the lead up to the 1972 election. Over years, he set out an ambitious program of reform, expanding the government's role in many areas of social life, and giving a degree of detail that no-one has done since.

Partly this reflected the times. There was more confidence in the capacity of governments to deliver. The 23 year old conservative government was very divided. Whitlam had stimulated a high level of press gallery support during his six years as opposition leader and was a much better television performer than his conservative opponents (Lloyd 1992: 120) That election is also remembered for the much more modern campaigning, and especially the theme song and slogan "It's Time".

The opposite approach is to seek to keep the media focus strongly trained on the defects of the incumbent. When a government has been divided with high levels of internal conflict and policy controversies, some opposition campaigns have sought to raise the political temperature by emphasising not so much their own agendas but the hopelessness of the current government. The two outstanding examples are Malcolm Fraser in 1975 and Tony Abbott in 2013. Fraser proclaimed "the action we have taken is right to remove from Australia the worst government since the beginning of Australia" (Kelly 1976: 282).

After the hung parliament following the 2010 election, "Knowing an election might be only a heart attack away, Abbott embarked on a permanent campaign". According to the doyen of the Canberra press gallery, Laurie Oakes: "His strategy was for the opposition to attack, oppose, provoke, block, sling mud, stir up anger, and generally make as much noise as possible, in the process creating an impression of disorder and instability" (Oakes 2013: ix). Abbott became renowned for his three-word slogans: "axe the tax", "repay the debt", "stop the boats", "stop the waste" and "open for business".

In both 1975 and 2013 disillusion with the incumbents was at such a level that the key to success was to keep the public focus on them. The oppositions were articulating and mobilizing a national mood.

A common recent addition to political jargon somewhat overlaps the positive and negative: big target and small target campaigns. When there is substantial disillusion, especially with a long-term government, opposition leaders may seek to keep the focus on the government, and in their own offerings seek to keep the political temperature relatively cool, and to offer reassurance. The key in this strategy is to pick the right fights, to have the focus on the weaknesses of the incumbents, but to avoid any policy proposals of their own that would be ripe for wedging or scare campaigns.

While suggestive, the phrases big and small target are too much in the eye of the beholder, and insufficiently precise to be very helpful in analysing elections. For example, after the Howard government's 2007 loss, Treasurer Peter Costello's staffer Nikki Savva said that Rudd "looked as safe as Howard. He looked like he could be Howard's son, he sounded like Howard, and did everything he could to encourage comparisons with Howard. It was creepy." "The electorate was looking for a younger version of Howard" (Savva 2010: 256).

In counterpoint to Savva, it was also true that, unlike Howard, Rudd was a Mandarin speaker with a long interest in Asia; who said that climate change was the most urgent moral question of our time; promised to roll out broadband; promised to withdraw troops from Iraq; was a republican, and wanted a much higher priority given to child care. Rudd's success was not in being a 'small target' but in choosing the right battles, putting the focus on to areas where the Howard government was weak and there was a strong constituency for change. Although very difficult to research, winning the agenda battles is a central part of successful campaigning.

Creditable losses?: No government in this half century lost government at its first attempt at re-election, although in nearly every case the opposition gained some ground, and often did better than initially expected.

Five of the six cases in the second row of the above table involve such first efforts at re-election and in all five the opposition cut the majority of the government. For example, Abbott in 2013 was elected with 53.5 per cent of the two-party preferred vote, while in 2016 Turnbull survived but with just 50.4 per cent against Shorten's Labor opposition.

Two oppositions came closest to winning. In 2010 the Abbott opposition reduced Gillard to a minority government, where she depended on Greens and some independents to maintain a parliamentary majority. Not coincidentally, that election followed the first ever overthrow of a leader who had won government, and the bitter internal conflicts that followed.

In only two of these 20 elections has a party securing under 50 per cent of the two-party preferred vote won government – Hawke in 1990 had 49.9 per cent, and Howard in 1998 won with just 48.9 per cent. So that year, Beazley won the largest losing share of the two-party preferred vote (51.1%) but still lost because of the distribution of support. Beazley campaigned strongly on education, but perhaps the more important factor was Labor's campaign against Howard's intention to introduce a GST.

Before the elections, the pundits gave Snedden (1974) and Peacock (1984) little chance, but both ended with much better results than predicted. In neither case was there any reason during the campaign to expect this. Snedden's campaign was littered with policy stumbles and disagreements with National Country Party leader Doug Anthony. The Coalition's strong showing in the results was probably an early sign that issues of stagflation and economic management were gaining traction, and that the Whitlam Government was becoming less attractive to voters in the outlying states.

No other government has entered an election campaign with the complacency and arrogance of the Hawke government in 1984. Full of confidence amid a recovering economy, the prime minister's record public approval levels, and with (for the first time) a majority of the nation's newspapers endorsing Labor, the path to victory seemed easy. Again during the campaign, few commentators thought there was any sign that Peacock's opposition was succeeding. The government began with a long campaign (seven weeks) into an election they had called early for no apparent reason beyond expedience. It is plausible some of the electorate wanted to punish the government for its arrogance. Neither Snedden nor Peacock survived to lead the opposition into the next election, so perhaps their colleagues shared the judgement of the pundits.

The loss of Beazley's Labor opposition in 2001 is unique in several ways. As noted above, Beazley had come very close to winning in 1998 on domestic issues. For at least two years after that, it looked likely that Labor would win the next election. Then in 2001 came the sharpest change in political agendas during this half century. First came the "Tampa", a Norwegian tanker which had rescued asylum seekers and then sought to give them safe landing in Australia. Against convention, the Howard government refused it permission to land. The government then dramatized its decision to take a very strong line against asylum seekers. A prominent Liberal advertisement had a clip of Howard's policy speech saying we will decide who comes to this country and the conditions under which they come (Wright 2022).

Whether or not this would have succeeded by itself, al Qaeda's 9/11 bombing in New York brought global attention to the threat of terrorism and changed the political agenda even more sharply. The polls showed a strong swing back to the government. After the election was called, Beazley managed to win back some of the lost support (Clune 2002, Marr and Wilkinson 2003).

Opposition failures: The old adage claims that 'oppositions don't win elections; governments lose them.' It has immediate plausibility for two reasons. The first is that if the public is happy, it is likely to opt for the status quo, to vote the same way it did last time, and so deliver the incumbents victory again. However happy publics seem to be in scarcer supply than they used to be. Secondly, as noted above, governments have many news generating advantages over oppositions, and more scope for influencing the political agenda.

The central flaw in such conventional wisdom is that elections involve a preferential rather than an absolute decision. If an opposition is not seen as a viable alternative, then an unpopular incumbent may survive, the lesser of two evils, or the most palatable among a limited menu.

What the final seven elections have in common is that the news focus turned strongly on to the opposition, and as a result its support went backwards rather than forwards.

The 1977 election is unique, in that Whitlam was the first leader since Ben Chifley in 1951 to contest the next election as opposition leader after losing office as prime minister, and it is safe to predict he will also be the last. He was leading a bitter, divided and disillusioned party. The Fraser Government campaign concentrated on what a disaster Whitlam had been in office. An effective Liberal advertisement had the music 'Memories' playing over negative headlines from the Labor years. Another called Whitlam the unemployment expert. The result was a loss almost as big as Labor's thrashing in 1975.

All the others were elections which the government could well have lost but which the opposition wasn't good enough to win. Hayden's Labor opposition was ahead in the polls and looked likely to spring a surprise. The Fraser government sought to portray him as weak, a 'sissy' said

Doug Anthony. The last week and a half of the campaign were dominated by charges that Labor would introduce a wealth tax, which would include taxing the family home. Labor seemed unable to take back any political initiative. The Hayden opposition secured a two party-preferred swing of 4.2 per cent, but Fraser held on to government with a small majority based on a two-party preferred vote of 50.4 per cent.

For much of the period of the Hawke government after 1984 it trailed the opposition in the polls. Nevertheless in both 1987 and 1990 it was able to retain office, with the campaign period leading to the opposition support falling. This was the era of Peacock-Howard conflicts in the Liberals. Bob Hawke exploited this with attack line: "if you can't govern yourselves you can't govern the country" (Bramston 2016: 328). Keating called the opposition leaders "vacuous" and "hopeless" and boasted that 'I used to throw the opposition around like rag dolls' (Bramston: 235). "Can a souffle rise twice?" Keating scathingly asked when Peacock resumed the leadership (SBS nd).

In 1987, under difficult economic circumstances for the government, Bramston observed that "by June 1987 Labor was winning back voters from the Liberals primarily due to their disunity" (Bramston: 285). Apart from Peacock supporters, Howard was also having difficulties with the "Joh for PM" insurgency. During the campaign Howard's promises of tax cuts and reduced public spending was painted by the government as a threat, and became more controversial as major errors in the figures were revealed. In 1990, according to ALP research, "There [was] a great deal of disillusion with Peacock, the Liberals' direction generally and their policy stuff ups" (Bramston: 334).

In 2004, the Howard Government was attempting its fourth election victory in a row, having been in power for eight years. Like all long governing parties, it had accumulated several scars and liabilities. In late 2003, Mark Latham had replaced Simon Crean as leader, and for the next several months seemed to be making progress. When Howard called the election, Labor was ahead in the polls. During the campaign, the Liberals concentrated on what they saw as Latham's lack of experience and lack of reliability. Their advertisements featured a capital L for 'Learner' whenever his name was present. They also sought to contrast their economic management credentials with his. Latham had put off announcing Labor's Tasmanian timber industry policy to the last week. When he did so it was denounced by prominent Tasmanian Labor figures, while Howard addressed cheering timber workers (Clune 2005).

In 2001 and 2004, Howard secured a swing towards the government and away from the opposition, the first time this had been achieved, as he pointed out on election night, since the elections of 1955 and 1958 at the height of the Labor split. It also became the first government since before the 1980 election to win control of the Senate.

In each of these four cases at the outset of the campaign, the government and opposition appeared to have roughly equal chances of winning, and in each the opposition wilted as the media attention was focused on it. This is even more starkly true of the two cases in the bottom row of the table.

John Hewson in 1993 and Bill Shorten in 2019 were both seen as losing the 'unlosable' election because their ambitious proposals presented targets for the opposing parties to mount scare campaigns. In 1993 the government started the campaign a long way behind and drew ahead in the last days before the election, while in 2019 it is more likely the polls had been wrong for some time (Goot 2019).

In 1993, the public was still suffering from what Keating called the recession we had to have, and the polling showed both Labor and Keating, who replaced Hawke in December 1991, trailing by a considerable margin. The Liberals under Hewson were very confident, and he proposed a GST as well as reforms in health and industrial relations. Labor operative and Keating confidante Peter Barron's "brutal advice was to run on the GST alone." Labor should not highlight its positive achievements, but rather keep the focus on the opposition, with Keating's memorable line: "If you don't understand it, don't vote for it, and if you do understand it, you'd never vote for it." (Maiden 2020: 4).

After Shorten had come so close to victory in 2016, and after considerable and obvious conflict among the Liberals in overthrowing Turnbull and installing Morrison as prime minister, Labor consistently led in the polls. Shorten "wanted to win big with a big agenda" (Errington and van Onselen 2021: 44). Labor put forward plans for tax reform, for increased spending in various areas, and for targets in CO_2 emissions. Journalist David Crowe observed that Morrison was weakened by any reminder of the divisions in the Liberal Party. "The Cabinet team was a liability. The Liberal brand was a problem. Morrison made the election a choice between himself and Shorten" (Crowe 2019: 313).

The government claimed that Labor's plans would lead to a higher tax revenue of $387 billion. Morrison thus "defined the Labor agenda with a single number" (Crowe: 320). The Liberals mounted a sustained charge on all fronts, claiming that Labor wanted to introduce an inheritance (death) tax, and that its franking credit policy was a "retirement tax". Shorten became the Bill Australia cannot afford. Barron's conclusion was that "There was an accumulation of risk factors. The electorate hates risk". "I don't think they liked Morrison any more at the end than they did at the start. But I think they thought he was less risky" (Maiden: 4).

These were the two strongest "scare" campaigns among the 20 elections. Scare campaigns are much more commonly used against oppositions because they are more of an unknown quantity to the public. Less often and usually less effectively they can focus on what a re-elected government might do. Labor supporters were able to conjure quite limited changes to Medicare into the mediscare campaign of 2016 (Eliot and Manwaring 2018).

The loss of these two "unloseable" elections provide a negative reference point for campaign professionals, and the lessons they take are not ones that will make for more constructive campaigning. Small target campaigns and keeping a negative focus on incumbents are seen as the path to victory.

The politics of explanations

Election results are often over-explained in two senses. First they picture the public and public attitudes as much more unanimous than they are. In most elections 47 per cent or more of the electorate effectively give their vote to the losing side. Rarely do all the public react one way or the other. Although easier said than done, more precision is needed about what influenced which voters and why. Secondly many developments are retrospectively interpreted in light of the result. There is a tendency to picture the victor as doing everything right and the loser everything wrong. But in very few election races is every post a winner. In 2022 Albanese won a clear victory, but for much of the campaign criticisms of his performances were plentiful. He had a bad start being unable to remember a key economic statistic on the first day, which began a game of the media playing 'gotcha' with him and made for unfavourable headlines. But these hiccups seemingly affected few votes. Nevertheless it is not because he waged a superior campaign that Albanese won.

For the participants, explaining election outcomes is always politically charged. It involves allocations of credit and blame, which play into internal conflicts and ambitions. For the losing side, at least in public, the challenge is less to explain and more to explain away. They need to find formulas that respect the will and wisdom of the people while also maintaining the essential rightness of their own party. There was nothing wrong with our message just with the way it was delivered, or misrepresented. So, explanations such as the other side had more resources than us, or played dirty tricks and lied are more palatable to the party faithful.

Comparisons of alternative explanations rarely have the finality of a Factcheck exercise. Key propositions are less tangible and less open to definitive verification and rebuttal. They can be much more subject to imagery and metaphor. For example in the lead-up to Howard's loss in 2007, Tony Abbott offered a unique psephological explanation: "the risk is that we might sleepwalk into changing the government in a fit of absent-mindedness". Afterwards Savva, thought the government "was punished severely by a sated electorate" (Savva: 275).

Perhaps the most bizarre judgement on a government losing office was by press gallery members Simon Benson and Geoff Chambers. They quote unnamed members "inside the Liberal and Labor camps [who] compared the [2022] outcome to Winston Churchill's postwar loss to Labour's Clement Atlee in the 1945 UK general election" (2022: ix). Whatever the plausibility of casting Morrison as a Churchillian figure, to then liken opposition leader Albanese to Clement Atlee involves a huge amount of rewriting history. According to them his "Atlee-inspired strategy" was "small target" (Benson and Chambers: 180). In fact, the Atlee Government was probably the most radical reforming British government of the twentieth century, and this was foreshadowed in its campaign. Atlee openly espoused socialism, nationalised some sectors, introduced a sweeping welfare state and founded the national health service (Howell 2006). None of this resembles Albanese in 2022, or a small target.

Although rarely as extreme as Benson and Chambers, journalists often do not have the same discipline in asserting explanations as they do in establishing facts.

Media and campaign momentum

In the twenty most recent elections, oppositions only won when they were already ahead before the election was called. During the campaign oppositions went backwards at least as often as they went forwards. This presents a puzzle because as noted election campaigns usually give the opposition more parity with the government. Goot found that in the ten elections between 1983 and 2007 incumbency was not the key to changing support during the campaign. Rather the party that started behind made up ground on the party that started ahead in all of them (2010: 69).

The evening television news, in particular, often said to be the most important medium, tends towards the most 'balanced' presentations, with equal time going to both leaders most nights. Other media, notably some commercial radio talk programs and newspapers, do not feel the need to become more balanced.

One explanation might be that the framing of news changes – from "how bad is the government?" to "will the opposition be any better?" and "can the opposition deliver?" The glaring examples are the loss of the two "unloseable" elections. During the 2019 campaign journalists, pollsters and politicians alike thought that Labor was on the road to victory, and overwhelmingly media attention was on what Labor would do in office. When the Morrison Government was re-elected there had probably been less attention to its future plans than to any other incumbent gaining another term.

In most of the seven elections which the opposition won, nearly all of them had if not a friendly media, then an accommodating one. Although the majority of newspapers were against Whitlam in 1972, the press gallery was very sympathetic to him and with close-up views of him and McMahon were much more impressed by Whitlam's grasp of issues. Likewise in 1983, the momentum towards a Hawke victory was manifested clearly in media coverage. Both in 1972 and 1983, even though the majority of editorials supported the Coalition, this was to some extent balanced by the press gallery's attitudes, and in both influence of editorial outlooks on news coverage was much less than in some other elections.

In all three occasions when the Coalition gained government, the Murdoch press was strongly supportive. In 1975, the Murdoch press, which had supported Labor in 1972, was so strongly anti-Labor that its journalists went on strike. On the first day of the 2013 campaign, the front page of *Daily Telegraph* was memorably headlined: "Kick this mob out".

Murdoch supported Labor in 1972. In 2007, the Murdoch press adapted itself to some degree to the likelihood of a Labor victory. The newspapers split in their editorial support, and although there were several stories and features that could be seen as anti-Labor there were also counter-examples.

The strongest exception to this ability to get some support from the

Murdoch press was Albanese in the 2022 election. Unlike 1983, Murdoch's populist feel had gone while unlike 2007 his desire to be at least somewhat on the winning side had faded. Instead, Albanese was faced with the tribal opposition of the Murdoch papers. However, the result was a dramatic example of how little direct impact its papers now had.

Although media bias is a common explanation by partisans for their election loss, this is more easily asserted than established. To some degree, but far from infallibly, a winning campaign creates a bandwagon effect in the media, with the side facing defeat being subjected to questions about their poor performance, their bleak prospects, and who is to blame.

Many criticisms of media performance about superficial coverage are easily made, and others about media agendas following political agendas are often debated. However even though partisanship among some media is readily apparent in some elections, it is a big, further step to establish any impact on votes.

It is easier to describe press content than it is to establish its influence. Whatever the Murdoch press had done in 1975 or 2013, for example, it is all but certain Labor would have lost. For at least the last decade, the Murdoch press and some commercial radio talk back hosts such as Alan Jones and Ray Hadley have been so consistent in their attitudes it is hard to imagine any of their regular consumers are going to change sides now.

It is not necessarily the most spectacular media coverage that may have an effect, but rather that which will affect voters whose mind is not yet made up. One possible example might be the 1980 election, which was very close, and where Murdoch newspapers gave ample coverage to the Fraser Government's scare campaigns about Labor wealth taxes in the last ten days.

There is a marked contrast between the parties and the news media. The parties are clear about their goals and the stakes are high. Aided by data from polls and focus groups, they seek to learn lessons from the last campaign for the next one. The news media do not give the same scrutiny to their own performance. For them the stakes are much lower – perhaps a blip in the TV ratings or readership figures or some fleeting professional kudos - and so their strategies for covering elections are far less dynamic. The charge of mediocrity is much more immediately persuasive than that of media power.

Media and political fragmentation – A changing future?

In 2022, the ALP gained government with just 32.6 per cent of the primary vote, by far the smallest percentage it had ever won with. Indeed its first preference share slightly declined – by 0.76% - almost certainly the first time a party winning government from opposition has had its vote fall. The two major parties combined gained just 68 per cent of the vote, continuing a long-term switch in first preference votes towards minor parties and independents. In 2022, the Coalition lost 19 seats, but of these, nine went to Labor and ten went to Greens and independents.

This long-term trend towards a decline in first preference votes for the major parties may or may not increase, but there is currently no sign it will go into reverse. Perhaps it is a symptom of how the old two-sided catch-all party competition is insufficient in the much more complex political environment we now have. Perhaps also though as politics has become more professional, the trend towards negative campaigning has contributed to growing public cynicism about and distaste for both the major parties. What may be best for advancing immediate party interests may not be best for contributing to long-term democratic efficacy.

The increasing political relevance of minor parties and independents creates problems for the news media. Young found that in the first three elections of the 2000s only 5 per cent of any newspaper articles, 4 per cent of radio news clips and 6 per cent of television clips quoted an independent or minor party representative (2011: 180). An independent candidate with strong support in his or her electorate does not necessarily carry wider significance for a national audience. Their rise also makes the reporting of polls more difficult. Nationally aggregated polls give no indication of whether an independent will win in a particular seat.

Moreover the audiences for the mainstream media are also becoming more fragmented, in addition to declining audiences for some of the most important media of the past (Young 2009). Although the role of social media and local campaigning are increasing, the news media are still the central arena in which the inter-party conflict is pursued, but at the least it no longer has the unchallenged dominance it once did.

These trends do not necessarily favour either government or opposition. They probably make governing more difficult, but the more fragmented politics and media make it more difficult for oppositions to mobilise majority size coalitions of support. So many conflicting forces are at work that the only safe prediction is that the future will not be a simple extrapolation from the past.

References

Benson, S., and Chambers, G., *Plagued: Australia's two years of hell – the inside story*, Sydney: Pantera Press, 2022

Bramston, T., *Paul Keating. The big-picture leader*, Melbourne: Scribe, 2016

Clune, D., "Howard at the crossroads. The October 2004 federal election" *Australasian Parliamentary Review*, 20(1), Autumn 2005, 3-20

Clune, D., "Back to the Future? The November 2001 federal election", *Australasian Parliamentary Review*, 17(1), Autumn 2002, 3-16

Crowe, D., *Venom. Vendettas, betrayals and the price of power*, Sydney: Harper Collins, 2019

Eliot, A., and Manwaring, R., "'Mediscare!' Social Issues" in Gauja, A., Chen, P., Curtin, J., and Pietsch, J., *Double Disillusion. The 2016 Australian Federal Election*, Canberra: ANU Press, 2018

Errington, W., and van Onselen, P., *How good is Scott Morrison?*, Sydney: Hachette, 2021

Goot, M., "Underdogs, bandwagons or incumbency? Party support at the beginning and the end of Australian election campaigns, 1983-2007", *Australian Cultural History*, 28(1), April 2010, 69-80

Goot, M., "Did late deciders confound the polls?", *Inside Story*, 19 September 2019

Hartcher, P., "Howard's instinct let him down", *Sydney Morning Herald*, 16 November 2007

Hawke, R., *The Hawke Memoirs*, Melbourne: Heinemann, 1994

Howell, D., *Atlee*, London: Haus Publishing, 2006

Kelly, P., *The Unmaking of Gough*, Sydney: Angus and Robertson, 1976

Kenny, M., "Opinion: Anthony Albanese, John Howard share many similarities" Canberra: Australian Studies Institute, 21 May 2023

Lloyd, C., "Prime Ministers and the Media", in Weller, P., (ed), *Menzies to Keating. The Development of the Australian Prime Ministership,* Carlton: Melbourne University Press, 1992

Maiden, S., *Party Animals. The Secret History of a Labor Fiasco*, Sydney: Viking, 2020

Marr, D., and Wilkinson, M., *Dark Victory. How a government lied its way to political triumph*, Sydney: Allen and Unwin, 2003

Oakes, L., *Remarkable Times. Australian Politics 2010-13: What really happened*, Sydney: Hachette, 2013

Savva, N., *So Greek: Confessions of a Conservative Leftie*, Melbourne: Scribe, 2010

SBS, "Top Paul Keating Quotes" https://www.sbs.com.au/news/article/top-paul-keating-quotes/r2jkhxv92

Wallace, C., *How to win an election*, Sydney: UNSW Press, 2020

Wright, T., "The year Howard drew a line in the sand and transformed Australia", *Sydney Morning Herald*, 1 January 2022

Young, S., "The decline of traditional news and current affairs in Australia", *Media International Australia,* 131, 2009, 147-59

Young, S., *How Australia Decides. Election reporting and the media*, Melbourne: Cambridge University Press, 2011

5

An Opposition Leader's Perspective

John Howard

There can never be an accepted approach to opposition. It will vary according to the myriad circumstances faced by Oppositions in a Westminster system.

Some opposition periods may be seemingly endless. The Labor Party was in opposition for 23 years between 1949 and 1972. It had four leaders, one of whom – Ben Chifley, the former Prime Minister – died in office. The last of those Opposition Leaders, Gough Whitlam, was elected Prime Minister in December 1972. By contrast, Bob Hawke never occupied the Opposition Leader's chair in federal parliament. He effectively became Leader of the federal parliamentary Labor Party the very day the 1983 election was called and went on to win that election convincingly and became the longest-serving Labor Prime Minister in Australia's history.

I was Opposition Leader for a total of four years and 10 months, broken into two separate periods *viz* between September 1985 and May 1989, then again between February 1995 and March 1996. It might be fair to say that I first became Leader of the Opposition by accident and lost it in May 1989 by ambush. My return to the leadership in 1995 was by consensus. I was unopposed. I became Prime Minister in March of 1996 and was in office for 11 years.

When I first became Leader the incumbent Labor Government led by Bob Hawke was electorally strong. Hawke and his Treasurer, Paul Keating, were an effective combination and had won a lot of support through implementing policies closer in substance to many associated with the

Liberal and National Parties.

I did not take the view that the Coalition should oppose just for the sake of being different. In my view, each policy initiative of the Hawke Government should be addressed on its merits. If it made sense and was in accord with the attitudes of the Coalition, the policy should be supported. Examples of such policies included deregulation of the financial system and reduction in levels of tariff protection.

Using ideological language, I wanted the Liberal and National Parties to attack Labor from the Right. If the Labor government felt it was good policy to deregulate Australia's financial system internationally by floating the dollar it should match that domestically by deregulating the industrial relations system. Not only was this good policy but, due to Labor's closeness to the union movement, it presented the then government with a dilemma. It could never support the Coalition in freeing the labour market, yet by accepting continued dictation from the ACTU it damaged its credentials as a reforming force as well as being seen to succumb to outside control.

Labor's decision to reduce tariff protection was the most courageous it took in government. Yet it almost certainly reasoned that the Opposition would not oppose this large policy change. High tariffs had been a bipartisan constant in Australian politics for decades. Once Labor decided to change, the Coalition had little alternative but to support it. In any event, the pressure for change within the Coalition had gathered momentum during the final years of the Fraser Government and the early years of Opposition.

The Coalition's approach of judging policy decisions on their merits was evident when the Higher Education Contribution Scheme (or HECS) was introduced. I had argued that the nation could no longer afford so-called free university education. The Labor Government responded with the HECS scheme. The only real opposition to the scheme came from student activists on university campuses.

When John Hewson became Opposition Leader after the 1990 election, he appointed me Shadow Minister for Industrial Relations. Thus commenced one of the most productive periods of my time in federal parliament. I immersed myself in the Industrial Relations portfolio and achieved real success in shifting public support in favour of a freer industrial relations system whereby individuals could strike direct bargains with their employers without the compulsory intervention of a union. My attack on the unfair dismissal laws of the time, which had deleterious effects on small businesses, was relentless. On the eve of the 1996 election Paul Keating indicated that he was open to change in this area.

An effective opposition is one which spends the minimum possible amount of time on the wrong side of the Speaker. This means that it must constantly have a policy agenda fit for the circumstances of the nation. It goes without saying that an Opposition should approach elections with detailed policies, yet present them in a way which does not leave it vulnerable to attack.

For example, the then Coalition position on health policy was more damaging to it at the 1993 election than its policy to introduce a GST. The Coalition's health policy for that election was confused and exposed it to damaging attacks particularly directed at female voters. That is why, shortly after I became Leader in 1995, I determined that the Coalition should accept the public's embrace of Medicare. We thus went to the 1996 election supporting Medicare but reinforcing that support with a commitment to revive private health insurance.

Internal unity is essential if the transition from opposition to government is to occur. The last year of opposition in the 1990s saw great unity between the Liberal and National Parties. There was a united determination to present a cohesive alternative to an increasingly out of touch government.

I had taken the view that effective opposition was a mixture of readily embracing policy with which the Coalition was comfortable as well as traditional denigration of bad policy, particularly in the arena of industrial relations. This approach won respect and support and was one of the main reasons why the Liberal and National Parties won convincingly on 2 March 1996.

6

The Changing Australian Federal Scene: The Role of the Senate Crossbench – A New Opposition?

Scott Prasser

Introduction

This chapter examines the impact of the substantial growth in recent decades of minor parties, independents and 'micro' parties in the Australian Senate. It examines the effect on the dynamics of opposition politics in the Senate and how this has affected both the nature of oppositional politics and the direction of national policy. Collectively known as the "crossbench" this group following the 2022 election has 18 representatives out of a total 76 in the Senate This large number of crossbenchers is in stark contrast to most of the Senate's history (see Table 1). The issue is whether this expanded, and as will be highlighted, increasingly diverse crossbench constitutes an additional opposition to that provided by the major opposition party that is formally recognised as "the opposition". The emergence of this expanded and diverse crossbench is important because of the Senate's pivotal constitutional, legislative, and political roles in Australian national government which is unmatched by upper houses in other Westminster democracies.

The pivotal place of the Senate in the Australian national government

The foremost issue about the Australian Senate is its entrenchment in the Australian Constitution.[1] This means it cannot easily be abolished or have its powers diminished by executive government *fiat* or legislation passed by the lower house, as has occurred in other Westminster democracies. Only a national referendum can alter the powers of the Senate and its very existence. Nor, as an elected chamber, can governments "swamp" its membership, as was threatened with the House of Lords in 1911. Nor can any Australian government threaten to stack the Senate with compliant lackeys to indulge in self-immolation as happened in Queensland in 1921-2 and New Zealand in 1950.

Second, as the Senate has been an elected chamber since its inception (unlike the American Senate),[2] it has a greater legitimacy to exercise its extensive powers than the appointed House of Lords or Canadian Senate. Nevertheless, the Senate's legitimacy is sometimes contested. It is argued that its equal number of senators from each State regardless of population, make it a less democratic body than the House of Representatives where the number of seats in each State reflects population size and shifts (Aroney 2001: 257-63). Further, full Senate elections only occasionally coincide with House of Representatives polls, consequently its composition is usually less current than the lower house. These, and other factors, provoked former Labor Prime Minister, Paul Keating, to label the Senate as "unrepresentative swill", lacking the legitimacy to oppose his government's legislative agenda (Keating 1992: 2549). Newly elected governments often claim that, as they reflect the most recent expression of the electorate's will, they have a mandate for their policies to be implemented without any Senate obstruction.

Third, the Australian Senate's extensive constitutional powers are co-equal with the House of Representatives, except in relation to the introduction of taxation bills and legislation authorising government spending. Even here, however, it can under the Section 53 of the Constitution, "return to the House of Representatives any proposed law … requesting … the omission or amendment of any item or provision therein". This has long been interpreted as meaning that the Senate can reject money bills (budgets) and other legislation indefinitely (Aroney 2009: 237-9). This is what occurred in 1975 when the Senate "exercised its legal power to deny supply to an executive government" causing a "constitutional crisis" and resulting in the Governor-General dismissing the Whitlam Labor Government on the grounds that it could not guarantee supply (Aroney 2009: 361). By contrast, the House of Lords since the *Parliament Act 1911* can only delay legislation for a short time and then be bypassed. While the Canadian Senate can reject legislation its appointed nature makes obstruction rare and easily overcome.

Fourth, the equal State representation and proportional voting system of the Senate affords more opportunities for minor parties and independents to exploit local and regional issues and gain election than in the House of Representatives. The initial emergence of the Greens in the Senate largely reflected environmental issues in Tasmania. Pauline Hanson's One Nation Party's Senate success was nurtured by Queensland's particular demographic base and economy.

At the same time the drivers of increased minor and independent members in the Senate have had an impact on their representation in the House of Representatives. Traditionally, because of its single member constituencies and preferential voting, minor parties and independents have only been able to gain small footholds in the House of Representatives. Since the late 1990s, however, this group has been enjoying a consistently growing share of the House of Representatives' vote and seats (Miragliotta and Ghazarian 2021: 171-3). In 2022, they hold a record 16 seats in the lower chamber, although not, as in the Senate, the balance of power.

The coming of the Senate crossbench

Although the Senate may have been originally seen as a States' house and even a house of review in keeping with then current Westminster views of bicameral legislatures, it has generally been regarded as performing the former not at all, and the latter only sporadically, depending on whether the government had a majority or not (McIntosh 1989). This was because, as Deakin and others had predicted at the Constitutional Conventions (Aroney 2009: 359-61), the Senate would soon be captured by the emerging political parties with their tightly disciplined regimes (Starr 1979). The Senate's voting systems – first past the post (till 1919) and then preferential (until 1949) – exaggerated majorities for one or other of the two major parties that dominated Australian national politics.[3] Consequently, for the first fifty years of federation, governments mostly controlled the Senate except for some brief interludes – 1913-14, 1929-31, and 1941-44. Generally, the Senate acted as a "rubber stamp" for government legislation. It was seen as the reserve of party timeservers, hacks and "meddlesome old men" – a backwater (Bennett 2003-4: 8). That the Labor Party had as part of its federal platform from 1918-1977 the objective of abolishing the Senate hardly added to its prestige.

What contributed to a changed role for the Senate was the Chifley Labor Government's decision in 1948 to increase its size from 36 to 60 seats accompanied by the introduction of the proportional voting system. At the same time the House of Representatives was also increased from 75 to 121 seats. The increase in both houses was because of the nexus requirement in the Constitution[4] (Gorman and Melleuish 2018). There were sound reasons for these increases given that Australia's population had increased from 3.8 million in 1901 to 7.6 million as measured by the 1947 Census. Proportional representation was also seen as being more democratic and would make it easier for small parties and independents to win Senate positions. The Chifley Government's motivation for these initiatives, however, was primarily partisan. It was to thwart the Menzies Coalition, expected to win the 1949 election, from gaining a Senate majority and to shore up positions for current Labor members in both houses, but especially in the Senate where the previous preferential voting system would have almost totally annihilated Labor in that chamber[5] (Bennett 2001; Mackerras 1995: 65-6). Labor was partly successful.

Menzies despite a near landslide election win in 1949 did not gain a Senate majority. In 1951, Menzies, confronted with Senate obstruction called a double dissolution election (Australia's then second only such double dissolution) and successfully gained a Senate majority.[6] Since then governments have only occasionally secured Senate majorities:[7] the last was by the Howard Government (2004-07). No Labor administration has enjoyed a Senate majority since 1949. It is now regarded as almost impossible for any government to gain a Senate majority.

While proportional representation and increasing the size of the Senate has often been used to explain the growth of the crossbench, at first these changes did not lead to an immediate influx of minor party or independent members. It was not until the mid-1950s that this began to occur (see Table 1). At that time this largely occurred because it was a breakaway group from one of the major parties, the Democratic Labor Party (DLP) which had split from the Labor Party, and thus had some profile and political salience with a group of disaffected ALP voters. The DLP reached its zenith in 1970 winning five Senate positions which, along with three independents, brought the crossbench to the then record total of eight senators. The DLP had considerable influence on Coalition government policy given that their House of Representatives preferences helped the Coalition retain office (Reynolds 1974). Ironically, it was during this latter period from 1967 when the Coalition government lacked a Senate majority that the DLP in conjunction with Labor, revamped the Senate committee system and enhanced its reputation as a house of review.

As the DLP's fortunes waned another breakaway party group emerged – the Australian Democrats (AD) led by former Liberal Party frontbencher, Don Chipp.[8] Initially winning two Senate seats in 1977, the AD numbers rose to nine by 1998. However, internal squabbling, competition from the Greens, and the view that they had become too supportive of the Howard Government[9] all combined to lead to the Australian Democrats' demise by 2007 (see Table 1).

Subsequently, the Greens and other more disparate small parties and mavericks have joined Senate ranks. Starting with a single Senate position in 1990, the Greens after the 2022 election had 12 senators – the largest number ever held by a minor party. Changes to the electoral laws introduced by the Hawke Government in 1984 led to the growth of micro parties, spectacularly seen at the 2013 election when six new crossbench senators from a diversity of groups joined the growing crossbench. This brought the crossbench total to 20 after the 2016 election or over 26 per cent of the Senate. It fell slightly to 18 senators following the 2022 election (see Table 1). Explanations for this growth of the crossbench are varied and include: declining support for the major parties; emergence of single issue groups; a more fragmented society which the major parties are often slow to accommodate; and the growth of an "anti-politics sentiment" (Kelly 2018; Lesh 2018; Marsh 1995; Wood and Daley 2018).

While the growing size of the crossbench has been one of the challenges facing governments, the other has been its changing composition. The crossbench has become more diverse, less connected to the major parties and thus less manageable and predictable (Ghazarian 2012; 2015; Miragliotta and Ghazarian 2021). Some, like the Greens are ideological, so, although they are less flexible, they at least have a consistent set of known views. Other single-issue parties or those focussed around particular personalities, have a less consistent set of views making it harder for governments to negotiate with these senators.

Roles and strategies of the Senate crossbenches

The crossbench, composed as it usually is of minor and micro parties and independents, has developed a different role compared to traditional oppositions and consequently pursues different strategies which affect its behaviour and interactions with any government. This also affects their stance on issues, what they may be wanting to bargain for and how hard the negotiations might become. By contrast, the traditional opposition of one of the major parties has a solid electoral base, usually a defined set of policies, a consistent philosophy and its own past record in government that affects its behaviour. As well, being the "government in waiting", it must exercise certain constraints in both what it opposes and what policies it proposes if it is to be taken seriously. Proposing alternative policies that involve unrealistic increases in public expenditure can prove electorally inept. This is what Labor Opposition leader H.V. Evatt did in his 1954 election platform and consequently attracted considerable criticism from not just the incumbent Menzies Government, but many media commentators too (Martin 1999: 259; McMullin 1992: 271-2). Similarly, opposing everything a government is doing can be counter-productive. Such antagonism and negativeness wears thin over time with the electorate and the media. It can sometimes be more electorally advantageous for an opposition to show its relevance by being able through negotiation to be seen to modify a government's policy and legislation for a better overall outcome. Of course, as highlighted earlier about the Australian Democrats, too much consorting with a government, especially on controversial issues, can alienate supporters.

Lastly, as highlighted in Chapter 3, the major parties when in opposition must be wary of trying to appeal too much to their base, their political supporters, always a temptation when a party moves from government to opposition. It has long been documented that party membership is not always a good reflection of wider public opinion and so a deft hand is needed to keep the party faithful onside while also appealing to the wider community. All this means that the major opposition party must adopt a certain degree of "reasonableness" in the policy stances it takes and its behaviour to be taken seriously as an alternative government and to allow parliament to work. After all, the opposition assumes that one day it will be the government and will want some level of co-operation with the opposition to have a workable parliament and administration.

All this indicates that for the major parties being in opposition requires considerable political skills and judgement in terms of adopting obstructionist or more compliant parliamentary tactics.

By contrast, minor and micro parties, independents, and mavericks, work under a different framework. None realistically see themselves as the "government in waiting" whatever their private aspirations. Their prime aim, like all political players, is to retain their parliamentary positions, but not to gain office, and their route to achieve success is different from that of the major parties when in opposition. For these crossbench members the strategy pursued is a combination of retaining their followers and gaining media attention for their stands. This can vary from being "principled", usually meaning intransigent, to any government proposal or being seen to influence or modify a government policy as long as it is in line with the party's core beliefs. The former involves attacks and non-co-operation. The latter requires well publicised negotiations – often deliberately drawn out and involving considerable brinkmanship – making them, rather than the government, appear to be the centre of the decision-making process. Cohesive, disciplined, experienced minor parties with a common philosophy like the Greens are in many ways more like major parties and are better able to perform these multiple tasks against a background of making strategic political choices.

Micro parties and single independent senators, often less experienced and with more diffuse policy frameworks, somewhat disparate membership, and aware that their electoral clock might be about to wind down, have more difficult choices to make. Their smaller numbers mean they will not be crucial to every Senate vote. While they have the same dilemmas as the larger crossbench representatives – to oppose or to support – their choices are more contingent on the issues, the number of votes the government needs, what other crossbenchers and the official opposition are doing. Their concern is whether to stand out from the crowd – the crossbench crowd – but be possibly irrelevant, or to join with the others and be lost in the crowd.

Some of these different dilemmas and choices are illustrated in the following case studies where crossbench support, or at least some of it, was essential for government to have its legislation passed.

Howard Government and industrial relations legislation 1996-8: The Mandate issue

One example concerns the Howard Coalition Government seeking to have its promised industrial relations legislation passed in 1996. This brings into focus a newly elected government with a large House of Representatives majority, and although having 37 senators still short of a Senate majority by two. The Howard Government faced a ten member crossbench[10] and 29 Labor opposition senators (see Table 1). The Howard Government wanted to implement changes to industrial relations by the *Workplace Relations and Other Legislation Amendment Bill* introduced two months after being elected. This reflected the Coalition's, and especially Howard's, long held industrial relations policy, often seen as controversial. Moreover, as the policy was part of the Coalition's 1996 election platform Howard argued his government had a clear mandate to implement the policy and that the Senate should not obstruct the legislation in any way (Howard 1996) – a common new government ploy. Of course, as has been pointed out (Evans 2000: 26-28) Howard's position was contrary to his previous views on such matters. When he was in opposition Howard expressed a willingness for the opposition in the Senate to reject Labor government legislation – a not unusual about face in federal politics with the oscillating fortunes of oppositions and governments.

The challenge for the Howard Government was whether to use its then large political capital, accept no Senate amendments and threaten to call a double dissolution election, that could possibly even culminate in a joint sitting to pass the legislation as occurred in 1974 under the Whitlam Government. Would such brinkmanship be both successful in terms of having the preferred policy implemented and be rewarded electorally at any new poll? Should the Coalition risk all for this one policy? After all, the Coalition had been in opposition for thirteen years. Howard thought it was not worth the risk (Howard 2010: 211-2). The better course was of action was to develop a compromise with the crossbench, with the aim having the most important parts of the policy accepted and thus implemented. As the Labor Opposition and the Greens were adamantly opposed to the legislation, as was independent Senator Harradine (former Labor Party member), the focus of negotiation shifted to the Australian Democrats. The additional risk of this approach was that in seeking to gain Australian Democrat support, the policy might be compromised too greatly.

The Australian Democrats too, faced several critical decisions. They could join the Labor Party and Greens to oppose and defeat the legislation. This might trigger a double dissolution election and then a joint sitting that would eventually pass the very legislation to which they were opposed. In so doing, the Democrats would be seen to be largely tagging along supporting Labor which would almost certainly take the lead and the limelight in all the debates and the media coverage. Alternatively, by negotiating directly with the Howard Government it would enable maximum concessions to be extracted, leading to better policy outcomes at least from their perspective. Politically, it would put the Australian Democrats at the centre of government decision-making, increase their profile, make them look relevant and influential, and sideline Labor and the Greens – their prime rivals.

Certainly, the Howard Government sought to negotiate with the Australian Democrats "in order to secure the principal thrust of their objectives even at the cost of modifications" (Singleton 2000: 3). In so doing, the Howard Government accepted 170 amendments to its most important legislation which was then passed with the support of the Australian Democrats. Meanwhile, the Labor Party opposition, along with the Greens, were made redundant. It was both a policy and political win for the Howard Government – and the Australian Democrats. As Howard later recalled, "although I was unhappy with the compromises ... with the Democrats, we were nonetheless able to achieve a substantial part of our workplace agenda" (Howard 2010: 242).

This episode highlights that even a government highly committed to a particular policy, extensively developed,[11] long advocated and publicly endorsed at a recent election – was prepared to accept modifications in response to crossbench pressure of a minor party as distinct from the formal opposition. Howard chose to work within the existing constitutional and institutional structures and boundaries, than to attempt to "crash through" by any form of brinkmanship. For a time, the focus of opposition shifted to a minor party. That the Australian Democrats increased their Senate representation to nine seats at the subsequent 1998 election suggests that they had pursued a politically astute strategy. However, not all Australian Democrats were happy with either the policy outcome of the negotiations or the public profile of being feted by the Howard Government.

The process was repeated two years later when the Howard Government, after the 1998 election based very much around the good and services tax (GST) again negotiated with the Australian Democrats given the rejection by the Labor opposition, the Greens and Senator Harradine (see Harvey 2023 concerning Harradine's views). Although Treasurer Peter Costello led the process, all accounts suggest that it was Howard's personal intervention that made it happen. This involved both a willingness as Howard said, "to give the Democrats something" in removing the tax on food (which Costello was against) and the warm manner, patience and open style by which Prime Minister Howard personally conducted the negotiations (Howard 2010: 314-15). The process was to have adverse impacts on the Australian Democrats far more than had occurred over the industrial relation legislation. That two of its members did not support the legislation, indicated this disquiet within the ranks. Subsequently, it led to its leader, Meg Lees, being replaced, further party fragmentation and consequential disintegration and by the 2007 election, complete disappearance from the political stage. This suggests that too close a flirtation with government can have adverse impacts on minor parties if supporters believe the party has veered too much from its core mission (see Bartlett 2002).

The success of the Howard Government in managing the crossbench on two major policy initiatives was the result of several factors. The Howard Government was not breaking an election promise, but in both cases delivering. The policies had long histories, had been articulated in detail, and examined in detail by Senate committees, was led by senior and capable ministers and, especially, by Prime Minister Howard whose interest and commitment to both policies, was known, strong and genuine.

The Abbott Coalition Government and the "feral" Senate

If the Howard Government was able to navigate its way through the Senate political labyrinth and successfully negotiate with the crossbench on its two major policy planks, the Abbott Coalition Government (2013-15) although elected by an almost as large a margin as the Howard 1996 win (Green 2015), and also without a Senate majority, was seen to have largely come unstuck in its dealings with the Senate on important legislation. The issue was whether this was ineptness on the part of the Abbott Government or changed political circumstances in the Senate given its quite different composition compared to the Howard period?

Initially, the Abbott Government was confronted with a hostile Labor-Greens controlled Senate until the six newly elected crossbench senators arrived in July and the rerun of the Western Australian Senate election was completed in early 2014 which slightly changed the overall results.[12] The final Senate configuration facing the Abbott Government was a crossbench of 18: 10 Greens and 8 others. After subsequent desertions and changes, the 8 evolved into six members linked to five micro parties and two independents (see Table 1). Certainly, the overall size was bigger than the 10 crossbench senators that faced the Howard Government. Importantly, it was more diverse – a culmination of the trends discussed above. In essence, the Abbott Government "faced the challenge of a diverse, complex, and to some parts unconventional crossbench" (Prosser, Warhurst and Dennis 2015: 60). While the Howard Government had to target just the Australian Democrats or only needed the support of two crossbench senators to have a majority, the Abbott Government needed six – a bigger challenge. Further, given the steadfast opposition from the Greens and, naturally, the Labor Party, such support could only come from these eight mixed crossbench senators.

What irked the Abbott Government more than perhaps other newly elected administration with a large lower house majority, was that most of these eight micro-party crossbench senators were elected by very small percentages of votes (less than one per cent in one case – see Green 2015: 407). From the Abbott Government's perspective, this further undermined their legitimacy to obstruct its program. It possibly affected its sometimes offhand approach in dealing with the crossbench and Abbott's reported intermittent attention. Abbott's labelling of the Senate as "feral" reflected this view. It was used too easily by the government, and especially the Prime Minister's Office (PMO), as an excuse for some of its policy failures – like the inability to have co-payments for GP visits passed, or the failure to pass higher education deregulation announced with great fanfare on the 2014-15 budget night.

Nevertheless, the Abbott Government was more successful than some of its own rhetoric suggested. Its core election promises to end the carbon and mining taxes and to introduce its Direct Action environment policy were supported by the Senate. Overall, some 92 per cent of its legislation was passed, almost comparable to previous governments while some rejections of bills were assessed as not being major (Mullins and Richertson 2016).

Where the Abbott Government came unstuck early, and with lasting harm, was with many different parts of its first Budget (for 2014-15) where issues like higher education changes, Medicare co-payments, pension and unemployment benefit cuts were rejected. They were portrayed by the media, as well as the Labor Party, as being not only unfair, but also as broken election promises. Some, like the higher education fee deregulation were a complete surprise until announced on budget night. It had no electoral mandate and there had been no preliminary discussions to build interest group support or to assess the policy's possible flaws. The policy was seen as increasing the cost of higher education (Bell and Probert 2016: 221-28) and thus was portrayed as being quite contrary to

Abbott's rash promise on the eve of the election of "no cuts to education, health, pensions, the ABC or SBS, and no changes to the GST" (Abbott 2013). Little wonder that an inexperienced crossbench, even those potentially sympathetic to a Coalition government, would be reluctant to support some aspects of the Abbott Government's first Budget. As Errington and Van Onselen (2015: 23) have argued, "After the Coalition fell achingly short at the 2010 election, Abbott failed to use the next three years to prepare for government by setting out a policy framework, as Howard had in just one." This contrasted with the Howard Government's industrial relations and GST proposals that had, as noted, long histories

Adding to these problems were the very different styles of leadership shown in the negotiation process. The general assessment was that Abbott's involvement in negotiations with the crossbench was a hit and miss affair, although this also owed a lot to the very different, diverse and large crossbench that had to be persuaded and the far greater range of issues under negotiation. The Howard Government on its major policy issues just dealt with one minor party, the Australian Democrats, which had all the numbers it needed and had members who had been in the Senate for some time and thus appreciated the policy process and the negotiating game. There were also personal relationships across the benches. Howard's interactions were regular and conducted with considerable respect. There was also a consistent government view.

In the end, though, it was the Abbott Government's failure to clarify its policy agenda, to co-ordinate its approaches and some issues of personality which combined with its quick loss of electoral appeal following its election, that made its management of the Senate less successful than it should have been. Indeed, very early on the Abbott Government was struggling to deal with the normal politics and processes of governing (Savva 2016), as its consistent poor opinion polls indicated (Grattan 2016: 11-12), let alone manage effectively the new, changed and very complex nature of the Senate. It should have done better. It should have prepared better.

Passing the Industrial Chemicals Act 2019 – up close and personal[13]

At the 2016 election, with Malcolm Turnbull since September 2015 as the new prime minister, replacing Abbott, the Coalition was returned with a slender one seat majority in the House of Representatives. Again, the new Turnbull Government did not have a Senate majority. The size of the Senate crossbench had grown to 20 senators and included 9 Greens and 11 others covering six different parties – with membership again unstable because of disagreements and ambitions (see Table 1).

A minor area of reform to be achieved concerned changes announced in the Abbott Government's 2015-16 Budget to the industrial chemical regulatory framework. These changes involved six bills. They sought to: deliver a $23m annual regulatory saving to industry; make regulatory efforts more proportionate to the level of risk to humans or the environment; and to provide a faster pathway to regulation to act as an incentive for the introduction of safer new industrial chemicals. In addition, during the 2016 election campaign, the Coalition released a press release in a marginal seat stating that the Turnbull Government would introduce an animal test ban for chemicals solely used in cosmetics in line with the European Union (EU) laws.[14]

While the legislation easily passed in the House of Representatives in October 2017, fifteen months later with the 2019 election looming, it was still stuck in the Senate due to opposition from Labor, the Greens, and most of the crossbench. Although this opposition was under the general mantle of concern for the environment and safety for humans, there were, in fact, other motivations. Labor wanted to increase regulations ostensibly to improve environmental standards, but these would make it more difficult for environmentally sound products to be imported in more economic quantities thus increasing the costs of the products for Australian industry. Labor's prime goal was political – to ensure the government could not honour its election promise and thus be embarrassed. The Greens demanded a more extreme regulatory regime that would have undermined the very aims of the legislation and to which the government could not agree. The crossbench, consisting of a variety of micro parties with limited resources and experience, was being heavily lobbied and influenced by international environmental activists like the Humane Society International (HSI). They claimed that the proposed new laws were not equivalent to the EU laws in relation to animal testing. These activists wanted to make Australia the new frontier in the fight to remove chemicals from the market by banning animal testing in any product used for cosmetics, even if it had other uses which would have significantly impacted on those uses by such actions.

Nevertheless, there was support for the legislation. Industry, including manufacturers and marketers of hygiene and cosmetic products, wanted the Turnbull Government to get the legislation passed in this session of parliament as they were concerned a change of government would produce unworkable laws and disadvantage Australian industry. The RSPCA was satisfied that the legislation, with some minor concessions concerning animal testing, was acceptable.

As the legislation was in the Senate, responsibility for its future passed to a Senate based Minister – in this case one of cabinet rank.[15] A strategy was developed and approval was sought and gained from the Prime Minister's Office (PMO) in late 2018 for the Minister's Office (MO) to take full carriage of negotiations. It was clear that HSI support was essential to swing the vote of the crossbench especially the micro parties but also, if achieved, and then pitched resolutely, even also that of Labor and the Greens.

The turning point came when the MO requested the Department of Health to seek written confirmation through a letter from the Executive Director of the European Chemical Agency that the draft legislation was equivalent to theirs. The MO then diligently worked on a process of building trust with advocate groups until they conceded that Australian laws were the equivalent of the European Laws. After lengthy negotiations the MO extracted their written admission that this was the case. This admission was pivotal in gaining support from the whole crossbench, as well as from Labor. Minor concessions were made to the Labor Party and to some crossbench members on several matters, confirmed almost immediately in writing by the Minister. The integrity of the original legislation remained intact. This was all achieved by a concerted process of interactions by the MO with all parties and which were characterised by being ordered, frequent, open, honest, but resolute. Agreements made were expected to be honoured by all sides. Informal discussions and negotiations were quickly followed by formal letters of exchange confirming and clarifying what had been agreed thus avoiding confusion, real or otherwise, and slippage. The result was the legislation was passed in the Senate on 19 February 2019 receiving the unanimous support from the whole of the crossbench including the Greens and Labor. Royal Assent was given on 12 March 2019. Consequently, the Morrison Government was able to go to the May 2019 federal election with the previous election promise honoured.

Conclusion

These case studies highlight that managing the Senate no longer means solely dealing with the formal opposition. Rather, given the increasing diversity of the Senate, to have legislation passed requires negotiations across a multiple range of players – minor parties like the now persistent Greens, micro parties whose existence is often ephemeral and whose views are diverse, and with mercurial senators who are often in conflict with each other even sometimes with those in the same party or alliance. These developments have challenged many once settled aspects of Australian government – executive government dominance over parliament, the acceptance of a government mandate (always a questionable argument), the hegemony of the two major party system, and the very role of the traditional opposition as it operates in the Senate (Chalmers and Davis 2000-01).

The Australian constitutional settings and the place of the Senate in those has not changed. For government policy to be enacted legislation must pass in the House of Representatives and then the Senate. What has changed is the diversity of the Senate's membership and the size of the overall crossbench. This makes the managing of this process considerably harder to achieve on a more regular basis than has occurred previously. It means that the formal opposition is no longer the only focus for a government desiring to have its legislation passed. The traditional opposition given its size is still important, but negotiations have partly moved to the ever widening crossbench which now acts, given its composition, as a secondary opposition group that has to be consulted and courted as much, if not even more so than the formal opposition.

Consequently, no government can afford to conduct its Senate negotiations in a haphazard manner. Prosser et al in identifying criteria for evaluating minority governments laid down the strategies and behaviours which governments need to follow if they are to exercise any semblance of control over the Senate and thus to have a viable and functioning administration. These are:

- developing respectful and trusting relationships;
- openness in negotiations – a more transactional approach;
- ensuring the central role of the prime minister in providing commitment to any proposals;
- being consistent in approach and keeping agreements once made (Prosser et al: 56-7).

Of course, the traditional major party opposition in the Senate, must adjust too to this growing crossbench. Not only must the opposition decide when to compromise and when to obstruct (see Chapter 3), it must also consider more carefully the tactics and strategies of the crossbench in negotiations and on the floor on parliament, to avoid being supplanted, wrong-footed and even made redundant. While this is not completely new, it is now a more serious challenge, given the size and diversity of the crossbench. This is certainly a development worth monitoring in the future as its impact on any government's legislative program will be important.

Table 1: Minor and minor parties and independents and minority parties in Senate 1901-2022

ELECTION	Total number of minor and non-major party members	Composition of minor and non-major members
1901	-	
1903	2	IND
1906	2	IND
1955	2	DLP
1958	2	DLP
1961	2	1-DLP 1-IND
1964	3	2-DLP 1-IND
1967	5	4-DLP 1-IND
1970	8	5-DLP 3-IND
1974	2	1-LM 1-IND
1975	2	1-LM 1-IND
1977	3	2-AD 1-IND
1980	6	5-AD 1-IND
1983	6	5-AD 1-Ind
1984	9	7-AD 1-NDP 1-IND
1987	10	7-AD 1-NDP 2-IND
1990	10	8-AD 1-GRN 1-IND
1993	10	7-AD 2-GRN 1-IND
1996	10	7-AD 2-GRN 1-IND (Harradine)

1998	12	9-AD 1-GRN 1-ON 1-IND
2001	13	8-AD 2-GRN 1-ON 2-IND
2004	9	4-AD 4-GRN 1-FFP
2007	7	5-GRN 1-FFP 1-IND
2010	11	9-GRN 1-DLP 1-IND
2013	18	10-GRN 2 -PUP 1-MEP 1-DLP 1-FF 1-LDP 1-XEN
2016	20	9-GRN 4-ON 3-XEN 1-DHP 1-FF 1-LN 1-LD
2019	15	9-GRN 2-ON 2-CA 1-LN 1-AC
2022	18	12-GRN 2-ON 2-LN 1-UAP 1-IND

AC Australian Conservatives
AD Australian Democrats
CA Centre Alliance
DHP Derryn Hinch Party
DLP Democratic Labor Party
FFP Family First Party
GRN Greens

INP   Independent
LDP   Liberal Democrat Party
LN   Lambie Network
MEP   Motoring Enthusiasts' Party
PUP   Palmer United Party
UAP   United Australia Party
XEN   Xenophon Party

References

Abbott, A., Media Statement, 12 September 2013

Aroney, N., *The Federal Commonwealth of Australia: A Study in the Formation of its Constitution*, Thesis submitted for Degree of Doctor of Philosophy, School of Law, Monash University, April 2001

Aroney, N., *The Constitution of a Federal Commonwealth: The Making and Meaning of the Australian Constitution*, Cambridge: Cambridge University Press, 2009

Aulich, C., (ed), *From Abbott to Turnbull: Australian Commonwealth Administration 2013-2016*, West Geelong: Echo Books, 2016

Bartlett, A., "The Australian Democrats", in Warhurst, J., and Simms, M., (eds), *2001: The Centenary Election*, St Lucia: University of Queensland Press, 2002, 139-44

Bell, S., and Probert, B., "Education policy: from bipartisan promises to radical agendas", in Aulich, *From Abbott to Turnbull*, 221-42

Bennett, S., *The Australian Senate*, Research Paper No 6, Canberra: Commonwealth Parliament, 2003-4

Brett, J., "Exit Right: The unravelling of John Howard", *Quarterly Essay*, Melbourne: Black Inc, 2007

Chalmers, J., and Davis, G., *Power: Relations between the Parliament and the Executive*, Research Paper No 14, 2000-01, Canberra: Department of Parliament Library, Commonwealth Parliament.

Errington, W., and Van Onselen, P., *Battle Ground: Why the Liberal Party Shirtfronted Tony Abbott*, Carlton: Melbourne University Press, 2015

Evans, H., "The Howard Government and Parliament", in Singleton. G., (ed)., *The Howard Government: Australian Commonwealth Administration 1996-1998*, Sydney: UNSW Press, 2000, 26-36

Evans, H., "The Case for Bicameralism", in Aroney, N., Prasser, S., and Nethercote, J.R., (eds), *Restraining Elective Dictatorship: The Upper House Solution?* Crawley: University of Western Australia, 2008, 67-80

Galloway, A., "Labor says greens blocking housing bill will be a betrayal", *Sydney Morning Herald,* 11 June 2023

Ghazarian, Z., "The Changing Type of minor Party Elected to Parliament: The Case of the Australian Senate from 1949-2010", *Australian Journal of Political Science*, 47(3), 2012, 441-54

Ghazarian, Z., *The Making of a Party System: Minor Parties in the Australian Senate*, Melbourne: Monash University Publishing, 2015

Gorman, Z., and Melleuish, G., "The nexus clause: A peculiarly Australian obstacle", *Cogent Arts and Humanities*, 5, 2018

Grattan, M., "There's never been a better time to change Prime Minister", in Aulich, *From Abbott to Turnbull*, 1-21

Green, A., "Explaining the Results", in Johnson, C., Wanna, J., with Lee, Hsu-Ann., (eds), *Abbott's Gambit: The 2013 Australian Federal Election*, Canberra: ANU Press, 2015, 303-410

Harvey, K., *Harradine,* Redland Bay: Connor Court Publishing, 2023

Howard, J., MP, Transcript of the Victory Speech of the Prime Minister Elect, Wentworth Hotel, 2 March 1996

Howard, J., MP, Address to the National Press Club, Canberra, 8 December 1997

Howard, J., MP, House of Representatives, *Commonwealth Parliamentary Debates*, 15 September 1987, 56

Howard, J., MP, "The Liberal-National Parties' Industrial Relations Policy: Deregulation by Providing a Enterprise Focus", *The Economic and Labour Relations Review*, 1(2), December 1990, 34-47

Howard, J., MP, House of Representatives, *Commonwealth Parliamentary Debates*, 19 August 1993, 331

Howard, J., *Lazarus Rising*, Sydney: HarperCollins, 2010

Keating, P., MP, House of Representatives, *Commonwealth Parliamentary Debates*, 4 November 1992, 2549

Kelly, P., *Triumph and Demise: The Boken Promise of a Labor Generation*, Carlton: Melbourne University Press, 2014

Kelly, P., "Disillusioned voters not keen to go to the big party?, *The Australian*, 14 March 2018

Lesh, M., *Democracy in Divided Australia*, Redland Bay: Connor Court Publishing, 2018

Mackerras, M., "Election and Party Performance", in Prasser, S., Warhurst, J., Nethercote, J.R., (eds), *The Menzies Era: A Reappraisal of Government, Politics and Policy*, Sydney: Hale and Hale and Iremonger, 1995, 60-79

Marsh, I., *Beyond the Two Party System*, Melbourne: Cambridge University Press, 1995

Martin, A., *Robert Menzies: A Life Volume 2, 1944-1978*, Carlton: Melbourne University Press, 1999

Mayer, H., "Introduction" in Mackerras, M., *The Australian Senate, 1965–1967: Who Held Control?*, Sydney Australasian Political Studies Association, Monograph No 9, 1968

McIntosh, G., "The Senate: States' House or Party House?, *Current Affairs Bulletin,* 65(10), March 1989, 25-7

McMullin, R., *The Light on the Hill: The Australian Labor Party 1891-1991*, Melbourne: Oxford University Press, 1992

Miragliotta, N., and Ghazarian, Z., "Minor Parties and Independents", in Fenna, A., and Manwaring, R., (eds), *Australian Government and Politics*, Melbourne: Pearson, 2021, 168-83

Prasser, S., "Controlling the Senate", in Frame, T., (ed), *The Desire for Change, 2004-2007: The Howard Government Volume IV*, Sydney: UNSW Press, 2021, 103-26

Prosser, B., Warhurst, J., and Dennis, R., "New wine, old wine skins: perspectives on the 'feral' Senate", in Aulich, *From Abbott to Turnbull*, 45-67

Reynolds, P., *The Democratic Labor Party*, Milton: The Jacaranda Press , 1974

Savva, N., *The Road to Ruin*, Melbourne: Scribe, 2016

Singleton, G., "Industrial Relations: Pragmatic Change", in Prasser, S., and Starr, G., (eds), *Policy and Change: The Howard Mandate*, Sydney: Hale and Iremonger, 1997, 197-207

Starr, G., "Introduction", in Starr, G., Richmond, K., and Maddox, G., (eds), *Political Parties in Australia*, Richmond: Heinemann Education, 1978, 1-10

Whiteley, A., "Is the party Over? The Decline of Party Activisms and Membership Across the Democratic World", *Party Politics,* 17(1) 2011, 21-44

Wood, D., and Daley, J., *A Crisis of Trust: The Rise of Protest Politics*, Melbourne: Grattan Institute, May 2018

Endnotes

1   Since federation in 1901 only 8 of the 45 attempts to change the Constitution have been successful. Changes are made by a referendum of the whole national voting electorate and to pass requires a majority of votes across the nation plus a majority of votes in a majority of the six States. This is called the "double majority" rule.

2   The American Senate was not directly elected until 1913.

3   For instance, at the 1919 election the Nationalist Party government (Liberal)

won 35 of the 36 Senate seats. Following the 1946 federal election the Coalition only had three of the 36 Senate seats.

4   S 24 states that, "The House of Representatives shall be composed of members directly chosen by the people … and the number of such members shall be, as nearly as practicable, twice the number of the senators".

5   See footnote 3.

6   Menzies had Senate majorities from, 1951-56 and from 1958-61.

7   The Fraser Coalition Government secured a Senate majority from 1975-81, followed by the Howard Government from 2004-7.

8   Chipp had been a prominent Liberal Minister in the Gorton and McMahon Coalition governments (1969-72), a shadow minister in opposition (1973-75) and a minister in Fraser's caretaker administration (November -December 1975). However, because of some comments he made during the 1975 election he was not appointed minister in the subsequent Fraser Government and subsequently resigned from the Liberal Party in 1977.

9   In particular, the Australian Democrats were seen to have been too supportive by many of their members of the Howard Government's GST changes.

10   This involved 7 Australian Democrats, 2 Greens and the Independent Senator Harradine from Tasmania.

11   The Coalition's industrial relations policy can be traced back to the early 1990s.

12   A Palmer United Party candidate replaced an Australia Sport's Party candidate.

13   The author was Senior Adviser to the Minister responsible for overseeing the passage of this legislation through the Senate.

14   Multi-use chemicals are those with uses in addition to cosmetics. The exception of multi-use chemicals recognises these uses may present a higher risk to human health and the environment and require consideration of animal test data to provide protection.

15   This was Senator Bridget McKenzie, National Party Minister for Regional Services whose portfolio also included health issues.

7

The Resources of the Federal Opposition

Liz Dowd and Scott Prasser

Introduction

In Westminster democracies, it has long been a fundamental principle that there is a recognised and institutionalised opposition with the right to hold the government of the day to account under the principles of responsible government and parliamentary accountability. As has been discussed in other chapters (see chapters 1 and 2) in Australia the opposition is not a formal part of the Australian Constitution but, as at Westminster, is clearly embedded in the Commonwealth Parliament's procedures and in long-standing practices. Indeed, the opposition is indisputably recognised in all its aspects and roles, as is the focus of this chapter, its resources, staffing and parliamentary pay and allowances.

This chapter focusses on the publicly funded resources available to an opposition at the Australian Commonwealth level and considers how and by whom they are determined. Most importantly for a democracy, it assesses how these arrangements and the level of support provided impact on the effectiveness of an opposition in holding executive government to account and being able to develop alternative policies to meet its prime role of being the alternative government – in effect a "government in waiting" ready to take over the reins of power.

In discussing the "opposition", although this is a term reserved for the largest party out of office which is given due recognition of its status, the growth of minority, micro parties and independent members in both the House of Representatives and the Senate also can at times act as a form of opposition to the government (see chapter 6). These minor parties and crossbench members also figure in discussions about resourcing in terms of their entitlements.

Significantly, there has been little consideration in Australia of the actual resource needs of an opposition but there is agreement that a properly resourced opposition is important if it is to serve its role in the Westminster democratic process. Possibly the best in-depth report that sought to consider what level of resources were needed for an opposition to be effective was the Queensland Electoral and Administrative Review Commission's (EARC) 1991 report, the *Review of Information and Resource needs of Non-Government Members of the Queensland Legislative Assembly* (EARC 1991). EARC was a body specifically created by the Queensland 1989 *Commission of Inquiry into Possible Illegal Activities and Associated Police Misconduct* (Fitzgerald Report) that highlighted how the opposition in Queensland had been unable to perform its functions effectively because it had been deliberately starved of resources by the then incumbent National Party government.[1] The EARC report noted that "the burden of ensuring accountability of government activity, and responsible government, is largely the task of the opposition" (EARC 1991: 11). Many of EARC's insights are relevant to the Commonwealth level of government.

A brief history of support for federal oppositions

Early support

It is important to appreciate that from the beginning of the Commonwealth Parliament in 1901 all parliamentarians were remunerated at a standard rate of pay. Their counterparts in the United Kingdom had to wait until 1911 before receiving such remuneration. Official recognition of providing extra resources in the form of additional remuneration for the opposition began in 1920, with the introduction of the *Parliamentary Allowances*

Act 1920 (Cth). It stated that: "In addition to any other allowance payable under this Act there shall be payable to the Leader of the Opposition in the Senate, an allowance at the rate of Two hundred pounds a year, and to the Leader of the Opposition in the House of Representatives, an allowance at the rate of Four hundred pounds a year". For the first time, the Act provided for payment of an allowance to leaders of the opposition. It was not until an enquiry into the salaries and allowances of parliamentary members in 1952 that a recommendation was also enacted for additional renumeration for the deputy leader of the opposition. Additional renumeration was later expanded to the positions of managers of opposition business and shadow ministers. However, currently this does not extend to a shadow assistant minister.

Staff support

At the commencement of the Commonwealth Parliament most parliamentarians, both government and opposition backbenchers, were not allocated any staff. Ministers received advice and administrative support from officers from the Commonwealth Public Service. Personal staff were rare and paid for by the minister or member themselves.

Gradually, staffing for all parliamentarians in their capacity as representatives of their electorates increased. By the time of the election of the Whitlam Labor Government in December 1972, each parliamentarian had a single electorate officer – usually a secretary. Travel to Canberra was capped for staff and was available only when Parliament was sitting. Ministerial staffs were small, comprising secretarial staff, a press secretary and a private secretary, usually all seconded from the minister's department (Tiernan 2004). The opposition too, had limited staff support mainly reserved for the leader of the opposition, with a small number shared among the shadow ministry.

Expansion of support under the Whitlam Government

The election of the Whitlam Labor Government in 1972 was accompanied by major changes in the support and remuneration provided to government and opposition members. These initiatives were driven by several motivations. Out of office for 23 years, the incoming Labor administration was anxious to implement its extensive program of election promises. It was suspicious of the Commonwealth Public Service that it had inherited and desirous of appointing staff who would be imbued with the same sense of urgency and ideological commitment as the Labor Party. Consequently, there was a desire to improve resourcing for the new ministers and backbenchers, with particular attention paid to increasing ministerial staff numbers, their classifications and, importantly, making appointments from outside the public service (Forward 1977; Smith 1977).

Other changes that affected the resourcing of all parliamentarians – government and opposition – were also initiated at this time. The Whitlam Government resuscitated the report by Mr Justice Kerr[2] which recommended increases in salaries for ministers and backbenchers. It had been presented to the McMahon Coalition Government in December 1971, but was shelved in the run-up to the 1972 election for fear of a political backlash. Under Whitlam, parliamentary wages were increased by $5,000 instead of $4,000 as recommended by Kerr – a 52 per cent rather than 42 per cent increase. Uniform tax free electorate allowances of $4,000, removing the distinction between country and city members, were also introduced at this time. With the Whitlam Government's passing of the *Remuneration Tribunal Act 1973* a new body was established to provide independent assessments of salaries for ministers, backbenchers, judges and permanent public service heads (Lloyd and Reid 1974: 177-8). Lastly, the former single electorate secretary was joined in 1975 by a research officer, although payment for such staff to travel to Canberra was restricted until a decision by the Remuneration Tribunal in 1977 relaxed these limitations. During subsequent decades there was a gradual accretion of electorate office resources and staffing.

Developments since 1984

The next major turning point concerning resourcing occurred when the Hawke Government passed the *Members of Parliament (Staff) Act 1984*, (MOP(S) Act) which set the parameters for members to employ personal staff, including for members of the opposition. Before this personal staff were engaged by either private contracts or seconded through the temporary employment provisions in the *Public Service Act* within a budget allocated to an office. This framework was provided for in Section 48A (introduced in 1930), which allowed for secondment of public servants as private secretaries to ministers and the leader of the opposition in both Houses.

For the first time, the *MOP(S) Act* gave the authority for relevant office holders to have personal staff allocations and that the opposition was recognised in the Act as a relevant office holder. Still in force today, the *MOP(S) Act* gives the authority to allocate resources to the prime minister and is not prescriptive about the numbers or levels that they must have regard to when making these allocations. This gives the prime minister of the day a great deal of flexibility to decide arrangements including the number of staff and the level of seniority of those staff allocated to the relevant office holders.

It is worth noting that staffing for both Australian ministers, the opposition and backbenchers was far better than for their United Kingdom (UK) counterparts at the time. Not only were more staff provided to members and ministers in Australia than the UK, but there was also far greater emphasis in Australia on making direct staff appointments that were more political or partisan based and from outside the confines of the public service (Maley 2018). At the same time, secondment of public servants to ministerial and opposition offices persisted, as it does today, reflecting the value such staff offer in terms of their experience and knowledge of particular policy areas (Maley 2017).

How staffing is allocated to federal oppositions

The *MOP(S) Act* requires the prime minister to have regard to the parliamentary duties of a senator or member when allocating personal staff. Interestingly, a definition of "parliamentary duties" is not provided in the Act, and there is little guidance available in other supporting materials. Generally, following every election, staffing allocations are reviewed and reallocated by the prime minister. This involves authorising the allocation of staffing for ministers, assistant ministers, backbenchers, the opposition, minority parties, independents and other office holders such as former prime ministers.

The two major parties which either form government or the official opposition have operated on a convention since at least 1995 of approximately a 21 per cent staffing ratio of opposition to government for personal staff. The 2009 Henderson Review of Government Staff recommended that this ratio continue to apply not just to the total staff numbers but to the classifications as well. It is likely that these recommendations were made to give formality to a convention that had long existed and to avoid previous interpretations that have been detrimental in providing resources to an opposition. If the government staffing numbers are increased or decreased by the prime minister of the day a proportionate change in opposition staff also occurs. Further cementing the recognition of the opposition in resourcing matters, the terms of reference for the Henderson Review stated that consideration be given to "the impact of any change in the number and classification of personal staff allocated to ministers and parliamentary secretaries on the number and classification of staff allocated to the opposition and minor parties". These arrangements remain in place today.

For minor parties, such as the Greens, there was a convention for a three per cent ratio of government staffing, which has been in place since they were designated as a minor party on 1 July 2008. Department of Finance advice was that this was consistent with the percentage allocation to the Australian Democrats when they were a minor party and was also a recommendation of the Henderson Review. To be considered a minor party, there is a definition, based on the *Parliamentary Business Resources Regulations 2017*, which requires a party to have at least five parliamentary members. Independent parliamentarians first received an allocation of one personal staff member in 2007. Since then, the allocations have varied between one and four personal staff (see below for recent developments).

The prime minister is not required to provide reasons for decisions on allocations. However, they do have to include expenditure allocations in the annual Federal Budget, but these are high-level, across all parliamentary resources. The most recent Budget (2023-24) provided for $500 million for Ministerial and Parliamentary Services including entitlements, salaries for staff employed under the *Members of Parliament (Staff) Act 1984,* and COMCAR services.

Issues in resourcing oppositions

Whilst opposition staffing levels have generally followed a consistent ratio over time, the same cannot be said for the Independents or the crossbench. As discussed earlier, the *MOP(s) Act* allows a prime minister significant discretion in allocating staff to the crossbenches and minor parties and there is no requirement to provide justification for these decisions. The rise and fall of the numbers of staff allocated to Independents over the years seems to be largely influenced by the overall balance of power in the parliament.

In June 2022, the just elected Albanese Labor Government made the decision to reduce the staff allocation to crossbenchers, citing the need for Budget repair and to bring their staffing allocations back into line with other government and opposition senators and members. This bought the allocation down to four electorate staff and a single fulltime adviser position. Under the previous Morrison Coalition Government the crossbench had been provided with up to four advisers and four electorate staff. Independent members and senators argued that this cut made it difficult for them to do their jobs properly. The example provided was that in the last parliamentary term 550 pieces of legislation needed to be considered, in addition to serving the needs of their electorates. However, after the last election, the Greens' staff levels remained almost the same even though the number of their representatives grew from 10 to 16. These were not popular decisions with the minor parties and the crossbench and generated adverse publicity from the crossbench with threats to withdraw support from the Albanese Government especially in the Senate where the government does not have a majority (Coorey 2022). To date, such obstruction does not seem to have materialised.

Importantly, the 2023-4 Budget, saw the announcement of a further staffing boost for all members and senators allowing them to increase their electorate office staff from four to five and, for those with large electorates, an additional staff member was provided in each additional electorate office. Importantly, part of this was a change in rules to enable one electorate staff member to travel for parliamentary business without debit from the Electorate Support Budget (ESB). Previously this was an entitlement that was provided only to certain parliamentarians, such as particular office holders and to parliamentarians who held responsibilities as chairs of parliamentary committees. The Budget announcement stated that "any single member of any MP's office will now also be able to travel to Canberra for parliamentary sittings" (Australian Government 2023). The decision to fund this centrally reflects the feedback about parliamentarians being adequately supported in their role when attending parliament in Canberra.

All this highlights that decisions about resourcing for parliamentarians and oppositions remain firmly in the hands of executive government with little real parliamentary oversight, let alone wider public consultation and discussion.

The resources of the government

Bob Hawke was reported as observing shortly after becoming prime minister in 1983 that the support he received in government compared to when in opposition was "unbelievable". As he said, "You know, you can have any queries followed through. You can have your views or the views of your advisers checked and rechecked so that gives you a confidence in the quality of your own work which you have never been able to enjoy before" (see Bowers 1983). Most who make the transition from opposition to government have had the same experience as Hawke, highlighting the disparity in the resources provided to oppositions compared to governments.

While resources for governments have always been greater than for oppositions, the level of personal support for the executive government has increased dramatically in the last fifty years.

Support for federal ministers

Currently, federal ministers, depending on the portfolio and whether they are part of the inner cabinet, can now enjoy a staff ranging from 8 to 19 in an office. These days a cabinet minister's office will generally include: a Chief of Staff; 5-6 Senior Advisers (including Media Advisers); 4-5 Advisers; 1-2 Assistant Advisers; and 1-2 administrative staff in addition to electorate staff. Ministerial staff can be based in Canberra, working in Parliament House, or in Commonwealth Parliamentary Offices in one of the capital cities across Australia or in the minister's electorate office.

In addition, a portfolio department provides to a ministerial office one or more Departmental Liaison Officers (DLOs) who manage the information required by the ministerial office and workflows between the department and the office. They also answer phones and can assist members of the public with portfolio related information. The department can also provide relief arrangements or secondments of staff for personal employees for up to 12 weeks. By contrast, opposition shadow portfolio offices need to fund replacements from their own office budgets.

A non-cabinet minister's office usually has a similar spread of levels but less of each and staff are often paid at lower salary levels. Assistant ministers usually are allocated two personal staff, consisting of one adviser and one assistant adviser, in addition to their electorate office staff. The government currently has a total of 472 personal positions available for allocation and has allocated 471. The last record from the previous Coalition government in March 2022 states that the government had 471.8 personal positions available for allocation and they had all been allocated.[3]

Resources for the prime minister have also increased. At the date of writing, current Prime Minister Albanese had 58 staff working in the Prime Minister's Office (PMO). In Sir Robert Menzies time, the PMO consisted of just nine staff – some of whom were secretaries and all of whom were seconded from the public service.

Departmental support for ministers

In addition to these large enhancements of personal staff in ministers' offices, government has access to extensive physical, intellectual and financial resources that are not available to any opposition parliamentarian through the Australian Public Service (APS). While the APS must remain apolitical, federal ministers and assistant ministers can, and do, access support from the relevant portfolio departments to undertake their official duties which of course aids them politically.

Generally, some of the day-to-day official duties which a portfolio department would provide to a minister's office include: answering or drafting correspondence; assisting with drafting possible questions and responses for Question Time; organising events; providing briefing notes on any topic pertinent to the portfolio; drafting speeches for portfolio related events; undertaking research and developing policy options; and providing meeting briefs for any stakeholder meetings the office may have. For the development of policy, the government can also through departmental budgets, contract external consultants or academics to provide further intellectual resources. By contrast, if the opposition wants to access the APS for information about a particular policy or program this usually requires the permission of the relevant government minister and an adviser from that office would likely attend any briefing provided.

If a minister is a member of cabinet, the portfolio department can develop a proposal and supporting material, provide briefings to the minister to support their role in cabinet and the various sub-committees of cabinet. The cabinet process is supported by the Cabinet Division of the Department of the Prime Minister and Cabinet, thus providing another resource for the government.

Governments can have policy proposals costed by the Departments of Finance and Treasury whilst the opposition is reliant on the Parliamentary Budget Office (a relatively new function with limited staff) and its own staff. Departments can also undertake media and communication support for ministers and assistant ministers via the drafting of responses to the media, media releases, transcription and media monitoring. In most departments there is a branch that manages media and communications issues.

Portfolio departments also support ministers and assistant ministers with office expenses and other resources. The Department of Finance's Ministerial and Parliamentary Services branch provides guidance on what support departments can provide. However, it also states that this does not prevent portfolio departments providing other resources the minister or assistant minister requires that are not listed. This support means that these expenses do not have to come out of annual electorate support budgets.

The opposition's resources

Elder and Fowler (2018: 543) stress the important role of parliament in a Westminster democracy:

One of the more important functions of the House is its critical review function. This includes scrutiny of the executive government,
bringing to light issues and perceived deficiencies or problems,
ventilating grievances, exposing, and thereby preventing the government from exercising, arbitrary power, and pressing the government to take remedial or other action.

Importantly, they note: "to call the government to account depends, in
large measure, on its knowledge and understanding of the government's
policies and activities" (Elder and Fowler: 543).

This is one of the prime roles of any opposition if they are to convince
the electorate that they deserve to replace the incumbent government.
Consequently, as the alternative government, the opposition's shadow
ministry is structured in a similar way to that of the government
ministry to closely monitor its activities and to highlight gaps in the
government's performance across these different portfolios. Similar to
cabinet processes in government, the opposition also has shadow cabinet
and other committees to develop approaches and alternative positions
to government policy. There are, however, no departmental resources
available to support this.

To be effective, resources are required to develop a knowledge of
the portfolio which often involves reviewing and researching many
departmental, public inquiry, and parliamentary committee reports and
financial statements which flow through parliament, land on members'
desks and are the grist to the mill in knowing any policy area well. Such
knowledge is then used in asking questions of ministers at Question Time
and for probing public servants about their department's programs and
policies at the regular Senate Estimates committee processes that occur
throughout the year. This involves seeking to embarrass the government
for any mistakes, highlighting inconsistencies from previous responses,
and in addition, procuring information not previously available about
different aspects of the government's activities to develop alternative
policy stands.

When parliament is sitting the opposition scrutinises a government's draft legislation and the policies underpinning it. Often governments seek to rush legislation through parliament to minimise opposition scrutiny. The challenge for any opposition is to be able at short notice to not just understand the proposed legislation and highlight its flaws, but just as importantly, to be able to propose amendments that reflect alternative policy perspectives. After all, the opposition, as the government in waiting, is supposed to be ready to govern and that means being more than just a critic by being able to expound viable alternative policy options.

In addition to working within the ambit of parliament, shadow ministers regularly meet with the many different stakeholders that are an integral part of every policy area. Such interactions are important if an opposition, without the support of a government department, is going to be able to understand key issues and become aware of interest group complaints. These might be the basis of criticising the government or help to develop new policies that give an opposition an electorally winning edge. While interest groups are a rich source of alternative advice care needs to be taken that the information provided is accurate and not biased. Information provided may be factually wrong or deliberately distorted to favour the interest groups. Also, an opposition should not appear to be just a front for some narrow interest group at the expense of the wider policy concerns. All this challenges oppositions. After all, unlike the government, an opposition does not have resources of the public service to check the information being presented by these interest groups or individuals. Coalition Opposition Leader, Malcolm Turnbull's uncritical acceptance of information provided by a disgruntled public servant in the "Godwin Grech" affair highlights what can go wrong. In that case, the information that was provided proved to be fabricated. This damaged both the credibility of the opposition and Turnbull's own personal reputation and contributed to his loss of the opposition leadership in 2009 (Tiffen 2017: 53-4).

As part of its role in holding government to account and persuading the public that it is a viable alternative worth supporting, oppositions seek to promote their views through all forms of the media. Nevertheless, an opposition cannot match the number of media staff supporting a federal minister along with the additional resources of the communications branches found in most departments these days. Nor can an opposition match the public funded advertising campaigns that governments now employ to 'explain' new programs. Also, government ministers can usually attract media attention more easily than oppositions. Ministers have something major and positive to announce like a new policy initiative, a major review, or new legislation. By contrast opposition shadow ministers by the very nature of their roles, usually have something to criticise, making it difficult to gain media attention.

In addition, parliamentary practice and procedure allows government and non-government members to have equal opportunity to speak. In Question Time, the asking of questions alternates between the government and non-government members (mainly the opposition). Much parliamentary business is initiated by an opposition, including debates like matters of public importance (MPIs), private members' business, censure motions of the government, and motions to suspend standing orders to debate certain matters. House, Senate, and joint parliamentary committees include opposition representatives who as well as providing input into their reports, can include minority reports if consensus cannot be reached across the partisan divide.

Generally, staff in an opposition office are divided between servicing the electorate and personal staff providing advice on political, policy and parliamentary processes. There is some overlap between diary management, research and media, with staff operating across these areas. This is similar to arrangements for government staffers. Opposition personal staff support their employers not only in the portfolio role but also in their non-portfolio functions, such as House or Senate business and constituency work.

In comparison to the current Albanese Government's 472 staff, the current opposition has been allocated a total of 102 personal staff. This is the same as under the previous Coalition government. Personal employees' salary rates are also divided into government and non-government components in the *MOP(S) Enterprise Agreement*, with the latter rates lower than government staffers, thus reducing the attractiveness of the positions, particularly given the hours worked and that prospects of returning to office may not be immediately foreseeable.

The opposition leader is allocated staffing by numbers and levels by the prime minister. The opposition leader then distributes this staffing depending on the shadow ministry portfolio and other responsibilities such as whips and leaders of opposition business. Neither the prime minister nor the opposition leader is required to publicly provide reasons for staff allocation decisions. The opposition's staffing provided to each office is only published for the leader, deputy leader, leader and deputy leader in the Senate. The rest is grouped under shadow ministers and there is an average allocation of about two staff.

Other entitlements for all parliamentarians – impacts for oppositions

All members and senators are provided with an annual, finite Electorate Support Budget (ESB). This can be used to pay for electorate employees' travel, additional employees for peak workloads or to cover staff absences. An annual office budget to cover office expenses is also provided for the purposes of undertaking parliamentary business. This would cover items such as printing, office stationery, cameras, signage, and media monitoring services.

In 1984, when the *MOP(S) Act* commenced, staffing in electorate offices increased from two to three positions for each senator and member and four for members serving geographically larger regional electorates which usually now includes a second electorate office. In 2007, there was a further increase in electorate offices staffing from three to four positions for each senator and member plus additional staff in the geographically larger electorates. As noted, all senators and members, government and opposition, can now employ five electorate office staff. In larger electorates, House of Representatives members can have two or three electorate offices and they are permitted to employ an additional staff member per office. One electorate officer can be nominated to come to Canberra during sitting weeks to assist with parliamentary duties.

These increases in staffing reflected acknowledgement that the workload for electorate offices had increased because of growth of emails, growing complexity of issues, the rise in community expectations of government services, the expansion of government programs, and increases in the nation's population. As well as playing a role for an opposition to persuade the electorate about being an alternative government, often an electorate office is where an opposition discovers information about how government policy is affecting citizens on the ground. Such was the case with the Robodebt issue[4] where complaints from constituents alerted Labor opposition members at an electorate level to the problems that this new program was causing to a growing number of individuals (Holmes 2023).

These large increases in electorate office staffing apply to all members – government, opposition and crossbench alike and can be to their benefit in servicing their electorates and constituents. Such additional staffing can also be a potentially valuable extra resource for an opposition in its role of holding a government to account and developing policies as the government in waiting. It depends on how an opposition chooses to use these additional resources. If it was solely at the discretion of individual members and senators to decide who to employ and what they do, then the opposition would accrue little benefit of this increase in electorate staff. If, however, these staff and their roles were more centrally co-ordinated across the opposition, they could enhance the total resources available and improve effectiveness if they were deployed for policy research activities in monitoring government rather than just electorate duties. However, individual opposition members, especially those without any shadow ministry duties, might be reluctant to allow their electorate staff to be pooled, undermining their efforts to retain their seats.

Conclusion

Bagehot commented that the importance of opposition is that "The nation is forced to hear two sides – all the sides, perhaps of that which most concerns it." (Bagehot 1971: 72). To undertake these functions, it is important in a democracy to have a properly resourced opposition enabling it to conduct research, develop policies and to be an effective critic of an incumbent government's policies and programs. The Queensland EARC noted that the resources made available to the opposition have to be balanced against not only the numbers of ministerial staff but also the entire resources of the Queensland State Public Service which are at the disposal of the government (EARC 1991: 114). This key principle is just as relevant at the Commonwealth level.

While there are examples across Australian jurisdictions where an opposition's lack of resources meant it was unable to hold a government to account as rigorously as it should, there are other factors that affect an opposition's effectiveness. These include, for instance, an opposition's real desire and drive to win office, to work hard and so as to make the maximum use of existing resources no matter how limited. Success also depends on an opposition's political guile – to know what to pursue and what not to pursue and its ability to project issues in ways so that the electorate can understand their importance.

Lessons from the past have also shown that when parliament's ability to carry out its traditional role is diminished there are consequences for democracy. The Fitzgerald Report noted: "Non-government party members must be provided with appropriate resources and detailed information to enable them to supervise and criticise, just as Governments naturally are well equipped and staffed. Without information, there can be no accountability" (Fitzgerald 1989: 123-4).

Leo Amery in his *Thoughts on the Constitution* is right when he says that the "main task of Parliament is still what it was when it was first summoned, not to legislate or govern, but to secure full discussion of all matters" (Amery 1953: 12). It is therefore fundamental that both sides of the discussion are equipped to be able to have it.

The recent *Review into the Members of Parliament Staff Act 1984* by the Department of Prime Minister and Cabinet (2022) found many instances of excessive workloads in offices. It recommended that a review should be undertaken into the resourcing of parliamentary offices to inform an evidence-based consideration of office and staffing resources and that review should recommend principles to be considered by the prime minister in determining staffing allocations. It also recommended that the *MoP(S) Act* should be amended to require the allocation of staff to be transparent through annual reporting arrangements. At the time of writing the current Albanese Government has agreed in principle with all the recommendations. The Parliamentary Workplace Support Service stated at Senate Estimates in October 2023 that this review is a priority deliverable.

References

Amery, L., *Thoughts on the Constitution*, Oxford: Oxford University Press, 1953

Australian Government, *Budget Paper Number 2*, 2023-4, Canberra: Commonwealth of Australia, 2023,

Bagehot, W., *The English Constitution*, London: Fontana, 1971

Bateman, J., *In the Shadows: The Shadow Cabinet in Australia*, Parliamentary Fellowship Monograph, Canberra: Commonwealth Parliamentary Library, Commonwealth Parliament, 2009

Bowers, P., "Help is unbelievable, says the new PM", *Sydney Morning Herald*, 2 April 1983

Coorey, P., "Albanese faces teal revolt over staff cuts", *Australian Financial Review*, 24 June 2022

Creighton, A., "How many staff members does it take to change the country?", *The Australian*, 28-29 June 2014

Department of Prime Minister and Cabinet, *Review of the Members of Parliament (Staff) Act 1984*, Canberra: Australian Government, 2022

Elder, D., and Fowler, P., (eds), *House of Representatives Practice, Seventh edition*, Canberra: Department of the House of Representatives, Commonwealth Parliament, 2018

Electoral Administrative Review Commission (EARC), Review of Information and Resources needs of Non-Government Members of the Queensland Legislative Assembly, *Report*, Brisbane: Queensland Government, December 1991

Fitzgerald, G.E., (Chairman), Committee of Inquiry into Possible Illegal Activities and Associated Police Misconduct, *Report*, Brisbane: Queensland Government Printer, 1989

Forward, R., "Ministerial Staff under Whitlam and Fraser", *Australian Journal of Public Administration*, 36(2), June 1977, 159-67

Henderson, A., *Review of Government Staffing,* Feb 2009 (tabled May 2009)

Holmes, C., (Chair), Royal Commission into the Robodebt Program, *Final Report*, Canberra: Australian Government, 2023

Lloyd, C.J., and Reid, G.S., *Out of the Wilderness: The Return of Labor,* Melbourne: Cassell, 1974

Maley, M., "Temporary partisans, tagged officers or impartial professionals: Moving between ministerial offices and departments", *Public Administration,* 95(2), 2017, 407-20

Maley, M., "Understanding the divergent developments of the ministerial office in Australia and the UK", *Australian Journal of Political Science*, 53(3), 2018, 322-35

Ng, Yee-Fui, *The Rise of Political Advisers in the Westminster System*, London: Routledge, 2018

Smith, R.F.I., "Ministerial Advisers: The Experience of the Whitlam Government", *Australian Journal of Public Administration*, 36(2), June 1977, 133-58

Tiernan, A., *Ministerial Staff under the Howard Government: Problem, Solution or Black Hole?* PhD Thesis, Department of Politics and Public Policy, Griffith University, 2004

Tiffen, R., *Disposable Leaders: Media and Leadership Coups from Menzies to Abbott*, Sydney: NewSouth, 2017

Legislation and government reports

Members of Parliament (Staff) Bill 1984 – Explanatory Memorandum

Members of Parliament (Staff) Act 1984

Parliamentary Allowances Act, Australian Government 1920

Department of Finance – *Personal Employee Positions as at 1 March 2022*

Department of Finance – *Personal Employee Positions as at 1 May 2023*

Department of Finance – *Annual Report* 21-22

Department of Finance Ministerial and Parliamentary Services, *Administration Responsibilities*, 2021

Finance and Public Legislation Committee, *Senate Estimates*, Canberra; Commonwealth Parliament, October 2023, 136

Endnotes

1   The National Party had been in coalition as the senior partner with the Liberal Party from 1957 to 1983 and then, following a split with the Liberals, governed in its own right from 1983 till 1989 when it was defeated by the Labor Party.

2   Kerr was a member of the Commonwealth Industrial Court at the time of this review. He had previously chaired the 1968 federal Administrative Review Committee. He was Chief Justice of the NSW Supreme Court when in July 1974 the Whitlam Government appointed him Governor-General.

3   It appears that recently there has been another increase in staffing allocations for both government and the opposition. However, at the time of writing these allocations had not been published.

4   The Robodebt program was a new income compliance program introduced by the then Coalition Government. It used data matching techniques to assess whether recipients of Commonwealth social welfare benefits were receiving income from other sources and therefore were committing fraud. It was found to have major flaws resulting in some welfare recipients wrongly been asked to pay back previously received benefits and threatened with prosecution. The Albanese Government appointed a royal commission into the issue in 2022 which reported in July 2023.

8

The Challenge of the COVID-19 Pandemic: Federal Labor in Opposition, 2019-22

Brendan McCaffrie

Introduction

When the COVID-19 pandemic reached Australia in 2020 it presented an enormous challenge for the Morrison Coalition Government both as a public health and economic emergency, but it also presented a conundrum for the Anthony Albanese-led Labor Opposition. The Opposition began the pandemic leading in all public polls, but as the pandemic hit and the Morrison Government acted to close the national border, to stimulate the economy, and to work with the States and Territories to implement significant public health measures, polls flipped to favour the Morrison Government. As this situation continued, Labor initially had few political opportunities, and unrest grew within the Labor Party.

This chapter examines how the Labor Opposition managed to navigate an unfavourable context to ultimately win government at the 2022 election. It explores Labor's strategy throughout the term, which was a traditional approach, ensuring the media and public paid more attention to the government than the opposition. And although Albanese emphasised Labor's "constructive" approach throughout the pandemic, Labor largely retained its traditional opposition strategy as COVID-19 emerged in

Australia. Labor supported the Morrison Government's legislation but barely slowed in its criticism of the government. Albanese and Labor struggled for media attention during the pandemic but patiently waited for the best timing to release policies rather than seeking to steal the focus early in the term. The chapter draws conclusions about the art of opposition in dealing with the political challenge of a time of intensified national unity brought about by a crisis. It demonstrates that, particularly with a long and drawn out crisis like the pandemic, the approach that worked for Labor was largely a traditional approach to Opposition that it could just as easily have followed in more "ordinary" times.

Context

Labor and a history of opposition

Histories of the Australian Labor Party (ALP) frequently refer to the federal party's poor electoral record. It has spent 51 of the 78 post-war years in opposition (as at 2023), and the Coalition parties have sometimes been described as the "natural parties of government" (eg Parkin and Warhurst 2000: 39). That the ALP has won the popular two-party preferred vote at 14 of the 29 elections in that time suggests a more even contest with the Coalition parties, though Labor politicians, officials, members and supporters are far from consoled by relative popularity without victory. The abundance of time in opposition has been in part a product of internal tensions. Factional rivalries, the Split of the 1950s, and a struggle to balance electoral popularity with purity of ideology and representation of working-class Australians, have all contrived to diminish Labor's electoral prospects.

This history weighs heavily on the modern ALP, which rarely feels confident of victory. However, the tension between following labourist ideological principles and seeking electoral success which long dogged the party is now usually resolved in favour of the latter. Modern opposition leaders would not console supporters with the message that an election loss should not discourage "members of the Labor Movement from fighting for what they think is right, whether it brings victory to the Party or not" as Ben Chifley did in 1951 (Chifley, in McMullin 1991: 261). Labor's identity as the party of major reform, seeing itself as the architect of the post-war Keynesian economic system under Curtin and Chifley, the expansive social welfare reforms under Whitlam, and the economic liberalisation under Hawke and Keating, further contributes to supporters' preference for an activist policy approach.

Unsurprisingly then, Labor under Bill Shorten established an expansive agenda during the 2016-19 parliamentary term. Shorten's policy agenda appealed to traditional Labor voters, while its ambitious targets on climate change were well-suited to a contest with Prime Minister Malcolm Turnbull. Labor's policy placed Turnbull in the awkward position of having to argue against policies he broadly agreed with but could not implement from within his own party, which had a significant climate change-sceptical element. However, once Scott Morrison assumed the prime ministership in 2018, the government was able to use his honeymoon period to attack Shorten Labor.

Albanese became Labor leader at a time when party MPs, members and supporters were distraught, having been shocked by the 2019 election loss (Manwaring and Foley 2023: 13). As the 2019-22 term began, the Morrison honeymoon quickly concluded, and Albanese was leading a Labor Party that had an opportunity to put pressure on an increasingly unpopular government. Morrison's unimpressive performance as prime minister during the long bushfire crisis of the 2019-20 summer (McCaffrie 2023: 279-82) saw Labor take the lead in national two-party preferred polling for the first time since the election, though few in the ALP were particularly optimistic about how this translated into election chances in three years' time.

Re-orienting Labor

Early in Albanese's term, Labor reviewed its surprise election defeat, with former Federal Labor minister Craig Emerson and former South

Australian Premier Jay Wetherill concluding that: there was no clearly defined election strategy, the Labor Opposition did not adjust to the Morrison prime ministership after Turnbull was deposed, and Bill Shorten was an unpopular leader (Emerson and Wetherill 2019). These were major problems and there was also a significant challenge in persuading Australians about the merits of a big, complex and, in the terms of the report, "cluttered" policy agenda. The Morrison Government was in a position to run a negative campaign, targeting new tax policies on negative gearing and franking credits. While these changes were designed to affect few people, most of whom were very wealthy, the communications challenge meant that many who would not be affected were worried about them (Grattan 2019: 134-5). Morrison also targeted Shorten Labor's climate change policy, which had a 45 per cent emissions reduction target by 2030. Morrison was supported by the Business Council of Australia which called Labor's position "economy-wrecking" (Manwaring and Foley 2023: 186). Climate policy particularly cost Labor votes in regional electorates in Western Australia and Queensland, where mining and agriculture are dominant industries (Megalogenis 2019).

These issues presented challenges for the party after Albanese took over. Climate policy was somewhat divisive internally. Similarly, the policy arguments for the taxation measures were strong, but they now carried negative political connotations. Albanese adopted a strategy of policy moderation, looking to find an uncontroversial middle ground, to ensure that the party would not be subject to the same criticism as in 2019. Similarly, he convinced shadow cabinet to support the Morrison Government's controversial Stage 3 tax cuts, which would reduce income taxes for wealthy Australians and were contrary to normal Labor principles (van Onselen and Errington 2022: 34).

COVID-19: Opposition during the Pandemic

At a superficial level, the pandemic was a major boost for the government. At a time when governments can struggle to gain the attention of voters, the stream of crucial daily press conferences allowed Morrison and other political leaders to provide reassuring communication on matters with life and death consequences, emphasising the importance of government itself, and of themselves as protectors of the population. Incumbent governments were returned at the first five state and territory elections after the pandemic reached Australia (Northern Territory, Australian Capital Territory, Queensland, Western Australia and Tasmania), with increased margins in some cases. While there were local factors at play in these elections too, there is little doubt that the pandemic had helped these governments. Even in South Australia, where Labor defeated the Liberal government in March 2022, the Liberals led in most polls during 2020 and 2021.

The pandemic represented a major challenge for Albanese Labor. The opposition clearly had less chance to make a mark on the politics of the day. Parliamentary sittings were curtailed, the media focused more on State governments than on the federal opposition, and the pace of events and the complicated nature of information made it hard for the opposition to make alternative suggestions on the health response (van Onselen and Errington 2022: 38-41). To be over-critical at a time of national crisis of the government would likely have been poorly received. As Albanese put it, Labor needed to "dive down deep, watch the wave go over … and wait for the right wave to come in" (Albanese, in Murphy 2022: 31). However, the pandemic also gave Labor an opportunity to adjust its policy positions without drawing too much attention to internal policy arguments.

Labor's opposition during the pandemic promised to be "constructive", but arguably, the approach was consistent with its already established, traditional approach to opposition. Under Albanese, Labor sought to ensure that public focus was on the Morrison Government and its weaknesses and problems, and not on Labor. Particularly with a government that was into its third term, this was a standard approach to opposition. Some called Albanese's approach a "small target" strategy (eg van Onselen and Errington 2022; McAllister 2023), though Manwaring and Foley (2023) argue that this label undersells the ideological, policy and spending distinctions between the two parties' platforms. "Small target" is not a term that has been clearly conceptually defined, and for our purposes it is more relevant that Albanese wanted a more balanced approach than his predecessor. As a corrective to the Shorten years, Albanese Labor presented a small*er* target, with many of Labor's more contentious policies removed or modified to reduce the opportunities for Morrison to attack, yet there remained substantial policy to promote, particularly on climate change and childcare.

Crisis management and 'constructive' opposition

The scale of the pandemic crisis, and its unprecedented nature made the job of opposition difficult. Taking a highly active approach would likely lead to criticisms that the opposition was being obstructionist, while taking a quieter approach could lead to the appearance of irrelevance. Albanese was eager to occupy the middle ground between these two positions, emphasising Labor's constructive approach. Deepening the challenge, the Morrison Government, like state and territory governments around Australia, made a virtue of heeding the scientific experts. Outright opposition would mean suggesting that Labor knew better than the medical scientists who had better access to information than they did; it would also have the potential to undermine confidence in the response in ways that could have had material negative effects.

In March 2020, in response to the Morrison Government's announcement of its first stimulus package, Albanese and Shadow Treasurer Jim Chalmers made clear that Labor would support these measures. "We will be as responsible and as constructive as possible and will work with the government to expedite legislation through the Parliament". However, they continued to criticise the Morrison Government's record of announcing measures but not actually delivering them, as well as arguing for a range of additional support that the package could provide, particularly to casual workers and the self-employed (Albanese and

Chalmers 2020).

Albanese himself described the opposition as "constructive" frequently in the early months of the pandemic, usually at the beginning of statements, speeches and opinion pieces (Albanese 2020a), before delivering criticisms of the government and taking credit for the adoption of a range of policy measures. For instance, during debate on the *Coronavirus Economic Response Package (Payments and Benefits) Bill 2020*, Albanese noted Labor's "responsibility to be constructive". He gave the Morrison Government a backhanded compliment, "We have called for a wage subsidy for weeks ... I congratulate the government on changing its view", and noted that Labor would move amendments but would support the legislation regardless of how the amendments fared. Albanese further took credit for changes in the government's approach on a range of issues on which it had pressed for more action: COVID testing for people arriving on international flights, increased use of Telehealth, a moratorium on evictions from residential properties, interest rate relief for landlords whose tenants had no income, and support for childcare centres (Albanese 2020b).

Overall, the approach was constructive, but it was also a carefully considered political strategy. Given the deep fear many Australians felt as the pandemic emerged, it was important not to appear to be scoring political points over a life and death issue. Analysis of the text of Albanese's speeches and media releases from this time reveals that alongside describing his opposition as constructive, Albanese continued to be highly critical of the Morrison Government, often personally attacking Morrison. In May 2020, Albanese criticised Morrison's insistence that the stimulus measures had been designed as temporary and would afterwards "snap back" to business as usual, and blamed him (and former Liberal Prime Minister Tony Abbott) for "ravaging Australian industry" so that necessary manufacturing of personal protective equipment was more difficult (Albanese 2020c).

The tone of Albanese's public statements differed little from a standard opposition leader's attack. In late June 2020, Albanese took the opportunity to call for a Royal Commission into the so called Robodebt scheme, which had unlawfully and frequently inaccurately assessed and recovered debts from citizens who had apparently been overpaid a range of welfare entitlements (Holmes 2023). Albanese reminded people of Morrison's role as Minister for Social Services when the scheme commenced, stating "the Prime Minister himself was the architect of this cruel scheme". Simultaneously, he attacked COVID-19 economic stimulus measures which had allowed people to withdraw from their superannuation accounts giving rise to a range of scams, and the HomeBuilder scheme, whose conditions were initially so restrictive that very few people used it. Albanese's central attack, that the "Morrison Government is all spin and no delivery" (Albanese 2020d), was one that he used repeatedly throughout the term with slightly different phrasing, from the bushfire response of 2019-20 (Albanese 2020e), to the 2021 failures of the vaccine rollout (Albanese 2021a). For Albanese then, constructive meant offering tangible support on legislation, but it did not mean offering a new, less combative form of politics.

Managing the party and maintaining the leadership

In recent years, Labor leaders who have not appeared likely to lead their party to victory have been in imminent danger of losing their position. Labor's highly entrenched system of factions (Bennister and Heppell, 2016) provides patronage and support to their own, motivates battles for influence and positions within the parliamentary party, and can be decisive in making or breaking party leaderships. For Labor leaders, failure to maintain support with factional powerbrokers has seen them removed swiftly, as happened to Kevin Rudd, who was not factionally aligned and did little to build support with the factions (Bennister and Heppell: 143).

The rules for replacing a Labor leader changed at Rudd's behest in 2013. When in opposition, a 60 per cent Caucus vote is required to remove a leader, and if there is more than one candidate for the leadership, votes are taken both within the parliamentary caucus and the wider party membership, with each of these having a 50 per cent weighting towards the outcome. The new rules make removing a leader far more difficult than was previously, when all that was required was a majority parliamentary caucus vote. However, when the media began speculating about the Labor leadership during Albanese's time as Opposition Leader, it was publicly noted by disgruntled former Albanese supporter Joel Fitzgibbon that the rules could be changed by a simple majority in the parliamentary caucus (Murphy and Karp 2021). Of course, to change caucus rules would be a significant step and one that would show disregard for party members, but party leaders cannot afford to disregard factions and caucus on an assumption that the rules would save them.

As a member of the smaller, Left faction Albanese was clearly conscious of the need to maintain support across Left and Right, but he was also eager not to be too focused on maintaining his own position. He had friendships throughout the party and was confident that his "cross-section of loyalists was very strong across the factions, across the states" and that "there wasn't a clear alternative" (Albanese quoted in Van Onselen and Errington 2022: 41-42). The key here was his relationship with Richard Marles from the Victorian Right. Albanese offered Marles the deputy leadership which he accepted, bringing Marles' significant support base with him (Van Onselen and Errington 2022: 5; Murphy 2022: 35-36). In 2021, the media reported that Tanya Plibersek was positioning herself as a rival (Murphy and Karp 2021), and that the Right faction might offer her backing to remove Albanese, though she later denied attempting to gather support for a leadership challenge (van Onselen and Errington 2022: 43).

In managing the factions, Labor's internal divide on climate policy was significant. While most favoured strong action, there was a range of views about how strong that action should be, given the competing scientific and political realities. Others felt that Labor should be more focused on winning back disaffected voters in traditional Labor territory such as in Joel Fitzgibbon's seat of Hunter, which Fitzgibbon had held in 2019 despite a 9.48 per cent swing, which had taken it from "safe" to "marginal" seat status. Fitzgibbon was the chief advocate for a far less ambitious climate policy, publicly advocating Labor adopt the same medium term emissions reduction target as the Coalition (Murphy 2020). Fitzgibbon resigned from the Labor front bench after failing to convince caucus and called for Mark Butler to be removed as Shadow Climate Change Minister (van Onselen and Errington: 49).

Labor's 2030 emissions reduction target was also a constant in media questioning. Albanese commented: "We were asked this every day for two years" (Albanese in van Onselen and Errington: 48). Albanese was keen to release the policy after UN Climate talks in Glasgow in November 2021, so that Morrison couldn't use Labor's position to define a more electorally palatable alternative to take to the talks. This meant that Albanese spent much of the term deflecting interest in defining Labor's climate policy both from media and from within the party: "I was determined to hold my nerve, people were looking for us to do more, come out with new policies, suggesting we do a climate policy in 2020. They were wrong. Including people who were close to me" (Albanese in Murphy 2022: 47).

Labor eventually settled on a 43 per cent by 2030 emissions reduction target, announced in December 2021, six months before the election. Notably, the target was only two per cent lower than Shorten's, but it was in a different context, with business and the population more receptive to the need for the target. It had clearly been a matter of some nervousness for Albanese Labor, but even though the target was similar, it avoided some of the mistakes of the previous term in making sure there was solid economic modelling to underpin the position, and making sure relevant industries had been consulted and broadly agreed with the position (van Onselen and Errington: 53).

As with Albanese's need to push back on party demands to act early on climate policy, Labor's identity as the party of progressive reform frequently led to demands to be bold from its MPs and its supporters. However, bold action is not always the most successful strategy for an opposition, as it shifts scrutiny from government to opposition. Oppositions typically are under-resourced, meaning that governments frequently find holes and errors in the evidence for their policies. The more frequent path to electoral success for Australian oppositions of both major parties has been to point out the flaws of the current government and promise to do more or better on a few key issues. This was certainly the path Albanese took, and the one that had succeeded for all opposition election victories since Gough Whitlam's success with an expansive policy platform in 1972. From opposition, Labor's tension between ideology and policy ambition on the one hand and electoral success on the other rarely align perfectly, and this places further pressure on the skills of an opposition leader to manage the party internally as well as shaping public perceptions about what an opposition should be doing.

Campaign

Overwhelmingly, Labor's 2022 campaign was focused on the failings of Scott Morrison as prime minister. Morrison was far from popular, and according to the Australian Election Study was the least popular Liberal leader since at least 1987 (McAllister 2023). Many Australians held grievances on account of his failure to lead meaningfully during the "Black Summer" bushfires (McCaffrie 2023), his incapacity to comprehend and act on a range of issues to do with women's safety and equality (Rowe 2023), and his perceived "drift and incompetency" over the COVID-19 vaccine rollout (Kefford and Mills 2023: 105). However, Albanese was not particularly popular either. The combination of the pandemic and his smaller policy platform meant that Albanese was not especially well known among the electorate (Kefford and Mills: 106).

As noted earlier, most governments facing elections had a significant incumbency advantage from the pandemic and this helped them retain power. The Morrison Government was rated far more favourably in polls in the early stages of the pandemic, but by the time of the election its performance on the pandemic was seen as a negative by a plurality of voters (37 per cent), with neutral (33 per cent) also outnumbering those who felt the government had handled the pandemic well (30 per cent) (McAllister 2023: 8).

Labor's negative campaign focused heavily on Morrison's failures to take responsibility, with television advertisements highlighting his phrase "that's not my job", and in relation to the bushfires "I don't hold a hose, mate" (Kefford and Mills: 116). The negative aspect of the campaign was effective, but a large portion of the vote accrued to Greens and independents. As McAllister's analysis in the Australian Election Study shows, "Leadership was the most important factor in shaping the vote, with those viewing Morrison negatively being more likely to vote Labor or Green, in roughly equal proportions" (2023: 12). Given the relative size of the Labor and Greens parties, a roughly equal split of the anti-Morrison vote is a surprising result. In part, the lack of an inspiring Labor agenda may have been to blame. While the traditional opposition strategy was electorally smart and by far the safer option, for the increasing number of voters disillusioned with both major parties, it was unlikely to encourage them to vote for the opposition. Labor's strategy, an unpopular Coalition Government, and the professional campaigns run by a series of "teal" independents combined to produce the lowest primary vote share for the major parties ever (68.3 per cent).

Conclusion: Lessons from Labor's opposition during the pandemic

Ultimately, what Labor itself chooses to learn from its victorious strategy is an open question. Nonetheless, one key lesson for oppositions is that of patience. Australian politics has become notorious for its ruthlessness with party leaders when polls do not suggest victory, and arguably the changes rarely make a lasting difference to party fortunes. Albanese's term as opposition leader demonstrated that patience and stability can help provide a path to victory. There is little doubt that a switch of leader would have undermined the party strategy of neutralising difficult issues and maintaining the media and public focus on the government and its many downsides. Unstable oppositions seldom prosper.

A second lesson is that it would take a seismic shift to see a truly constructive form of opposition emerge in Australian politics. Even in the context of the pandemic, constructive opposition was as much a strategy based on Labor's own interest as it was a genuine effort to help the Morrison Government. That is not to say that Labor did not help the government in battling the pandemic, but it never missed a beat in pointing out the Morrison Government's errors either. Even a few months into the pandemic, Labor's criticism of the Government was of similar intensity to its criticism of the Government in "normal" times. This worked because the Morrison Government had many perceived failures to answer for. A newer, more popular government may have been harder to attack in this same way, but it is also remarkable how in the crisis context of the pandemic, the media frequently reported Albanese's self-assessment that Labor was constructive, with few, if any, analysing what that entailed.

The final lesson is the one that Labor may find hardest. The lessons above largely support the conventional wisdom about the battle between Australian governments and oppositions. In a two-party contest, being more appealing than the alternative is frequently enough. However, the biggest electoral surprise in 2022 was the emergence of the teal independents and the surge of the Greens. Should minor parties and independents continue to grow in strength, the conventional approach of being more appealing than the other major party may not be enough. A politics in which both major parties' traditional supporters have palatable alternatives to vote for is one in which the major parties will need to work harder to appeal to those supporters. Arguably, this could make the traditional "small target" version of opposition harder to prosecute. As the old certainties of Australian politics die, it may well be that Australia's most common, and most successful approach to opposition must die with it. However, the Shorten Labor opposition provides counsel against a swift change to expansive policy agendas. Opposition strategy has never been particularly easy, but the path to victory from opposition may have become much harder.

References

Albanese, A., "Coronavirus Response: Labor Backs the Right Decision", *The Australian*, 6 April 2020a.

Albanese, A., "Reply to Ministerial Statement on COVID-19 Crisis", *House of Representatives, Parliament House,* Canberra, 8 April 2020b. https://anthonyalbanese.com.au/anthony-albanese-speech-reply-to-ministerial-statement-on-covid-19-crisis-canberra-wednesday-8-april-2020

Albanese, A., "Australia Beyond the Coronavirus". Vision Statement 6: Address to Federal Labor Caucus, 11 May 2020c. https://anthonyalbanese.com.au/anthony-albanese-speech-australia-beyond-the-coronavirus-canberra-monday-11-may-2020

Albanese, A., "It's Time for a Royal Commission into Robodebt", Media Release, 23 June 2020d. https://anthonyalbanese.com.au/media-centre/anthony-albanese-bill-shorten-mark-dreyfus-linda-burney-media-release-its-time-for-a-royal-commission-into-robodebt-tuesday-23-june-2020

Albanese, A., [@AlboMP] "The Morrison Government promised $200 million a year for bushfire preparation. They've spent zero dollars. All announcement, no delivery", [Video attached] [Tweet], *X,* 2 December 2020e. https://twitter.com/AlboMP/status/1334065016186806273

Albanese, A., "The PM's Shambolic Vaccine Rollout Is Missing All Its Targets", *The Age*, 22 April 2021a

Albanese, A., and Chalmers, J., "Statement on Coronavirus Economic Stimulus Package", 12 March 2020, https://anthonyalbanese.com.au/media-centre/albanese-chalmers-media-release-statement-on-coronavirus-economic-stimulus-package-thursday-12-march-2020

Bennister, M., and Heppell, T., "Comparing the Dynamics of Party Leadership Survival in Britain and Australia: Brown, Rudd and Gillard", *Government and Opposition*, 5 (1), January 2016, 134-59

Emerson, C., and Weatherill, J., *Review of Labor's 2019 Federal Election Campaign*, Australian Labor Party, 2019. https://alp.org.au/2019_campaign_review

Grattan, M., "Labor in Opposition: When the Favourite Loses", in Evans, M., Grattan, M., and McCaffrie, B., (eds), *From Turnbull to Morrison: The Trust Divide*, Melbourne: Melbourne University Press, 2019, 127-43

Holmes, C., (Chair) Royal Commission into the Robodebt Scheme, *Report*, Canberra: Commonwealth of Australia, 2023

Kefford, G., and Mills, S., "Strategy and leadership in the Labor and Liberal campaigns", in *Watershed: The 2022 Australian Federal Election"*, Sawer, M., and Sheppard, J., (eds), *Watershed: The 2022 Australian Federal Election*, Canberra: ANU Press, 2023, 101-20

Manwaring, R., and Foley, E., "The Australian Labor Party", in Gauja, Sawer, and Sheppard, *Watershed: The 2022 Australian Federal Election*, 181-202

McAllister, I., "Party explanations for the 2022 Australian election result", *Australian Journal of Political Science*, Advance online publication, DOI: 10.1080/10361146.2023.2257611

McCaffrie, B., "Scott Morrison's Crisis Leadership", in McCaffrie, B., Grattan, M., and Wallace, C., (eds), *The Morrison Government: Governing through Crisis, 2019-22*, Sydney: NewSouth Publishing, 2023, 278-89

McMullin, R., *The Light on the Hill: The Australian Labor Party 1891-1991*, Oxford: Oxford University Press, 1991

Megalogenis, G., "2019 election: The shock of the new normal", *The Monthly*, June 2019

Murphy, K., "Joel Fitzgibbon quits shadow cabinet after dispute over Labor's climate policy", *The Guardian*, 10 November 2020

Murphy, K., "Lone Wolf: Albanese and the new politics", *Quarterly Essay*, 88, November 2022

Murphy, K., and Karp, P., "Joel Fitzgibbon calls for changes to Labor's leader selection rules as Albanese finalises reshuffle", *The Guardian*, 28 January 2021

Parkin, A., and Warhurst, J., "The Labor Party: Image, History and Structure", in Warhurst, J., and Parkin, A., (eds), *The Machine: Labor Confronts the Future*, St. Leonards: Allen and Unwin, 2000, 21-48

Rowe, P., "From 'daggy dad' to 'woke agendas': Women and equality", in McCaffrie, Grattan, and Wallace, *The Morrison Government: Governing through Crisis, 2019-22*, 154-65

van Onselen, P., and Errington, W., *Victory: The Inside Story of Labor's Return to Power*, Sydney: Harper Collins Publishers, 2022

9

The Opposition in New South Wales

Rodney Smith

*"I spent the day like a doomed man, taking phones calls and draft-
ing a statement, saying to the press I wasn't shifting [to federal
politics]. I feel a jolt in the stomach at what I'm letting myself in
for. It will destroy my career in four years. Everything's altered. It's
my fate . . . ".*

Bob Carr, 27 March 1988 (quoted in Dodkin 2003: 6)

Bob Carr's fears, expressed as it emerged that he was to become leader
of the opposition in the Legislative Assembly of New South Wales
(NSW) following Labor's defeat at the March 1988 election, were
understandable. After all, Labor had governed for the previous 12
years, during which time the Coalition Opposition had been led by no
fewer than six different politicians. Labor had just suffered an electoral
swing of 10.3 per cent, reducing it to 43 seats in the 109 seat Legislative
Assembly. Seven ministers had lost their seats (Hagan and Clothier 2001:
272-4). The expectation was that it would take at least two terms for
Labor to claw its way back into government (Dodkin: 5). Carr might also
reasonably have expected the new Coalition Government to follow in the
footsteps of past Labor and Coalition ministries, using its parliamentary
numbers ruthlessly to dominate the Labor Opposition in the NSW "bear
pit" (Parker 1978: 223).

Carr's predicament could be seen as the inevitable consequence of
deep structural forces that tend to result in weak oppositions in NSW.

On the other hand, the fact that Labor bounced back at the 1991 NSW Election, reducing the Coalition Government to minority status, and then won a narrow victory in 1995, suggests that a talented group of politicians lead by a skilful and energetic figure can overcome the structural disadvantages that frustrate lesser opposition teams. These two possibilities, the pessimistic and the optimistic views, are reflected in the literature on NSW oppositions, as they are more broadly in writings on parliamentary opposition (Ionescu and de Madariaga 1972; Fletcher 2011). The pessimistic view tends to be taken by authors who focus on parliament as a democratic institution and see the role of opposition as something more than that of a government-in-waiting (Thompson 1985; Clune and Griffith 2006; Rozzoli 2006). The optimistic view tends to be taken by authors who adopt a biographical leader-centred approach and measure oppositions by their electoral success or failure (Steketee and Cockburn 1986; Dodkin; West and Morris 2003; Abjorensen 2007; Hancock 2013).

The rest of this chapter outlines historical patterns of oppositions and opposition leadership in NSW, analyses the structural constraints on oppositions and their available resources, and assesses their performance in keeping executives accountable and dealing with legislation. It concludes with some reflections on what NSW experience suggests about the workings of opposition more generally. The chapter mainly focuses on the period since the Second World War but it also draws on earlier evidence for comparative purposes. Its broad theme is that neither the optimistic nor the pessimistic views properly capture the recent dynamics of opposition in NSW. The optimistic view underestimates the difficulties of winning office, even with talented leadership. Following 1995, the Coalition endured 16 years in opposition, after which Labor took 12 years to regain government. The pessimistic view has become outdated because developments within and outside the NSW Parliament have strengthened the opposition's capacity to scrutinise the Executive and influence legislation.

Broad patterns of opposition in NSW since 1901

Duration

The history of NSW opposition since Federation divides into two distinct periods: 1901 to 1932; and 1932 to the present. During the first 32 years, government changed hands nine times. The average period a party or coalition spent in opposition before winning power was just three and a half years. At that rate, the opposition and government should have swapped places some 25 times since 1932. Instead, there have been only seven such changes, with the average period in opposition increasing to just over 13 years (see Table 1).

Table 1: Parties of Government and Oppositions in NSW, January 1901-March 2023

YEARS	GOVERNMENT	OPPOSITION
1901-04	Protectionist	Liberal-Reform
1904-10	Liberal-Reform	Labor
1910-16	Labor	Liberal
1916-20	Nationalist	Labor
1920-22	Labor	Nationalist
1922-25	Nationalist-Progressive	Labor
1925-27	Labor	Nationalist-Country
1927-30	Nationalist-Country	Labor
1930-32	Labor	Nationalist-Country
1932-41	UAP-Country	Labor
1941-65	Labor	UAP/Democratic/Liberal-Country
1965-76	Liberal-Country	Labor
1976-88	Labor	Liberal-National/National Country/National
1988-95	Liberal-National	Labor
1995-2011	Labor	Liberal-National
2011-2023	Liberal-National	Labor

This pattern has been uneven in partisan terms. Since 1932, Labor has spent an average of 10 continuous years in opposition before regaining government, compared with 17 years for the Coalition parties. This difference is partly a matter of historical electoral geography. Until recently, the Coalition's support has tended to be concentrated in safe seats in the northern suburbs of Sydney and in rural NSW. Labor's support, although highest in working class Sydney and the Illawarra and Hunter regions, has been spread more evenly throughout NSW. These patterns have weakened in the past few decades, with Labor winning fewer rural and regional seats and the Liberals becoming more competitive in western Sydney (Clifford et al 2006; Green 2012: 291-296; Clune and Smith 2019). The difference is also a matter of NSW Labor's character since the late 1930s. Having endured the instability and splits of the Lang years, Labor has been pragmatic, aiming to gain and retain power rather than pursue ideological causes. In the 1950s, NSW Labor avoided the splits that kept Labor in opposition for decades in Victoria and Queensland (Hagan and Turner 1991; Smith 2003: 43, 60-63).

Leadership

Forty politicians – 38 men and two women – have served as leader of the opposition over 45 separate periods in NSW since 1901 (see Table 2). They have all been the leaders of the second largest party grouping in the Legislative Assembly, either Labor or the Liberal Party (and its predecessors). The only major, if brief, confusion about which party would provide the opposition leadership occurred immediately after second "Wranslide" election in 1981. The Coalition was reduced to 28 MLAs, 14 from each party. Country Party Leader Leon Punch savagely criticised the Liberal Party's performance and was reportedly prepared to take over the leadership of the opposition. He reluctantly backed down, since pressing his claim would have destabilised other aspects of the Coalition agreement, notably the avoidance of three-cornered electoral contests (Davey 2006: 274-5).

Leaders of the opposition in NSW have served, on average, 988 days in the role (see Table 2). The vast majority did so over a single period, with only three leaders serving in two separate periods and just one – Jack Lang – in three. Non-Labor leaders of the opposition have averaged shorter periods than their Labor counterparts, a difference that has remained constant over time. This gap may well reflect differences in the cultures and ideologies of the two parties, with the Liberal Party placing greater emphasis than Labor on leaders and therefore exhibiting greater impatience with those who are seen to struggle in the job (West 1965; Hancock 2007; Smith 2012).

Table 2: Tenure and Change in NSW Opposition Leaders, 1901-2012

Opposition Leader	Party	Years	Days as Opposition Leader	Changes of Government per Decade (1901-1910, etc.)	Changes of Opposition Leader per Decade (1901-1910, etc.)
Charles Lee	Lib-Ref	1901-02	545		
Joseph Carruthers	Lib-Ref	1902-04	713		
James McGowen	ALP	1904-10	2,223		
Charles Wade	Lib	1910-16	2,218	3	3
Ernest Durack	ALP	1916-17	90		
John Storey	ALP	1917-20	1,147		
George Fuller	Nationalist	1920-22	730	2	3
James Dooley	ALP	1922-23	462		
Greg McGirr	ALP	1923	39		
William Dunn	ALP	1923	107		
Jack Lang	ALP	1923-25	688		
George Fuller	Nationalist	1925	94		
Thomas Bavin	Nationalist	1925-27	755		
Jack Lang	ALP	1927-30	1,114		
Thomas Bavin	Nationalist	1930-32	498	4	8
Bertram Stevens	UAP	1932	39		
Jack Lang	ALP	1932-39	2,632		
William McKell	ALP	1939-41	620	1	3
Alexander Mair	UAP/Dem	1941-44	998		
Reginald Weaver	Dem/Lib	1944-45	642		
Alexander Mair	Liberal	1945-46	128		
Vernon Treatt	Liberal	1946-54	3,066	1	4
Murray Robson	Liberal	1954-55	400		
Philip Morton	Liberal	1955-59	1,397		

Robert Askin	Liberal	1959-65	2,128	0	3
John Renshaw	ALP	1965-68	1,167		
Patrick Hills	ALP	1968-73	1,953	1	2
Neville Wran	ALP	1973-76	894		
Eric Willis	Liberal	1976-77	581		
Peter Coleman	Liberal	1977-78	296		
John Mason	Liberal	1978-81	949	1	4
Bruce McDonald	Liberal	1981	134		
John Dowd	Liberal	1981-83	505		
Nicholas Greiner	Liberal	1983-88	1,838		
Robert Carr	ALP	1988-95	2,555	1	4
Peter Collins	Liberal	1995-98	1,344		
Kerry Chikarovski	Liberal	1998-2002	1,208	1	2
John Brogden	Liberal	2002-2005	1,254		
Peter Debnam	Liberal	2005-07	581		
Barry O'Farrell	Liberal	2007-11	1,453	0	3
John Robertson	Labor	2011-14	1,364		
Luke Foley	Labor	2015-18	1,404		
Michael Daley	Labor	2018-19	136		
Jodi McKay	Labor	2019-21	700	1	4
Chris Minns	Labor	2021-23	660		
N=41			Ave 988	Total = 16*	Total = 43*

*Excludes 2020s. Source: Parliament of New South Wales. "Facts and Figures - Leaders of the Opposition in the NSW Legislative Assembly, 1901 – Present". Available at: http://www.parliament.nsw.gov.au/prod/web/common.nsf/key/ResourcesFactsopplead

If winning government is seen as the benchmark for a successful opposition leader, around two-thirds must be counted as failures. Only 14 opposition leaders have taken their parties from opposition to government; Lang was the only one to achieve this feat twice. Nine won at the first election they fought as leader; in most cases taking over their party after previous leaders had failed to unseat the government. The other five required two elections to win. The greater focus in recent decades on leaders – sometimes called the "presidentialisation" of

Australian politics (Hart 1992; Strangio et al 2017: 5) – might provide a reason for opposition parties to give their leaders less time to win government than they once did. There is little evidence of any such trend. The average period served as NSW opposition leader increased from the 1940s and has not decreased in recent decades. Four of the six leaders of the opposition to become premier since the Second World War (Robert Askin, Greiner, Carr and Barry O'Farrell) all served well over the average term of an opposition leader before winning government, with Neville Wran and Chris Minns the exceptions. Longevity as leader of the opposition does not guarantee eventual victory (consider Vernon Treatt's 3066 days, or the 2632 days of Lang's third period in the role). Nonetheless, it does allow a leader of the opposition time to establish an agenda and gain a public profile.

Organisation

The current division of NSW oppositions into backbenchers and frontbenchers, with the individual frontbenchers holding specific portfolios and forming a "shadow ministry" or "shadow cabinet", is relatively recent. Lang's Labor Opposition introduced such a division in the 1930s (Parker: 230); however, it was not adopted as normal practice by Coalition or Labor oppositions until the 1970s. Instead, the oppositions of the 1940s to the 1960s were characterised by a committee structure. Between 1941 and 1965, the Parliamentary Liberal Party divided the work of examining bills between a number of standing committees. Katharine West noted 13 such committees operating in 1959: Rural, Transport, Local Government, Education, Legal, Miscellaneous, Housing, Health, Labor and Industry, Finance, Public Works and Conservation, Mines, and Publicity. These committees were chaired by senior MLAs. The opposition leader and committee chairs led parliamentary debates on their subject areas. Committee chairs had the expectation that they would become ministers when the Coalition won government. Some committees were active; however, according to West, most of them were characterised by "apathy". According to the Liberal backbencher Douglas Darby, most of the policy work of opposition fell on the leader: "The Leader of the Opposition has a task more onerous than a Minister of the Crown, for he has critically to observe the work of all Ministries" (West 1965: 153-4; 166).

When Labor was defeated in 1965, Opposition Leader Jack Renshaw adopted the Coalition's committee approach, "set[ting] up six watchdog committees of seven or eight members each, covering a group of portfolios. They would report to Caucus, from which all statements were to be issued through a publicity committee" (Hagan and Turner: 228). By the early 1970s, Labor had adopted something much more like the current system, with a distinct frontbench of 18 individual "shadow ministers" elected by the Caucus, supported by policy committees (Steketee and Cockburn: 99-100). In reality, Leader of the Opposition Wran acted as a "one man band", centralising policy announcements through his office and rarely allowing his shadow ministers to make media appearances (Dale 1985: 49-64).

In 1976, the Coalition under Opposition Leader Eric Willis reverted to a committee structure. Willis and his Deputy Leader aside, legislative responsibilities were divided between 16 committees, each chaired by a member of one of the Coalition parties, with the other Coalition partner providing a deputy chair. When Peter Coleman became leader of the opposition in 1977, the Coalition adopted the individual shadow minister system that it has used ever since (Parliament of New South Wales no date a). One obvious factor behind the move away from a more collegial committee structure was the need for oppositions to respond to the demands of an increasingly rapid news cycle, something achieved more easily with a single, clearly-defined spokesperson for each portfolio area.

Table 3: Average Shadow Ministry Membership, MLC and Portfolio Numbers, 1973-2020.

Decade	Average overall number of members per shadow ministry.	Average number of MLCs per shadow ministry.	Average number of named portfolios covered by a shadow ministry.
1970s*	20.6	0.4	25.8
1980s	21.7	3.0	33.8
1990s	21.4	4.0	41.8
2000s	22.1	4.1	50.8
2010s	20.3	6.7	49.0

*Excludes 1971-72. Source: Parliament of New South Wales, "Opposition Shadow Ministries from 1973": http://www.parliament.nsw.gov.au/prod/web/common.nsf/key/OppositionShadowMinistriesfrom1973

The number of shadow ministers has not increased significantly since shadow ministries became the norm (see Table 3). The noticeable growth of MLCs in shadow ministries – from almost none throughout the 1970s to around seven over the last complete decade – is largely accounted for by the growing professionalisation of the upper house (see below), one of whose effects was the formal inclusion in shadow ministries of the leader and deputy leader of the opposition in the Legislative Council. By contrast with the relatively stable number of shadow ministers, the number of identified portfolios shared among the opposition frontbench has doubled, from around 26 in the 1970s to around 50 since the 2000s. In 2023, the Minns Government had 50 separate portfolios, while the Opposition boasted 55 (see Table 4).

Some of this growth in portfolios is mere differentiation of areas that once had a broader single title. It also reflects a genuine expansion of responsibilities across the State level of Australian government since the 1970s. The expansion of opposition portfolios has largely followed the expansion of government portfolios (Moon and Sayers 1999). As Table 4 indicates, shadow portfolio titles generally mimic those of ministries. This makes sense in terms of the role of the opposition in trying to keep government ministers accountable within the Parliament and the opposition's need to have readily identifiable spokespeople to present its perspective to the media. Sometimes oppositions have been the innovators in portfolios, creating new titles to emphasise specific concerns. In the early 2000s, the Coalition did this effectively with portfolios named for particular regions ("Shadow Minister for Western New South Wales", etc.), a practice that Labor followed after 2011. More recent examples include Labor's shadow portfolios for the "gig" and "night-time" economies (see Table 4).

Table 4: Comparison of Government and Opposition Portfolios, February 2023.

Government Portfolios	Opposition Portfolios
Premier	Leader of the Opposition
Treasurer	Shadow Treasurer
Attorney General	Shadow Attorney-General
Minister for Police	Shadow Minister for Police
Minister for Health	Shadow Minister for Health
Minister for Education and Early Learning	Shadow Minister for Education and Early Childhood Learning
Minister for Corrections	Shadow Minister for Corrections and Juvenile Justice
Minister for Families and Communities	Minister for Family and Community Services
Minister for Finance	Shadow Minister for Finance, Industry and Trade
Minister for Planning	Shadow Minister for Planning and Public Spaces
Minister for Homes	Shadow Minister for Housing and Homelessness
Minister for Transport	Shadow Minister for Transport
Minister for Metropolitan Roads	Shadow Minister for Roads
Special Minister of State	Shadow Special Minister for State
Minister for Energy	Shadow Minister for Energy and Climate Change
Minister for Employee Relations	Shadow Minister for Industrial Relations
Minister for Local Government	Shadow Minister for Local Government
Minister for Sport	Shadow Minister for Sport
Minister for Enterprise, Investment and Trade	Shadow Minister for Finance, Industry and Trade

Minister for Tourism	Shadow Minister for Jobs, Investment and Tourism
Minister for Women	Shadow Minister for Women
Minister for Women's Safety and the Prevention of Domestic and Sexual Violence	Shadow Minister for Prevention of Domestic Violence and Sexual Assault
Minister for Mental Health	Shadow Minister for Mental Health
Minister for Skills and Training	Shadow Minister for Skills, TAFE and Tertiary Education
Minister for Science, Innovation and Technology	Shadow Minister for Better Regulation and Innovation
Minister for Customer Service and Digital Government	Shadow Minister for Customer Service; Shadow Minister for Digital
Minister for Veterans	Shadow Minister for Veterans
Minister for Lands and Water	Shadow Minister for Natural Resources; Shadow Minister for Water
Minister for Disability Services	Shadow Minister for Disability Inclusion
Minister for Regional Transport and Roads	Shadow Minister for Regional Transport and Roads
Minister for Emergency Services and Resilience	Shadow Minister for Emergency Services
Minister for Small Business	Shadow Minister for Small Business, Property and Multiculturalism
Minister for Environment and Heritage	Shadow Minister for the Environment; Shadow Minister for Heritage
Minister for Multiculturalism	Shadow Minister for Small Business, Property and Multiculturalism
Minister for Seniors	Shadow Minister for Seniors
Minister for Regional Youth	Shadow Minister for Youth
Minister for Juvenile Justice	Shadow Minister for Corrections and Juvenile Justice
Minister for Agriculture	Shadow Minister for Agriculture
Minister for Aboriginal Affairs	Shadow Minister for Aboriginal Affairs and Treaty
Minister for the Arts	Shadow Minister for Arts; Shadow Minister for Music
Minister for Regional New South Wales	Shadow Minister for Regional New South Wales
Minister for Western New South Wales	Shadow Minister for Western New South Wales
Minister for Western Sydney	Shadow Minister for Western Sydney
Minister for Infrastructure	---
Minister for Fair Trading	---

Minister for Cities	---
Minister for Active Transport	---
Minister for Flood Recovery	---
Minister for Hospitality and Racing	---
Minister for Regional Health	---
---	Shadow Minister for Medical Research
---	Shadow Minister for the Night-Time Economy
---	Shadow Minister for the Gig Economy
---	Shadow Minister for Justice
---	Shadow Minister for Counter-Terrorism
---	Shadow Minister for the Central Coast
---	Shadow Minister for the North Coast
---	Shadow Minister for the Hunter
---	Shadow Minister for the Illawarra and South Coast

For Labor oppositions, the distribution of shadow portfolios has been partly a matter of balancing competing factional and sub-factional interests and strengths. For the Coalition, the balancing act has had to take into account both internal Liberal factions and the relative strengths of the Liberal and National parties. The typical balance since the 1970s has been roughly two Liberal shadow ministers to one National shadow minister, reflecting the strengths of the Coalition partners in the Assembly. When the "Wranslide" elections produced parity between the Coalition party numbers (18 Liberal to 17 Country in 1978 and 14 each in 1981), the shadow ministries were also shared equally. Unsurprisingly, the National Party has typically claimed, and been given, shadow portfolios related to primary industry, agriculture and regional services (Chaples et al 1985; Parliament of New South Wales no date a).

The structural context of opposition in NSW

The previous section of this chapter demonstrates that, while the basic functions of opposition may not have changed in NSW since 1901, the durations, leadership, size and organization of oppositions have gone through important developments. This section explores the main structural context in which oppositions in NSW have had to operate. One structural feature affecting the opposition's success – the presence of disciplined party blocs – has remained constant since the early 20th century. Other structural elements have changed quite significantly.

Opposition and the Legislative Assembly

Strong party discipline combined with majority government has generally allowed governments to control the business of the Legislative Assembly, introducing and changing standing and sessional orders to disadvantage oppositions. In the 1920s and 1930s, standing orders were amended to speed up passage of bills through the Assembly. Throughout this period, Labor and Coalition governments alike applied the gag and guillotine. Premier William McKell adopted opposition amendments and refused to cut off debate during the 1940s; however, his approach was unusual. His immediate Labor successors quickly reverted to use of the gag and guillotine, as did Liberal Premier Askin and Labor Premier Wran (Clune and Griffith: 158-538).

There is a strong element of socialisation through the experience of opposition in this repeated pattern. Clune and Griffith (429) write of the late 1960s:

> Askin was on top and he meant to stay there using every means at his disposal. Any hope that his experiences in Opposition would translate into an attempt to make the Assembly operate in a freer, fairer, more effective manner quickly evaporated. The new Premier's attitude was that he was going to mete out to the ALP the treatment that it had given him – with interest.

In 1973, Wran, a particular target of Askin's gag, expressed his "hope . . . that we shall behave more like civilised human beings, rather than like animals setting upon each other in a situation where, if one party has the numbers, it tramples the other to death" (quoted in Steketee and Cockburn: 102). Once Wran secured office, the trample of hooves drowned out the call of civilisation.

Oppositions have also been hampered in the Assembly by the reluctance of Coalition and Labor governments to develop a committee system in the lower house that would aid in legislative work and scrutiny of the executive. After a strong start – 82 select committees were formed between 1901 and 1910 – governments rapidly reduced their use. By the 1960s, Askin had rejected any need for select committees. Wran allowed select committees to investigate several policy matters in the 1970s but resisted establishment of standing committees until 1982.

The Greiner Government showed equally little interest in reforming lower house procedures or allowing committees to develop until 1991, when it found itself in minority in the Assembly. Relying on the support of three non-aligned Independents, Greiner signed a Memorandum of Understanding with them that contained a range of changes to Parliament. These included provision of parliamentary counsel services to all members; constitutional recognition of the independence of the presiding officers; establishing all-party committees with a veto power over cabinet nominations for the Auditor-General, Independent Commission Against Corruption Commissioner, Ombudsman and Director of Public Prosecutions; reforming parliamentary pecuniary interest disclosures; instituting a parliamentary code of ethics; establishing estimates and legislation committees; reform of Question Time and an overhaul of Legislative Assembly standing orders. These reforms were not fully achieved; however, enough were to make the Assembly a more rewarding place for opposition activity (Smith 1995; Clune and Griffith: 540-67).

After Labor won the 1995 election, it began to reimpose many of the obstacles to effective opposition examination in the Legislative Assembly. The committee system was scaled down, bills were examined more perfunctorily and passed with fewer amendments. The Labor Government commonly used sessional orders to circumvent the standing orders established during the period of minority government (Clune and Griffith: 614-21; Smith 2012). This pattern of a disciplined government majority minimising opportunities for effective opposition continued during the Coalition governments of 2011 to 2023. Small moves towards greater scrutiny emerged as the Coalition gradually fell into minority throughout 2021 and 2022 (Legislative Assembly 2022: 5). The opposition and crossbenchers quickly took advantage of the election of a minority Labor Government in March 2023 to revive key scrutiny measures (see, for example, *NSWPD Legislative Assembly*, 23 May 2023, 47-48).

Opposition and the Legislative Council

The Legislative Council has provided a mixed set of constraints and opportunities for parliamentary oppositions in NSW. From the advent of bicameralism in 1856, the Council has been constitutionally powerful, with virtually the same legislative powers as the Assembly, buttressed by a cumbersome procedure for resolving deadlocks between the houses (Twomey 2004: 246-67). Until the 1960s, there was no official opposition in the Legislative Council, in some part to maintain the fiction that it was a non-partisan chamber. In 1962, Liberal MLC Arthur Bridges permitted himself to be called "Principal Representative of Members who are not Supporters of Government" and in 1965, Labor MLC Reg Downing became the first "Leader of the Opposition" (Parker: 206-7). The absence of formal opposition did not, however, mean the complete absence of opposition in the upper house, even when it was an appointed house and later an indirectly elected house. Government bills were regularly opposed in debates and occasionally defeated in the Council (Turner 1969; Clune 2022).

The advent of directly elected MLCs in 1978 had three effects that dramatically strengthened the role of the opposition in the Council. First, the proportional representation system used to elect MLCs meant that no government since 1988 has had a majority in the upper house. Governments have thus had to find support from the opposition or crossbench MLCs to get their legislation passed (Smith 2006: 120-6). Second, direct election by the people of NSW gave MLCs a newfound democratic legitimacy that those MLCs were increasingly willing to assert against the Executive (Clune 2017a). Third, the introduction of full payment for MLCs in 1985 to reflect their new status underlined the

Council's position as a full-time house of review. Labor MLCs became members of the Caucus and Coalition MLCs took on shadow ministries for the first time. Before 1985, Council sittings were limited to allow MLCs to pursue paid occupations and business activities. This "gentleman's club" culture meant that the Council had lacked the capacity to undertake activities associated with the ideals of opposition in a systematic way (Page 1991; Clune and Griffith: 524).

A full-time directly elected Council not under the control of the Government resulted in the expansion of Council committees into a full committee system and the revival of accountability measures – such as disallowance of regulations and motions for the production of state papers – that had lain dormant for decades. These reforms have added a strong forensic element to opposition in NSW that is generally missing in the more combative "bear pit" politics of the lower house (see below).

Formal recognition of the opposition

As the foregoing account suggests, for much of the NSW Parliament's history, the opposition received little protection, or, indeed, recognition, from the standing orders of either House. The leader of the opposition was first mentioned in the Standing Rules and Orders of the Legislative Assembly as late as 1994, although the standing orders had made reference to "Party Leaders" from the 1920s, particularly in relation to time limits on speeches (Parliament of New South Wales 1994; Clune and Griffith: 242). From 1928, the leader of the opposition (as a party leader), along with the premier or the minister leading the government's side of a debate, were granted "unspecified" time periods to speak on most subjects, while other MLAs' speaking times were specifically limited. With each major reform of the standing orders, the specified time limits were shortened – speeches on the Address-in-Reply, for example, were gradually reduced from 60 minutes to 15 minutes between 1928 and 2009 – however, the right of the leader of the opposition to speak for an unspecified period was preserved throughout (Parliament of New South Wales, Legislative Assembly 1976: SO 142A; 1994: SO 95; 2009:

SO 85; Hawker 1971: 247; Clune and Griffith: 242, 550). Other reforms to Legislative Assembly Standing Orders that recognised the opposition concerned questions. From 1994, the leader of the opposition was granted the right to ask the first question during Question Time and since 2015 the opposition leader has been granted more written questions per sitting day than other Members (Legislative Assembly 1994: SO 140 [now SO 131]; 2023: SO 132).

The opposition was not specifically mentioned in the Legislative Council Standing Rules and Orders until the 1990s. Since then, Standing Rules and Orders have recognised the opposition in various ways. Over the same period, however, they have also reflected the diverse composition of the chamber. Until 2011, for example, speeches in the Council were generally not restricted by time limits. When time limits were introduced for debate on government bills, the first opposition speaker and the minister leading the debate were each accorded 40 minutes, with 20 minutes for other speakers. By 2022, the 40-minute limit was extended to include the first crossbench speaker in a debate. Similarly, the processes for the scheduling of private members' business developed since 1999 have acknowledged a need for parity between government, opposition and crossbench members. Representation of crossbenchers as well as the opposition on the Council's committees has been either explicitly mandated or implied in recent versions of the Standing Rules and Orders (Legislative Council 2004: SO 48, 183-185, 200, 201, 205, 210; 2022: SO 144, 190-195, 211, 217; Want et al 2018: 596-619; 821). In these ways, the Standing Rules and Orders have moved away from a government versus opposition model to one of multi-party negotiation.

Formal and informal resources

While NSW government ministers have considerable publicly provided resources at their disposal, most shadow ministers receive no additional funding or resources in recognition of their roles. In 1912, the NSW Parliament was the second in the British Commonwealth to grant the leader of the opposition an additional salary, eight years before the

Australian House of Representatives took the same step (McHenry 1954: 447-50). In 1959, the resources provided to the opposition leader were "an extra £1000 salary, £250 expense allowance, a car with driver, an office and a staff of three" (West 1965: 165). The current allowance, established by the *Parliamentary Remuneration Act 1989* (NSW), gives the leader of the opposition a salary loading of 57 percent over the parliamentary base salary, as well as an expense allowance of 26 percent, the equivalent loadings to those provided for junior ministers. Opposition whips gained salary allowances in 1932, while deputy leaders of the opposition, along with the leaders of "third parties" with ten or more MLAs, did so in 1956 (Parker: 189). Extensions of payments and allowances to a small number of other opposition roles in the Legislative Assembly and Legislative Council have followed (Parliament of New South Wales no date b). Taking these loadings and entitlements as a whole, the opposition leadership group across both houses currently receives parliamentary resources roughly equivalent to those available to between four and five junior ministers.

Interestingly, the "third party" leader allowance was introduced under a Labor government, although its only likely beneficiaries were the Coalition parties. Since the 1920s, the NSW National Party has more or less willingly followed its Commonwealth counterpart's practice of relinquishing the official position of deputy leader of the opposition to the Liberal Party when the Coalition has been in opposition. Regardless of the formal arrangements, the National Leader considers him or herself the second most important person in the Coalition (Davey: 40; West: 158-9). Since the 1950s this practice has maximised the Coalition's resources when in opposition, by allowing Liberal deputy leaders of the opposition and National (Country) Party leaders to claim separate allowances.

Few other avenues exist for oppositions to boost their statutorily-provided resources, which are covered by strict rules and an enforceable Code of Conduct (Twomey 2004: 459). The fate of Labor's Shadow Transport Minister, Brian Langton, established the pitfalls of an opposition pooling its resources. In 1998, the Independent Commission against Corruption

(ICAC) found that Langton had acted corruptly in 1994 by using other Labor parliamentarians' travel warrants and falsely recording the details, even though Langton had used them to pursue legitimate opposition duties related to his portfolio (NSW Independent Commission Against Corruption 1994; Smith 1999). Opposition MPs and their staff do have access to the NSW Parliamentary Library to help in researching policy issues. Their use of this resource has varied considerably (Parr 1995). Oppositions also rely on volunteer labour from party supporters and free policy advice provided by interest groups (Collins 2000: 264-5; Rozzoli: 63-6).

Perhaps the most versatile official parliamentary resource through which oppositions can develop policy ideas, examine legislation and pursue suspected government failures is the extensive committee system of the Legislative Council, which currently includes three standing subject committees addressing Law and Justice, Social Issues and State Development, eight Portfolio Committees, a Public Accountability and Public Works Committee, select committees established periodically to inquiry into specific matters, and regulation and selection of bill committees. In addition, MLCs serve on joint standing, statutory and select committees with MLAs. In contrast to the usual practice in the Assembly, Council committees generally do not have a majority of government members, which gives the opposition more influence over their inquiries and reports (Parliament of New South Wales no date c).

The Council committee system has continued to evolve and grow. The new Public Accountability and Public Works Committee, for example, combines two committees that were first established in 2018. The powerful Portfolio Committees have grown over the years from five General Purpose Standing Committees established in 1997, which were in turn replacements for the joint budget estimates committees created in 1991. The current Portfolio Committees cover Premier and Finance, Health, Education, Regional NSW, Justice and Communities, Transport and the Arts, Planning and the Environment, and Customer Service.

Each Portfolio Committee has three Coalition, two Labor and two crossbench members, roughly representing the proportions of MLCs in the Legislative Council. They can inquire into public policy issues without requiring a referral from the Council as a whole. Their inquiries attract submissions from a range of interest groups and community members, which can be supplemented by public hearings. Inquiry processes are supported by secretariats, who manage submissions and hearings and assist the Committee chairs with their reports. The Committees also act as estimates committees, questioning relevant ministers and senior public servants on their portfolio expenditure and administration in NSW. Once a relatively limited exercise, these estimates hearings now provide an opportunity for opposition and crossbench interrogation that extends over two and sometimes three rounds of questioning per Committee (Smith 1995; Smith 2012: 68-71; Parliament of New South Wales no date d).

The tasks of opposition in NSW have been made easier since the 1970s by the development of extra-parliamentary resources in the form of "watchdog" bodies that monitor, audit and investigate government activity. The three most significant watchdogs are the Audit Office, the Ombudsman and the Independent Commission Against Corruption (Smith 2005). The Audit Office can trace its history to 1870 but has only played a systematic role monitoring public sector finances since the 1980s (Parker: 283-4; Funnell and Cooper 1998: 282-6). The Audit Office's new activism was accompanied by a stronger role for its parliamentary partner, the Legislative Assembly's Public Accounts Committee. The Committee was seen as having an "ignominious history" until the late 1970s, when it became a stepping stone for ambitious MLAs such as Laurie Brereton, Greiner and Carr, who used it to scrutinise government expenditure (Parker: 236; Cumming 1991: 298-300; Funnell and Cooper: 286; Collins: 139-40; West and Morris: 134-5). The Ombudsman was established in 1974 to hear and investigate complaints against public agencies (Parker 441-4). Initially a weak body, its powers have been modified over time, generally to strengthen it and broaden its scope. One significant responsibility since 1989 has been oversight of "freedom of information" measures in NSW. Although these measures, now governed by the *Government Information (Public Access) Act 2009*, are often criticised as restrictive and costly, they have been used by the opposition and news organisations to gain access to government information that would otherwise have remained hidden.

The most formidable (and controversial) body is the Independent Commission Against Corruption (ICAC), established as a "standing royal commission" to combat corruption in 1988 by Greiner's newly elected Coalition Government. As previous leader of the opposition, Greiner had been frustrated by failures to have alleged corruption within the Wran Government properly investigated. The new leader of the opposition, Carr, supported establishment of ICAC against the strong wishes of some within Labor (Chaples and Page 1995; Dodkin 13-15; West and Morris 168-74, 206, 258-9). Perhaps unsurprisingly, since the mid-1990s, the strongest criticisms of the ICAC have come from whichever party has been in government, as oppositions have made political mileage from referring matters to ICAC and from ICAC findings against premiers and cabinet ministers, including Greiner (see below).

The news media, and particularly the NSW Parliamentary Press Gallery, has always been a potentially valuable resource for oppositions. The Gallery has changed over time, with fewer media organisations represented and fewer journalists stationed at Macquarie Street; however, major newspapers, radio and television channels retain a presence in and around the Parliament (Chase 2006). Their audience reach is still significant, despite the rise of social media (Park et al 2022). The media's focus on the government both hinders and helps oppositions. On the one hand, governments dominate the media agenda through media releases and announcements; on the other, the media and the opposition both have an interest in government failure. Opposition leaders who have rapport with state political reporters and understand what makes news can disrupt the government's media dominance and deflect attention away from the opposition's own failings. The most successful exponent of these arts was undoubtedly the former journalist Carr (Chase; Carr 2018).

The performance of NSW Oppositions

Oppositions can be judged by a range of criteria (Ionescu and de Madariaga). The two broad criteria adopted here are holding the executive accountable for its actions and contributing to the legislative program of the Parliament. Both of these criteria can be divided into several sub-categories.

Executive Scrutiny (I): General

For most of the 20th century, oppositions in NSW lacked parliamentary mechanisms for general scrutiny of the executive beyond Question Time. Since 1988, NSW oppositions have been aided in their scrutiny function by the continuous minority position of government parties in the Legislative Council (Evans 1997; Smith 2001: 375-6; Clune and Griffith: 651-6). The Council committee system, discussed above, has resulted in a large number of committee inquiries and reports across a wide range of public issues. In the five years between mid-2017 and mid-2022, for example, Council committees held 210 public inquiries and produced 158 reports. While the outcomes of individual inquiries have varied considerably, their overall effect has been to produce greater transparency in the State's public administration. The formal requirement that governments respond to committee recommendations within three months also puts the onus on the executive to justify its previous and proposed actions (Clune and Griffith: 658-65; Department of the Legislative Council 2022: 7).

Government minorities in the Legislative Council have also led to a revival of motions for the production of state papers relating to policy and administrative decisions. In 1995, the Opposition and minor parties in the Council began passing motions that papers relating to decisions by the Carr Labor Government be made available for scrutiny. The Labor MLC and Treasurer, Michael Egan, resisted these motions and was in turn censured and suspended from the Parliament. Egan pursued legal action in two cases taken to the NSW Supreme Court, the first of which he pursued further via appeal to the High Court. The result was that the right of the Council to order the production of state papers, along with its generally powerful constitutional position, was affirmed by the courts. Hundreds of successful motions for the production of papers have since been passed in the Council, and the types of papers demanded has also broadened. Critics such as Egan have claimed that the material produced is often not properly examined by anyone and has not led to greater accountability. The most obvious counter-argument is the instances in which the production of papers has provided critical information for effective opposition. In addition, the mere possibility that an opposition may uncover damaging information through the release of documents should make governments and their agencies more careful in their decision-making and processes (Clune and Griffith: 651-6; Twomey 2008; Lovelock 2009; Mihaljek 2017; Clune 2017b; Clune 2022: 197-9).

Executive Scrutiny (II): Bringing down ministries

Party discipline in the Legislative Assembly makes the chances of an opposition bringing down a government exceedingly slim. The closest that oppositions have come to this achievement in the post-war period occurred in 1992, after the Greiner Coalition Government lost its majority. A core element of the 1991 Memorandum signed by Greiner and the three non-aligned Independent MLAs bound them to support the government in no confidence motions except "where matters of corruption or gross maladministration are involved". The Independents threatened to vote with the Labor Opposition against the Greiner Government after the ICAC found against Greiner and the Environment Minister, Tim Moore, for their involvement in appointing former Liberal Minister turned Independent MLA Terry Metherell to a Senior Executive Service post in the public service. Faced with a choice between collective and individual ministerial responsibility, Greiner and Moore reluctantly resigned. The Independents voted against Labor's subsequent no confidence motion in the government, and John Fahey succeeded Greiner as premier (Gleeson et al 1992).

NSW oppositions sometimes have an interest in keeping governments in power. Premier Wran's power to call a snap early election in 1984 almost certainly won him another term that a later election may well have prevented. This vexed then Opposition Leader Greiner and the Independent MLA John Hatton (Chaples et al; Hancock: 119-139). The 1991 Memorandum included a provision for fixed four-year parliaments, which were subsequently introduced. In 1993, Opposition Leader Carr believed that Governor Peter Sinclair might grant Premier Fahey an early election, which the Coalition was likely to win in the euphoria of Sydney's successful bid for the 2000 Summer Olympics. The Opposition sent the Governor legal advice that an early election would be unconstitutional. As it transpired, Fahey did not seek an early election and Carr was victorious in 1995 (Smith 2009).

Executive Scrutiny (III): Bringing down ministers

Oppositions in NSW have frequently called for the resignation or dismissal of ministers. Such calls are often made in the hope of drawing public criticism of the government, rather than in the genuine expectation of taking ministerial scalps. NSW premiers tend to resist calls for ministerial sackings, attempting to "tough out" opposition attacks and preferring to replace troublesome ministers quietly as part of later ministerial reshuffles (Thompson and Tillotsen 1999). Between 1901 and 1988, only three ministers were forced to resign: William Grahame in 1920, Joshua Arthur in 1953, and Rex Jackson in 1983. All three resignations concerned improper or corrupt relationships between the ministers and others. Each followed opposition pressure, bolstered by media attention and official investigations (Evatt 1940: 470-83; Clune 2001: 17-18; Steketee and Cockburn: 306-11).

Since 1988, the number of forced ministerial resignations and sackings has increased significantly, affecting Coalition and Labor governments alike. Seven Coalition ministers resigned or were dismissed between 1988 and 1995; ten Labor ministers and three parliamentary secretaries resigned or were dismissed between 1995 and 2011; and 11 Coalition ministers and one parliamentary secretary were forced out between 2011 and 2023. All these cases concerned personal ministerial impropriety, rather than more systemic problems of policy failure, maladministration or public sector corruption (see Table 5).

Table 5: Forced Ministerial Resignations and Dismissals in NSW, 1988-2023.

Minister	Issue	Key players	Year
Matt Singleton	Rezoning conflict of interest.	Opposition; media.	1989
Terry Metherell	Taxation.	Australian Taxation Office	1990
Phillip Smiles	Taxation.	Australian Taxation Office	1992
Nick Greiner	SES appointment.	ICAC; Opposition; Independents.	1992
Tim Moore	SES appointment.	ICAC; Opposition; Independents.	1992
Ted Pickering	Misleading Parliament.	Police Commissioner; Parliamentary committee.	1992
Terry Griffiths	Sexual harassment of female staff.	Opposition; media; staff whistleblowers.	1994
Brian Langton	Travel when in Opposition.	ICAC.	1998
Richard Face	Post-ministerial employment.	Self; media.	2003
Tony Stewart (i)*	Drink driving.	Police; Premier; ALP.	2006
Carl Scully	Misleading Parliament.	Self.	2006
Milton Orkopoulos	Sex and drug offences.	Police.	2006
Matt Brown	Inappropriate behaviour; lying.	ALP; Premier.	2008
Tony Stewart (ii)	Bullying of staff member.	Whistleblower; Premier; independent inquiry.	2008
John Della Bosca	Sexual affair.	Media.	2009
David Campbell	Visiting gay sex venue.	Media.	2010

Karyn Paluzzano*	Misuse of staff allowance.	ICAC.	2010
Ian Macdonald	Travel while minister.	Media.	2010
Paul McLeay	Accessing internet pornography and gambling.	Department of Parliament staff member; media.	2010
Angela D'Amore*	Misuse of staff allowance.	ICAC.	2010
Greg Pearce	Appointment conflict of interest.	Media.	2013
Chris Hartcher	Political donations.	ICAC.	2013
Barry O'Farrell	Gift; testimony to ICAC.	ICAC.	2014
Mike Gallacher	Political donations.	ICAC; Premier.	2017
Daryl Maguire*	Developer commissions.	ICAC.	2018
Don Harwin	Covid rules breach.	Police; media.	2020
Gladys Berejiklian	Funding conflict of interest.	ICAC.	2021
John Sidoti	Improper influence in property development.	Opposition and Greens; ICAC.	2021
Gareth Ward	Sexual violence allegations	Police; media.	2021
Eleni Petinos	Bullying of staff.	Staff whistleblowers; Premier.	2022
Stuart Ayres	Intervention in trade role recruitment.	Opposition and Greens MLCs.	2022
Damien Tudehope	Shares conflict of interest.	Media.	2023
*Parliamentary Secretary.			

Examination of these 32 forced resignations and sackings suggests that opposition demands for a ministerial exit are only effective if other actors such as the media, premiers, police, integrity agencies such as the ICAC and whistleblowers are already involved, or become involved because of opposition claims of ministerial misbehaviour. In some cases, the opposition has played no obvious role at all, as when Liberal Premier O'Farrell sacked his Finance Minister Greg Pearce in August 2013, following media revelations of Pearce's conflict of interest when making a board appointment to Sydney Water (*Sydney Morning Herald*, 1 August

2013). More commonly, the opposition has used parliamentary processes to help maintain media interest in allegations of ministerial impropriety and maintain pressure on premiers to act. A good example of this was provided by the resignation of Trade Minister Stuart Ayres over his involvement in the appointment of former Deputy Premier John Barilaro as NSW Trade Commissioner to the Americas. Barilaro's appointment was announced in June 2022, sparking public debate about "jobs for the boys". The Legislative Council's Public Accountability Committee began investigating almost immediately, with its public hearings keeping the issue in the news over the next five months. Ayers resigned in August after Premier Dominic Perrottet confronted him with sections of a separate draft inquiry report by Bruce McClintock SC. Although McClintock's final report and another later independent inquiry ultimately found Ayres had not breached the Ministerial Code of Conduct, the Public Accountability Committee's more critical judgements resonated with the public and he was not reappointed to cabinet (Parliament of New South Wales no date; *Sydney Morning Herald*, 3, 12, 16, 27 August 2022).

Even in the post-1988 context, oppositions cannot force ministers out against determined government resistance. Motions of no confidence in ministers are very rarely put in the Council and their effect is symbolic. Disciplined majority party support for a minister in the Assembly means opposition no confidence motions in that chamber are doomed to fail. They can only succeed in a hung parliament, and only then if the opposition can persuade enough crossbench MPs that a minister has acted sufficiently badly to deserve removal. The 1992 resignations of Greiner and Moore, discussed above, provide a rare example of such success. In October 2020, by contrast, the Coalition used its slim majority in the Assembly to defeat Opposition Leader Jodi McKay's no confidence motion in Liberal Premier Gladys Berejilklian. Three of the eight crossbench MPs who voted (Independents Greg Piper, Joe McGirr and Alex Greenwich) also opposed the motion. McKay's motion was grounded in claims that the Premier Berejilklian had been aware of corrupt activity by Liberal MP

Daryl Maguire but had failed to act on it or report it to ICAC. These allegations had emerged as part of an ongoing ICAC investigation. Premier Berejilklian. resigned almost a year later on 1 October 2021, when the ICAC announced it was extending its investigation of her relationship with Maguire (*The Guardian*, 14 October 2020; *Sydney Morning Herald*, 1 October 2021).

Legislative Role (I): Amending legislation

Whether or not oppositions should attempt to improve government bills has long been a matter of debate (Birch 1964: 166). Disciplined party government in NSW since the early 20th century has meant that these attempts have usually relied on the goodwill of the government, which has rarely been forthcoming. In the 1940s, Premier McKell was open to opposition amendments; however, his successors did not follow his lead. In periods when the opposition held majorities in the indirectly elected Legislative Council before 1978, it sometimes insisted that government bills be amended if they were to be passed (Turner: 43-8). Much more frequent amendment of government bills has been a feature of NSW politics since 1988, when the crossbench and opposition have been able to form combined majorities in a directly elected Legislative Council. Between mid-2017 and mid-2022, for example, 2609 amendments were moved in the Council and almost exactly one-third (866) were passed (Legislative Council 2022: 7). Because both the government and opposition know that controversial government bills will pass the lower house without amendment but face amendment and possible committee referral in the upper house, debate on these bills in the Assembly is sometimes perfunctory, so that the business of negotiating amendments in the Council can proceed as quickly as possible.

Legislative Role (II): Defeating government bills

Oppositions are rarely able to defeat government bills in the Legislative Assembly, except during periods of minority government when they can combine with crossbenchers to do so. Opposition attempts to defeat government bills in the Council since 1988 have rarely been successful, largely because the minor parties have preferred to amend government bills rather than reject them outright (Smith 2006: 160-1). On occasions, the government has withdrawn bills rather than seeing them unacceptably amended. In one notable example, the Coalition Government withdrew its 1990 *Industrial Relations Bill*, for example, after the Opposition and the Australian Democrats passed more than 300 amendments in the Council. The bill was reintroduced and passed by the Government, with Christian Democrat support, after the 1991 election altered the balance of power in the Council (Page: 26; Smith 1997: 215-9; Clune and Griffith: 575-87).

Legislative Role (III): Initiating bills

When the government has a majority in the Legislative Assembly, the prospects for successful private members' bills initiated by the opposition are miniscule. The 1991 to 1995 period of minority government provided an unusual opportunity for the opposition, crossbench and government backbench MLAs alike to propose private members' bills with some chance of success. One hundred and fifty were introduced between 1991 and 1995, with 16 making it to the statute book. While some Labor Opposition MLAs took to this law-making opportunity with enthusiasm, others wondered whether the energy involved in negotiating the passage of opposition bills would have been better spent on bringing down the Coalition Government (Smith 1995: 33-4). More recently, the only successful private members' bills have been ones in which party discipline has been removed to allow free votes on "conscience" issues, such as Independent MP Alex Greenwich's Voluntary Assisted Dying Bill in 2022 (Legislative Assembly: 48-49). Although the quality of the debates on such bills is often praised, party discipline quickly returns as the norm.

Conclusion

This survey of opposition in NSW suggests some broad points about the success or failure of oppositions. The first is that the structural constraints and opportunities for NSW oppositions have varied quite considerably over time. The constraints on Coalition oppositions of the 1950s, facing Labor governments that controlled both houses of Parliament, were very different from those confronting Coalition oppositions in the 2000s, which benefited from Labor's minority position in the Legislative Council, as well as from the activities of independent watchdog agencies such as the ICAC.

Second, these constraints must affect the strategy adopted by an opposition if it is to be successful. An opposition with no prospects of a constructive scrutiny or legislative role must simply attempt to win office. As Ionescu and De Madiagara (123) suggest:

> Once it is realized that the minority party has no power whatsoever to affect the course of action and the permanence in power of the government, it is bound to consider the years of opposition as a [four]-year-long purgatory, during which it must do all in its power to win the next election by cajoling the electorate and playing to the gallery.

On the other hand, an opposition with the opportunity to exercise the scrutiny and legislative roles outlined in this chapter for the period since the late 1980s clearly has a wider range of strategic options available to it.

Third, given the right structural opportunities, there is no necessary contradiction for an opposition between pursuing electoral victory and enhancing the contribution of parliament to democracy while still in opposition. The scrutiny and legislative successes of Labor (in combination with the crossbench) when in opposition between 1988 and 1995, followed by Labor's 1995 narrow election victory, is probably the best example of this; however, most subsequent oppositions have combined playing to the electorate and engaging with parliamentary processes to produce better legislation and more transparent government.

Finally, this chapter suggests that despite the structural disadvantages of NSW opposition, agency remains an important factor. The more rapid success of the Labor Opposition of 1988 to 1995 compared with its Coalition and Labor successors cannot be explained by differences in their structural situations. As Ionescu and De Madiagara (134) write: "A lot depends on [an Opposition's] own will . . . the skill, ingenuity and tenacity displayed by political leaders or parties, starting from what has always been an unfavourable position".

References

Abjorensen, N., *Leadership and the Liberal Revival: Bolte, Askin and the Post-War Ascendancy*, Kew: Australian Scholarly Press, 2007

Birch, A., *Representative and Responsible Government*, London: Allen and Unwin, 1964

Chaples, E., Nelson, H., and Turner, K., (eds), *The Wran Model: Electoral Politics in New South Wales 1981 and 1984*, Melbourne: Oxford University Press, 1985

Chaples, E., and Page, B., "The New South Wales Independent Commission Against Corruption", in Laffin, M., and Painter, M., (eds), *Reform and Reversal: Lessons from the Coalition Government in New South Wales 1988-1995*, Melbourne: Macmillan, 1995, 55-72

Chase, S., *You Didn't Get it from Me: A Reporter's Account of Political Life in New South Wales from 1988-2001*, Sydney: ABC Books, 2006

Clifford, E., Green, A., and Clune, D., (eds), *The Electoral Atlas of New South Wales, 1856-2006*, Bathurst: New South Wales Department of Lands, 2006

Clune, D., "1953", in Hogan, M., and Clune, D., (eds), *The People's Choice: Electoral Politics in Twentieth Century New South Wales, Volume Two 1930 to 1965*, Sydney: Parliament of New South Wales and University of Sydney, 2001, 297-322

Clune, D., *Connecting with the People: The 1978 Reconstitution of the Legislative Council*, Sydney: Legislative Council of NSW, 2017a

Clune, D., *The Legislative Council and Responsible Government: Egan v Willis and Egan v Chadwick*, Sydney: Parliament of New South Wales, 2017b

Clune, D., "The Legislative Council of NSW: A Progressive Conservative Institution", in Ergas, H., and Pincus, J., (eds), *Power, Parliament and Politics: Essays in Honour of JR Nethercote*, Redland Bay: Connor Court Publishing, 2022, 185-205

Clune, D., and Griffith, G., *Decision and Deliberation: The Parliament of New South Wales, 1856-2003*, Leichhardt: The Federation Press, 2006

Clune, D., and Smith, R., "Back to the 1950s: the 2019 NSW Election", *Australasian Parliamentary Review*, 34(1), Autumn/Winter 2019, 86-101

Collins, P., *The Bear Pit: A Life in Politics*, Sydney: Allen and Unwin 2000

Cumming, F., *Mates: Five Champions of the Labor Right*, North Sydney: Allen and Unwin, 1991

Dale, B., *Ascent to Power: Wran and the Media*, Sydney: Allen and Unwin, 1985

Department of the Legislative Council, *Annual Report 2022*, Sydney: Parliament of New South Wales, 2022

Dodkin, M., *Bob Carr: The Reluctant Leader*, Sydney: UNSW Press, 2003

Davey, P., *The Nationals: The Progressive, Country and National Party in New South Wales 1919 to 2006*, Leichhardt: The Federation Press, 2006

Evans, J., "State of Play in the NSW Legislative Council: Minorities in Upper Houses", *Legislative Studies*, 11(2), 1997, 46-50

Evatt, H., *Australian Labour Leader: The Story of W.A. Holman and the Labour Movement*, Sydney: Angus and Robertson, 1940

Fletcher, N., (ed), *How to Be in Opposition: Life in the Political Shadows*, London: Biteback, 2011

Funnell, W., and Cooper, K., *Public Sector Accounting and Accountability in Australia*, Kensington: UNSW Press, 1998

Gleeson, M., Allan, T., and Wilkins, M., *An Act of Corruption? Nick Greiner's Years in Power and His Unorthodox Demise*, Sydney: ABC Books, 1992

Green, A., "The Results", in Clune D., and Smith R., (eds), *From Carr to Keneally: Labor in Office in NSW 1995-2011*, Sydney: Allen and Unwin, 2012, 282-97

Hagan, J. and Clothier, C., "The 1988 Election", in Hogan, M., and Clune, D., (eds), *The People's Choice: Electoral Politics in Twentieth Century New South Wales*, Volume Three 1968 to 1999, Sydney: Parliament of New South Wales and University of Sydney, 2001, 251-81

Hagan, J. and Turner, K., *A History of the Labor Party in New South Wales 1891-1991*, Melbourne: Longman Cheshire, 1991

Hancock, I., *The Liberals: A History of the NSW Division of the Liberal Party of Australia, 1945-2000*, Leichhardt: The Federation Press, 2007

Hancock, I., *Nick Greiner: A Political Biography*, Ballan: Connor Court, 2013

Hart, J., "An Australian President? A Comparative Perspective", in Weller, P., (ed.), *Menzies to Keating: The Development of the Australian Prime Ministership*, Carlton: Melbourne University Press, 1992, 183-201

Hawker, G., *The Parliament of New South Wales 1856-1965*, Ultimo: NSW Government Printer, 1971

Ionescu, G., and de Madariaga, I., *Opposition: The Past and Present of a Political Institution*, Harmondsworth: Penguin, 1972

Legislative Assembly, *Standing Rules and Orders* Sydney: Parliament of New South Wales, 1976

Legislative Assembly, *Standing Rules and Orders*, Sydney: Parliament of New South Wales, 1994

Legislative Assembly, *Standing Rules and Orders*, Sydney: Parliament of New South Wales, 2009

Legislative Assembly, *Annual Report 2021-2022*, Sydney: Parliament of New South Wales, 2022

Legislative Assembly, *Standing Rules and Orders*, Sydney: Parliament of New South Wales, 2023

Legislative Council, *Standing Rules and Orders*, Sydney: Parliament of New South Wales, 2004

Legislative Council, *Standing Rules and Orders*, Sydney: Parliament of New South Wales, 2022

Lovelock, L., "The Power of the New South Wales Legislative Council to Order the Production of State Papers: Revisiting the Egan Decisions Ten Years On", *Australasian Parliamentary Review*, 24(2), 2009, 197-218

McHenry, D., "Formal Recognition of the Leader of the Opposition in Parliaments of the British Commonwealth", *Political Science Quarterly*, 69(3), 1954, 438-52

Mihaljek, K., "Fifty Shades of Grey(Hounds): The Extent of the NSW Legislative Council's Power to Order Papers from Organisations Not in the Control of a Minister", *Australasian Parliamentary Review* 32(1), 2017, 74-91

Moon, J., and Sayers, A., "The Dynamics of Governmental Activity: A Long-Run Analysis of the Changing Scope and Profile of Australian Ministerial Portfolios", *Australian Journal of Political Science*, 34(2), 1999, 149-168

NSW Independent Commission Against Corruption, *Investigation into Parliamentary and Electorate Travel: First Report*, Sydney: Independent Commission Against Corruption, Sydney, April 1998

Page, B., "Developments in the Legislative Council of New South Wales Since 1978", *Legislative Studies*, 5(2), 1991, 23-31

Park, S., McGuinness, K., Fisher, C., Lee, J.Y., McCallum, K. and Nolan, D., *Digital News Report: Australia 2022*, Canberra: University of Canberra, 2022.

Parker, R., *The Government of New South Wales*, St Lucia: University of Queensland Press, 1978

Parliament of New South Wales, "Opposition Shadow Ministries from 1973". Available at: http://www.parliament.nsw.gov.au/prod/web/common.nsf/key/OppositionShadowMinistriesfrom1973 no date a

Parliament of New South Wales, "Salaries and Allowances for Members". Available at: https://www.parliament.nsw.gov.au/members/Pages/salaries-and-allowances-for-members.aspx no date b

Parliament of New South Wales, "Committees", available at https://www.parliament.nsw.gov.au/committees/listofcommittees/pages/committees.aspx no date c

Parliament of New South Wales, "Budget Estimates", available at https://www.parliament.nsw.gov.au/committees/Pages/budget-estimates.aspx no date d

Parliament of New South Wales, "Appointment of Mr John Barilaro as Senior Trade and Investment Commissioner to the Americas", available at https://www.parliament.nsw.gov.au/committees/inquiries/Pages/inquiry-details.aspx?pk=2891 no date e

Parr, E., "'Good' Information and Two Parliamentary Libraries", in Cope, R. (ed.), *Government and Parliament: Information Issues in the 1990's*, Sydney: The School of Information, Library and Archive Studies, The University of New South Wales, 1995

Rozzoli, K., *Gavel to Gavel: An Insider's View of Parliament*, Sydney: UNSW Press, 2006

Smith, R., "Parliament", in Laffin, M., and Painter, M., (eds), *Reform and Reversal: Lessons from the Coalition Government in New South Wales 1988-1995*, Melbourne: Macmillan, 1995, 22-39

Smith, R., "The Australian Democrats in NSW Politics", in Warhurst, J., (ed.), *Keeping the Bastards Honest: The Australian Democrats' First Twenty Years*, North Sydney: Allen and Unwin, 1997, 213-33

Smith, R., "Australian Solitudes: Citizens, Parliamentary Party Politics, Corruption Agencies and Political Ethics", *Legislative Studies*, 14(1), Spring 1999, 36-46

Smith, R., "1999", in Hogan, M., and Clune, D., (eds), *The People's Choice: Electoral Politics in 20th Century New South Wales*, Volume Three 1968 to 1999, Sydney: Parliament of New South Wales and University of Sydney, 2001, 369-413

Smith, R., "New South Wales", in Moon, J., and Sharman, C., (eds), *Australian Politics and Government*, Cambridge: Cambridge University Press, 2003, 41-73

Smith, R., "Mapping the New South Wales Public Integrity System", *Australian Journal of Public Administration*, 64(2), 2005, 54-61

Smith, R., *Against the Machines: Minor Parties and Independents in New South Wales 1910-2006*, Leichhardt: The Federation Press, 2006

Smith, R., "Peter Ross Sinclair", in Clune D., and Turner, K., (eds), *The New South Wales Governors*, Leichhardt: The Federation Press, 2009, 587-602

Smith, R., "The Liberal Party", in Clune D., and Smith, R., (eds), *From Carr to Keneally: Labor in Office in NSW 1995-2011*, Sydney: Allen and Unwin, 2012, 15-26

Smith, R., "Parliament", in Clune, D., and Smith, R., (eds), *From Carr to Keneally: Labor in Office in NSW 1995-2011*, Sydney: Allen and Unwin, 2012, 55-71

Steketee, M., and Cockburn, M., *Wran: An Unauthorised Biography*, North Sydney: Allen and Unwin, 1986

Strangio, P., 't Hart, P., and Walter, J., *The Pivot of Power: Australian Prime Ministers and Political Leadership 1946-2016*, Melbourne: Miegunyah Press, 2017

Thompson, E., "The New South Wales Parliament, 1978-81", in Chaples, E., Nelson, H., and Turner, K., (eds), *The Wran Model: Electoral Politics in New South Wales 1981 and 1984,* Melbourne: Oxford University Press, 1985, 69-78

Thompson, E., and Tillotsen, G., "Caught in the Act: The Smoking Gun View of Ministerial Responsibility", *Australian Journal of Public Administration*, 58(1), 1999, 48-57

Turner, K., (eds), *The Wran Model: Electoral Politics in New South Wales 1981 and 1984*, Melbourne: Oxford University Press, 1985, 69-78

Turner, K., *House of Review? The New South Wales Legislative Council, 1934-68*, Sydney: Sydney University Press, 1969

Twomey, A., *The Constitution of New South Wales*, Annandale: The Federation Press, 2004

Twomey, A., "Executive Accountability to the Australian Senate and the New South Wales Legislative Council", *Australasian Parliamentary Review*, 23(1), 2008, 257-273

Want, S., Moore, J., and Blunt, D., *Annotated Standing Orders of the New South Wales Legislative Council*, Sydney The Federation Press, 2018

West, A., and Morris, R., *Bob Carr: A Self-Made Man*, Sydney: Harper Collins, 2003

West, K., *Power in the Liberal Party: A Study in Australian Politics*, Melbourne: Cheshire, 1965

10

Parliamentary Oppositions in Queensland, 1860-2023

Paul D. Williams

Introduction

Well-resourced parliamentary oppositions are essential to any Westminster polity laying claim to democratic heritage. But opposition parties and the role they play at state and territory level are often covered superficially in the Australian news media, and have certainly been under-analysed in the Australian scholarly literature. For reasons explored below, this is especially the case in Queensland. This chapter aims to correct this oversight by exploring the types, roles and conditions shaping Queensland oppositions and their leaders since 1860. In so doing, several research questions emerge: Are oppositions in Queensland different from those in other states and territories? Why have oppositions found themselves especially constrained in Queensland? What has caused defeated parties to languish for decades on Queensland's opposition benches, and what does it take for oppositions to "break through" to government? I offer six arguments: first, oppositions in Queensland are indeed different from those of any other in Australia; second, those differences are borne of a unique political culture underpinned by a peculiar geography, economy and demography; third, key institutional differences, such as Queensland's unicameralism and a (now defunct) system of electoral malapportionment, have helped marginalise successive oppositions; fourth, marginalisation often fractures opposition parties which, in turn, further hampers electoral success; fifth, these factors allow governments to occupy the Treasury benches for decades on end (with little or no interruption) to effectively create electoral hegemonies[1]; and, last, oppositions tend to win in Queensland only when calamitous economic or political events disrupt a government's hegemony.

Method

This chapter employs several methods. The first is the construction of a theoretical framework that anatomises Queensland's populist political culture and offers causes behind long-enduring governments and often-diminished oppositions. A second is the identification of the themes, patterns and principal characteristics of Queensland oppositions since 1860, with a view to determining the forces shaping oppositions over 160 years. Third, the chapter adopts periodisation as a method of historiography before identifying ten distinct phases in the evolution of oppositions in Queensland. While periodisation in the writing of history can be both "limited" (Friedman 2019: 398) and "arbitrary" (Guillaume 2021: 564), the method remains useful because "cultures and social groups did and do fix the boundaries between past, present and future in different ways" (Lorenz 2017: 110). Ultimately, as Green (1993: 13) argues, "[s]cholars assert that history constitutes a seamless garment, but they cannot render the past intelligible until they subdivide it into manageable and coherent units of time". The chapter concludes with discussion of the factors that have allowed oppositions in Queensland to make that uncommon move to the government benches.

Queensland's political culture

Politics in Queensland can be properly understood only through the lens of the state's unique political culture - one cultivated via local geographic, economic, demographic and institutional differences that, in turn, have shaped the way Queenslanders 'think' and 'do' politics, from the rhetoric leaders use to the way policy is made to the vote choices Queenslanders make. This Queensland "difference" has long been acknowledged (Murphy 1978; McQueen 1979; Charlton 1983), with numerous studies identifying "populism" as the core element of Queensland's political culture – a conclusion drawn from the state's agrarian industries and decentralised population cultivating among leaders and voters a deep suspicion of "elites" and "outsiders" (Walter and Dickie 1985; Mullin 1986: 132-62; Stokes 2000; Williams 2009; Williams 2011a).

Populism in Queensland further adapted to local conditions to become a unique local variety comprising five core elements: voters' reverence for strong, avuncular leadership; a pragmatism in policy development and delivery that too often sees compromised accountability; an emphasis on state development, especially the building of infrastructure; a focus on developing that infrastructure in regional and rural Queensland where the bulk of state budgets are expended; and a state parochialism that, in cultivating a sense of moral superiority over other Australians, contributes significantly to a perceived "Queensland exceptionalism" (Williams 2009; Bleakley 2022).

Critically, these unwritten rules of "doing" politics have applied not only to premiers and their governments but also to oppositions hoping to engage meaningfully with electorates sensitive to parochial values. To win the confidence of a majority of voters, oppositions have also found it necessary to appeal not to abstract political ideas but to lowest common denominators. Indeed, Colin Hughes (1980: 5) described the concerns of Queenslanders as "the politics of development, concerned with things and places and not people and ideas", that is, a concern for the material progress of roads, bridges, police stations, schools, hospitals and dams. In an economy dominated by regionally-based primary industries, and where residents are acclimatised to authoritative leadership (and not drawn-out public consultation) to quickly facilitate much-needed infrastructural development, the root source of such appeals is clear. With a harsh climate and rugged terrain, it is also easy to understand how a tough "pioneer" mentality evolved, and how a unique "country-mindedness" (Aitkin 1985) allowed Queenslanders to feel separate from, and superior to, other Australians. This bucolic mindset, where parochialism and regionalism subsumed globalism and centralism, also forged cultural prejudices in Queensland – a state that, even in the 2020s, is still home to more residents living outside the capital city than within it. In that sense, Brisbane has never dominated the state as Sydney and Melbourne have dominated New South Wales and Victoria. Indeed, north Queensland has long regarded not only Canberra but Brisbane as "southern" and, therefore, worthy of suspicion. Strains of anti-intellectualism and sexism – derived from lower levels of completed tertiary education – have also contributed to a masculine, blue-collar political culture, with threads of racism, borne of below-average levels of migration, also present (Williams 2023a; Williams 2023b).

There is little doubt these traits are generally more pronounced in regions outside the capital, which explains why far-right populist candidates can win Legislative Assembly seats in regional Queensland but not in Brisbane City. Indeed, scholars have historically described "two Queenslands": the southeast in and around Brisbane where more progressive social attitudes have much in common with southern capitals, and a western and northern Queensland where more conservative behaviours are recorded (Mackerras 1973: 238; Holmes 1994; Kraaier 2018). Distance explains much of this phenomenon when one remembers Brisbane is farther from Cairns than it is from Melbourne. But my research has found not two but six distinct Queenslands, each with its own unique geographic and economic characteristics, and each making unique vote choices (Williams 2018a; Williams 2023b). Oppositions failing to acknowledge regional differences do so at their peril.

The power of rural and regional identity therefore cannot be overstated in Queensland politics for either governments or oppositions, and it is the state's historically agrarian character – and its significantly smaller manufacturing and professional middle classes – that inverted a party structure typical in southern states. In Queensland for most of the 20th century, the Country (later National) Party won a greater share of parliamentary seats (but often fewer votes) than the Liberals and, therefore, assumed senior partner status in successive coalitions in both government and opposition. The resulting tension between the two parties - and between the Queensland and the federal Coalition parties, as demonstrated during the 1987 "Joh for PM" campaign (Davey 2015) – was often palpable but unsurprising in a state comprised of two very different non-Labor constituencies. Even when enjoying healthy parliamentary representation, the Liberals were relegated to virtual insignificance within cabinet and shadow cabinet and, between the 11 years and four election campaigns between 1983 and 1992 – the Liberals were excluded altogether. Despite re-uniting in 1993 under Nationals leader Rob Borbidge and Liberal leader Joan Sheldon – and forming minority government between 1996 and 1998 – Coalition precariousness still haunted the National and Liberal parties. This came to a head during the 2006 Queensland election campaign when newly-installed Liberal leader Dr Bruce Flegg conceded that, even if the Liberals won more seats than the Nationals, Nationals leader Lawrence Springborg would become the State's premier (Koch 2016).

The Labor Party in Queensland, too, enjoyed a different history. Where working class consciousness in New South Wales developed strongly in the inner suburbs of Sydney and among workers in rural districts (Clune 1984), Labor in Queensland found its strongest base almost exclusively among rural farm workers and regional miners (Fitzgerald 1982: 151, 176; McMullin 1991: 6-7; Williams 2023a: 262). Indeed, the "Tree of Knowledge" in rural Barcaldine, 900 km north-west of Brisbane, still marks the Labor Party's birth after pastoral workers had failed to win improved conditions via strikes. Interestingly, even early regional Labor organisers mistrusted their Brisbane counterparts – the "Brisbane junta" – for its attempted "centralization of authority" (Dalton 1970: 5).

Patterns in Queensland opposition politics

Several interconnected patterns shaping opposition politics in Queensland can be identified. The first is that governments often remain in office for such excessively long periods that "hegemonies" - or "natural parties of government" – emerge which, in turn, marginalise oppositions in voters' cognisance. The Ministerialists constituted the first hegemony when the liberal Samuel Griffith forged a coalition with his conservative rival Thomas McIllwraith in 1890 to form the "Griffillwraith" Continuous Ministry. With McIllwraith already twice serving as premier and Griffith once, the Continuous Ministry dominated the Legislative Assembly for 13 years, with a smattering of Labor MPs and a few liberal dissidents (the "Remnant") offering the only opposition (Hughes 1980: 13-14; Beanland 2013: 250-51). Following a decade of non-hegemonic volatility during which the major parties found modern form, a second hegemony can be identified in the 42 years Labor governed between 1915 and 1957 (with a single term of non-Labor rule, 1929-32). A third hegemony is found in the 32 years of uninterrupted Coalition (and later National Party alone) governments between 1957 and 1989, while a fourth is found in the 35 years of Labor governments between 1989 and 2024 punctuated by two, single-term conservative administrations (1996-98 and 2012-15). Clearly, elections in Queensland confirm governments in power and rarely change them (Reynolds 2010: 160).

Table 1: Parliamentary and electoral hegemonies in Queensland, 1890-2024

Hegemony	Party	Years	Interruptions	Premiers
First	Ministerialists	1890-1903	1899 (Dawson - Labor)	Griffith, McIllwraith, Nelson, Byrnes, Dickson, Philp
Second	Labor	1915-1957	1929-32 (Moore - Country and Progressive National Party)	Ryan, Theodore, Gillies, McCormack, Forgan-Smith, Cooper, Hanlon, Gair
Third	Country (later National)-Liberal; later National alone	1957-1989	None	Nicklin, Pizzey, Chalk, Bjelke-Petersen, Ahern, Cooper
Fourth	Labor	1989-2024	1996-98 (Borbidge-National-Liberal); 2012-15 (Newman - LNP)	Goss, Beattie, Bligh, Palaszczuk, Miles

A related trait is that governments often win – and maintain over many years – enormous parliamentary majorities: a phenomenon assisted between the 1940s and the 1980s by a zonal system of electoral malapportionment that over-represented rural seats to initially benefit Labor and, later, the Country (National) Party, but never the Liberals (Reynolds 1990; Wear 1990). Appendix Two notes that Campbell Newman's Liberal-National Party (LNP) won 88 per cent of the Legislative Assembly seats in 2012 (Australia's largest parliamentary majority to that point), with Joh Bjelke-Petersen's Coalition winning 85 per cent in 1974. Similarly, Labor's William Forgan-Smith and Peter Beattie each attained 74 per cent of the Assembly in 1935 and 2001 respectively. The corollary is that oppositions often netted tiny seat shares despite much larger primary vote totals. In 2012, for example, Labor won just eight per cent of the seats despite attracting more than a quarter of the state's support while, in 1974, the party won just 13 per cent of the seats despite attracting more than a third of the vote.

A third characteristic has been the substantial presence of minor party and non-aligned independent MPs in the Legislative Assembly, even after the formalisation of oppositions in 1898 and the crystallisation of the modern binary party system in the early 1910s. In fact, Australia's only Communist Party MP, Fred Paterson, represented regional Bowen between 1944 and 1950. Only in a few recent parliaments (1977-80; 1980-83; 1986-89; 1989-92; 1992-95) was the Legislative Assembly comprised of only Labor, Liberal and National MPs. More recently, major party hegemony has been challenged by Pauline Hanson's One Nation (PHON), which won 11 seats in 1998, and by Katter's Australian Party and the Queensland Greens which, after the 2020 election, held three and two seats respectively. Independents have also featured prominently in recent hung Queensland parliaments: Liz Cunningham (Gladstone) held the balance of power for most of the 48th Parliament (1996-98), with Peter Wellington (Nicklin) sharing the balance of power for part of the 49th (1998) and for the entire 55th Parliament. The effect of a substantial crossbench in successive parliaments has seen anti-government forces rarely speak with one voice.

The propensity for oppositions to learn the styles, strategies and tactics from their governing opponents comprises a fourth pattern – one especially pronounced in the 19th century when, in absence of party organisations, parliamentarians received little formal guidance. Yet this practice continued into modern times. Despite ostensibly championing democratic socialism, William Forgan-Smith, for example, adopted the agrarian conservatism of his predecessors, while Joh Bjelke-Petersen assumed the almost ruthless attitude toward Labor oppositions that Labor governments had shown him (Williams 2009). LNP Premier Campbell Newman was similarly accused of treating the Labor opposition with disdain when, in 2012, he moved its seven Labor MPs from Parliament House to offices several blocks from the parliamentary precinct (Williams 2018b).

A fifth pattern is found in the institutional impediments, unique to Queensland, that have made parliamentary life difficult for opposition parties. The first, and arguably the most recognisable distinction separating Queensland's parliament from those of other states, is unicameralism. With scores of Labor bills savaged by the conservative and unelected Legislative Council, Labor Premier T.J. Ryan held a referendum in 1917 to abolish the Legislative Council. The referendum failed, and Ryan's successor, Ted Theodore, was sufficiently frustrated to "swamp" the Legislative Council in 1922 with new appointees who soon voted to dissolve their own chamber (Evans 2007: 164; Williams 2022). The long-term effect was profound: both Labor and conservative governments, free of upper house scrutiny, would now engage in authoritarian and corrupt behaviour over the next seven decades.

A second institutionalised impediment has been successive governments' manipulation of the electoral system for political advantage. In 1893, for example, the liberal-conservative government, fearful of an emerging Labor Party, changed the first-past-the-post (FPTP) method (employed since 1860) to a "contingent" (optional preferential) method where non-Labor support could be coalesced. Labor reverted back to a FPTP system in time for the 1944 election at which Labor faced both the Country Party and Queensland People's (later Liberal) Party. The Nicklin Coalition then moved to compulsory preferential voting (CPV) in 1962 to ensure the National and Liberal parties enjoyed the full benefit of preference exchanges, with the Goss Labor Government introducing Optional Preferential Voting in 1992 on the recommendation of the Fitzgerald-inspired Electoral and Administrative Review Commission. Interestingly, the LNP Opposition criticised the Palaszczuk Government in 2016 when, during the Second Reading debate on legislation to hold a referendum to increase the parliamentary term to four years, Labor attached (with just 18 minutes' notice) an amendment to return Queensland to CPV (Williams 2016: 631).

After the 1929 election, the merged Country and Progressive National party (CPNP) Moore Government thwarted the opposition with an unfavourable electoral redistribution. This paled in comparison with the Hanlon Labor Government's 1949 zonal system of electoral malapportionment – the widely despised instrument partly responsible for the parliamentary "lopsidedness" that maximised Labor support while minimising that of the Country and Liberal parties' seat share. The tables were turned in 1958 when the new Country-Liberal Coalition Government introduced its own zonal system, one refined to enormous Country Party advantage (at the expense of both the Liberal and Labor parties), and further so at subsequent redistributions in 1971, 1977 and 1985. Other factors, such as weak leadership, internal factionalism, trade union links and policy platforms unpalatable to a burgeoning middle class, also kept Labor from office. Indeed, Labor before 1989 never attracted a sufficient vote to win a majority of seats even under one-vote, one-value terms.

A third impediment has been the near total control by governments over the Legislative Assembly. While there have been parliamentary committees, for example, since the first Queensland parliament (1860-63), their mundane briefs – library and refreshment rooms, standing orders and privileges – meant committees until the post-Fitzgerald reforms of the late 1980s were never instruments of government accountability (Wanna and Arklay 2010: 23-24). Indeed, the Standing Orders Committee did not even meet between 1962 and 1982 (Coaldrake 1989: 59).

Even after subordinate legislation committees were introduced in 1975, scrutiny of government was negligible; the Legislative Assembly still resembled the "sausage machine" it had been since 1922 where bills entered at one end of the parliament and legislation emerged, quickly and virtually unchanged, at the other (Bernays 1931: 209; Fitzgerald 1984: 27). Executive control also extended to numerous Speakers of the Legislative Assembly who eagerly deferred to government interests. One egregious example is found in Selwyn Muller's 1979 assertion that his role as Speaker was to "apply the wishes of the government he represented" (Morley 2008). Indeed, of the 41 MPs suspended (for up to 14 days) from parliament between 1957 and 1989, all but two were Labor (Wanna and Arklay 2010: 497-98). Executive control even extended to the parliamentary mace. When first presented to the Parliament in 1978, the mace's inscription read "Government of Queensland", a misnomer not corrected till the Goss Government new inscription of "Parliament of Queensland" (Wanna and Arklay 2010: 21). Moreover, *Questions Without Notice* during Question Time were not permitted until 1970 (Wanna and Arklay 2010: 199). In what appears to have been a lack of comprehension of the due constitutional role of Her / His Majesty's Loyal Opposition, successive governments often showed unabashed contempt for those on the left of the Speaker, and frequently denied opposition parties adequate resources such as staff and office space. Few and infrequent parliamentary sitting days also curtailed oppositions' opportunities to hold governments accountable, with the 1983 parliamentary year, which saw just 14 sitting days, marking a low-point (QPD 22 November, 1983: 9).

A sixth pattern is what Paul Reynolds (2010: 5) describes as "Connectional Politics" – the propensity for informal power networks to emerge, with government patronage (via such ministries as Public Works, Housing, and Main Roads) delivering infrastructure to electorally sensitive (and ideally appreciative) constituencies, especially in regional Queensland. It also created a path for local councillors to enter the Legislative Assembly via the parties' networked pre-selection processes. It is self-evident that connectional politics significantly hindered opposition inroads into established power structures.

The prosaic nature of election issues in Queensland constitutes a seventh pattern. Consistent with a bipartisan commitment to (especially regional) economic development, campaigns have largely been "bread and butter" affairs (Hughes 1970: 54-5), with electoral contests resembling auctions between parties over infrastructure, irrigation, roads, hospitals, schools, and law and order. Queensland's emphasis on strong leadership has also seen campaigns develop into quasi-presidential contests, with National Party campaigns under Joh Bjelke-Petersen especially indicative (Lunn 1984; Wear 2002).

The above created a ninth pattern: frustrated oppositions beset by leadership tensions, internal dissent and open factionalism which, in turn, diminished electoral appeal. For example, rivalries between the liberals and conservatives were put aside in the last decade of the 19th century, but spilled over in the first decade of the 20th. After often testy coalitions, the non-Labor parties merged into the single CPNP in 1925, but split again in 1936 after successive election defeats. After two more losses, the parties attempted a second merger into the Country National Party (CNP) – with a dissident Queensland Country continuing to operate separately in western Queensland – in 1941. After losing yet another state election, the CNP again split in 1944 into the Country Party and a new Queensland People's (later Liberal) Party (Cribb 1983). Even after returning to government in 1957, the often more progressive urban Liberals feuded with the rurally conservative Country (National) Party, with Liberals especially divided over how to deal with the autocratic Joh Bjelke-Petersen (1968-87). Indeed, when Bjelke-Petersen dissolved the Coalition in 1983 after a Liberal "ginger" group supported a Labor move to establish a Public Accounts Committee – a proposal vehemently rejected by Bjelke-Petersen – the Liberals remained out of government for another 13 years (Walter 1990: 504). In more recent times the merged and ostensibly united LNP has also suffered tensions over such issues as daylight saving and whether infrastructure expenditure or debt-servicing should be an LNP government's priority (Williams 2018b).

Labor, too, has fallen foul of factionalism. During its earliest years in the 1890s, Labor fought internal ideological battles as to whether the party was socialist or merely the reformist parliamentary wing of industrial trade unions (Dalton 1970: 3-5). And while Queensland Labor managed to avoid the splits of 1917 and 1931 – over conscription and depression-induced economic recovery respectively - that so damaged other state parties, it could not survive the 1957 split – ostensibly over industrial relations but, in reality, over attitudes towards communism – that saw Premier Vince Gair take 25 Labor MPs out of caucus to form a rival Queensland Labor Party. Labor was heavily defeated at the following election and its factionalism – fuelled by ongoing battles between the Australian Workers' Union and the Trades and Labor Council for control of the party (Fitzgerald 1984: 220-21) – helped keep Labor out of office for another 32 years. Federal intervention in 1980 and a subsequently organised power-sharing "consociational" factional system (with party positions apportioned by a proportional representation vote) have since mitigated internecine warfare (Wanna 2000). But rivalry between the Labor Forum (AWU), Labor Unity (Old Guard) and Left factions was evident well into the 21st century.

The last identifiable theme is the propensity for Queensland oppositions to seize government only when major economic or political crises have beset incumbent governments. As discussed below, the Denham Liberal Government decayed after the 1912 General Strike, while the McCormack Labor Government came to grief over the *Mungana* mine corruption scandal (also involving former Premier and Federal Treasurer Ted Theodore) in 1929. Similarly, Labor's first hegemony ended when the party split in 1957, while the Nationals' rule came to an end when, in 1989, Royal Commissioner Tony Fitzgerald exposed wide and longstanding corruption stretching from police ranks to cabinet ministers. Critically, Labor's reign was interrupted in 2012 after voters felt Premier Anna Bligh had misled them over the sale of state assets – a touchstone of economic faith in Queensland – an issue which also ended the LNP Newman Government in 2015 (Williams 2018b).

The evolution of the Queensland opposition

Parliamentary oppositions in Queensland today are hardly the same species as those sitting to the left of the Speaker in the 19th century. While opposition to executives and government policy certainly existed from 1860, it was only in 1898, with Labor's Thomas Glassey, that a formal Leader of the Opposition emerged. In 1909, an additional salary was assigned to the role and, since 1898, 37 individuals – 35 men and two women – have served as the Leader of His or Her Majesty's Loyal Opposition. One served on four separate occasions, one on three, and four leaders have served twice.

For more than a century, opposition leaders had been MPs, and had been elected by fellow MPs in their respective party rooms. But tradition was broken in 2011 when Campbell Newman – the popular Lord Mayor of Brisbane (Australia's largest local government authority) – was elected LNP leader without holding a seat in parliament.[2] After the unpopular Labor Premier Anna Bligh received a public opinion boost in the wake of her government's widely approved handling of the Queensland floods (2010-11), LNP chieftains convinced opposition leader John-Paul Langbroek to step down in Newman's favour (Wardill 2011). Interestingly, while Newman immediately became Queensland's *de facto* opposition leader for campaign and news media purposes, former Nationals leader Jeff Seeney served as the "interim" or *de jure* opposition leader inside the Parliament until the 2012 election (Williams 2011b). In 2014, tradition would again be broken when Queensland Labor's organisational wing, mirroring leadership rule changes in the federal Labor Party, broadened leadership ballots beyond the party room to also include grass roots members and affiliated trade unions, with each base comprising a third of the elective power (Fraser 2014).

Periodising the Queensland opposition

As outlined above, the evolution of parliamentary oppositions in Queensland can be plotted across ten distinct phases, described below.

Pre-Ministerialist: 1860-90

In the first phase after separation from New South Wales and the granting of full responsible government in 1859, *"pre-Ministerialist"* oppositions comprised loose groupings of MPs fleetingly aligned in opposition to government policy on an *ad hoc* basis. Long before organised political parties, and in the absence of strong ideological cleavages, MPs in this period – overwhelmingly mature, wealthy male farmers – were largely homogenous in composition; divergence of interest was found only among types of primary industry and the specific demands of local constituents. Opposition to government therefore evolved from urban and rural, and northern and southern, economic rivalries. Moreover, a lack of organisation meant governments could easily escape rigorous scrutiny, with the earliest ministers requiring little political acumen and even less parliamentary skill (Joyce 1990a: 9-43). More substantial opposition emerged towards the end of the period, however, and the most notable battles occurred between the two political giants of the age: the conservative Premier Thomas McIlwraith and his liberal rival, Samuel Griffith.

Ministerialist: 1890-98

A new phase in opposition politics began in 1890 when Premier Morehead (1888-90) proposed an unpopular property tax. In a vein typical of Queensland politics, the wealthy McIlwraith and Griffith allowed pragmatism to override difference, and the two joined forces to defeat Morehead by forming a coalition government colloquially labelled the

"Griffillwraith" coalition. The McIlwraith-Griffith alliance thus formed the initial phase of the eminently successful "continuous ministry" that survived, under successive premiers, until 1903 (Hughes 1980: 13-14). The implications for opposition politics are self-evident: the combined liberal-conservative forces almost wholly dominated the parliament and ensured their own survival by steadily promoting potential rivals into their own ministerial ranks. A small group of disaffected liberals who refused to support the new arrangement, known as the "Remnant", became a *de jure* opposition (Joyce 1990b; Waterson 1990). Yet this phase remains critical as it also saw the birth of a party system and, with it, the emergence in 1891 of the Australian Labor Party.

From 1891, a multi-party system would thus exist, offering a more organised, albeit restrained, opposition voice. Elections from 1893 were contested under party labels, and electoral returns only underscore the parliamentary lopsidedness of the day. After the 1893 election, for example, the ruling Ministerialists claimed 42 of the 72 Legislative Assembly seats (until 1907, 22 were dual member constituencies), while only seven "opposition" candidates were returned. Labor enjoyed relatively rapid progress, but still held just 16 seats in 1893, and only 20 by 1896. The Queensland Farmers' Union (amalgamating with the Liberals to form the Nationalists in 1917) and Independents comprised a small remainder (Campbell 1996).

Official Opposition (Multi-party): 1898-1908

The decade 1898-1908 saw the previous multi-party environment continue, with the Ministerialists in direct competition with "Oppositionists", Labor and, occasionally, a "Farmers" group. Yet the period remains distinctive because of the formal status now accorded to the Leader of the Opposition. Indeed, the vigorous flavour the first incumbent, Thomas Glassey, gave the position became a model for future leaders under which Queensland opposition politics would become increasingly combative. Importantly, this period also saw Glassey's successor, Anderson Dawson, lead the world's first Labor ministry, albeit for just a week in December 1899, after several Ministerialists crossed the floor to defeat a railways bill and, with it, the conservative Dickson Government. After modest gains in 1902, Labor secured 34 seats at the 1904 election. The following year, 1905, was key to Queensland politics: plural voting was abolished and universal suffrage established. In 1906, William Kidston formed a second minority Labor Government, but it was short-lived: the Labor Government fell in 1907 when Kidston, protesting Labor's "socialist objective", sided with the conservative Robert Philp (Fitzgerald, Megarrity and Symons 2007: 50).

Official Opposition, Two Party, Pre-Hegemony: 1908-15

The phase initiated by the Kidston-Philp alliance saw two important developments. First, the new Labor Opposition boasted just two leaders in seven years, thereby introducing degrees of stability and continuity. The first of these, the colourful David Bowman (1908-12), marked out a new level of public recognition for the Leader of the Opposition as he became something of a "household name" (Bernays 1919: 162). The second leader, T.J. Ryan (1912-15), made an even greater impression. A Brisbane-dwelling teacher-turned-lawyer who represented a rural seat, Ryan won support across the geographical, industrial and class divides with a middle-class professionalism and support for workers during the General Strike of 1912. Articulate, urbane and doggedly determined, Ryan forever changed the face of Queensland opposition politics (Johnston and Murphy 1988).

A second and more important development brought by the Kidston-Philp coalition was the emergence in 1908 of a two-party system. In 1909, the conservatives won 41 seats, and Labor 27. In 1912, the governing party, now branded the Liberals, won 46 seats to Labor's 25. The propensity for administrations to rise and fall between elections had now passed: from this point, Queensland would boast a modern binary system (notwithstanding later coalitions) mirroring the federal model, with the contrast between governments and oppositions coming into sharper focus.

The First Labor hegemony – pre-malapportionment: 1915-1949

The year 1915 saw Queensland allow women to stand for parliament, with the state becoming the first polity in the British Commonwealth to introduce compulsory enrolment and voting. The year also marks the beginning of the first Labor hegemony after Ryan crushed Denham's Liberals. Ryan had broken through as Leader of the Opposition by sewing together coalitions of hitherto disparate constituencies, especially among sugar cane farm owners and workers (Shogren 1980: 181-83). Opposition strategy of casting a wider net of electoral appeal was now entrenched. Yet Labor also owed its success to the initially popular program of establishing government-owned industries that ranged from an insurance company to hotels to butcher shops. A dispirited conservative opposition thereafter floundered, dissolved and reformed itself in various incarnations, including under the Nationalist (1917-20) and Queensland United Party (1923-24) labels. A separate Country Party, borne from earlier farmers' groups, was founded in 1920. The birth of this third party formalised the triangular character of Queensland party politics still evident today. But opposition leaders continued to arrive and depart with frequency, and included Edward Macartney (twice), William Vowles, Charles Taylor, and Arthur Moore, who became premier in 1929. For much of this period, Labor controlled two-thirds of the seats of the Legislative Assembly - an executive dominance magnified immeasurably after Labor's abolition of the Legislative Council in 1922.

Labor's hegemony was interrupted by CPNP's breakthrough at the 1929 election. Several factors allowed this to occur. First, Arthur Moore had begun his campaign a year before the poll was due. Second, Labor Premier William McCormack was an unpopular figure, even within his own party. Third, the brewing *Mungana* mining scandal implicating both Theodore and McCormack – later the focus of a Royal Commission – sullied Labor's credentials (Costar 1990: 382-83; Kennedy 1990: 369) and, fourth, the conservatives throughout the 1920s had successfully galvanised their forces. In 1921, for example, Northern Country Party MPs were absorbed into the official Country Party and, in 1925, the

United and Country parties created a new Country-Progressive Party. When the remaining conservatives joined a few months later, a new and united CPNP was born (Hughes 1980: 17).

Blamed for the Great Depression, the Moore Government also suffered increasing disunity before losing the 1932 election. But the passionate William Forgan-Smith, the new Labor Opposition leader, was also sufficiently hard-headed to forcibly unite a squabbling Labor Party while simultaneously shifting attention to the Moore Government and economic malaise. In pioneering yet another Queensland tradition, Forgan-Smith also extracted political capital from attacks on conservative Prime Minister Joe Lyons and the federal Coalition's tough measures for economic recovery (Carroll 1990: 405-06).

Labor won the next eight elections, and the CPNP Opposition retreated to virtual irrelevancy before reverting to its Country Party and United Australia Party (the latter renamed the Queensland People's Party in 1943, and the Liberal Party in 1949) elements in 1936. Even so, the period saw a new level of stability in the conservative opposition. After Ted Maher's unsuccessful term as Country Party leader (1936-41), Frank Nicklin's (1941-57) "calming influence" reset the opposition standard (Stevenson 1990: 475). Yet, in losing five elections before taking office in 1957, Nicklin – opposition leader for 16 years - also set a new benchmark for patient resilience. In the interim, Forgan-Smith's strong leadership and regional focus became a model not only for Labor successors Frank Cooper (1942-46), Ned Hanlon (1946-52) and Vince Gair (1952-57), but also for subsequent non-Labor premiers.

The First Labor hegemony – Malapportionment, 1949-57

This phase remains distinctive for Hanlon's introduction of a zonal electoral system (with electorates of unequal voter enrolments) which significantly disadvantaged the opposition. In 1956, for example, Labor won 65 per cent of the seats with 51.2 per cent of the vote, while the Opposition won 44.3 per cent of the vote but only one-third of the seats.

Opposition leader Nicklin knew the impossibility of his task when he said in 1955 that "it would take something of an electoral earthquake to bring about a change" (Stevenson 1990: 478). That seismic event arrived unexpectedly in 1956-57 when Premier Vince Gair refused a Labor Party Central Executive order to introduce three weeks' leave for State government employees (Fitzgerald, Megarrity and Symons 2009: 178). The Premier was expelled from the party and Gair, with the support of 25 MPs, formed a rival Queensland Labor Party (QLP) which, in 1962, merged with the Democratic Labor Party. The effects of the split were immediate. At the 1957 election, under a FPTP system, Labor won just 28.9 per cent of the vote and 20 seats; the rival QLP attracted a sizeable 23.4 per cent and won 11 seats. A unified opposition in the face of a fractured government had paid huge electoral dividends.

The Country (National)-Liberal hegemony: 1957-83

Like so many predecessors, Premier Nicklin combined strong leadership with an appeal to regional agrarianism. His popularity, the zonal electoral system and Labor's war with the QLP wholly marginalised the new opposition for more than a decade. But the new conservative hegemony was clearly assisted by three lacklustre opposition leaders in Leslie Wood (1957-58), James Donald (1958) and Jack Duggan (1958-66). The last opposition leader Nicklin faced, Jack Houston (1966-74), breathed some life back into Labor when, in 1966, he marshalled an informal shadow cabinet where frontbenchers would "look after" ministerial portfolios (Wanna and Arklay: 193). Before 1966, Labor tactics were organised by a "parliamentary executive" of five MPs; it was not until 1970 that Labor's shadow cabinet was formalised (Wanna and Arklay: 170; 193).

As uncompromising as previous premiers of both sides had been, few were prepared for the new level of contempt National Party leader Joh Bjelke-Petersen (1968-87) would show opponents. Parliamentary resources for the opposition remained scarce: while Bjelke-Petersen enjoyed the benefits of a taxpayer-funded private jet, opposition leaders were relegated to commercial flights (Wanna and Arklay: 494). It appears Bjelke-Petersen regarded Labor not as Her Majesty's Loyal Opposition – and therefore constitutionally entitled to resources to critique Her Majesty's Government – but instead as a personal foe and enemy of the people. Put simply, to oppose Bjelke-Petersen was to oppose Queensland, and even virtue itself.

The period also saw a tougher redistribution in 1971 that also expanded the Legislative Assembly to 82 seats. In 1974, Labor fell to a new low in representation of just 11 districts, with leader Perc Tucker (1974) losing his own seat. Tom Burns (1974-78) found some electoral traction to deliver 6.8 per cent primary swing in 1977 – when the Nationals' primary vote overtook the Liberals' for the first time – before Ed Casey's leadership (1978-82) saw a small swing back to the Coalition in 1980. Critically, civil opposition to the Bjelke-Petersen Government increased from the late 1970s, with Bjelke-Petersen responding in brutal kind: street marches were banned in 1977, "state emergencies" were declared to extend police powers over protestors (during the 1971 Springboks' rugby union tour, the 1982 Commonwealth Games, and the 1985 SEQEB power worker strike), while the notorious 1981 *Queen Street Mall Act* prohibited political communication and assembly in Brisbane's main street. Despite, or perhaps because of, Bjelke-Petersen's "law and order" mantra, the Nationals in 1983 won majority government "in their own right" (Metcalf 1984).

The National Party hegemony: 1983-89

Strains within the Coalition Government increased in the early 1980s and – as on previous occasions when strong governments faced weak oppositions – more substantial challenge to the ruling party emerged from the government's own side. For example, while a clique of progressive Liberal MPs – disparagingly labelled "trendies" by conservatives (Callick 1988) – had previously supported the Labor Opposition on Legislative Assembly reform, tensions boiled over in August, 1983, when Liberal Health Minister Terry White and his progressive faction voted with Labor to establish a Public Accounts Committee (Wear 2002: 164-65). Bjelke-Petersen dismissed White from Cabinet (who then won the Liberal leadership from Llew Edwards) but Bjelke-Petersen refused to work with White, and the Coalition was immediately dissolved. The Premier, now leading a minority government, adjourned the parliament before winning a narrow majority (with the assistance of two Liberal MPs defecting to the Nationals)[3] at the October election.

The early 1980s strengthened the Labor Opposition's stocks. In 1981, Peter Beattie and Denis Murphy – mortified by a moribund Labor Party, years of defeat and undemocratic organisational structures in the hands of the "Old Guard" – convinced federal Labor leader Bill Hayden to intervene and democratise the Queensland branch. Despite some resistance, intervention resulted in power-sharing arrangements, ballots conducted on proportional representation, and an ordered factional system. The Labor Opposition was now more transparent, more policy-focused and more inclined to pre-select women and high-profile candidates such as Brisbane lawyer Wayne Goss.

But immediate success eluded Labor. The 1983 election saw the Nationals win 41 seats (or 43 with the two defectors), the Liberals just 8 (a loss of 14) and Labor 32 (an increase of 7). Critically, it appeared voters opted for stability as they blamed the Liberals for the Coalition's demise while largely overlooking a refreshed Labor Opposition, led by the more polished Keith Wright (1982-84), which had seen a modest primary swing of 2.5 per cent. An even tougher 1985 redistribution (and a Legislative Assembly expanded to 89 members) and a populist anti-union election campaign saw the Nationals retain majority government in 1986 with a vote of 39.6 per cent: its highest tally ever. The Liberals won two extra seats, and the Labor Opposition lost two under the tepid leadership of Nev Warburton (1984-88).

An "earthquake" like that described by Nicklin turned Queensland politics on their head when, between 1987 and 1989, long-suspected police and political corruption – implicating some of Queensland's most senior figures – was confirmed by the Fitzgerald Royal Commission. The Nationals' spell of invincibility was now broken, and Bjelke-Petersen resigned in late 1987. He was succeeded as Premier by Mike Ahern (1987-89) who, in late 1989, was himself ousted by Russell Cooper. When the Labor Opposition elected the intellectually adroit Wayne Goss as leader in early 1988, the effect was profound. Goss's urbane style and focussed appeal for accountability and reform contrasted sharply with the lukewarm Ahern and the relatively unknown Cooper. Importantly, from 1988 – under the direction of Peter Beattie as Labor State Secretary and Wayne Swan as Campaign Director – the Labor Opposition began its campaign for election more than a year early, with reader-friendly policy documents on key issues widely distributed. Thus, it can be argued that allegations of corruption were insufficient to bring down the Nationals; voters also demanded inspiring Labor leadership, party unity and a credible policy program from their alternate government (Swan 1991: 98). Importantly, Labor's campaign targeted the Liberals as complicit with the Nationals: a tactic that saw Labor win government with 54 seats, the Nationals relegated to opposition with 27, and the Liberals winning just eight.

The Second Labor hegemony vs Coalition: 1989-2008

The Fitzgerald reforms of the early 1990s created the most level playing field for oppositions in Queensland history. The public service was remodelled, a Criminal Justice Commission (later the Crime and Corruption Commission) was established, and cabinet and parliamentary processes reformed. While Public Accounts and Public Works committees had already been established under Ahern, other committees with genuine powers of scrutiny were established, including, in 1994, Queensland's first Budget Estimates. The zonal electoral system was also abolished, and the 1992 election was the first since 1946 to be fought on a "one vote-one value" basis[4] (Stevens 1993: 124). The 1992 election also saw the Liberals and Nationals contest separately and, when neither improved its position over 1989, a new Coalition – the first in nine years – was formed late in 1992. For the following three years, Nationals (and Opposition) leader Rob Borbidge (1996-2001) and Liberal (and Deputy Opposition) leader Joan Sheldon (1991-98) presented a harmonious public relationship – the "Rob and Joan show" (Madigan 1998) – that seized eight Labor seats to produce a hung parliament (after the Court of Disputed Returns overturned Labor's win in Mundingburra) at the 1995 election. But the Goss Government's growing reputation for a "centralised approach to public policy [that] left many interest groups dissatisfied" (Fitzgerald, Megarrity and Symons 2009: 213) – including an unpopular Brisbane to Gold Coast road – hardly assisted Labor. When Independent Liz Cunningham threw her support behind the Coalition in early 1996, Labor was returned to opposition, with the high-profile Peter Beattie elected as Opposition leader in something of a "dream ticket" with Deputy Jim Elder (Wanna and Williams 2005: 67). Beattie defied even the most optimistic expectations when he led a chastened Labor Opposition – now committed to listening to the people – to minority government at the 1998 election after a single term in the wilderness; majority government came at the Mulgrave by-election six months later. The 1998 election also saw the rise of the populist, anti-globalisation PHON which, under the tutelage of federal MP Pauline Hanson, won seats from both Labor and the Coalition. The question of preferences to PHON, and strategies for dealing with gun control (after the Port Arthur massacre) and Indigenous reconciliation (after the *Mabo* and *Wik* High Court decisions), soon exposed rifts in the conservative opposition.

When, in 2001, Labor was plagued with accusations of internal vote rorting[5], the opposition undoubtedly expected an easy return to government. Beattie, however, adopted a novel *mea culpa* approach to political *faux pas* and, promising to rid his party of rorters, wrong-footed the opposition with decisive action and a ubiquitous media presence (Williams 2005). Labor at the 2001 election won 48.9 per cent of the primary vote and 66 seats, the Nationals 14.2 per cent and 12 seats, and the Liberals 14.3 per cent and just three seats. The Coalition was again dissolved, with the Nationals becoming Her Majesty's Opposition, and the Liberals consigned to the cross-benches.

Despite public policy failures in health and water, Labor easily retained large majorities at the 2004 (63 seats) and 2006 (59 seats) elections. The opposition's woes were compounded by the disunity caused by "on again-off again" Coalition agreements, and the inability of rural-based National Party leaders Mike Horan (2001-03), Lawrence Springborg (2003-06; 2008-09) and Jeff Seeney (2006-08) to resonate with Brisbane voters. The Liberals, too, underwent leadership transition, with David Watson (1998-2001), Bob Quinn (2001-06), Bruce Flegg (2006-07) and Mark McArdle (2007-08) all failing to find traction.

The Second Labor Hegemony vs the LNP: 2008 to present

The most recent phase in the evolution of oppositions in Queensland – a return to a single conservative non-Labor party – can be traced to 2002 when the Nationals returned to the long-mooted question of full amalgamation with the Liberals. Springborg, the most ardent supporter of a merger, met resistance during intermittent negotiations, especially from state and federal Liberals, including Prime Minister John Howard (Davis, Scott and Hughes 2006). Spurred on by their 2006 defeat, the conservative parties negotiated in earnest from 2007 and, in mid-2008, a merged LNP was born. The new party made progress at the 2009 election, winning an extra nine seats in a 3.7 per cent primary swing. But the LNP's real potential emerged when Labor found itself accused of a breach of public faith after Premier Anna Bligh privatised several major state assets immediately after the election despite no mention of the plan during Labor's campaign (Walker 2009). Public anger was palpable and, by late 2010, a *Galaxy* public opinion poll found Labor's primary vote has collapsed to 28 per cent (its record low), with 2PP support for the LNP Opposition – now under the leadership of John-Paul Langbroek – soaring to 60 per cent (Lion 2010).

But the disastrous Queensland floods in January 2011, and category five Cyclone Yasi just weeks later, soon reversed Labor's fortunes. According to *Newspoll*, Premier Bligh, widely praised for decisive leadership and grasp of detail during the crises, by March enjoyed a surge in support (Walker 2011). As outlined above, LNP powerbrokers, fearful of losing yet another election, adopted in early 2011 one of the most radical approaches to opposition politics ever seen in Australia: the dumping of Langbroek and the installation of the popular Campbell Newman – whose profile had been similarly enhanced by flood crisis management – as LNP leader, despite the fact Newman did not hold a Legislative Assembly seat. The Newman leadership experiment soon paid dividends. At the 2012 election, the LNP attained a 13.7 per cent 2PP swing that captured 78 seats (or 88 per cent) in the Legislative Assembly. Labor won just seven seats – the party's lowest total since the party's formation in 1891 – with Annastacia Palaszczuk becoming the State's first female opposition leader. Labor soon found life difficult inside the chamber but, critically, Palaszczuk found traction during successive Budget Estimates hearings where she embarrassed the government with allegations of cronyism (Williams 2014). Yet the LNP's dominance continued and, in late 2013, Newman unilaterally dissolved the parliamentary committee overseeing the Crime and Misconduct Commission (renamed the Crime and Corruption Commission in 2014) – the only committee not to enjoy a government majority – with commentators later joking "here we Joh again" (Syvret 2014).

The defeat of a government after a single term despite boasting the then-largest parliamentary majority on record remains of enormous scholarly interest. Indeed, Labor's return to (minority) government in 2015 on a 14.0 per cent 2PP swing is explained not only by Newman's unpalatable personal leadership and the LNP's unpopular privatisation program. Like the Goss Opposition between 1988 and 1989, Palaszczuk needed to rebuild Labor's community relationships, especially with regional voters. Not unexpectedly, Queensland's trade unions were instrumental in disseminating Labor's anti-privatisation message (and urging voters to number the LNP last on ballot papers), with the Left faction – having seized control of the party's state conference from the right-aligned AWU (Labor Forum) in 2014 – arguably the best-placed to prosecute Labor's case (McKenna 2014).

A demoralised LNP, once again in opposition, turned for a third time to the rural-based Lawrence Springborg – the "father" of the merged party – to steer it through recovery. Brisbane-based MP Tim Nicholls then assumed the Opposition leadership in 2016, before losing the 2017 election in yet another negative swing. Despite the leadership then moving back to the LNP's Nationals faction under Deb Frecklington – Queensland's first female conservative leader – the opposition, now marginalised by the Covid-19 pandemic, led the LNP to yet another defeat (despite an increased primary vote) at the 2020 election. With the party leadership again returning to the Liberal faction under the moderate David Crisafulli, the LNP Opposition found traction during Labor's third term as integrity crises plagued the Labor Government, and as Palaszczuk – now dubbed the "red carpet premier" (Mackay 2022) for an allegedly glamorous lifestyle - herself fell from public favour (McCormack 2023). At the time of writing, Palaszczuk's replacement as Premier by the Left-aligned Steven Miles in December, 2023, appeared to do little to lift Labor's fortunes.

Conclusion

The role of parliamentary oppositions can be obscure for voters who commonly look upon a critical opposition leader as a "whinger" or a "knocker", and not as the head of His Majesty's Loyal Opposition whose constitutional role is to criticise the government. This perception is undoubtedly fuelled by a far too superficial coverage in the news media, and is especially strong in Queensland where, due to institutional factors such as unicameralism and (formerly) electoral malapportionment – and owing to such cultural factors as voters' reverence for strong leadership, policy pragmatism and local parochialism – governments have enjoyed long electoral hegemonies that have marginalised parliamentary oppositions.

This chapter has explored the types, roles and conditions shaping Queensland oppositions and their leaders since 1860. It has found that oppositions in Queensland are different from those of any other Australian state or territory – a difference borne of a separate political culture itself shaped by a unique geography, economy and demography. It has also found that oppositions in Queensland – subjected to four electoral hegemonies – have evolved through at least ten distinct phases since 1860, with the expectation that oppositions will continue to adapt to meet changing conditions.

Considering this ongoing evolution, this chapter offers several lessons for oppositions in Queensland. The first is that, on those rare occasions when governments have been defeated, they have usually fallen only as a result of major economic or political "earthquakes". Second, government crisis alone is insufficient to induce defeat; mediocre administrations often win successive elections because voters have little confidence in lacklustre oppositions. The key to a transition to government in Queensland therefore rests with the quality of oppositions - party unity (and unity between parties in coalitions), the appeal of policy platforms, and accessible "strong" leadership – as a measure of readiness for government. Last, this chapter demonstrates that the Newman example of appointing a popular figure from another tier of government - or, indeed, from any part of the public sphere, including celebrity – as *de facto* party before winning a seat in parliament can allow an opposition to "break through" to government. Given Australians' growing mistrust of established political institutions and practices, and given how increasing numbers of voters place a premium on leadership as a determinant of vote choice, it seems almost inevitable future oppositions will again attempt this experiment.

Appendix 1: Queensland Opposition Leaders, 1898-2024

Name	Party	Opposition Tenure	Elections contested as Opposition leader	Premiership(s)
Thomas Glassey	Labor	1898-99	1898	None
Anderson Dawson	Labor	1899; 1900	None	1899
Robert Philp	Ministerial; Conservative	1899; 1903-04; 1904-07; 1908	1907	1899-1903; 1907-08
Billy Brown	Labor	1900-03	1902	None
Arthur Rutledge	Conservative	1904	1904	None
William Kidston	Kidstonite; Liberal	1907-08	1908	1906-07; 1908-11
David Bowman	Labor	1908-12	1909; 1912	None
T. J. Ryan	Labor	1912-15	1915	1915-19
Edward Macartney	Liberal; National	1915; 1918-20	1918	None
William Vowles	National; Country	1920-23	1920; 1923	None
Charles Taylor	Queensland United	1923-24	None	None
Arthur Moore	Country; CPNP	1924-29; 1932-36	1926, 1929, 1935	1929-32
William Forgan Smtih	Labor	1929-32	1932	1932-42
Ted Maher	Country	1936-41	1938; 1941	None
Frank Nicklin	National-Country; Country	1941-57	1944; 1947; 1950; 1953; 1956; 1957	1957-68
Les Wood	Labor	1957-58	None	None
Jim Donald	Labor	1958	None	None
Jack Duggan	Labor	1958-66	1960; 1963; 1966	None
Jack Houston	Labor	1966-74	1969; 1972	None
Perc Tucker	Labor	1974	1974	None
Tom Burns	Labor	1974-78	1977	None
Ed Casey	Labor	1978-82	1980	None
Keith Wright	Labor	1982-84	1983	None
Nev Warburton	Labor	1984-88	1986	None
Wayne Goss	Labor	1988-89	1989	1989-96

Russell Cooper	National	1989-91	None	1989
Rob Borbidge	National	1991-96; 1998-2001	1992; 1995; 2001	1996-98
Peter Beattie	Labor	1996-98	1998	1998-2007
Lawrence Springborg	National; LNP	2003-06; 2008-09; 2015-16	2004; 2006; 2009	None
Jeff Seeney	National; LNP	2006-08; 2011-12*	2012*	None
John-Paul Langbroek	LNP	2009-11	None	None
Annastacia Palaszczuk	Labor	2012-15	2015	2015-present
Tim Nicholls	LNP	2016-17	2017	None
Deb Frecklington	LNP	2017-20	2020	None
David Crisafulli	LNP	2020-present	None	None

Note: *Jeff Seeney was the "interim" opposition leader inside the parliament while Campbell Newman was the LNP leader outside the parliament while campaigning for the seat of Ashgrove, 2011-12.

Appendix 2: Primary Vote (%) and Seat Share (%), Queensland Parliament, 1915-2020

Election	Labor	Liberal*	National*	Other	Gov't seat share	Opp'n seat share
1915	52.1	42.0	-	0.9	63	29
1918	53.7	44.6	-	1.7	67	30
1920	47.8	26.7	24.7	8.3	53	43
1923	48.1	36.1	12.1	4.9	60	40
1926	48.0	49.2		2.8	60	39
1929	40.2	54.2		5.6	60	37
1932	49.9	45.2		4.9	53	45
1935	53.4	33.8		12.8	74	26
1938	47.2	14.0	22.6	16.2	71	27
1941	51.4	15.6	20.9	12.1	66	29
1944	44.7	24.7	17.6	13.0	60	30
1947	43.6	25.7	19.5	11.2	56	38
1950	46.9	29.9	19.3	3.9	56	42

1953	53.2	21.3	18.8	6.8	67	31
1956	51.2	25.1	19.3	4.5	65	22
1957	28.9	23.2	20.00	27.9	56	26
1960	39.9	24.0	19.5	16.6	59	32
1963	43.8	25.1	19.0	12.1	59	33
1966	43.8	25.5	19.3	11.4	61	33
1969	45.0	23.7	21.0	10.3	57	40
1972	46.8	22.2	20.0	9.0	57	40
1974	36.0	31.1	27.9	5.0	85	13
1977	42.8	25.2	27.2	4.8	72	28
1980	41.5	26.9	27.9	3.6	70	30
1983	44.0	14.9	38.9	2.2	50	39
1986	41.4	16.5	39.6	2.5	55	34
1989	50.3	21.1	24.1	4.5	61	30
1992	48.7	20.4	23.7	7.1	61	29
1995	42.9	22.8	26.2	8.1	49	49
1998	38.9	16.1	15.2	29.8	49	36
2001	48.9	14.3	14.2	22.6	74	17
2004	47.0	18.5	17.0	17.5	71	22
2006	46.9	20.1	17.8	15.2	66	28
2009	42.3	41.6		16.1	57	38
2012	26.66	49.66		23.68	88	8
2015	37.47	41.32		21.21	49	47
2017	35.43	33.69		30.88	52	42
2020	39.57	35.89		24.54	56	37

Source: M. Campbell. 1996. *Queensland's Electoral History.* Electoral Commission of Queensland [ECQ]: Brisbane; ECQ. 2010. *Election Information and Results.*
Various Returns. https://www.ecq.qld.gov.au/elections/election-events
Note: Italics denotes winning party or coalition of parties
*Liberal and National includes respective non-Labor antecedents.

References

Aitkin, D., "Countrymindedness: The spread of an idea", *Australian Cultural History*, 4, 1985, 34-41

Beanland, D., *Sir Thomas McIllwraith: The Queensland Caesar*, Brisbane: Booralong Press, 2013

Bernays, C.A., *Queensland Politics During Sixty Years, 1859-1919*, Brisbane: Government Printer, 1919

Bernays, C.A. *Queensland: Our Seventh Political Decade, 1920-1927*, Sydney: Angus and Robertson, 1931

Bleakley, P., "Queensland Exceptionalism and the Construction of 'Southern Folk Devils' in Twentieth Century Public Rhetoric", *Australian Journal of Politics and History*, 68 (1), 2022, 36-53

Carroll, B., "William Forgan Smith: Dictator or Democrat?", in Murphy, D., Joyce, R., and

Cribb, M., (eds), *The Premiers of Queensland*, 2nd ed, St. Lucia.: University of Queensland Press, 1990, 397-432

Campbell, M., *Queensland's Electoral History*, Brisbane: Electoral Commission of Queensland, 1996

Charlton, P., *State of Mind: Why Queensland is Different*, Sydney: Methuen-Haynes, 1983

Clune, D., "The State Labor Party's Electoral Record in Rural New South Wales 1904-1981", *Labour History*, 47, 1984, 91-9

Coaldrake, P., *Working the System: Government in Queensland*, St Lucia: University of Queensland Press, 1989

Costar, B., "Arthur Edward Moore: Odd Man In", in Murphy, Joyce and Cribb, *The Premiers of Queensland*, 375-96.

Callick, R., "Fitzgerald jolts the state of Amnesia", *Australian Financial Review*, 9 December, 1988

Cribb, M.B., "Hunter, James Aitchison Johnston (1882–1968)", Australian Dictionary of Biography, Vol. 9, Canberra: Australian National University, 1983. https://adb.anu.edu.au/biography/hunter-james-aitchison-johnston-6770/text11707

Dalton, J.D., "An Interpretative Survey: The Queensland Labour Movement", in Murphy, D., Joyce, R.B., and Hughes, C.A., (eds), *Prelude to Power: The Rise of the Labour Party in Queensland, 1885-1915*, Brisbane: Jacaranda Press, 1970, 3-27

Davey, P., *Joh for PM: The Inside Story of an Extraordinary Political Drama*, Sydney: NewSouth Publishing, 2015

Davis, M., Scott, S., and Hughes, D., "Lib, Nats merger: never, says Howard", *Australian Financial Review*, 30 May 2006

Evans, R., *A History of Queensland*, Melbourne: Cambridge University Press, 2007

Fitzgerald, R., *A History of Queensland: From the Dreaming to 1915*, St. Lucia: University of Queensland Press, 1982

Fitzgerald, R., *A History of Queensland: From 1915 to the early 1980s*, St. Lucia: University of Queensland Press, 1984

Fitzgerald, R., Megarrity, L. and Symons, D., *Made in Queensland: A New History*, St Lucia: University of Queensland Press, 2009

Fraser, K., "Still power in the union", *Courier Mail*, 25 August 2014

Friedman, S., "Alternatives to Periodization: Literary History, Modernism, and the 'New' Temporalities", *Modern Language Quarterly*, 80(4), 2019, 379-402

Green, W., "Periodization in European and World History", *Journal of World History*, 3(1), 1992, 13-53

Guillaume, X., "Historical Periods and the Act of Periodisation", in Costa Lòpez, J., de Carvalho, B. and Leira, H., (eds), *Routledge Handbook of Historical International Relations,* Oxfordshire: Routledge, 2021, 562-70.

Holmes, J., "Coast versus Inland: Two Different Queenslands?", *Queensland Review*, 1(1), 1994, 14-27

Hughes, C.A., "Queensland", in Rorke. J., (ed.), *Politics at State Level - Australia*, Sydney: University of Sydney, 1970, 44-59

Hughes, C.A., *The Government of Queensland*, St Lucia: University of Queensland Press, 1980

Johnston, W.R., and Murphy, D., "Ryan, Thomas Joseph (1876 - 1921)", *Australian Dictionary of Biography*, Volume 11, Carlton: Melbourne University Press, 1988, 496-500

Joyce, R. B., "George Ferguson Bowen and Robert George Wyndham Herbert: The Imported Openers", in Murphy, Joyce, and Cribb, *The Premiers of Queensland*, 9-44

Joyce, R.B., "Samuel Walker Griffith: A Liberal Lawyer", in Murphy, Joyce and Cribb, *The Premiers of Queensland* 1990b, 143-76

Kennedy, K., "William McCormack: Forgotten Labor Leader', in Murphy, Joyce and Cribb, 341-74

Kraaier, N., "How the 2017 same-sex marriage postal survey and the 2017 Queensland state election underscore the 'two Queenslands' thesis", *Queensland Review*, 25(1), 2018, 39-49.

Koch, T., "Beattie enjoys a poll gaffe", *The Australian*, 16 August 2006

Lion, P., "Premier says job safe despite poll", *Sunday Mail*, 28 November 2010

Lorenz, C., "'The Times They Are a-Changin'. On Time, Space and Periodization in History", in Carretero, M., Berger, S. and Grever, M., (eds), *The Palgrave Handbook of Research in Historical Culture and Education*, London: Palgrave, 2017

Lunn, H., *Johannes Bjelke-Petersen*, St Lucia: University of Queensland Press, 1984.

Mackay, J., "Labor in renew or die scenario", *Courier Mail*, 19 June 2022

Mackerras, M., "The Swing: Variability and Uniformity", in Mayer, H., (ed), *Labor to Power: Australia's 1972 Election*, Sydney: Angus and Robertson, 1973, 234-41

Madigan, M., "Pete and Jim put on show of unity", *Courier Mail*, 6 April, 1998

McCormack, M., "Poll: Labor in losing position', *Courier Mail* 6 July 2023

McMullin, R., *The Light on the Hill: The Australian Labor Party, 1891-1991*, Melbourne: Oxford University Press, 1991

McQueen, H., "States of the Nation – Queensland: A State of Mind", *Meanjin*, 38, 1979, 41-51

Metcalf, A., *In Their Own Right*, St Lucia: University of Queensland Press, 1984

Morley, P., "Speaker's gaffe caused uproar", *Courier-Mail*, 29 February 2008

Milner, C., "With right campaign, state election is Labor's to lose," *Courier Mail*, 11 December 2014

Mullins, B., "Populist politics and development", in Head, B., (ed), *The Politics of Development in Australia*, Sydney: Allen and Unwin, 1986, 138-62

Murphy, D., "Queensland's Image and Australian Nationalism", *Australian Quarterly*, 50, 1978, 77-91

QPD. *Queensland Parliamentary Debates*. 22 November, 1983. https://documents.parliament.qld.gov.au/events/han/1983/1983_11_22.pdf

Reynolds, P., "Problems and Prospects for Electoral Reform After Fitzgerald", in Prasser, S., Wear, R., and Nethercote, J., (eds), *Corruption and Reform: The Fitzgerald Vision*, St Lucia: University of Queensland Press, 1990, 245-9

Reynolds, P., *The Politics of Queensland: 1980 to the Present*. Unpublished manuscript. Brisbane, 2010

Shogren, D., "Agriculture: 1915-29", in *Labor in Power: The Labor Party and Governments in Queensland 1915-57*, St Lucia: University of Queensland Press, 1980, 178-93

Stevens, B., "Reform of the State Electoral System", in Stevens, B., and Wanna, J., (eds), *The Goss Government: Promise and Performance of Labor in Queensland*, South Melbourne: Macmillan, 1993, 117-32

Stevenson, B., "George Francis Reuben Nicklin: Honest Frank: The Gentleman Premier", in Murphy, Joyce Cribb, 475-94

Stokes, G., "One Nation and Australian Populism", in Leach, M., Stokes, G., and Ward, I., (eds), *The Rise and Fall of One Nation*, St Lucia: University of Queensland Press, 2000, 23-41

Swan, W., "The Labor Party", in Hughes C.A., and Whip, R., (eds), *Political Crossroads: The 1989 Queensland Election*, St Lucia.: University of Queensland Press, 1991, 96-112

Syvret, P., "Operation fire up support," *Courier Mail*, 9 September 2014

Walker, J., "Bligh braves backlash over sell-offs", *The Australian*, 5 November 2009

Walker, J., "Rein in Bligh bounce, LNP told", *The Australian*, 9 February 2011

Walter, J., and Dickie, K., "Johannes Bjelke-Petersen: A Political Profile", in Patience, A., (ed), *The Bjelke-Petersen Premiership, 1968–1983: Issues in Public Policy*, Melbourne: Longman, 1985, 33-52

Walter, J., "Johannes Bjelke-Petersen: 'The Populist Autocrat'", in Murphy, Joyce and Cribb, 495-526

Wanna, J., "Queensland: Consociational factionalism or ignoble cabal?", in Warhurst, J., and Parkin, A., (eds), *The Machine: Labor Confronts the Future,* St Leonards: Allen and Unwin, 2000

Wanna, J. and Williams, P.D., "Peter Beattie: The 'Boy from Atherton' Made Good", in Wanna, J., and Williams, P.D., (eds), *Yes, Premier: Labor Leadership in Australia's States and Territories*, Sydney: University of New South Wales Press, 2005, 61-87

Wanna, J., and Arklay, T., *The Ayes Have It: The History of the Queensland Parliament, 1957-1989*, Canberra: Australian National University Press, 2010

Wardill, S., "LNP opens door and Bligh hints at an early poll", *Courier-Mail*, 23 March, 2011

Waterson, D.B., "Thomas McIlwraith: A Colonial Entrepreneur," in Murphy, Joyce and Cribb, 119-42

Wear, R., "The Weighting Game: Do the Nationals have a Case?", in Prasser, Wear and Nethercote, 1990, 259-67

Wear, R., *Johannes Bjelke-Petersen: The Lord's Premier*, St Lucia: University of Queensland Press, 2002

Williams, P.D., "Peter Beattie's Strategies of Crisis Management: *Mea Culpa* and the Policy "Backflip"', *Australian Journal of Public Administration*, 64(4), 2005, 41-52

Williams, P.D., "Leaders and Political Culture: The Development of the Queensland Premiership", *Queensland Review*, 16(1), 2009, 15-34

Williams, P.D., "How did they do it? Explaining Queensland Labor's Second Electoral Hegemony", *Queensland Review*, 18(2), 2011a, 112-33

Williams, P.D., "House on the line in Can Do gamble", *Courier-Mail*, 23 March, 2011b

Williams, P.D., All's not necessarily fair in the wars of public office", *Courier-Mail*, 15 April, 2014

Williams, P.D., "Political Chronicle: Queensland", *Australian Journal of Politics and History*, 62(4), 2016, 635-32

Williams, P.D., "One, Two or Many Queenslands? Disaggregating the Regional Vote at the 2017 Queensland State Election", *Australasian Parliamentary Review*, 33(2), 2018a, 55-79

Williams, P.D., "Leadership or Policy? Explaining the 2015 Queensland Election Result", *Australian Journal of Politics and History*, 64(2), 2018b, 260-76

Williams, P.D., "Queensland's Quandary: To reintroduce a Legislative Council?", *Queensland Review*, 29(1), 2022, 36-48

Williams, P.D., "Queensland", in Chen, P., Barry, N., Butcher, D., Clune, D., Cook, I., Garnier, A., Haigh, Y., Motta, S., and Taflaga, M., (eds), *Australia's Politics and Public Policy*, 2nd ed, Sydney: Sydney University Press, 2023a, 245-64

Williams, P.D., "Revisiting Six Queenslands: Disaggregating the Regional Vote at the 2020 Queensland State Election", *Australasian Parliamentary Review*, 38(1), 2023b, 108-27

Endnotes

1   For detailed discussions around Queensland's electoral hegemonies, see: Williams, P.D., "The Queensland Election of 17 February 2001: Reforging the Electoral Landscape?", *Australian Journal of Political Science*, 36 (2), 2001, 363-71; Williams, P. D., "The Queensland Election of 7 February 2004: The Coming of the Second Labor Hegemony?" *Australian Journal of Political Science*, 39 (3), 2004, 635-44; Williams, P.D., "Defying the Odds: Peter Beattie and the 2006 Queensland Election", *Australasian Parliamentary Review* 22 (2), 2007, 212-20; Williams, P.D., "The Queensland Election of 21 March 2009: Labor's swim against the tide", *Australian Journal of Political Science*, 45 (2), 2010, 277-83; Williams, P.D., "How did they do it? Explaining Queensland Labor's Second Electoral Hegemony", *Queensland Review*, 18 (2), 2011, 112-33; Williams, P.D. "Leadership or Policy: Explaining the Queensland Election of 31 January, 2015", *Australian Journal of Politics and History*, 64 (2), 2018, 1-17; Williams, P.D. "Back from the brink: Labor's re-election at the 2017 Queensland state election", *Queensland Review*, 25 (1), 2018. 6-26; Williams, P.D. "The Grateful State: The 2020 Queensland Election", *Queensland Review*, 28 (1), 2021, 57-72.

2   In March 2011, the LNP preselected Newman for the Brisbane seat of Ashgrove, which he easily won in 2012, and which he just as easily lost in 2015 to become just the second premier, after Digby Denham, to lose his seat in a general election. Newman was thus the only Queensland premier never to have served in opposition.

3   Brian Austin had been Liberal MP for Wavell before defecting to the Nationals to provide Bjelke-Petersen a parliamentary majority in 1983; Austin then

represented Nicklin as a National MP (1986-89). Don Lane had been a Liberal MP for Merthyr (1971-83) before also defecting to the Nationals (1983-89). Austin and Lane, with fellow ministers Leisha Harvey and Geoff Muntz, were later imprisoned for misappropriation of public moneys.

4   Seats with areas greater than 100,000 km^2 were excluded from the "one-vote, one value" principle under the 1991 redistribution. Five western and northern seats qualified: Charters Towers, Cook, Gregory, Mt Isa and Warrego.

5   The Shepherdson Inquiry, 2000-01, found evidence of fraudulent voter enrolments ahead of internal party plebiscites inside the Queensland branch of the Australian Labor Party, with the AWU (Labor Forum) faction at the heart of the allegations. See CJC, *The Shepherdson Inquiry: An Investigation into Electoral Fraud.* Criminal Justice Commission: Brisbane, 2001. https://www.ccc.qld.gov.au/sites/default/files/2020-01/The-Shepherdson-inquiry-Report-2001.pdf

11

Opposition in the Queensland Parliament: Some Observations from a Chief of Staff

Kevin Martin

In this chapter I draw on my practical experiences as Chief of Staff to three leaders of the Opposition in the Queensland Legislative Assembly to provide an account of how opposition works in the unicameral Queensland Parliament.

The background

It is often remarked that much of the constitutional practice and procedures under which governments operate in Australia is determined by understandings and practices inherited, with our Westminster foundations, from our British forbears. In effect, the fundamental presumption is that democracy itself requires that there be a government and an opposition. In the case of Queensland, with its unicameral parliament, the *Constitution of Queensland Act 2001* does not even mention the term "opposition". The *Parliament of Queensland Act 2001* makes several mentions of the opposition without defining it or prescribing how it is to be identified. There is thus no statutory provision that defines what government is and what opposition is, save in passing as outlined above. Rather, both terms must be understood from a consideration as to how the political system operates in reality and from passing mention in statutes. This lack of constitutional and statutory recognition, however, belies the reality that the institution of an opposition is one of the essential elements that underpins our whole system of government and politics and thus our democracy.

The role of the opposition in the Queensland Parliament has been officially described in a Queensland Parliament Fact Sheet.[1] This statement reflects the common roles Bateman (Bateman 2009) has identified for a shadow cabinet:

- Organising the opposition
- Providing an alternative government
- Serving as an arena for training and testing potential future cabinet ministers.

Without an opposition to provide focus for the political contest, conducted both in parliament and the community, democratic government would rapidly disintegrate into dictatorship by those who comprised the government of the day. Where it has been institutionalised, the opposition is the mechanism whereby a government is held to account in a parliament and in the broader community.

Whilst over recent years there has been community and academic support expressed for an enhanced role for minor parties and independent or non-aligned members of parliament, the reality of political life in a unicameral system is that it is only where a government lacks command of a majority on the floor of the lower house that independent or minor party members can play any significant role in the political life of parliament.

Queensland has had recent examples of this phenomenon. The first was the Borbidge-Sheldon Coalition Government (1996-98) which was dependent on the support of the Independent Member for Gladstone. The second was the first Beattie Labor Government (1998-2001) which depended on the support of the Independent Member for Nicklin. The third was the first Palaszczuk Labor Government (2015-17) when, after defeating the Newman LNP Government, Palaszczuk was again able to rely on the Independent Member for Nicklin to form government. It is interesting to compare the political tenor of these experiences. Overall, they would indicate that government, in a parliamentary setting, functions best when that government is faced with an opposition that matches, so far as possible, the government's numbers in the parliament and the resources available to it.

Institutional domination by government

In the modern era, a government formed on the floor of a parliament is led by a cabinet and executive that has available to it immense resources. The government can draw upon the full intellectual, financial and administrative resources of the public service. Frequently, the longer a government is in office the more the policies and attitudes of the government and the public service come into parallel. In addition, government has the financial resources to purchase the best possible assistance from the private sector to achieve its objectives. The increasingly symbiotic relationship between government and the major private sector financial services providers in the development and implementation of solutions to policy problems facing government is an area where further research is needed, particularly from public integrity agencies. Some individuals seem to slip seamlessly between the roles of ministerial adviser, political operator, financial services partner and senior public service or statutory appointee. All this assists in developing a commonality of purpose between the areas that should be displaying creative tension to achieve the best possible community outcomes.

Through the power of appointment, and particularly through the transformation of the senior ranks of the public service from tenured to short-term contract employment, the self-interest of the government and the individuals comprising the senior ranks of the public service tends to coincide. CEOs are thus beholden to the government that appointed them and have a strong personal survival interest in successfully implementing government policies (whatever their objective worth may be) in order to maintain their employment and the significant emoluments that go with it. What this means, so far as the opposition is concerned, is that not only does the opposition have to confront the government as formed on the floor of parliament, it has to confront the power, might and resources of the whole public service as well.

Resources for members of the Queensland Parliament and the opposition

Members of the Queensland Parliament are now provided with a variety of resources, fully accountable through the Australian Tax Office, to enable them to carry out their parliamentary duties. These resources include an office in their electorate fully equipped with modern communication tools, staff (minimum of two), travel entitlements, and allowances to be expended on electorate related expenses (such as motor vehicles, telephones, necessary expenses at functions and so on).

These resources are provided by, and were formerly controlled through, the Queensland Parliamentary Service established under the *Parliamentary Service Act 1998* which was under the control of the Speaker and the Clerk of the Parliament. Following the introduction of the Committee of the Legislative Assembly (CLA), established under amendments to the *Parliament of Queensland Act 2001* that commenced on 18 August 2011, the CLA determined the major policies that the management of the Parliamentary Service was required to follow.

In 2013, by the *Queensland Independent Remuneration Tribunal Act 2013,* the parliament vested an Independent Tribunal (appointed by the government) with the capacity to make determinations (which are not legally challengeable) on issues such as remuneration (Subdivision 2 of Division 1) and entitlements of crossbench members to additional staff (Subdivision 3 of Division 1).

Employees of the Queensland Parliamentary Service support all MPs but only in their role as members and not in any other role they might occupy. Separate provision is made in the budget for the parliament to vote funds to meet the annual costs of the Queensland Parliamentary

Service which are separately accounted for and examined through the committee process.

Disparity of resources

The resources available to ministers are enormous. Not only are they provided with specific resources to staff their ministerial as well as their parliamentary offices, they also have available an enormous range of assistance provided by the relevant government department. This includes experts in policy formulation and advice, administration and management, media management and representation and public relations. In addition to this direct assistance, ministers are able, through their departments, to purchase from the broad community expertise not available in-house in the department or ministerial office.

Office accommodation for the opposition

During my experiences as chief of staff to leaders of the opposition, the Queensland Parliamentary Service provided some assistance to the opposition, at no budgetary charge, by way of office space and furniture in the parliamentary precinct. This can be contrasted to the position that had prevailed until 2001 where the opposition, in addition to space within the parliamentary precinct, had been supplied, through the annual budget process controlled by the Premier's Department, with office accommodation, furniture and telecommunications facilities in a Brisbane CBD office tower. This outside accommodation was abandoned at the insistence of the newly re-elected Beattie Government following the 2001 election at which the formal opposition, the National Party, had been reduced to 11 MPs.

Accommodation for the opposition within the parliamentary precinct meant that when any individual wished to contact the opposition (members or staff) in person they had to go through, and be observed by, staff of the State Government Security Service, an organisation controlled by a department, not the Parliamentary Service. This inhibited anyone from business, community groups or the public sector who wished to discuss an issue of concern with the opposition; they feared naturally that, given the nature of the political process, they would be identified and be disadvantaged for dealing with the opposition. This fear was exacerbated when, as has occurred in Queensland for many years, there was a consensus community view that the odds were very much against an incumbent government being defeated, so do not get offside with the government.

This has meant that the democratic right of an individual to approach a member of parliament (a right supposedly protected by the Standing Orders of the Parliament) was significantly eroded in Queensland through institutional dominance by the government. This had the effect of strengthening the political position of the incumbent government by practically limiting access to the opposition. Consequently, there grew up a "secret squirrel" mentality in relation to dealings with opposition members of parliament during that time whereby open discussion of problems in public service delivery became surrounded in secrecy. This reinforced a "them and us" mentality from the government which concentrated its efforts on producing a positive media spin to satisfy the ever-growing demands of the 24-hour news cycle.

However, the demand for space in the parliamentary precinct meant that the opposition is now provided with accommodation in a building outside the parliament precinct, albeit still under government control and with similar problems of access by the public. The unspoken fear of being seen to be acting contrary to the interests of the government of the day thus continues. It would only be alleviated if the opposition was granted its own budget resources to enable it to obtain premises for its operations entirely separate from any form of government or public sector control or oversight.

Staff resources – government vs opposition

There is a large disparity in staff resources available between ministerial offices and the opposition office:

- Ministerial staff as at 9 February 2010 totalled 217.9[2] which rose to 223 in 2010-11. By contrast, the maximum staff number then available to the Opposition was 22, a ratio approaching 10:1 favouring the government.
- By 31 March 2022, ministerial staff numbers had increased to 229 whilst opposition staff resources increased by 1 to 23, maintaining this 10 to 1 ratio.

In addition, ministerial offices are nearly always supplemented by departmental staff appointed as liaison officers, allegedly to facilitate information flows and co-operation between the department and ministerial offices. This directly increases resources available to ministers funded by departments. The employment classifications in a ministerial office are significantly higher than in the opposition office. This is often a detrimental factor in recruiting suitably qualified opposition staff.

According to the *Service Delivery Statement for the Department of Premier and Cabinet* for the State Budget 2010-2011 (pp 1-11) the total budget for ministerial offices and parliamentary secretaries was $35.3m. The total budget for the Office of the Leader of the Opposition was $3.1m. As at December 2022, total ministerial expenses for the period from July 2022 (tabled 15 March 2023) were $26.45m for ministerial offices whilst the total for the opposition office was $1.7m. The premier alone had ministerial expenses of $4.6m.

The Office of the Premier at 31 March 2022 contained 35 staff members in contrast with the Opposition Office's 22. The number of staff in individual ministerial offices ranged from 8 to 35 averaging at least 9 per office. From the total of 22 to 23 staff members, the leader of the opposition normally has to employ the following: chauffeur, personal or diary secretaries for the leader and deputy, receptionist/front office, clerical and administrative support, policy researchers, political advisers and media advisers. The maximum size of any unit within the opposition office, because of the necessary areas to be covered, is thus four to six persons.

Government control of opposition resources

Opposition Expenses and Ministerial Office Expenses are both provided for in the Annual Budget of the Department of the Premier and Cabinet.[3] The Director-General of the Department of the Premier and Cabinet is the accountable officer for all expenditures by the opposition office in accordance with the provisions of the *Financial Accountability Act 2009*.

Following the Fitzgerald Commission in 1989 and the charging of certain ministers with offences in relation to their expenditures, the incoming Goss Government established a unit of the Department of the Premier and Cabinet, the Ministerial Services Branch (MSB) to act as the accountability mechanism for all expenditures by both ministers and the opposition office.

General experience over the years was that confidences between the opposition office and MSB were maintained and respected.

During my time as a Chief of Staff, as the likelihood of a change of government in Queensland had become less remote, the then Director-General became more actively involved in monitoring the fine details of expenditures by the Opposition Office. This culminated in June 2010 with a ban by the Director-General on the expenditure of any moneys from the opposition office on any form of advertising or publicity despite such advertisements being in accordance with the controls and conditions contained in the *Opposition Handbook* approved by the MSB. The ban was only lifted after new advertising controls, which applied to both government and opposition advertising, were imposed in August 2010.

Why the Director-General adopted this approach is unclear. It certainly is clear, however, that in Queensland all directors-general are employed directly under a contract with the premier and relevant minister and are under a contractual duty to implement the policies of the premier and thus of the government. There is thus a convergence of interests between the government of the day, the premier and ministers and the personal employment and thus economic interests of a director-general in the maintenance of that government and that premier in office. To suggest that a director-general in those circumstances will always act in the allegedly impartial manner of classic Westminster-style public servants is to ignore the reality of the modern situation of contract employment for senior public servants. This view is strengthened when one considers that the advertisements that the then Director-General banned were extremely critical of the policies of the government he was contractually bound to serve. It is not difficult to perceive a potential, if not a real, conflict of interest in those circumstances.

In December 2021 a government *Advertising and Marketing Communication Code of Conduct* was issued. The Code's stated objective was "to ensure advertising and marketing communication is objective, factual and an efficient use of funds". However, the very next sentence goes on to state the Code did " not apply to advertising and communication actively undertaken and paid for by Ministerial Offices." It did apply to the Office of the Leader of the Opposition, however. The willingness of a government to use government resources to support its own version of policy, whatever the true position might be, has rarely been more clearly illustrated. Opposition expression on that same policy is subject to constraints whilst ministerial offices, and thus governments, are not.

Contrast in roles and powers between government and opposition

Government, by its very nature, is always taking positive action - it has the option to do or refrain from doing something. Because it is the government, it has the financial and other resources to implement its decisions. The opposition, on the other hand, is by its very nature nearly always negative. It is the role of the opposition to hold government to account, to identify failures in government policy and administration, to criticise what is occurring or what will occur as a result of government actions. It is rare, except in the period immediately before an election, for the opposition to advance in the media suggestions that can be portrayed as positive, as against those the government has been putting into practice.

This negativity of opposition is reinforced by the modern media cycle with its demand for 24-hour news. Government is far better equipped with resources and the potential to take positive action to meet the needs of this cycle, particularly by utilising its large numbers of media advisers to feed positive stories to the media. Oppositions, with fewer resources and a negative role, are limited in their approach, and thus are portrayed as "whingers", lacking any positive message.

Compared to the opposition, the resources available to government to generate positive media coverage are immense. Firstly, it has the largest number of MPs, and thus the largest number of electorate staff to offer assistance. Being the government, it has the capacity to initiate actions and make decisions guaranteeing that it can generate the greatest amount of publicity for itself and its actions. Controlling the public service, it can employ the largest number of media and other advisers to generate this publicity. Controlling the budget, it can expend such sums as it can get away with publicly on paid media advertising to support its policy positions. Government is able to reap the most donations from individuals and groups who seek to curry favour and influence decisions to their advantage.

It is commonly accepted that the political battle conducted on a daily basis between government and opposition is, in reality, a battle between Goliath (government) and David (opposition). Unlike the Biblical story however, Goliath normally wins.

Financial accountability and impacts on opposition

Not only are the resources available to the opposition substantially less than those available to the government, the use of those resources is subject to controls designed to ensure that only minimum impact can be had in criticising government actions and policy. The Office of the Leader of the Opposition is treated as if it were a ministerial office with day-to-day financial and administrative accountability being exercised through the Ministerial Services Branch of the Department of the Premier and Cabinet.

This system has several disadvantages. Whilst expenditures are undertaken in accordance with the provisions of an *Opposition Handbook*, which parallels much of the material contained in the *Ministerial Handbook*, the exercise of any discretion as to whether expenses are or are not allowable is undertaken initially by public servants of the Ministerial Services Branch and ultimately by the Director-General of the Department of Premier and Cabinet. Many in the opposition hold a well-founded view that, when it comes to the exercise of discretion as to whether or not a particular expenditure is allowable in accordance with the guidelines, that discretion will be exercised to the detriment of the opposition.

The Queensland Opposition has for many years consistently argued that expenditure and financial controls in relation to the opposition should be exercised by independent and impartial authorities, either the Parliamentary Service or the Auditor-General or some similar official body responsible to the parliament as a whole.

Dealing with the media

The media today is a constantly changing environment. Whereas once media could be confined to newspapers which were published on a regular basis with relatively long lead times to publication, and to pamphleteering of various types, nowadays, the growth of electronic media has opened up many battlefields for both government and opposition.

Electronic media, in particular, has moved from that of a limited number of radio stations and then television stations to the 24-hour news cycle which uses, as well, internet sites and other self-published forms of social communication such as Facebook, Twitter, and blogs. Media today is instantaneous with journalists regarding themselves not just as reporters of other people's views but personalities and commentators playing an active role in the political process.

This news cycle must constantly be fed with breaking news and comment. Government devotes considerable resources to feeding it through its employment of large numbers of media advisers/public relations/social media consultants both within ministerial offices and also within departments. The opposition must basically seek to counter this constant flow through information generated within, and communicated through, the very small media unit attached to the Office of the Leader of the Opposition. At best, during my employment, the opposition media unit consisted of no more than four or five persons whose task it was to attempt to communicate the opposition position through the various media outlets.

A worrying trend has been the capacity of government to "buy" the most successful and experienced members of the parliamentary press gallery by offering salaries and emoluments in excess of that which their media employers can offer. Collective knowledge, particularly of Queensland political history, has declined, in what remains of the gallery, as senior operatives have been replaced by more junior and inexperienced ones who often defer to the so-called wisdom and experience of those who have "taken the government's shilling".

The parliamentary press gallery is of particular importance in portraying to the community what happens in parliament. In doing this, because of the importance of television and the desire for some colour in their presentation, a heavy concentration is placed upon the daily theatre of Question Time. It is only up until the conclusion of Question Time that the television media will have cameras in the Chamber recording what happens. For this reason, the Opposition spends an inordinate amount of time seeking to utilise Question Time to produce "gotcha" moments which will play well on the news that night. The actions of both questioners and those questioned during Question Time over a consistent period create an image for government and opposition as a whole. This is the reason why the performance of both the Premier and the Leader of the Opposition in asking and answering questions is of vital significance.

All ministers have individual ministerial media advisers (often two or more) as part of their office together with government public relations units in individual departments. Opposition shadow ministers, by way of contrast, unless they themselves are self-starters who personally approach particular media operatives and endeavour to brief them on stories, rely to a large degree on media releases generated from within the opposition office. Given the small number of media staff available, this means that there is often significant internal tension within the opposition office as shadow ministers compete with one another to issue press releases.

Press releases are largely only effective in providing material to provincial newspapers (where they still exist) whose economics mean they can only employ a few local reporters and largely rely upon the stories generated through the AAP Network to fill the blank spaces between advertisements in their newspaper. Given the degree of syndication that exists in relation to both television and radio in Queensland, it is only if something is picked up following a press release by the hubs of those respective organisations that coverage throughout Queensland can be obtained.

In the field of paid advertising, the disparity between government and opposition is again clear. Government, controlling the purse strings, has the capacity to spend millions of dollars on running various forms of campaigns which allegedly merely explain government policy or are "educative" in value, for example, drive carefully so as not to run down road workers who are, of course, building wonderful new roads for you, or eat more beneficial foods - your government really cares for you!

By contrast, any advertising conducted by the opposition (other than that which the relevant supporting political party machine funds) must be paid for from the opposition budget which, after paying for salaries and necessary expenses, means that there is at best a few hundred thousand dollars of discretionary expenditure available.

Whilst, as mentioned previously, politics is conducted in a largely presidential style, the reality is that the leader of the opposition has, in many ways, a more important individual leadership role than that of the premier. This stems from the fact that ministers, as well as the premier, are able to generate media publicity to a significantly greater degree than can ever be generated by members of the shadow cabinet. An examination of the records of Media Monitors indicates that in relation to political issues the only member of the opposition who ever really generates consistent media coverage is the leader of the opposition. It would be very rare for even one other member of shadow cabinet to feature in the top ten political media coverage in any one week. Consistently, however, in addition to the premier, the deputy premier and up to six senior ministers feature consistently in the weekly top ten. This outcome is assisted by the resources available to, and the opportunities available from, government actions and decisions.

While a premier may sometimes suffer some weakness in media profile, the actions of other ministers tend to support the image of the government as a whole. On the other hand, where media coverage is focussed largely, if not exclusively, on the leader of the opposition, their failings and weaknesses are more readily publicised.

Shadow ministers' roles and functions

If an opposition is supposed to be an alternative government, then there is a necessity for it to have sufficient numbers on the floor of the Legislative Assembly to mirror the government of the day. Queensland, over the first decade of the century, has not had sufficient parliamentary representation in the opposition to make this contest work.

Following the 2001 election, the official Opposition, the Nationals, was reduced to 12 seats then 11. The fact that it consisted only of 11 members meant that everyone became a shadow minister, often covering more than one portfolio. This meant that the dynamic between a shadow cabinet and a backbench comprised of people aspiring to become shadow ministers was missing from the Queensland Opposition for a long period of time.

Even when various coalitions were formed between the National and the Liberal parties prior to the 2004 and 2006 elections, the paucity of numbers meant that this dynamic remained missing. This "every player receives a prize" syndrome meant that for virtually a decade the incentive for a shadow minister to perform was missing in Queensland.

The lack of the skills and personality necessary to be an effective shadow minister or minister has been a weakness of the opposition. Even after the 2009 election, where the LNP had sufficient numbers (34) to enable a distinction to be drawn between a shadow cabinet and backbench, the paucity of numbers since 2001 meant that, because of their longevity as MPs and shadow ministers, many retained shadow positions because of the lack of parliamentary experience of new MPs. Proposals to renew the shadow cabinet after the 2009 election necessarily caused internal political tensions. The ascension of Campbell Newman to extra-parliamentary leadership of the LNP and the shadow cabinet reshuffle to reward those who supported his move did not remove such tensions.

Since the defeat of the Newman Government in 2015, the shadow cabinet has been dominated by those members who had achieved ministerial or other senior positions in the Newman Government. These, for too long, were focused on the justification of decisions made during the Newman regime and not on the challenges posed by the increasingly confident Palaszczuk Government.

There has been no real incentive for shadow ministers to undertake the necessary skills training to be an effective minister should the opposition achieve government. Given the complexity of government today, it is clearly arguable that ministers should possess skills that ape, to at least some degree, the skills required of directors of large-scale corporations: a capacity to determine strategic policy, to "read the balance sheet", and to provide clear policy directives to the public service. In Queensland, such training of opposition members for those necessary skills has been lacking. This is also a weakness when it comes to election campaigns.

Whilst politics is often regarded as a quasi-presidential race between a premier and the leader of the opposition, there is at least some support for the suggestion that an important political element for the community as a whole is the comparison of competence between government and opposition front benches. Unless a shadow minister possesses extraordinary talents the resources available to ministers, particularly so far as media advisers, speech writers and so on are concerned, means that this comparison largely favours ministers. This again feeds into the lack of competition for shadow ministerial positions and means that there is little incentive for shadow ministers to perform above and beyond the minimum in order to maintain their positions.

Internal procedures of oppositions

If an opposition is supposed to be a government in waiting, it is necessary, to some degree, for the opposition to operate in a way similar to that of the government of the day. It is for that reason that opposition shadow ministers are normally appointed with the same title as ministers and with the same areas of policy responsibility. This means that when a minister introduces particular legislation emanating from one of their areas of policy responsibility, the shadow minister best able to respond immediately is readily identified. This paralleling between minister and shadow minister normally occurs but can at times be varied, particularly as an election approaches and the opposition seeks to restructure its shadow cabinet to reflect the organisation of government it would adopt if successful. The resources available to a shadow minister (at best, part of a policy adviser employed in the leader of the opposition's office and any party-associated policy committee) are limited, especially when compared with the resources of the whole of the public service available to a minister.

Internal procedures within the opposition office when it comes to the determining of a response to government legislation, the possible introduction of private members bills by the opposition, and formulation of opposition policies tend to ape the procedures adopted by government. This is often done as part of the process of attempting to educate shadow ministers about how Government operates. In Queensland, there is available, under the title *Governing Queensland*, a whole suite of procedure manuals, one of which particularly deals with cabinet procedures, including how cabinet submissions are to be prepared, circulated for comment and then submitted to cabinet. This has its counterpart in an opposition shadow cabinet manual that applies many of the same procedures although, given the resources available to opposition as opposed to government, without the level of input that occurs prior to a matter being considered by cabinet.

Whilst in government ministers other than the premier have a capacity to raise a public profile and develop a public personality, such opportunity is virtually lacking for shadow ministers. An examination of media monitoring would indicate that consistently, in the Queensland media, the premier of the day completely dominates with average coverage of at least twice that of the leader of the opposition, unless there is a major internal dispute occurring in the opposition. Consistently, apart from the leader of the opposition, it is extremely rare for any shadow minister to appear in the top ten of weekly media coverage.

Policy formation and advice

The formation of policy is a complex process. Political parties, by their very nature, comprise people who exhibit and support particular philosophies. These philosophies do not always lead to adoption of policies that are practical and objective.

Government usually formulates policy through the prism of the advice received from the public service and from parties who will be affected in their business and social activities if particular policies are implemented. Thus, to a large degree, the political philosophies of the government of the day are affected in their implementation by the realities of public administration and the fact that, if the philosophies have an adverse impact upon any particular element of the community, that adverse impact will be readily communicated to the government and become the subject of major public complaint.

The opposition, on the other hand, suffers because it neither has immediately available to it the practical advice of the public service nor, depending upon the community's view about the likelihood of the opposition ever achieving government, does it receive objective advice from community groups. Indeed, given the nature of society today, the opposition usually finds it very difficult to establish dialogue with community groups who interact with government.

The government has increasingly adopted the policy of providing various forms of subsidies and grants to community groups. These grants are often conditional on a requirement that groups in receipt of the grants do not publicly criticise the policies of the government. Many of these community groups have built substantial infrastructure upon these grants. The threat of their removal is sufficient to ensure that, not only do these groups not comment in any critical way about the government, but there is also a tendency for those groups to avoid any meaningful contact or dialogue with the opposition lest their actions put the continued receipt of such grants in jeopardy.

Opposition parties, when seeking to develop policy, find that the limit of the resources available to them means that generally they only receive effective advice from people who are ideologically committed to the cause. Whilst this may have the effect of reinforcing continued support from these groups, there is an adverse impact upon the opposition as it is not receiving assistance in the development of policy which may appeal to community interest groups who are not ideologically attuned to the attitudes of the opposition. Again, the resources available to the opposition mean that it is unable to obtain advice either from many full-time employees or through the commissioning of consultants, contractors and experts who can provide that advice.

The community's judgement about the likelihood of the opposition winning government also influences the level of community support which the opposition receives in its policy formulation process. The further the opposition appears to be from government, the less likely it will be that anyone in the community will seek to associate themselves with it lest they be punished by the government of the day.

Access to information – parliamentary processes

The opposition suffers significant disadvantages in the way in which information is conveyed from government to the general community. Much of the government's investment in media adviser and public relations consultants is focussed upon portraying the deluge of information that is released by government on a regular basis in the best possible light. All government departments and agencies now, as a matter of course, deliver annual reports outlining their activities. Often full of photos of the minister and other members of the government, these publications usually display favourable outcomes and seek to hide problems with obscure references.

It is a favourite ploy of government to claim that it is accountable by saying that it details in its annual reports, which are tabled in parliament, the outcomes of its various activities. However, the processes utilised to make those reports public detract from any capacity to have any form of critical examination of the matters contained therein.

Traditionally, such reports are not tabled when parliament is sitting but out of session. Often, they are tabled in a great number at the one time, usually on the last possible day for tabling. The tabling usually occurs after the media stories of the day are settled, thus limiting the capacity of the opposition to make any adverse comment upon any matter contained in such reports. Given the lack of resources available to the opposition, it is physically impossible to do more than give a cursory examination to these reports. If one matter in relation to the reports can be utilised by the opposition as a foundation for a press release, then the situation can be regarded as lucky. Given the nature of the news cycle, the information contained in most annual reports is regarded by the media as stale by the next day. Thus, issues contained in annual reports rapidly pass from the media's consciousness.

In addition to the annual reports from departments, formal processes exist through the estimates process for an examination of the service delivery statements of each department. The Queensland Parliamentary Estimates process has been subject to considerable academic and political criticism over the years. It suffers from several significant defects including:

- Estimates committees are portfolio committees with the government normally having the majority of members and thus the chair of the committee.
- The government chairs of such committees normally maintain a blocking role when non-government, particularly opposition members, seek to pursue in detail a particular expenditure.
- The total time available to consider the estimates of departments with tens of thousands of employees and billions of dollars of expenditure is limited.
- The time for questioning of individual elements of departments is limited with time being shared in blocks between government and non-government questioners. Often the maximum time available to ask questions is a block of 20 minutes or so.
- All questions are normally only answered by ministers. As occurs on the floor of the Legislative Assembly, ministers may answer any question in whichever way they choose to do so; there is no obligation on ministers to answer the questions posed directly.
- Departments that may be politically sensitive at any particular time are often scheduled for the estimates process at times beyond the normal media deadlines. The capacity to pursue issues in estimates and ask supplemental questions is restricted.

The opposition has the opportunity to ask questions during Question Time which is held on each parliamentary sitting day. Again, however, this process is open to considerable criticism as a mechanism to enable the Opposition to discover legitimate information about the Government's activities.

Question Time in the Queensland Legislative Assembly suffers from the following defects:

- Government and opposition members basically take turn and turn about to ask questions. That means that of every hour allocated to Question Time, at least half an hour is devoted to government members asking "Dorothy Dix" questions of ministers who are able to give scripted and structured responses either extolling the government's virtues or attacking the Opposition.
- Supplementary questions have not generally been permitted.
- In Queensland, answers need not have any relevance to the question asked. Consistent rulings of Queensland Speakers have been that the minister can answer a question in any way the minister likes. Most answers to opposition questions are a diatribe of abuse from ministers against the opposition with no restraint being imposed by speakers appointed from the government ranks.

Question time is basically a theatrical performance with the opposition largely concentrating on "gotcha" questioning rather than undertaking any serious analysis of government failures and certainly no suggestion of offering any alternative policy solutions.

In addition to questions without notice, each member is entitled to ask at each parliamentary sitting, one question on notice to which the government is required to respond within one month. Again, answers to questions on notice do not have to be relevant to the questions asked. An examination of answers to questions on notice reveals that they, too, contain a large amount of partisan rhetoric and invective.

In addition to the process of obtaining information through questions, the opposition also has a right to seek information under Right to Information Legislation (RTI). However, the government limits the capacity of the opposition to exploit this source of information by requiring not only that the opposition pay the standard fee for lodging an RTI application, but also insists on charging the opposition for the supply of any information which the opposition identifies that it wishes to receive. All these costs have to be met from the budget allocated to the opposition. There is thus a consistent constraint upon the opposition in having to pay government-imposed charges from an already limited budget.

The absence of an upper house in Queensland – impacts on oppositions

Since 1922, Queensland, unlike other Australian States, has had a unicameral parliament. This has meant that the party that wins majority status in the Legislative Assembly completely controls executive government through the cabinet and is able to dominate the whole process of government and parliament. So long as the party in government maintains its own internal discipline, long-term political dominance is achievable. The opposition in eras of long-term government has generally been weak, divided and largely ineffectual. Both the Borbidge and Newman governments were defeated because of their own internal problems or ill-advised policy decisions, not because of the effectiveness of the Labor opposition.

Because of government dominance of the only chamber of parliament there is no alternative power base from which a dominant executive government can be attacked as can potentially occur in parliaments containing second chambers. Second chambers are often elected on electoral systems other than single member electorates, such as proportional representation. This means that a government will often not control both houses. Even if it does control the upper house, there is a difference in approach demonstrated by members, even of the same party, in the two houses given the different ways in which they are elected and the different constituencies which they are required to service.

There is thus greater potential in a bicameral system for an opposition to be able to exercise more effective political power through the necessity of passing legislation in an upper house. This has a significant impact upon factors that in a unicameral parliament bedevil an opposition, namely, the attraction of suitable candidates and thus MPs and the raising of donations from community groups and individuals who seek to advance their interests through the political process.

It is thus clearly arguable that opposition in Queensland has been, and continues to remain, significantly weakened through the unicameral structure of the Parliament.

Conclusion

An effective opposition is vital to the functioning of a parliamentary democracy. Without an opposition using the forum of parliament to hold the government of the day accountable for its policies and administration the vital tension that underpins the democratic process will not occur. Any government without this brake on its activities will thus tend to slide towards authoritarianism which is a threat to the very existence of the democratic process.

Queensland with its unicameral parliament and executive domination of government needs an effective opposition to counter the extremely long terms of one party domination of the parliament. Apart from short interregnums, Queensland has been dominated by three long terms: ALP 1915 to 1957; Coalition 1957 to 1989; since 1989 Labor. Interruptions to these dominations have been short-term only and have usually disintegrated largely through the inexperience of those thrust into government.

In the absence of the brake of a second chamber on the powers of executive government, Queensland needs to explore enhancing the role of the opposition through providing it with resources that are independent of the intense oversight and control of the government of the day and which the opposition can utilise in whatever way it believes to be politically effective in holding government to account. Unless this occurs, one party domination of parliament and thus executive government will continue to be the rule. This is not good for the maintenance of democracy in Queensland.

References
Bateman, J., *In the Shadows: The Shadow Cabinet in* Australia, Canberra: Commonwealth Parliamentary Library, 2009

12

Opposition in South Australia

Clement Macintyre, John Williams, and Rob Manwaring

Introduction

The behaviour of parliamentary oppositions is inevitably shaped by the overarching institutional characteristics that define Westminster-style parliaments. At the same time, to a large degree, it is also shaped by the circumstances that are found in the various parliamentary practices and cultures that are specific to each parliament. In South Australia, one of the most notable political features is that the election outcomes regularly produce governments with small majorities that have sometimes included, or minority governments that have had to include, independent members of parliament. In six of the 16 state elections from 1970 – 2022, the party winning office has not achieved a majority of seats. This is partly because the South Australian Parliament is relatively small by Australian standards (with only the Tasmanian Parliament and the two unicameral Territories having fewer members). It is also because, after the passing of the *Referendum (Electoral Redistribution) Act 1990* (SA), until its repeal in 2018, there was a constitutional requirement which stipulated that electoral districts were redistributed after each election to ensure that any party securing more than 50 per cent of the valid two-party preferred vote should expect to win a majority of seats in the House of Assembly. Reflecting the distinctive electoral demography of South Australia, this led to frequent election results where the numbers in the South Australian House of Assembly were fairly evenly divided.

Parties that govern in minority or with a bare winning majority are often thought to be more disciplined and more focussed in their behaviour. In his comments on the swing away from the Rann Government on the night of the 2010 election, Kevin Foley (then Labor Deputy Premier and Treasurer) admitted the first Rann Government (2002-06) may have been a "better government because [its minority status meant] it had a sharper focus" (ABC *Election Broadcast*, 20 March 2010). Similarly, Steve Bracks (Labor Premier of Victoria 1999-2007), when discussing the prospects of a hung parliament in Canberra in August 2010, acknowledged his experience of minority government led, in some respects, to better government: "We had to discipline legislation better, we had to articulate it more precisely and we had to persuade and argue and that wasn't a bad thing" (ABC, *7.30 Report*, 26 August 2010). However, whether or not oppositions perform at an optimum level when they are within a few seats of government is less certain. The party room can often be distracted by the frustration of having just failed to win, by some recriminations over (perhaps critical) campaign errors, or by some ill-disciplined manoeuvring in anticipation of potential ministerial roles following the next election. This chapter will examine the distinctive patterns of South Australian political history and assess the role of the opposition and the development of the oppositions' parliamentary tactics in the context of a small parliament that has experienced a significant number of very close election outcomes.

Historical Background

The introduction of responsible government in South Australia brought with it, by default, many of the constitutional institutions and parliamentary conventions of Westminster. The Constitution enacted following the passage of the *Australian Colonies Act 1850* (Imp) stipulated there would be a House of Assembly, a Legislative Council and an executive that would be drawn from the elected members of these two chambers. The *Constitution Act 1856* (Imp) stated in section 1 that:

> There shall be, in place of the Legislative Council now subsisting, a Legislative Council and a House of Assembly, which shall be called "The Parliament of South Australia", and shall be severally constituted in the manner hereinafter prescribed, and such

> Legislative Council and House of Assembly shall have and exercise
> all the powers and functions of the existing Legislative Council.

As was the case with the Australian Constitution, the South Australia
Constitution was silent on the existence and role of political parties and
on the structural arrangements of the government until 1985 (when a
constitutional change required that any casual vacancy in the Legislative
Council be filled by a person "publicly recognised by a particular political
party as being an endorsed candidate of that party"). There was in 1856,
for example, no reference to a head of government, to the electoral
arrangements that were to be used, or to the existence of political parties.
As was the case in the other self-governing Australian Colonies, it was
assumed the conventions and practices that had evolved over time at
Westminster would be adopted and developed to suit the particular local
circumstances. Accordingly, the South Australian Parliament that first sat
in 1857 was recognisably a product of the Westminster system, although
it had several distinctive features reflecting local preferences. One of
the most notable of these was the democratic franchise used to elect
members. Every South Australian male (including Aboriginal men) over
the age of 21 was eligible to vote in 1857, and while the franchise for the
Legislative Council was restricted to those with property, it was at least
an elected chamber, unlike the House of Lords. Similarly, the disposition
of the House of Assembly in its early years, with some members seated at
desks looking directly at the presiding officer (rather than in oppositional
benches as was the case in Westminster), suggests a different initial
conception of the role of government and opposition.

In fact, the absence of clearly defined parties in the first few decades after
self-government meant the administration of South Australia was far from
the more stable and predictable model of government and opposition that
eventually became the norm by the last years of the nineteenth century.
For instance, the balance of numbers, and the fluid and shifting allegiances
of members of parliament in the early years, ensured governments were
frequent and short-lived. In the 44 years between 1857 and federation
in 1901, there were 36 separate governments led by 21 different men.

Each administration lasted on average about one year and four months. In contrast, in the following 120 years, there have been only 21 changes of government, with just 29 men as head of government. The advent of four-year terms in 1985 with limited opportunities for early elections, followed by fixed four-year terms after the 2002 election means greater stability has now been literally entrenched. It can thus be seen that, again reflecting patterns seen in Westminster and elsewhere in Australia, it was not until the emergence of more settled and disciplined political parties that governments became more stable. A parallel development was that those opposed to the government began to see themselves as constituting a formal parliamentary opposition in the sense we understand it today.

The emerging concept of opposition

The idea of a "loyal opposition" existing in Westminster parliaments as a group of members who opposed the government of the day, voiced criticism of it, and who sought to replace it on the treasury benches (Johnson 1997: 489), does of course pre-date self-government in South Australia. The historic battles between the Crown and the Parliament in England eventually resulted in the Parliament winning the right to exercise sovereign power. In turn, the capacity of members of parliament to voice criticism of the administration, which had once been limited to "private, local and special grievances" with no opportunity to criticise the Crown over the conduct of matters of State, moved to the point where groupings in the Parliament could legitimately seek to "check the excesses of ministries" (Hockin 1966; Potter 1966: 6). In other words, opposition moved from being little more than the expression of local concerns, to a position where the constitutional authority of the government of the day was recognised. Accordingly, the direction of government and the policies of the government could be legitimately challenged without at the same time challenging the constitutional authority itself. Yet, even with this development, blurred party allegiances in the British House of Commons meant it was not until the 1840s that a party presenting itself as the alterative government won power at an election, and most opposition consisted of little more than a critique of the government rather than the positive promotion of an alternative program. Only when the settled two-party system was stabilised after the Reform Act of 1867 did a clear pattern of government and alternative government emerge (Johnson: 488-89, Hanham 1966: 38). So an *organised* Opposition (with a capital 'O') as distinct from *ad hoc* criticism of the government of the day really did not emerge in Westminster parliaments until well after self-government was established in South Australia. There the same informal conception of opposition to the government of the day, gradually and similarly evolved into a formally recognised position as the party system became established in the 1890s.

Prior to self-government the notion of opposition in the formal sense was contested, even within the South Australian Parliament itself. A debate in the Legislative Council on possible constitutional amendments in October 1852 shows that the term "leader of the opposition" was used in a way completely at odds with the modern understanding. Robert Torrens (the Registrar-General) pointedly noted an amendment "would have been carried, had not the Advocate-General (Richard Hanson) – the leader of the opposition, with his own peculiar tact, moved the adjournment of the House". Hanson, a fellow office holder in the Legislative Council, queried Torrens' description and the following sharp exchange was recorded:

> ADVOCATE-GENERAL: He did not know what was meant by that; he sat there as one of the members of Her Majesty's Government, and–
>
> The REGISTRAR-GENERAL would not leave the hon. and learned member under a misapprehension. When he spoke of the opposition, he meant those opposed to his own views.
>
> The ADVOCATE-GENERAL must say then that anything more arrogant and contemptible he never heard uttered. For one member of the Government to express his own opinions, and to term those who differed from him the opposition, certainly showed a degree of–
>
> The REGISTRAR-GENERAL must again prevent his sentiments being misunderstood or misrepresented. He had stated, when he first spoke upon the question, and had been followed by others in that course, that he did not speak as a member of the Government,

but simply as Robert Torrens; and he could not suppose that any hon. Member who had heard him could imagine he meant to arrogate to himself the post of the Government, or term those who differed from him the opposition, in the sense which was now sought to be put upon his words. When he spoke of the leader of the opposition he only meant the leader of those who were opposed to him in argument.

The ADVOCATE-GENERAL had certainly attached its ordinary meaning to the word opposition; and he must say it would have been very much better if the hon. member had explained at the time that he had used it in a non-natural sense. He might remark, however, that as far as there was any opposition in the matter, it was the Registrar-General, who was opposing the motion before the House (*South Australian Register*, 21 October 1852).

The slow development of the concept of opposition and the delay in according formal recognition to the opposition party is reflected in the official records of the South Australian House of Assembly. The *Statistical Record of the Legislature* contains a list the recognised "Leaders of the Opposition" from 1884. By the 1880s the office was well recognised in South Australia and the other colonies. *The Advertiser*, reporting on the opening of the fourth session of the twelfth parliament in 1889, lamented the "absurd practice" that the Governor's Speech would not be made available to the public until it was published. It acknowledged the reality of political life that "probably the idea of communicating, as an act of Parliamentary courtesy, the opening speech to the leader of the Opposition would not commend itself to the Ministry" (*The Advertiser*, 6 June 1889).

Notwithstanding the institutional acknowledgement, the accompanying notes to the *Statistical Record of the Legislature* point out that the term was not used consistently in the *Parliamentary Debates* of that period, and it was not until 1919 that an allowance was provided for the leader of the opposition under the Estimates of Expenditure. While provision had be made for remuneration of the Leader of the Opposition, other support was limited. During debate in the Assembly in November 1920 the plight of John Gunn, the Labor Leader of the Opposition, was discussed. *The*

Advertiser reported:

> Mr. Denny called attention to what he described as the inadequate provision for the leader of the Opposition. He should have some clerical assistance.
>
> Mr. Hill – He is getting only a clerk's salary.
>
> Mr. Petherick – 1 would like to see him get another £100 a year.
>
> Mr. Denny – So would I.
>
> The Premier agreed that Mr. Gunn was hard worked. In other Oppositions, however, the work had been distributed.
>
> Mr. Hill – That is only side-stepping.
>
> The Premier – 1 am prepared to take the provision of clerical assistance into consideration next session.
>
> Mr. Hill said the Government should increase the salary. The leader of the Opposition was at the beck and call of the whole State – as the Premier would realise after next election. (Laughter.)
>
> Mr. Butterfield did not think the leader of the Opposition had ever been properly treated. He should have a State motor car, the same as a minister (*The Advertiser*, 4 November 1920).

Since 1948 the salary of the opposition leader has been covered by the Act that regulates the payments to members of parliament. Surprisingly, despite the late adoption of the formal description of the leader of the largest non-government party as the leader of the opposition it was introduced several decades before the term "Premier" was officially used (despite its fairly common use in debates and the media). The *Statistical Record* shows that Frank Walsh (ALP Premier 1965-67) was the first head of government to have the formal title of Premier (*Statistical Record of the Legislature*, 118). Before this, the head of government usually (but not always) held the post of Treasurer, but was not officially described as Premier (Jaensch 1977: 108).

The South Australian political culture

There has been a total of 44 leaders of the opposition since 1884 (with 9 serving more than one term in this position). The first 40 were men while Isobel Redmond, (Liberal) Opposition Leader from July 2009 to

February 2013, is the only woman to have led a major party in the South Australian Parliament.[1] The average tenure of office of a leader of the opposition is just under two and a half years. However, just as the term of office enjoyed by a premier has tended to be longer in more recent years as the patterns of government have become more stable, so the tenure of opposition leaders has also increased. Between 1884 and 1949, leaders of the opposition averaged less than two years in the position. Since 1949, the average period has been just under four years.

So, in common with most of the majoritarian Westminster style parliaments around the world, the South Australian Parliament has adopted and evolved a set of structural arrangements that see the formal recognition of a government (based on the capacity of one party to command a majority on the floor of the lower house) opposed by an official opposition (made up of the next largest party). Such formality continues today. Yet despite the South Australian Parliament acknowledging the existence and role of the opposition, legislation rarely does. Only a handful of Acts passed by the South Australian Parliament make reference to the Leader of the Opposition. In general, this merely recognises a nomination by the opposition to a statutory committee or reference to remuneration.

In South Australia, the emergence of a dominant party political culture at the end of the nineteenth century, subsequently strongly reinforced in the House of Assembly first by electoral reforms that introducing contingency voting in 1929, then preferential voting, and by the use of single-member electoral districts from the 1938 election, has meant two party blocks have been entrenched over the past 120 years. One of these parties, the Australian Labor Party, has remained a constant political presence through the whole period. The other (variously called Conservative, Liberal, Liberal Country League and, since the 1970s, the Liberal Party) has been the dominant anti-Labor grouping. While minor parties have succeeded in winning seats in the House of Assembly, as have a few independents, the Liberals and Labor are the only parties that have formed government or had the status of official opposition. The main periods of government in South Australia since the 1940s are outlined in Table 1.

Table 1: South Australian Governments and Premiers

1940s	Playford				
1950s	Playford				
1960s			Walsh	Dunstan	Hall
1970s		Dunstan			Corcoran
1980s	Tonkin	Bannon			
1990s		Arnold	Brown		Olsen
2000s	Kerin	Rann			
2010s	Weatherill				Marshall
2020s	Mali-nauskas				

Legend: LCL/Liberal
**   Labor**

One of the characteristics of the South Australian electorate is that support for these dominant blocks has been fairly stable and fairly evenly divided. Since the formation of the Liberal Country League in June 1932, the LCL (later Liberal Party) first preference lower house vote has averaged about 40 per cent, while the ALP has enjoyed about 44 per cent support. With their average share of the vote since the 1938 election (the first with single member constituencies and preferential voting) exceeding 80 per cent, this domination made it very difficult for a third party to challenge the major parties' ascendency. More recently there has been some erosion in support for the major parties – a trend in common with the rest of Australia and many comparable advanced industrial democracies. For example, in the nine state elections held between 1970 and 1993 first preference support for the major parties fell blow 80 per cent just once. In the following seven elections (1993-2022), the major party first preference vote has gone above 80 per cent only once.[2] In sum, while the major party axis is still a dominate feature of government and opposition in South Australia, it is now a more fluid one. An overview of party competition is shown in Table 2.

Table 2: South Australian State Elections 1970 - 2022

Election	Labor	Liberal	Other	Gov	Seat Diff between ALP & Lib Seats	ALP First Prefs	LIB First Pref	Combined First Prefs	ALP TPP	LIB TPP
2022	27	16	4	ALP	11	39.97	35.67	75.64	54.6	45.4
2018	19	25	3	LIB	-6	32.79	37.97	70.76	48.1	51.9
2014	23	22	2	ALP	1	35.80	44.78	80.58	47.0	53.0
2010	26	18	3	ALP	8	37.47	41.65	79.12	48.4	51.6
2006	28	15	4	ALP	13	45.22	33.97	79.19	56.8	43.2
2002	23	20	4	ALP	3	36.34	39.97	76.31	49.1	50.9
1997	21	23	3	LIB	-2	35.16	40.40	75.56	48.5	51.5
1993	10	37	0	LIB	-27	30.37	52.80	83.17	39.1	60.9
1989	22	22	3	ALP	0	40.09	44.21	84.30	48.0	52.0
1985	27	16	4	ALP	11	48.19	42.15	90.34	53.2	46.8
1982	24	21	2	ALP	3	46.28	42.67	88.95	50.9	49.1
1979	20	24	3	LIB	-4	40.86	47.94	88.80	45.0	55.0
1977	27	17	3	ALP	2	51.64	41.21	92.85	53.4	46.6
1975	23	20	4	ALP	3	46.32	31.53	77.85	49.2	50.8
1973	26	20	1	ALP	6	51.52	39.79	91.31	54.5	45.5
1970	27	20	0	ALP	7	51.64	43.76	95.40	53.3	46.7

NB: Shaded totals are Two Party Preferred vote where party with plurality did *not* win office.

Yet, despite the dominance of the two major parties, the South Australian Parliament is unusual in the Australian context in that most elections have seen the return of at least one minor party or independent to the lower house. Since 1938 only three elections (1968, 1970, and 1993) have not seen a minor party or independent member of parliament elected to the House of Assembly. Since 1973, the average number of "others" elected at each election is 2.9 – remarkable given the size of the house, and the plurality electoral system. Minor parties such as the Nationals (and their Country Party predecessors), the Liberal Movement and the Australian Democrats have won seats, but the most regular non-major party presence has been provided by independents. To be sure, many of the independents were originally elected as a member of, or aligned to, one of the major parties, but even so many subsequently won their seats against endorsed major party candidates at later elections. This relatively even support for the major parties, together with the regular election of a small number of cross-benchers in a small Parliament of only 47 members (39 members of parliament from 1938-70) means numbers on the floor of the House are often fairly even, and that would suggest government and opposition should be regularly exchanged.

In fact, this is only half true. Consistent with the regular election of cross-benchers, the South Australian Parliament has frequently experienced bare winning majority governments or minority governments formed in a hung Parliament. However, the turnover of government has been less regular, and both of the major parties have, in turn, been able to enjoy long periods of political ascendency. A notional division of South Australia's political history since the 1933 election (the first following the formation of the Liberal Country League) into two blocks, shows that the LCL dominated the first 32 years, holding office uninterruptedly from 1933-65, while Labor has been the natural party of government since and been in office for 40 of the subsequent 58 years, interrupted only by four periods of Liberal government in that time. The obvious consequence of this pattern is that each of the major parties has had to endure long periods of opposition. A sustained time in opposition bring its own problems, not the least of which is a tendency to low morale and real difficulties in recruiting the most able candidates. A further (often related) problem is that frustrations and inexperience can sometimes leave the opposition exposed and appearing to the public to be unready for government. Yet, while long terms in opposition have been the norm in South Australia, for most of the time the opposition has faced a government with a very small majority, or one that has been returned as a minority government. Of the 24 elections held between the Second World War and 2022, seven resulted in a hung parliament, while another eight saw the government elected with a majority of just one or two seats. In only one election, in 1993 following the collapse of the State Bank, has a government been returned with a majority of more than five seats. So, the nature of South

Australian politics over the past few decades has meant extended time in opposition (mainly for the Liberal Party) but opposed to a government with a bare winning majority or holding office as a minority government. In this respect South Australia does not follow the examples from other Australian jurisdictions, and the strategies of opposition have been partly shaped by the experience of these particular circumstances.

The role of opposition

The general role of the oppositions in Westminster parliaments has been described by numerous commentators. Common to nearly all accounts is that the prime role of the opposition is to oppose the government of the day. However, an essential part of the model is that the process of opposition to, and criticism of, the government must be conducted within the accepted constitutional rules. A "loyal" opposition is one that wants to win, but not at the expense of breaking the system (Norton 2008; Potter 1966). It has been argued that parliaments have three principal functions: legislation or law-making, oversight of the executive, and representation (with legitimation of the constitutional process as a fourth function) (Donahoe 2002: 111-2). Given this, oppositions, in turn, have several distinct roles of their own. These are to monitor the integrity of the executive, to argue for action in relation to perceived needs, to ensure transparency of process and access to open information and provide an alternative interpretation of government policies and actions (Schmitz 1998: 9). In essence, within the accepted constitutional boundaries, an opposition should challenge the government of the day, force the government to justify itself, and offer an alternative government. Those conceptual and constitutional boundaries themselves reflect the superior place of the government. Consistent with the Commonwealth and other State Constitutions the South Australian Constitution deposes critical functions to the government. So, for instance, money bills must originate in the House of Assembly thus denying the opposition the capacity to control the budget. So too the sitting of Parliament is controlled by the government of the day. In turn, the legislature must recognise the legitimate role of the opposition through the provision of adequate resources, and the government of the day must accept the right of the opposition to voice its views. As Philip Norton has said, "the government is entitled to get its business, but the opposition is entitled to be heard" (Norton: 245).

By definition, an opposition does not have the numbers to win a vote on the floor of the lower house. If it is to be heard it partly relies upon the established procedures of the parliament and, to a large extent, it therefore relies upon the government which has the capacity to schedule debates and arrange the business of the House. Of course, governments cannot dismiss the claims of the opposition out of hand. As all political parties know, in time the wheel will turn and those in government today will one day themselves be in opposition. Increasingly, the opposition relies upon an attentive media to pick up and respond to the issues it raises (though from time to time the relationship is reversed and the opposition will take up a matter first raised in the press). In the South Australian Parliament, oppositions have traditionally targeted the scheduled Question Time to attract media attention. While Matters of Urgency and Grievance Debates and Estimates Hearings are also used to explore particular areas of opposition concern, Question Time in the South Australian Parliament lasts for sixty minutes each sitting day and is the only session of the day's sitting when the media are certain to be present. Successive oppositions have thus built their political strategies around briefing the press before and after Question Time and co-ordinating the focus of the questions that go to the government.

The Opposition today

For the Liberal Opposition in South Australia in the first decades of the twenty-first century, one of the consequences of this day-to-day concentration was a tendency to use Question Time to chase different issues rather than build and sustain pressure on weak points in the government. A combination of the fact that the Liberal opposition has often been in a position where it is close to government (in the sense that it is only a few seats short of a majority) and has, at the same time, often had to deal with internal pressures means it has concentrated on short-term strategies rather than drawn-out long term tactical assaults upon the government.

Any examination of the Liberal Party in South Australia over the past 50 years shows there have been two strong factions in the party vying for dominance. The divisions date from the original rift in the Party experienced before Steele Hall formed the Liberal Movement in 1972 as a result of the tensions between the more conservative rural-based members of the Party and the more moderate (often younger and urban-based) Liberals who argued for electoral reform and some more progressive social reforms (Jaensch and Bullock 1978). Despite efforts over the years to downplay the divide, there is no doubt there have been intergenerational tensions between sections of the Liberal Party and these have made it difficult for Liberal Party leaders – whether in government or opposition – to concentrate their full resources on their Labor opponents. Indeed, the frustrations proved too much for former Liberal leader Martin Hamilton-Smith, who resigned from the Liberal Party in 2014 to join the Labor cabinet while sitting as an independent liberal. Factionalism within the South Australian Liberal Party remains an enduring problem.

In the period between Sir Tom Playford's retirement in 1966 and the election of David Speirs in 2022, the Liberal Party has had thirteen leaders (including two separate periods as leader by John Olsen). Over the same years, Labor has had just seven leaders. This relative instability has meant Liberal leaders of the opposition have perhaps been under more pressure than their opponents (or some colleagues in other jurisdictions). This, as a consequence, suggests they do not have the luxury of an extended time frame to build long term political strategies. Often, when in opposition, the South Australian Liberals have therefore sought ephemeral political gains rather than building long, more telling attacks on the government of the day. It might also be fair to surmise that in recent election campaigns

Labor has often demonstrated more ruthless and, at times, questionable tactics, especially in the critical marginal seats. Two examples will serve here. At the 2010 election, Labor volunteers were accused of misdirection by wearing blue "Put your Family First" T-Shirts and handing out misleading "how to vote" cards, seeking to siphon preferences from the socially conservative Family First Party (ABC Radio Adelaide *News*: 24 March 2010). In 2014, Labor was accused of using racist campaign material with a tagline of "Can you Trust Habib?" targeting the Liberal candidate Carolyn Habib in the seat of Elder (ABC Radio Adelaide *News*: 12 March 2014). This relates to one of the key factors in explaining opposition performance – "unity and vigour" (Ball 2003: 24). At crucial elections, the ALP has shown not only a much stronger sense of internal unity, but also a much greater appetite either in government, or more rarely in opposition, to secure the keys to office. The unexpected ALP win in 2014 is a good example, and also the Liberals' loss in 2022. A key point is that the two major parties can operate differently when in opposition.

Two otherwise contextual factors are worth noting in understanding the opposition today; the changing media environment, and the advent of a more leader-centric and personalised polity. The desire to get a story on the main evening electronic news bulletins or the front page of the (only) local daily newspaper often means the opposition will focus upon different issues on successive days. As a result, the slower, more forensic attacks upon particular ministers or policy issues are less evident, and the concentration has been placed on more immediate campaigns. The so-called 24 hour news cycle, even the localised one, arguably makes it harder for the opposition to reach public consciousness.

A second contextual factor which might be shaping the dynamics of opposition behaviour and tactics are the claims that the wider political environment is more personalised and leader-centric (Walter, t'Hart and Strangio 2017). In political science scholarship there remains a debate about the extent to which a new focus on individuals and leaders, especially amplified through digital media, is displacing traditional political institutions. If there is currency to this trend, it might mean at the state level, that individual leaders have greater importance in shaping political debates and, as a result, opposition strategy might well focus on elevating strong leaders and targeting perceived weak leaders. Attacks on leaders are not new, and South Australia has had a long history of charismatic leaders (notably Sir Tom Playford and Don Dunstan); but the key issue is that personalisation might be shaping political and opposition strategies in more pronounced ways. Liberal opposition leader Rob Kerin faced strong attacks from the ALP government at both 2002 and 2006 elections. Most recently, Labor was strongly critical of Liberal Premier Steven Marshall's management of COVID-19 restrictions and placed a strong emphasis on its own leader, the more charismatic Peter Malinauskas, which was a central part of its successful 2022 campaign.

In terms of strategy and approach to reach public consciousness, South Australian oppositions have realised Question Time offers the most public forum within the Parliamentary sitting schedule. Even then, under the Standing Orders of the House of Assembly, there are strict rules over the way questions can be framed and put to the government: "a Member may not offer argument or opinion, nor may a Member offer any facts except by leave of the House and only so far as is necessary to explain the question" (South Australian House of Assembly, *Standing Orders* No 97). Questions in the House cannot contain contextual explanations ahead of the question and cannot contain supposition as a prelude to the question. The House of Assembly Standing Orders, in fact, act to limit the approach that can be taken by the opposition – or more accurately allow the government greater license to avoid the intent of the question. It is true that in the Legislative Council, members of the opposition questioning ministers have fewer constraints than do their colleagues in the lower house, but it is in the lower house that government is formed and where most of the key ministers sit. Also, importantly, the level of media coverage of the South Australian Legislative Council is minimal. However, as is ever the case, the reforms proposed by oppositions (of whichever party) from time to time to make Question Time a more useful exercise – with greater scope in the nature of the questions and supplementary questions, limits to the time taken by each question and answer, more rigour in ensuring the relevance of answers and other similar proposals – tend not to be supported by the government of the day and tend not to survive when a party moves from opposition to government.

In the South Australian Parliament there are other particular circumstances that also have to be accommodated. The most pressing of these for the opposition is the limited resources that can be called upon. So, for example, while the leader of the opposition has a staff allowance and has office space (roughly equal to that of a minister) allocated within the Parliamentary building, the capacity of the opposition to sustain a critical oversight of the government is limited. The leader has fewer staff than the lowest ranked minister in the government and there is some evidence that with a growth in ministerial allowances that has not been matched for the opposition, the ratio of opposition staff is declining. A recent senior opposition member of parliament suggested the sum of the staff and ancillary resources available to the opposition leaves the opposition disadvantaged in relation to the government by a ratio about 32:1 (private communication with authors).

The more general support services available to opposition members of parliament are, of course, the same as all other members enjoy. But these, as is the case with most entitlements, are largely at the discretion of the government. All members of the parliament are entitled to an office in the Parliamentary Building. Members of the House of Assembly also have an electorate office with modest staffing. The final determination of staff numbers follows a formula determined by the Treasurer and detailed in the "Electorate Services Handbook". Back-bench members of parliament have an entitlement to 1.6 FTE staff (sometimes supplemented by some trainee positions). Ministers, the speaker and the whips have larger electorate office staff. Members of the Legislative Council have accommodation in the Parliament, but do not have separate electorate offices and have more modest staffing allowances. Over time, governments have used the allocation of staff in quite deliberate ways, and some minor parties and independents have been able to make a case to the government that they need additional support. Depending upon the mood of the government at the time and their attitude towards the minor parties, this extra entitlement can be withdrawn. All members receive entitlements in the form of a global allowance to defray the costs of travel, accommodation, stationery and related expenses. The 2021 Annual Report of the House of Assembly reported that the total cost of supplies and services for members was $453,000 in 2021 (an average of $9,638 per Member) (Parliamentary Service of the House of Assembly, *Annual Report, 2021-2022*, Financial Statements, 13).

The opposition is clearly disadvantaged in terms of research facilities available in that opposition members cannot, of course, use the research facilities open to members of the executive through their ministerial offices (and indirectly to government party back-benchers through the Public Service). Nevertheless, all members have equal access to the Parliamentary Library and opposition members and government back-bench members have access to the Library's research services. Given the relatively small size of the South Australian Parliament, the Parliamentary Library offers a wide range of research services.

Opposition members of committees also have access to the support services provided for each of the ten Standing Committees of the South Australian Parliament as well as the more transitory Select Committees. The Standing Committees are a mixture of House of Assembly Committees, Legislative Council Committees and Joint Committees. Reflecting the fact that the government does not have a majority in the Legislative Council (where no government has held a majority since 1975 – the first election after the major electoral reforms of the early 1970s), most Legislative Council and Joint Committees have Members drawn from the parties in such a way as to ensure no single party holds a majority. In contrast, government members constitute a majority of the two House of Assembly Committees (Public Works and Economic and Finance). The recent pattern for Select Committees is that the governing party will not hold majority membership and the Chair or

Convenor is drawn from the opposition or cross-benches. The capacity of an opposition member to subject the government to scrutiny through membership of a committee depends upon the specific membership and focus of each committee. Nevertheless, active opposition use of opportunities arising in committee hearings and deliberations can be a useful part of process of keeping governments accountable. Committees, despite the constraints experienced by the opposition in the South Australian Parliament, provide one of the more valuable institutional avenues available to oppose a government. Observers of the Westminster system have pointed out that governments' capacity to set the agenda, together with oppositions' inability to enforce a veto gives great power to the governing party (Kaiser 2008: 25-8, Helms 2008: 10-2).

As noted above, the opposition is less hampered in the Legislative Council. Since 1975, the South Australia Legislative Council has been elected using proportional representation (PR). There are 22 Members of the Legislative Council and the whole of the State constitutes a single electoral district with 11 Members elected every four years for eight-year terms. The introduction of PR in the early 1970s resulted in no single party (or coalition of parties) being able to win a majority of the seats in the upper house since 1975. As a consequence, none of the governments since then has been able to guarantee the passage of legislation, and a combination of the opposition party of the day together with minor parties (first the Liberal Movement, then Australian Democrats, then Family First and more recently the Greens and SA Best) has had a blocking power. In fact, despite the long absence of a government majority in the Legislative Council, the general practice is that most bills are passed (albeit often with some amendment) after negotiation and consultation between the government, the opposition and cross-benches. It was estimated that between 1975 and 1998, only 1.8 per cent of all government bills were rejected outright (Davis 2001, Macintyre and Williams 2008: 220). So, while there appears to be a less combative relationship between the government of the day and the opposition in the Legislative Council, it is, in fact, the constant presence of the minor parties and independents since the electoral reforms of the early 1970s that has contributed to the more moderated role for the opposition. This different political culture in the upper house is important as, under the terms of the South Australian Constitution, the Legislative Council has the power to block all legislation. In other words, unlike some other State upper houses which can only delay, the South Australian Legislative Council has the same (relatively) unfettered powers as the Australian Senate.

Future prospects

As discussed above, the capacity of the South Australian opposition to act as a check upon the executive government of the day is partly a function of the legal and parliamentary frameworks within which it operates. Some of these are long-standing and entrenched and hence not susceptible to easy change or reform. Others, however, are part of the evolving political culture of South Australia in particular, and the changing modern government practices found more generally in Australia. There are clear limits upon the ability of political parties to shape these while they are in opposition, and then considerably less incentive for them to do so when they have won office and have formed a government. Nevertheless, in South Australia, (as is the case elsewhere in Australia), the nature of state government is changing and, as a direct consequence, the patterns of political opposition need to evolve at the same time.

Perhaps the clearest evidence of this is the more restricted policy roles assumed by State governments.

In the past few decades the changing nature of the relationship between Australian governments and the State governments has resulted in the Commonwealth actively shaping many of the States' policy decisions. Whether it be through tied grants or through incentives for greater collaboration via the Council of Australian Governments (and more recently the National Cabinet), there can be no doubt that in areas such as health, education, industrial relations among others, the States' role has increasingly become one of service provision rather than outright policy determination. In this context, inevitably, the task of opposition falls more to the opposition party in the Federal Parliament than it does to the State oppositions. That is one change that the South Australia opposition will have to accommodate (as will other State oppositions). Yet so far we have not seen much evidence of new party structures and strategies being put into place to reflect this new environment. The COVID-19 pandemic also placed new pressures on the federal dynamics, and to some extent, there was a resurgence of the states, especially on border control. This proved a difficult context for the (then Labor) South Australian opposition, since much of the government's policy response was driven and shaped by statutory offices – especially the Chief Health Officer and the Police Commissioner. With a broad bi-partisanship around the State's response, it was a particularly difficult period for the opposition to navigate, but still formed part of their successful critique of the government at the 2022 election.

Another change that oppositions will have to deal with is the increasing trend across Australia for governments to work more and more through complex financial relationships with private investors to build and manage public infrastructure projects. This has allowed governments to shelter behind "commercial in confidence" agreements and deny parliamentary oppositions full access to the financial arrangements. A text search of *Hansard* in the South Australian Parliament reveals many instances when opposition questions to ministers and public servants at Estimates are avoided by reliance upon commercial in confidence agreements. In South Australia these have been regularly used to evade scrutiny on recent major infrastructure projects such as the desalination plant and the construction of the new Royal Adelaide Hospital, as well as the cost involved in luring celebrities cyclists to the Tour Down Under, or well-known musicians to promotional events, or agreements over hosting golf tournaments. This trend of governments shielding themselves from formal parliamentary scrutiny and denying transparency of process means the opposition's ability to monitor the activities of the government and to act as a check upon the executive is severely curtailed. Increasingly, the only real opportunity to ensure oversight of process falls to agencies like the Auditor-General. In South Australia – the last state jurisdiction to introduce an anti-corruption agency – any hindrance upon the ability of the opposition to perform its role must be seen as a cause for concern.

One response to the changing role of the States and the changing political behaviour of State governments might be to argue oppositions have to change to adapt to the new contemporary political patterns. In fact oppositions will not so much have to change their role, as reinforce one aspect of it. As long ago as 1914 Lord Robert Cecil, giving evidence to the Select Committee on Procedure at Westminster made the point that the opposition should not measure its performance by winning battles in the House. Rather, he argued, "the tactics of an opposition are devoted, not to obtaining any result in the House itself, but to producing some effect among the electorate" (Cecil 1966: 8). In other words, much of the work of the opposition should always be devoted to ways it can shape the outcome of the broader public debates, rather than concentrate on less telling skirmishes in the House. The fact that governments have moved to close down the opportunities for scrutiny within parliaments does not mean oppositions cannot play a critical role in forcing the government of the day to justify itself. In South Australia it is fair to say that this "alternative" role has not always been embraced by the opposition.

A further change might well be the changing character of the South Australian party system. Whilst on the face of it, it might still be viewed as a classic two-party system, it might better be understood as a dominant party system, given the ascendency of Labor in winning 12 of the 16 elections since 1970, albeit with a number of small majorities (or in minority government) (Arian and Barnes 1974). While to some extent this reflects a structural disadvantage in the Liberal vote – which is highly concentrated in regional areas (which return fewer members than metropolitan Adelaide), it has also exposed issues in the Liberal Party's ability to straddle both factional and policy coherence. Further, the party risks losing significant institutional memory of governing. A strong opposition can often rely, and needs to draw upon, governing experience, not least to sharpen its parliamentary performance. With a decline in

311

the major party vote, there are potentially growing new stresses on both major parties.

Conclusion

There can be no doubt that in a Westminster-style parliament good government relies upon strong opposition. As Ivor Jennings wrote in his classic study of cabinet government, "if there be no Opposition, there is no democracy ... Her Majesty needs an Opposition as well as a Government" (Jennings 1961: 490). Over the past 50 years, the Parliament of South Australia has seen a fairly stable pattern of government and opposition. Most oppositions in that time have been close to government in terms of bare numbers on the floor of the House of Assembly. Yet despite this, since 1970 only two governments lost office after a single term and most have lasted for long enough to leave a considerable policy legacy in South Australia. Through this time, oppositions have struggled to be heard. There are only a few examples of an opposition attack making a significant mark upon the government of the day. It is true that oppositions have been limited in their role by the way in which the Parliamentary processes are determined by the government. At the same time it is also true (especially over most of the past 50 years) that several (Liberal) oppositions in South Australia have allowed internal disagreements and a lack of discipline to distract them from the valuable contribution a strong opposition should make. South Australia can only benefit from an opposition that ensures there is effective scrutiny of the government, and makes the government of the day accountable through the Parliament to the people of South Australia.

References

Arian, A., and Barnes, S., "The Dominant Party System: A Neglected Model of Democratic Stability", *The Journal of Politics*, 36(3), 1974, 592-614

Ball, S., "The conservatives in opposition, 1906-1979: a comparative analysis", in Garnett, M., and Lynch, P., (eds), *The Conservatives in Crisis,* Manchester: Manchester University Press, 2003, 7-28

Cecil, R., cited in Beattie, A., "British Coalition Government Revisited", *Government and Opposition*, 2(1), October 1966, 3-34

Davis, J., "The Upper House: a 'snap-shot' of the South Australian experience, 1975-1998", cited in Griffith, G., and Srinivasan, S., "State Upper Houses in Australia", New South Wales Parliamentary Library Research Service, Background Paper, 1/2001, 34

Donahoe, A.R., "The Value of Parliament", *Australasian Parliamentary Review*, 17(1), 2002, 109-18

Hanham, H.J., "Opposition techniques in British politics (1867-1914)", *Government and Opposition*, 2(1), 1966, 35-48

Helms, L., "Studying Parliamentary Opposition in Old and New Democracies: Issues and Perspectives", *Journal of Legislative Studies*, 14(1/2), 2008, 6-19

Hockin, T.A., "The Roles of the Loyal Opposition in Britain's House of Commons: Three Historical Paradigms", *Parliamentary Affairs*, 25(1) 1971, 50-68

Jaensch, D., *The Government of South Australia*, St Lucia: University of Queensland Press, 1977

Jaensch, D., and Bullock, J., *Liberals in Limbo: Non-Labor Politics in South Australia 1970–1978*, Richmond: Dominion Press, 1978

Jennings, I., *Cabinet Government*, 1961, cited in Johnson, N., "Opposition in the British Political System", *Government and Opposition*, 32(4), 1997, 487-510

Johnson, N., "Opposition in the British Political System", *Government and Opposition*, 32(4), 1997, 487-510

Kaiser, A., "Parliamentary Opposition in Westminster Democracies: Britain, Canada, Australia and New Zealand", *Journal of Legislative Studies*, 14(1/2), 2008, 20-45

Macintyre, C., and Williams, J., "The Embattled South Australian Legislative Council", in Aroney, N., and Prasser, S., (eds), *Elective Dictatorship: The Upper House*, Perth: University of Western Australia Press, 2008, 204-18

Norton, P., "Making Sense of Opposition", *Journal of Legislative Studies*, 14(1-2), March/June 2008, 236-37

Parliamentary Service of the House of Assembly, *Annual Report, 2021-2022*, Financial Statements

Potter, A., "Great Britain: Opposition with a Capital "O"", in Dahl, R., (ed), *Political Oppositions in Western Democracies*, New Haven: Yale University Press, 1966, 3-33

Schmitz, G., *The Opposition in a Parliamentary System*, Ottawa: Canadian Parliamentary Library Research Branch, 1998

South Australian House of Assembly, *Standing Orders*

Statistical Record of the Legislature, SA Parliamentary Paper No. 116 of 1978, revised and continued to 24 April 2007, 118

Walter, J., t'Hart, P., and Strangio, P., *The Pivot of Power: Australian Prime ministers and Political Leadership 1949-2016*, Melbourne: Melbourne University Press, 2017

Endnotes

1 It is notable that the South Australian Parliament, despite being the first to enable women to stand as candidates, has had a long-standing under-representation of women. It remains the only jurisdiction in Australia to have not had a woman as Premier or First Minister. It also lags in other ways in comparison with the other states and territories. For example, research found only 29 per cent of parliamentarians in 2020 were women, the lowest rate across *all* Australian parliaments (the national average was 37 per cent).

2 A striking measure of this trend was the rise of Nick Xenophon. At the 2018 state election, after Xenophon had had a stint as a federal Senator, he reverted to state politics, and his Nick Xenophon Team (NXT) polled strongly as a third party throughout the state. A poll in late 2018 saw Xenophon attract 41per cent support as preferred Premier, threatening the two party axis. This briefly interrupted the usual patterns of opposition, for example, Xenophon was included in a number of televised leader debates, which is customarily between the two major party leaders. The two major parties secure only 61 per cent of the first preference vote in 2018.

13

Opposition in the Tasmanian Parliament: Some Consequences of Reducing an Already Small Parliament

R.A. Herr

The State of Tasmania has a number of features that distinguish it and its parliament from the other five Australian States. The most commonly recognised descriptor for the State is "small". It is the smallest State by area, population and economy. Not necessarily concomitantly, it also has the smallest parliament.[1] Apart from its Lilliputian characteristics, perhaps the most visibly idiosyncratic aspect of the Tasmanian parliamentary system is the method of election, which reverses the mainland pattern. It is Tasmania's House of Assembly, the lower house, that is elected on a proportional representation basis; the Legislative Council, the upper house, is elected on a single-member preferential system. As a consequence, the Tasmanian Parliament tends regularly to produce close results for control of the House of Assembly with a history of minority governments. Its diminutive size and recurrent forays into non-majority government have frequently encouraged active opposition – both parliamentary and extra-parliamentary. The principal focus of this chapter is the effect of reducing the size of the Tasmanian Parliament on His Majesty's Opposition.

Parliamentary opposition can be expressed through a number of channels, not just through the formal structure of His Majesty's Opposition. Indeed, although the "official" Opposition has the most readily identified role, at least in the public's mind, it is often less effectual than other sources. The government's own backbench is generally a far more significant restraint in contemporary parliamentary practice. Moreover, the opposition has itself become something of a contentious concept recently in Tasmanian politics as two political parties have laid claim to the title. The contested status of the formal parliamentary opposition has been more than merely an argument over ceremonial recognition. It has a practical constitutional bearing since a distinction has to be made regarding which is the "official" opposition to be designated as the alternative government. The Legislative Council also provides a third oppositional arena within the parliament for overseeing the executive and managing its agenda.

Of course, there are extra-parliamentary sources of opposition such as community groups, the media, lobbyists and the like. These non-parliamentary sources of opposition are not treated in this chapter but this is not to minimise their significance especially in a small jurisdiction like Tasmania where the politics of personality frequently trump institutional processes. All the parliamentary sources of opposition in Tasmania were significantly affected by a decision in 1998 to accentuate the characteristic of smallness. As the subsequent twelve years demonstrated, not only did the reduction in the size of the Tasmanian Parliament challenge the capacity of the reduced parliament to replicate Westminster traditions, it compelled oppositional forces to find new outlets for expression.

The Tasmanian Parliament: 1998 – 2010

Prior to 1998, the Tasmanian Parliament comprised the Governor, 35 members of the House of Assembly and 19 members of the Legislative Council, a configuration that had been in place since 1959. By year's end, the two houses had been reduced to 25 in the House and 15 in the Council. The professed reasons for the reduction were that Tasmania was "over-governed" and too subject to "hung parliaments" although a number of politicians admitted *sotto voce* that it was to avert a public backlash against "politicians" for a 40 per cent pay rise they awarded themselves several years earlier.[2] A former Liberal leader, Bob Cheek, later validated what many believed was the real reason behind the concern for "hung parliaments", the power of the Tasmanian Greens on the crossbenches.[3] The shared experience of both the ALP (1989-92) and the Liberals (1996-98) in governing in minority with the support of the Greens helped to manufacture a sense of common purpose between the two major parties to clip the electoral prospects of the minor party.[4]

It is one of the enduring ironies of Tasmanian politics that it has proved easier to change the Tasmanian Parliament than to reform the electoral system which produces the outcomes so vexing to the major political parties. In 1958, the issue of "hung parliaments" provoked an increase in the size of the House of Assembly from 30 to 35 to eliminate tied results.[5] In 1998, the change was in the other direction; to reduce the number of seats.[6] The motivation in the case of the reduction in 1998 was to curtail the electoral prospects of minor parties and independents by taking advantage of the State's Hare-Clark electoral system and its effect on proportionality. With fewer members being elected from each constituency, the bar for election was raised significantly for each candidate. From 1959 through 1996, the Hare-Clark quota was 12.5 per cent but, since 1998, the quota has been 16.67 per cent. The Tasmanian Greens averaged around 12 per cent on a state-wide basis in the three elections from 1989 to 1996. Thus, the higher quota was predicted to diminish seriously, if not destroy, the party's prospects for seats in succeeding parliaments. It was expected that the new quota would renew, effectively, the traditional partisan duopoly within the state.[7]

The antagonism toward the Greens that drove the 1998 reduction stemmed from the direct experience both major parties had of governing in minority with the Greens. Neither minority government enjoyed public, business and/or media support during their abbreviated tenures in office.[8] Both were soundly defeated at the next election. Thus, each of the major parties nursed grievances against the Greens and each toyed with a variety of schemes over several years prior to the 1998 change on the appropriate way to shed parliamentary seats. In the event, it was not the Government but the Labor Opposition that introduced the *Parliamentary Reform Bill* in 1998. The Liberal Premier, Tony Rundle, had preferred a unicameral parliament of 44 but his proposal could not carry the support it would need to pass the Legislative Council.[9] The Labor leader Jim Bacon, had a plan to preserve the bicameral structure of the parliament but required the Legislative Council to share some of the pain by also shedding seats. Despite public demands for a referendum or some other demonstration of community support for the change and two previous commissions of inquiry finding against any reduction, the bill went forward quickly and without even a cursory investigation by a parliamentary committee. It passed both houses quickly and received Royal Assent on 27 July 1998 only a month before a state election was held on 29 August.

The subsequent state election not only returned 10 fewer members of the House of Assembly, it defeated the minority Liberal Government and produced a majority for the ALP. The Greens lost the most, proportionally, under the new arrangement, as many of the proponents of the new system hoped. The number of Greens fell from four MHAs to a single member despite a loss of less than 1.0 per cent in electoral support. The Liberals lost the most in absolute terms and went into opposition with ten seats, having held 16 in the previous parliament. Labor achieved victory by electoral stasis, winning a majority on the floor in the reduced House of Assembly by retaining its 14 seats albeit with some change in personalities in the Caucus. The Liberal Government's decision to support the reduction in the size of the parliament had been secured even though the reversal in electoral fortunes had been anticipated. Premier Tony Rundle and his party expected that they would be "punished" for having accepted minority government with the support of the Greens. However, they thought the setback would be temporary – a one-off spanking. The Liberals were not prepared for the institutional consequences for a party in opposition in the smaller parliament.

The Liberals lost even more heavily at the state election on 20 July 2002. The cause was more the adventurous "crash-through-or-crash" approach of Liberal leader Bob Cheek than the party's policies prior to 1998 but the effect on the opposition proved to be dramatic whatever the immediate electoral cause. The Liberals only held seven seats. The Greens, with an almost 8.0 per cent swing, regained their party status in the parliament by winning four seats, thus recovering almost all their 1998 losses. Labor retained its 14 seats but with a much-increased margin of votes. Astonishingly, the 2002 result was repeated virtually down to the votes in March 2006. Every recontesting member was returned and the party balance unchanged.

The identical electoral outcome in 2006 had a very real impact on attitudes toward the 1998 reduction as well as on the operation of the opposition. Clear evidence that the difficulties experienced since 1998 were not transitory but substantive and inherent in the ultra slim parliament helped to convince the parliamentary parties that the 1998 reduction needed to be reviewed. There was apparent agreement shortly before the 2010 election on this. However, inexplicably the ALP retreated at the last minute from discussions with the Liberals, Greens and the Legislative Council on ways to restore the parliament to its former size. The opportunity to undo the damage of the 1998 decision for the parliament was lost, at least for the time being, as some ALP strategists thought the party could repeat the electoral upset of 2006. They were wrong.

After three terms in office, a number of scandals and spectacular public controversies about resources and development matters, there was a palpable mood of change in the air as the State went to the polls in March 2010. The polls had been predicting a "hung parliament" for many months but, then, the same polls had made similar prognostications in

2002 and 2006. The difference in 2010 was that the election campaign did not shift voter intentions. The outcome on election night was precisely as predicted – at least in numerical terms. Labor lost four seats and the Liberals and Greens shared the spoils. The Liberals won three additional seats; the Greens picked up one. The swing against the Labor Government was an impressive 12.4 per cent. It seemed evident to all in the tally room that the Labor Party had lost both its majority and its mandate.

A tally room address by the Liberal leader, Will Hodgman, appeared as much a victory speech as Labor Premier David Bartlett's appeared to be a concession speech. The Greens leader, Nick McKim, made it clear he would talk with both parties but few thought any arrangement would be with Labor given so many years of strident criticism from the opposition benches of Labor in government (Caples 2002).[10] As it happened, the Liberal Party did not "pick up the phone" to talk with the Greens. Unaccountably, Will Hodgman seemed to have expected the Governor, Peter Underwood, to force the Greens to support the Liberals in minority without this party having to negotiate with the Greens. The strategy failed. The Labor Party, to the surprise of many, did seek an accommodation with the Greens and a bargain was struck. Labor retained office. The power-sharing arrangement between the two former opponents provided places for two Greens in Cabinet in their personal capacity while the Greens, as a party, moved to the cross-benches but under a confidence and supply agreement with Labor.

The backbench as opposition

Institutionally, one might expect to focus on the parliamentary sector dedicated to opposing the Government in a book reviewing parliamentary opposition. Practically, however, it is the governing party's own parliamentary members sitting on the benches behind their ministerial colleagues who exercise the real, practical day-by-day restraint on the government. By definition, the opposition does not have the numbers to defeat the government through its own strength. The government's backbench can impose this threat against its frontbench on a routine basis – provided it has the numbers. It is essentially for this reason that the framers of the Papua New Guinea (PNG) Constitution included a provision (Section 144) that sets the maximum number of minsters at no "more than one quarter of the number of members of the Parliament".[11] Since it requires two quarters plus one to form a majority government, the general likelihood is that the backbench will have numerical superiority over the frontbench. It may not always be the case. Given that the prime minister is exempted from the Section 144 restriction, the provision does not quite guarantee that the backbench will be larger than the ministry but it does assure a very near parity at worst. The Papua New Guinea standard for the ratio of backbench to frontbench recognised in 1975 that the backbench would be an important source of opposition to the government in a parliament dominated by partisan politics. Thus, the Constitution sought to preserve this capacity for restraining the government by its own party processes.

The "PNG Standard" in the Australian States 2012

State Parliament	Ratio of ministers to minimum MPs for majority government	Ratios as a percentage
Queensland	18:45	40%
NSW	21:47	45%
Victoria	20:44	45%
WA	14:29	48%
Tasmania pre-1998*	9:18	50%
SA	14:24	58%
Tasmania post-1998	9:13	69%

* The number of ministers varied prior to 1998 but was never more than 10. The current legislation permits nine ministers and this figure is used for illustration.

The value of the government's backbench as oppositional influence does not rest on the capacity of the backbench to bring down a government. It is scarcely credible to expect members of a party routinely to threaten their own frontbench with dismissal.[12] The power of the backbench rests with its numerical strength in the party room, the ambitions of backbenchers for a ministerial commission and, if necessary, a willingness to cross the floor to defeat a government proposal. The rough and tumble of the party room can be important in forcing a degree of openness and prudence on a party especially if ministers rely on advisers who are not effectively responsive to public opinion. Political ambition, perhaps, may be more important in terms of executive responsibility since it is increasingly rare for a minister to lose a want of confidence motion or a censure motion in parliament. In recent decades, ministerial resignations are more commonly effected by party pressure to save the party, not the parliament, embarrassment.[13] Thus, backbench ambition for promotion to the ministry is, perhaps, the most effective mechanism for holding weak minsters accountable even though it is far from certain.

In Tasmania in 1998, the size of the backbench was not an issue with any popular resonance in the public arena. Backbenchers were just "politicians", a class of humanity very much on the nose following the 40 per cent pay rise issue, without a particularly visible or important role. There were occasional references to the risks of a "shallow political gene pool" if the numbers in parliament were reduced but this was concern more for the capacity of the executive rather than the oppositional value of an effective and robust backbench. Campaigning for the change, then Leader of the Opposition, Jim Bacon, did make a gesture toward the PNG standard when he promised to reduce the size of the ministry to ensure there was some backbench.[14] Following the poll on 29 August, now Premier Bacon kept his promise to limit the ministry to seven. Thus, the ALP, having won 14 of the 25 seats in the downsized House, had an apparently respectable backbench, excluding the Speaker, of six. In reality, it was seven in the House since a Legislative Councillor, David Crean, was appointed Treasurer. Moreover, there were three other Labor MLCs[15] so that the ALP caucus had a numerical edge on the ministry.

This balance lasted only to the next election. The Bacon Government increased the maximum number of minsters to eight and later to nine. Greater use of parliamentary secretaries further shrank the backbench

– not formally but in terms of the way these informal officer-holders viewed their careers. Tasmanian parliamentary secretaries do not have commissions nor can they answer questions on any administrative responsibilities. Yet, along with the public, parliamentary secretaries regard the status as signifying a halfway house to becoming a minister and so they identify with the executive arm of governance rather than with the parliamentary. Therefore, in practical terms, the 1998 reduction in the size of the House of Assembly and government adjustments since have gutted the backbench role in parliamentary opposition.

His Majesty's Opposition

The first Bacon Government was formed after the 1998 reduction. It faced an opposition that was smaller than previously but otherwise looked fairly traditional. There was a shadow ministry that provided a full alternative government and a very small backbench. The Tasmanian Greens, had been reduced to a single member, Peg Putt. Putt chose a novel way to demonstrate her disgust at the electoral neutering of her party. She brought in a deck chair to sit where she once sat in the empty space created by the removal of the ten seats from the chamber. The gesture was immediately ruled out of order but it proved a publicity stunt with a political punch as cartoonists used her deck chair as a symbol for the parliamentary victimisation of the Greens. Putt chose to remain unaligned on the crossbench with either major party although neither side needed her support or wanted it. Nevertheless, although alone, the redoubtable Greens "leader" proved an adept politician and an able critic of the government. Indeed, the difference in the quality of leadership between the Liberals with 10 members and the Greens with one played a significant role in the 2002 State election.

The voter backlash against Bob Cheek undoubtedly aided Peg Putt and the resuscitation of the Tasmanian Greens at the 2002 poll but Putt herself had done much to make the Greens acceptable as an oppositional vote. Winning four seats crossed an important parliamentary threshold for the Greens. It enabled the Greens to reclaim parliamentary party status.[16] The fact was not lost on the victorious Labor Premier, Jim Bacon. In his election night victory speech, he announced that the opposition was now composed of *two* parties. It was a masterstroke in partisanship. The Bacon Government appeared magnanimous in improving the parliamentary capacity of a party in opposition. The gesture excited the Greens who saw themselves as winning public credibility but, in reality, underscored for voters the ALP's opposition to the Greens. The announcement further embarrassed the Liberals who, in losing three of their 10 seats, were made to appear not fully effective as *the* Opposition. There was the added bonus of setting up an almost guaranteed struggle for dominance between the two opposing parties and so reducing their effectiveness against the government - or so Premier Bacon hoped.

The Greens had the fewer adjustments to make, at least initially, in moving from the crossbenches to the opposition side of the chamber. They had rarely supported the government and had no real interest in collaborating with the Liberals. Perhaps the only aspect of their new posture on the floor of the House concerned the perks of being a part of His Majesty's Opposition. The Liberals resented the Greens "pretentions" in claiming to be an opposition party as the Liberals held that there could be only one opposition in the Westminster system. While the Greens felt they should share in the procedural benefits that the official opposition enjoyed, the Liberals had practice and precedent on their side.[17] There could be two parties in Opposition but procedurally only one could be the "official" opposition.[18] That status went to the Liberals, the larger of the two. In the meanwhile, the Bacon Government enjoyed the sport of irritating the Liberals by referring to the opposition parties in the plural. Outside of the parliament and its internal procedures, the media and the public cared little about the "official" opposition issue. For many, the Greens were the "real" opposition, as they had been on the crossbenches for a variety of reasons. They played the more visible political gadfly role and proposed the more innovative policy options, thereby attracting greater media attention despite their numerical inferiority on the opposition benches.

Perhaps the most institutionally challenging aspect of the 2002 election result was the incapacity of the Liberals to fill out a full shadow ministry. Being unable to match the ministry from its own membership, it was not an effective alternative government. This might appear to be a fine point of parliamentary pedantry given the extreme unlikelihood that the Liberals would be called upon to form a government without an intervening election. Nevertheless, there was an important and very practical flow-on effect for the Liberals from this deficiency. Attempting to be an alternative government with inadequate personnel seriously affected its other roles including constituency work that would normally be facilitated by the Opposition "backbench". When the March 2006 election resulted in a virtual rerun of the 2002 State election, the Liberals found themselves struggling for a further four years to find ways to lift their public profile without any additional parliamentary resources. The election brought no change in personnel on the Liberal side so the party could not claim a new look. Moreover, two disastrous elections made recruitment difficult for the party. There was little incentive to put careers at risk when the chances of a parliamentary seat were so low. Rather than pursuing government through positive initiatives for policy and grassroots activities in the constituencies, the Liberals appeared dependent on the old adage that governments lose elections.

On the other hand, the Greens in opposition failed to win any visible credibility as an alternative government despite such symbolic gestures such as routinely presenting an alternative budget and nominating shadow spokespersons. Their real success in opposition might have been in their use of parliamentary procedures that allowed them to put pressure on the Labor Government through question time, the adjournment debate and the like. None of these depended on being designated formally a part of the opposition. These mechanisms were equally available to the Greens from the crossbenches.

In reality, the critical change for the Greens was the return to parliamentary party status from the 2002 election. There may have been some recognition of this with the change in the Greens leadership. Peg Putt retired in July 2008. She was succeeded by Nick McKim, her "generation X" deputy. McKim continued the Greens designation as an opposition party but did attempt sometime before the 2010 State election to change this back to the crossbenches. It was a rather desultory gesture that did not resonate in the media or with the public. The logic for the move was that the crossbenches do not cross the floor regardless of which way they vote. The immediate motivation was to position the Greens more neutrally before the 2010 election so the party would be freer to support whichever major party it might choose should the expected "hung parliament" eventuate. Philosophically, the idea of being on the crossbenches made sense but after about seven years of self-identification as an opposition party, few in the media or public took on board a half-hearted arcane shift in professed parliamentary status.

The March 2010 State election returned a minority government but with some surprises. As far the Liberal Party was concerned, there was profound disappointment and some heads rolled but, after the tears and recriminations, the Liberals were still sitting on the Speaker's left notwithstanding their increased numbers and popular support. The party was torn between two responses. The prevailing view in private maintained an outraged "we wuz robbed!" Publicly, the Liberals attempted to turn necessity into a virtue by claiming to be the only party with principle, having refused to "do a deal" with the Greens, just as they had promised during the election campaign. Regardless of their feelings, the Liberals were now indisputably His Majesty's Opposition as the Greens now sat clearly if somewhat ambiguously on the crossbenches. While technically able to support the Liberals from the crossbenches there were practical complications. The Tasmanian Greens were, as a party, committed to a confidence and supply agreement with the Labor Government. Two Greens sat in Cabinet and a third, Tim Morris, was elected Deputy Speaker, a post that did not oblige him to support the Government but probably encourages a certain interest in its survival.

In opposition after the 2010 election, the Liberal Party did not prove especially adept at using the government's minority situation to its own advantage with regard to policy. Even when Premier David Bartlett resigned the leadership in January 2011 for family reasons, Opposition Leader Will Hodgman harped on the theme of an "illegitimate government" rather than seizing on policy consequences that might attract some crossbench support. Procedurally, however, the opposition has enjoyed rather more success.

There had been only one House of Assembly select committee from 1998 to the advent of the 2010 minority government. This was a partisan-driven investigation by the Labor Government into the Federal Liberal Government's *Workchoices* scheme. After the 2010 State election, more select committees were established. These had a capacity to embarrass the minority government. Simply, commissioning them served as a shot across the bow of the new minority government. Yet the lack of human resources to staff them and of time to meet severely limited the capacity of these House committees and even made timely reporting problematic for them. On the other hand, the government members on these committees were all neophytes in Parliament. This, it was said, restricted the government's influence on the new House committees.

The Legislative Council as opposition

The Tasmanian Legislative Council has most of the usual Westminster restraints and democratic reservations about an upper house acting in opposition to the government. It is unusual in two key respects, however, that make its critics believe it is less democratic than most other upper houses. The Legislative Council has never been dissolved since its creation in 1856; it cannot be dissolved as a house regardless of what it does to the government's legislation or budget. Secondly, the Legislative Council can refuse supply absolutely. Thus, a government can be forced to the polls if the Council refuses it supply but there is no capacity to compel the Council to go to the voters itself to defend its decision. Moreover, there is no established mechanism for parliamentary reform that does not involve the Legislative Council so the Council's powers cannot be amended without its acquiescence. The Council has immense potential power to obstruct or oppose a government while remaining unaccountable to the people. These factors make all Tasmanian governments aware that disputes with the Legislative Council can be very one-sidedly risky.

As real as the potential legislative power is, it remains latent given the likely public reaction were the Legislative Council actually to refuse supply. The Council's power can be used more practically to threaten key policy initiatives requiring legislation. Here, the threat of legislative obstruction can be a useful and useable lever against a government even if the threat is largely a political bluff. Given that the ALP has predominantly controlled government, it is scarcely surprising that the conservative cast of the Legislative Council has made the Council appear an ally of the Liberals ideologically. There is some evidence that members of the Legislative Council have indeed been "closet" Liberals and so acted at times in ways favourable to the opposition in the House of Assembly. Yet, the Liberal Premier, Tony Rundle, found the Council uncomfortably obstructionist to his minority government at times. In general, there has been public support for the Legislative Council as a house of independents and some antagonism when partisan politics influence its work. This generalisation has been challenged at times; most recently in Bacon's attempt to secure control of the chamber by endorsing candidates to stand for the ALP. While this challenge was said to have been abandoned, Labor continues both to endorse candidates and encourage Labor-leaning candidates to stand without endorsement.[19] The Legislative Council's power over legislation is not its primary mechanism for opposing a government, however.

In reality, the Legislative Council's primary parliamentary weapon remains its powers to scrutinise the government. Perhaps the main scrutiny function historically was expressed through the committee system. A secondary mechanism, more widely employed by other upper houses in Australia, questions without notice, has been slow to develop. The Tasmanian Legislative Council has not had a long tradition of ministers from its chamber. As a consequence, it is only in recent years that the Council has begun to pursue accountability through questions without notice. Even when used, questions for information display a feature that may be unique to Tasmania. The Leader of Government Business answers all questions on behalf of the government other than those that go to an MLC minister. The Leader of Government Business is not a minister and, as far as is known, has never been a member of the Executive Council.

The oppositional role of the Legislative Council changed noticeably after the reduction in the size of the parliament. Relations between the two houses have been affected by the pressures of coping with the dynamics of opposition in the much-reduced parliament. One early sign of recognition came with an attempt to strengthen the committee system as one form of compensation for the loss of critical mass. A Working Arrangements of Parliament Committee review reported in 2000 that the committee system should be enhanced by establishing two new joint standing committees in the wake of the reduced size of the parliament. This arrangement nevertheless itself fell foul of the reduced size of the House of Assembly. With too few MPs[20] available to allow for the timely and effective functioning of the joint committees, the Legislative Council grew increasingly disaffected by an arrangement that appeared to favour the government over the parliament. The frustration of the Legislative Council built to a point that, in 2010, the Council moved to set up two standing committees of its own to oversee government.

Similarly, in some respects, the Legislative Council found problems with the development of questions for information after 1998. The perceived need for recruiting ministers from the Legislative Council became more trenchant after 1998. Apart from the obvious limitations of the much smaller House of Assembly, there was another reason for this development. The Labor Party had been seeking control of the Legislative Council for some time with a view, in the eyes of its critics, to winning the numbers in the Council to secure a vote for unicameralism. Having to abandon (or, put on hold) this ambition, the post-1998 Labor governments resorted to a tactic seen by supporters of the Legislative Council to be unicameralism by stealth. This revolved around amending standing orders to permit ministers from one house to appear in the other. The government wanted the peripatetic ministers to go in both directions, but the Council was only willing to allow its ministers (at the time, the Treasurer and Human Services Minister) to attend Question Time in the House of Assembly provided this did not interfere with their responsibility to the Council.[21]

Although the post-1998 Legislative Council has taken steps to preserve and protect its role as an oppositional influence in the Tasmanian Parliament, in some areas it appears to have yielded to executive dominance. Allowing a party representative to respond to questions without notice even when there are ministers available in the Council and cancelling Legislative Council sittings for want of government business, are examples from the pre-1998 period that continued. Ceding ministerial visits to the House of Assembly is directly related to the reduction in the size of the parliament. So too may be the increased use of "briefings" to the Legislative Council mainly by the bureaucracy. In addition to such issues as to whether such arrangements are protected by privilege as part of the proceedings of parliament, there is the diminution of the transparency required to hold the government to account. These arrangements are not serviced in the manner of committee hearings so there is no record of what has been argued and resolved. Thus, unlike debates and statements in the chamber, briefings cannot serve as extrinsic material to assist the courts in understanding the intention of parliament. Basically, briefings provide the government an opportunity, sometimes in secret, to advance its own case without the public scrutiny the Legislative Council ought to provide.

Resources for parliamentary opposition

Tasmania's small size and limited resources are a fact of political life across the board for the Apple Isle. These resource constraints have been reflected historically in the means available to the parliamentary Opposition as well. Direct financial support for the official opposition is constrained and focused on and through the Leader of the Opposition. The Leader of the Opposition receives a supplementary stipend for the office equivalent to that of a minister while the Deputy Leader receives a supplementary stipend roughly half that. In addition to a chauffeur driven motor vehicle for each recognised party leader, there is an allowance to the Opposition Leader for shadow ministerial staff, aka "political minders". This allowance is administered through the Department of Premier and Cabinet (DPAC), based on a formula related to the number of MPs in the House of Assembly rather than directly on the number of shadow ministers. In 2010, financial resources came to the opposition by virtue of its status and size as a party not specifically for its role as the opposition.

The rise of the Tasmanian Greens Party as a continuing parliamentary party has shifted the focus from the traditional government and opposition structure to one that has responded to parliamentary needs in terms of party. The Greens have adopted a position in the House of Assembly that has vacillated between the crossbenches and opposition (see below). Thus, the 2010 funding formula gave the leader of each recognised non-governing party an allocation to support the parliamentary activities of that party regardless of its role in opposition.

A second significant development arose from the uncertainties in Tasmanian politics due to the electoral strength of the Greens. The ALP had been in power continuously from 1934 to 1982 with only one brief lacuna from 1969 to 1972. Being in opposition from 1982 to 1989 drove home for Labor the reality of operating without support staff while the 1989-92 experience of minority government imbued Labor with the fragility of future prospects. A second period in opposition provoked substantive action when the ALP returned to power in 1998. MPs and MLCs were given an entitlement to individual electoral office staffed with a full-time electorate officer. These entitlements are administered through the Premier's Department for the House of Assembly but by the Legislative Council for MLCs. Later, Premier Paul Lennon significantly upgraded the facilities in Parliament House to improve working conditions and capacity for individual MPs. Thus, while not specifically intended to compensate for reduced numbers, the post-1998 Tasmanian Parliament found some resources for opposition significantly enhanced.

However, perhaps the most important recent addition to oppositional resources came as a result of the formation of the 1989 minority government. The Green Independents insisted on a parliamentary research service for their support from the crossbenches. Again, this was not specifically designed to assist the formal opposition. Rather it was intended to strengthen the parliament against the Executive and, indeed, this is its continuing effect. The Tasmanian Parliamentary Research Service has been much used by Legislative Councillors, government backbenchers, crossbench members as well as the opposition since its establishment. Thus, while it has enhanced oppositional capacity, the research service has genuinely strengthened parliament institutionally.

The longevity of Labor's reign in power clearly weakened the parliamentary capacity of the opposition for several decades. Yet, it is intriguing to note that the Liberal Party during its three periods in Government (1969-72; 1982-89; and 1992-98) failed to address the weakness in oppositional resources despite its intimate knowledge of the weakness of opposition. The ALP, by contrast, became acutely aware of the disparity and seeing the implications of a majority third force in Tasmanian politics updated parliamentary, if not opposition, resources. This is not to say that support for parliament in general has been embraced wholeheartedly. Both major parties have kept their eye on executive power when considering the reversal of the 1998 reduction in the size of the Tasmanian Parliament. At various times since 1998 both have resisted increasing size of parliament with the expectation of enjoying the benefits of executive dominance. Moreover, even when supporting a return to an effective size, they have generally couched their arguments in executive terms, notably to augment the ministerial "gene pool", rather than to promote parliamentary capacity.

Conclusion

The decision to reduce the size of the Tasmanian Parliament in 1998 without reference to any parliamentary review of the consequences or to some form of public endorsement revealed the depth of the two major parties' determination to circumvent third party opposition The traditional "Government and Opposition" model was acceptable but something that reduced the predictability of single party control of executive power was not. The resolve of the two major parties to eliminate the crossbench "threat" was evident in the limited consideration allowed for reduction in the size of the parliament as an institution at any level. This was clear from the way they proceeded to implement their decision without an inquiry by the Parliament or by any recourse to public opinion whether through an election or a referendum.

All elements of parliamentary opposition were damaged by the reduction in the size of the parliament. The government backbench is the structure that suffered most obviously especially since the 2002 election when the Greens recovered a substantial share of parliamentary representation. Arguably, no opposition party since 1998 has had any backbench at all. This has reinforced an executive focus as to their perceived role in the House. Indeed, the official opposition was so bereft that, from 2002 to 2010, it was unable even to adequately fulfil its role as an alternative government much less sustain a backbench. The effect of this diminution of backbench capacity was evident in less effective participation in Question Time, fewer hours spent in debating legislation and less time in responding to constituency matters.

Some compensatory adjustments were made to rebalance the relationship between government and parliament-based opposition, but these were constrained to a notable degree by the overall reduction of parliamentary numbers. The committee systems in both the House of Assembly and Legislative Council were revamped or revitalised, although without a significant impact. The House committees were too resource-constrained to be more than a symbolic gesture. The Legislative Council's reformed committee had promise, although the chamber itself mitigated some of its oppositional role by an increased dependence on Government briefings.

One interesting, albeit largely tangential development in parliamentary opposition, was the distinction drawn between His Majesty's Opposition and the official opposition. The period of two parties, not in coalition with each other, choosing to stand in formal opposition to the government provided a reminder that His Majesty's Opposition was not always a synonym for the alternative government.

Fortunately, the case for restoring the Tasmanian Parliament to a size commensurate with Westminster processes, including that of an effective opposition, was made effectively in the public arena. The major parties recognised, belatedly, that the 1998 reduction was a mistake and that it had seriously compromised the parliament in every direction, but nowhere more importantly than in its roles of oversighting and checking the government of the day. Nevertheless, a fear of a voter backlash, essentially a fear of leadership in defence of the parliament as an institution, continued to allow the presumed cost of "more politicians" to stay their hand.[22]

In 2014, the ALP Government led by Lara Giddings was defeated in a landslide by the Liberals under Will Hodgman. He was re-elected in 2018, again as head of a majority government. Hodgman was succeeded as Premier in January 2020 by Peter Gutwein who won an early election in 2021. After Gutwein resigned, Jeremy Rockliff became Premier in April 2022.

In May 2022, Rockliff, announced that his government would restore the House of Assembly to its pre-1998 number of 35 members. With some resistance from the business community and surprisingly little pushback from the public, the *Expansion of House of Assembly Bill 2022* passed the Tasmanian Parliament with tri-partisan support. It received the royal assent on the 14 December 2022.[23] Although the Act reversed the effects of the 1998 reduction on the House, the numbers lost to the Legislative Council were not returned to it. No one, not even the MLCs, wanted to disturb the agreement brokered by the Premier. The next House of Assembly election, due in early 2025, will be fought once again across five electorates to fill seven seats in each.

The general drivers for this decision were essentially those canvassed in this chapter. However, there were several key "final straws". Undoubtedly the principal one was the emergence of a premier with the courage to face down the critics who had promoted the reduction of the size of the parliament in the second half of the 1990s. Rockliff's stated primary motivation was the need to better equip the Parliament to represent the diversity of opinion in a state dealing with an increasingly complex agenda for change.[24] He also acknowledged that he recognised the need for more depth in the backbench to provide for a viable committee system in the lower house. Nonetheless, there will also be direct benefits for the executive branch with the addition of one more Minister (11 up from the current maximum of 10) and somewhat less risk of political parties not being able to fill casual vacancies from their own candidates list.

Endnotes

1   Being small does not necessarily produce small legislatures. For example, the US State of New Hampshire ranks 41st in population in the United States but its 400 member lower house ranks as the largest in size amongst the 50 States. http://www.ncsl.org/default.aspx?tabid=13527

2   Summaries of the steps leading to the reduction in the size of the Tasmania in 1998 can be found in: Tasmanian Parliamentary Library, "Parliamentary

Reform – Downsizing Parliament" accessed at http://www.parliament.tas.gov.
au/tpl/InfoSheets/reform_1998.htm and Scott Bennett, "The Reduction in the
Size of the Tasmanian Parliament", Parliament of Australia, Department of the
Parliamentary Library, Research Note 2 1998-99 accessed at http://www.aph.
gov.au/library/pubs/m/1998-99/99m02.htm.

3   Bob Cheek, *Cheeky: Confessions of a Ferret Salesman* (Hobart: Robert
Cheek, 2006). David Llewellyn confirmed this recently from the Labor side.
See: Tim Walker, "Parliament size reduction was a 'conspiracy'", 936 ABC
Radio, Hobart, 13 May 2011. Accessed at: http://www.abc.net.au/local/
audio/2011/05/13/3216303.htm?site=hobart

4   I have assessed the origins and nature of this common purpose see Herr,
R.,"Reducing Parliament and Minority Government in Tasmania: Strange
Bedfellows Make Politics — Badly", *Australasian Parliamentary Review*,
20(2), Spring 2005, 130-43.

5   As luck would have it, the first election after the enlargement produced
a minority Labor Government with 16 Labor MHAs, 17 Liberals and two
Independents.

6   Some argue also that the reduction in the size of the House of Assembly in
1906 from 35 to 30 was sparked by the extension of the franchise to women in
1903 although the precise mechanism for this is not entirely clear.

7   Despite its Hare-Clark electoral system and until the advent of the Greens,
Tasmania long had one of the tightest two-party systems of any State in the
Commonwealth. See R.A. Herr, "Hare-Clark: The Electoral Legacy", in
Haward, M., and Warden, J., (eds), *An Australian Democrat: The Life Work
and Consequences of Andrew Inglis Clark*, Hobart: Centre for Tasmanian
Historical Studies; University of Tasmania, 1995.

8   Yet, in each case, the Government failed to go to full term by their own choice
not through an expression of a want of confidence by the House of Assembly.

9   For some of this background see: Australian Bureau of Statistics, Feature
Article - Tasmanian election 1998: a background report, 1384.6 - Statistics -
Tasmania, 2002. Accessed at http://www.abs.gov.au/Ausstats/abs@.nsf/7d12
b0f6763c78caca257061001cc588/efe8de28755c3a08ca256c320024154e!Op
enDocument

10   John Caples, "State Election 2002: The Decision. Landslide Win For Labor",
The Examiner, 21 July 2002.

11   Constitution of the Independent State of Papua New Guinea, http://www.
paclii.org/pg/legis/consol_act/cotisopng534/

12   Naturally, the same dynamics do not apply in the case of a coalition
arrangement and not at all in the case of a minority Government. This was a

significant factor in the Tasmanian minority government of 1989-92 when the Green independents threatened to support a no confidence motion against then Education Minister Peter Patmore. Premier Michael Field asserted he would treat such a move as a want of confidence in his government. Patmore averted the crisis by offering his resignation to the Governor without the knowledge of Field.

13   Patrick Weller in his *Cabinet Government in Australia, 1901-2006: Practice, Principles, Performance*, Sydney: UNSW Press, 2007 explores this issue in detail making the point that typically party not parliament sacks ministers in Australia.

14   Just before the 1998 change, the Tasmanian Government was set at ten and, at least initially, after the election that brought Labor to power, Bacon attempted to operate with seven ministers only six of whom were in the House of Assembly.

15   Michael Aird, Doug Parkinson and Silvia Smith.

16   Tasmania, House of Assembly, Standing Orders, 42 (4).

17   The *House of Representatives Practice* (p. 77) is clear on the "official" Opposition. When the Opposition consists of more than one party opposed to the Government, and the parties prefer to remain distinct, the single party having the largest number of members is recognised as the 'official Opposition'. If the official Opposition is not clear by virtue of numbers, it is for the Speaker to decide which group shall be so called, and who will be recognised by the Chair as the Leader of the Opposition.

18   The Tasmanian House of Assembly Standing Orders and Sessional Orders do not specify that there is an "official" Opposition but these make clear that there is only one "leader of the Opposition" and that the party led by this individual is invested with the formal activities of the Opposition although there may be allowances for other parties to be regarded as oppositional (see S.O. 148 (1.v). This interpretation is reinforced by the *Parliamentary Salaries, Superannuation and Allowances Act 1973* and its definition of the "Opposition Whip".

19   The Greens Party regularly endorses candidates for the Council but the Liberals have done so very rarely and express a philosophical reluctance to do so.

20   In 2006, the House of Assembly changed its post-nominal from MHA to MP but the MLCs retained theirs'.

21   Premier Bartlett claimed the initiative was part of a broader agenda for promoting the role of Opposition in the Parliament. In his press release on the Upper House ministers visiting the Assembly, he noted: "This year the Government has provided more sitting days, more question times, more time

for Opposition parties to propose policies on the floor of the House, and more time for scrutiny of Government policy, not just legislation." See David Bartlett, "Another step in open government" 23 March 2009. Accessed at: http://www.media.tas.gov.au/print.php?id=26266

22   Craig Hoggett, "Greens hold to MPs aim" *The Mercury*, 14 January 2012. Accessed at: http://www.themercury.com.au/article/2012/01/14/292311_tasmania-news.html and David Killick, "Labor to expand Parliament", *The Mercury*, 24 January 2012. Accessed at: http://www.themercury.com.au/article/2012/01/24/294891_tasmania-news.html.

23   *Expansion of House of Assembly Act 2022* (Tas) https://www.legislation.tas.gov.au/view/whole/html/inforce/2022-12-14/act-2022-040

24   Parliament of Tasmania, "Draft Second Reading Speech Hon Jeremy Rockliff MP, Premier Of Tasmania". Accessed at: https://www.parliament.tas.gov.au/Bills/Bills2022/pdf/notes/47_of_2022-SRS.pdf

14

The Victorian Coalition 1999-2023: A Permanent Opposition?

Terry Barnes

Introduction

Government is, for a party that aspires to government, the place to be. Opposition is a lonely and unwanted place, condemning members of parliament (MPs) party organisations and rank-and-file members to years of "wandering in the wilderness". It not only is being out-of-office; it is being out of power. While "the other mob" holds the reins of government, and its programs and agendas are able to be implemented and dominate the public discourse, oppositions are incidental and impotent. They can talk as much as they like, but unless the government of the day accepts what they propose, an opposition is barely relevant, little more than the obligatory quote for balance at the end of a political news story.

The purpose of an opposition is not simply to oppose. It has parliamentary, policy, and political roles, by which its success or failure should be measured:

- Parliamentary: Scrutinising the performance of the incumbent government and holding it to account, and providing a party leader and Members of Parliament capable of providing that scrutiny.
- Policy: To debate the government's policies, and to develop and promote alternative policies in the best interest of the nation or State.
- Political and leadership: To return to government by offering voters a strong, viable and effective alternative to the incumbents. This

includes providing a Leader of the Opposition and an opposition team of Members of Parliament seen as a viable alternative government.

For Members of Parliament, and those aspiring to be MPs, opposition is all too often a soul-destroying place. On both sides of politics, the careers of talented and committed people have been wasted as their expertise and careers are shunted aside by voters. If not defeated in a general election, experienced MPs, including former ministers, are often quick to make their exit rather than stay for the long haul. And, as the days in government recede further into the past, the only thing helping opposition MPs in maintaining their commitment and morale is that each new day in opposition is, hopefully, one day closer to government. In short, giving some hope that the time in the wilderness ultimately will be worth it.

However, in some jurisdictions, there seems to be little hope. The political scene has become so weighted in favour of one party of government, winning election after election, that the other is left in a state of near-permanent opposition, its frustration and powerlessness leading it to feed on itself and put a return to government even more out of reach.

Such a fate has befallen the Coalition parties in Victoria, particularly the Liberal Party, which for decades have failed so spectacularly that they have become, in effect, Labor's permanent opposition, to the point where, in his near-decade in office, Labor Premier, Daniel Andrews, routinely denounced his official opponents as "irrelevant", if indeed he ever mentioned them at all.

Most commentators note that the Coalition has been out-of-office for all but four years since Jeff Kennett's Government was defeated unexpectedly in late 1999. The full story is, in reality, far worse: since nearly three decades of continuous Coalition government was broken by Labor's John Cain junior in March 1982, the Coalition has been in government for less than eleven of the following 41 years and, as of mid-term in Labor's third consecutive term, seems to have little hope of regaining government at the 2026 state election or, possibly, at the following election in 2030. Such has been the political dominance of Andrews and Labor, and the sorry state of the Liberals as the primary Coalition partner. Indeed, the election result in November 2022 was more a vote against a hapless Liberal-led Coalition than a positive endorsement of Andrews and Labor.

For the party of Sir Henry Bolte, when Victoria was the "jewel in the Liberal crown", the Andrews years have been an unending nightmare, that the 2023 change of premier will not end. A progressive but far from universally-loved Labor government that seemingly "does things"; a premier in Andrews whose dominance was all but absolute; Covid-19; adverse flow-ons from federal factors; internal party factionalism and turmoil; and the simple equation of serious numerical inferiority in the Victorian parliament and consequently a talent pool shallower than a muddy puddle, have all played their part in ensuring the state Liberals are seemingly doomed to a state of permanent despair that, even in the decades of the Cain-Kirner and the Bracks-Brumby governments, never quite eventuated.

How did the Coalition get there?

To understand the current predicament of the Victoria's seemingly permanent opposition we need an appreciation of the effects of the decade and a half before Andrews regained office for Labor in November 2014. How the Coalition, and especially the Liberals, arrived in its slough of permanent opposition despond in the Andrews era is not down to a single factor. Effectively, it was both the author of its own misfortunes, as well as a victim of what British Prime Minister Harold Macmillan would describe as "events, dear boy, events". The decline started with the unexpected fall of the Kennett Government in 1999 and continued, with only the relief of the accidental one-term Ted Baillieu-Denis Napthine Government of 2010-14.

1999: The accidental opposition

In 1999, instead of the healthy re-elected majority the government and almost all public opinion polls predicted, a poor Liberal campaign, centred almost entirely on a hubristic premier, brought to a sudden and totally unexpected end the seven-year government of Jeff Kennett. An important factor was a new, non-threatening Labor leader, Steve Bracks, who benefited from his predecessor, John Brumby's clever concentration on dissatisfaction with the Kennett Government outside greater Melbourne.

In the unexpected cliffhanger election, the Coalition lost 13 members and majority government. After a supplementary election in Frankston East, where the incumbent died just hours before polls closed, the crossbench backed Bracks over Kennett and forced a policy-effective, but politically arrogant and complacent, government from office. Kennett himself resigned both as premier and as an MP when it became clear the numbers were against him.

The signs were there before the 1999 election, especially from by-election losses, that support for Kennett was soft. Nevertheless, after the shock loss, the mood in the Coalition was that 1999 was an aberration, a protest vote gone wrong. Polls suggesting the Kennett Government would be returned comfortably may have assisted a late swing to Labor, but also fuelled the party faithful's feeling that the next election would be a correction, and normal service would be resumed. Not near enough was done, under Napthine's decent but undynamic leadership, to ask hard questions of the Coalition's own performance in government and show the Victorian electorate that it had listened and learned from its Kennett-era mistakes.

The Liberals (but not the Nationals) after a late Liberal leadership change from Napthine to Robert Doyle reaped the whirlwind of complacency in 2002 when Bracks won re-election in a landslide, taking 20 seats from the Liberals. It was enough not just to entrench Labor but gut the parliamentary talent pool of their opponents. Liberal casualties notoriously included shadow Treasurer Robert Dean, who failed to register to vote in his own newly redistributed seat.

The year 2006 saw the both the Liberals and Nationals (for the time being out of Coalition[1]) under new Opposition leader Ted Baillieu clawing back some lost seats, but falling well short of threatening Labor. After three straight election losses, however, Labor's political dominance was largely unquestioned by the Coalition and the Liberals' mindset and culture switched firmly to opposition mode. Not expecting a return to government in the foreseeable future, the Coalition was used to playing the negative carping role against Bracks and his successor Brumby, while preoccupying itself with factional party games with MPs fighting each other over the scraps of opposition. The Brumby Government's well-regarded response to the tragedy of the 2009 Black Saturday bushfires also battered the restored Coalition's morale, and reinforced a widespread perception that Labor was unbeatable in 2010.

2010: The accidental government

But Labor was beatable, and beaten. In the 2010 state election, Labor finally experienced a "reverse 1999". Against poll indications, the Brumby Government suffered a seven per cent swing against it and lost 13 seats, giving Baillieu's Coalition a single-seat majority in the Legislative Assembly and, even more surprisingly, the same margin in the Legislative Council. This unexpected Coalition victory was assisted by a principled decision by Baillieu to preference Labor ahead of the major parties' common enemy, the Greens.

On paper, the surprise result giving control of both houses augured well for a prolonged period of Coalition government. It was, however, not to be: it proved to be the most Pyrrhic of Pyrrhic victories.

The reasons for the Baillieu-Napthine government's one-term failure essentially are threefold. First, in 2010 the Coalition expected only to build on 2006 and reduce Labor's majority still further. It did not, however, expect or plan to win. Consequently, most of the policies taken to the election were little more than statements of intent – "thought bubbles" that were never expected to be implemented. Instead of hitting the ground running with detailed and costed programmes, the Baillieu Government wasted nearly six months between its election and first budget to design the policies to match its campaign press releases, mostly contracting out that work to the Labor-friendly Victorian Public Service, which grasped the opportunity to frame the new government's policies for it.

This bureaucratisation of policy-setting was aided by the new government's inexperience. While some had served as senior ministerial advisers in the Kennett and Howard governments, with one exception,[2] no Baillieu minister, including the Premier, had prior personal ministerial experience. Additionally, the government was determined to honour an election promise to reduce Labor's ministerial staff numbers by a quarter and, for those eventually appointed, party and personal loyalties too often prevailed over competence and experience. Furthermore, too few staff actually appointed were experienced or confident enough to take on a public service monolith which was very comfortable working with Labor and Labor values.[3] That lack of experience, and the lost six months developing policy for the first Baillieu budget, ultimately proved fatal for the government (see Kemp 2015: 46-7).[4]

Second, the tightness of the government's majority gave otherwise obscure backbenchers power well beyond their actual competence. The biggest thorn in the government's was the eccentric, bagpipe-playing, self-important Member for Frankston, Geoff Shaw. He was a classic accidental MP: he was preselected for a seat the Liberals did not expect to win; there were questions about his suitability that should never have survived vetting; allegations about conflicts of interest with his private business and his using a government vehicle in that business. Shaw's awareness that his being crucial to the Baillieu Government's precarious majority, gave him a power his ineptness and unsuitability for public life did not deserve.

Shaw resigned from the Liberal Party in March 2013 over an unrelated scandal,[5] threatening to bring down the government if Baillieu did not resign as Premier. Baillieu immediately complied, to be replaced by Napthine. The Premier's resignation was arguably an over-reaction, but some suggested that Baillieu simply had had enough. This arguably marked the point when the Coalition's 2014 defeat became all but inevitable.

Third, the government was confronted by an opposition that actually knew how to oppose and took full advantage of the government's precarious majority. Replacing Brumby as Labor leader, Daniel Andrews proved a ruthless tactician who gave his opponents no quarter, let alone breathing space, homing in laser-like on Shaw and the Liberal instability he caused. Andrews also succeeded in achieving what rarely happens after a shock defeat: keeping his caucus largely unified. Over four years, Labor proved an implacable opposition, despite in that time proposing only two positive policies of its own: a gimmick commitment to an AFL Grand Final Eve public holiday, and a highly electorally effective but loosely-costed plan to remove dangerous level crossings around Melbourne, many coincidentally in target seats.[6]

Although the Coalition managed to survive in government until 2014, it was kept constantly off-balance by Andrews's parliamentary tactics and Labor-allied public sector union industrial campaigns. Andrews was not interested in any suggestion that stable government was in Victoria's best interests: as far as he was concerned as Opposition leader, the state's interest was best served by removing the Coalition government in one term and installing himself as Premier.

So it came to pass, with the defeated Baillieu-Napthine Government leaving just one tangible policy legacy: Protective Service Officers patrolling suburban railway stations at night. The 2014 election loss may have been relatively narrow,[7] but the accidental Coalition interregnum vanished, Ozymandias-like, overnight.

The entrenchment of permanent opposition: 2014 to today

The pathetic plight of the Liberal and National parties over the decade since November 2014 is illustrated by the parliamentary arithmetic, as Table 1 shows:

Table 1: Seats won in the Victorian Legislative Assembly, 2010-22

	Liberal	National	ALP	Greens	Other
2010	35	10	43	0	0
2014	30	8	47	2	1
2018	21	6	55	3	3
2022	19	9	56	4	0[8]

While an opposition losing seats in the next election following loss of office is not uncommon, as one-term governments are rare in Australia, it is highly unusual for an opposition to lose seats to the government in two elections running.

In Victoria's circumstances, this is extraordinary. The Coalition should have regained seats in 2022, given the Andrews Government's increasingly dubious record on debt and infrastructure delivery, internal Labor party infighting and branch-stacking scandals, and, above all, Andrews's heavy-handed and authoritarian approach to Covid-19 in which individual rights and liberties were trampled for what was spun successfully by Labor as being for the common good. Yet, notwithstanding the incompetence that marked the Andrews Government's Hotel Quarantine Program in 2020, and Victoria's Covid lockdown fatigue, it was the hapless Coalition, not Labor, that was pulverised at the ballot box.

The reasons for the Coalition's now seemingly entrenched opposition are many, but it is useful to evaluate its performance since the 2014 election.

Post-2014: aimlessly wandering the wilderness

The Coalition had an honourable loss after a difficult single term of government, and many Liberals believed that Andrews would return to his left-wing roots and prove beatable in 2018. Outgoing Planning Minister, Matthew Guy, became opposition leader.

Yet the Coalition was thrashed comprehensively by Andrews and Labor in 2018 and, humiliatingly, further ravaged in 2022.

Labor's behaviour in office gave some comfort to his opposition. The so-called "red shirts scandal", involving Labor staffers being diverted from official business to Labor campaigning (hence the red shirts), distracted politicians and media, as did Andrews's falling out with the powerful United Firefighters Union, and consequent turmoil within the government. The short-term fallout was that, in the 2016 federal election, Labor in Victoria underperformed relative to other States and helped barely return Malcolm Turnbull's Coalition Government.

The story of the Victorian Coalition since the 2014 loss is a complex and extensive story, far more extensive than can be covered in one chapter. Essentially, however, it comes down to five factors: failure to learn from defeat; leadership; the parliamentary talent pool; policy; factionalism; Covid; and the Liberals' lack of a clear values consensus.

Failure to learn from defeat

The Liberals failed to capitalise on Labor's internal troubles. More tellingly, the opposition failed to reflect on why it lost and renew both policies and people.

The 2015 Liberal post-election review,[9] by former Howard cabinet minister, David Kemp, provided an incisive and trenchant analysis of the 2010-14 government, the election campaign, and set out a comprehensive blueprint for what the Liberal Party needed to do to be electable in 2018. Suffice it to say, great lip service was paid to the Kemp Report by the parliamentary and organisation leaderships, but effectively little was actually implemented. Had it been, the disastrous story of the following terms might have been very different.

Indeed, the post-election review of the 2018 landslide defeat, conducted by party elder Tony Nutt had as its first recommendation the wholesale adoption of Kemp's recommendations.[10] Not that it was a lesson learned: after the 2022 loss, the then State President declared there was no need for such a review at all, as the lessons of the defeat were obvious. At least they were to him.

Leadership 2014-22

While the Coalition did take a wide range of policy statements to the 2018 election, Matthew Guy strove to keep the Liberal Party united. Like his successors Michael O'Brien and John Pesutto, Guy struggled to keep a lid on personal and factional tensions, both in the party room and wider party.

Guy's opposition spent relatively little time in hard policy development in its first term. Guy himself was seriously compromised in August 2017, when he unwittingly attended a fundraising dinner where a person with alleged criminal connections also attended, a dinner forever labelled as "lobster with a mobster".[11] Labor capitalised on the negative headlines and the questions it raised about Guy's political judgment not only in 2017-18, but again when he returned to the leadership in 2021.

After the 2018 defeat, Guy resigned was replaced as leader by his deputy, Michael O'Brien. O'Brien had proved to be an outstanding Treasurer under Napthine, and his aptitude for policy development was one of the opposition's few assets especially after fellow policy "wonk", Pesutto, unexpectedly lost his seat of Hawthorn in 2018.

O'Brien's leadership became a Covid victim. Too mild-mannered and gentlemanly to be a political mongrel, and despite being respected by the rank-and-file membership, disgruntled Liberal MPs and party figures turned against him. In 2021 O'Brien survived a near-successful challenge by frontbencher Brad Battin,[12] before he was deposed by the previous leader, Guy, a few months later.

Guy in his second incarnation failed to right the Liberal ship, although in the months before the 2022 election it appeared the Liberals could seriously reduce Labor's majority. He could not, however, achieve vital party unity and, worse, own goals including rogue MPs and his new chief-of-staff lobbying party donors for a salary supplement, did not help. Despite Guy's solid 2022 personal campaign, striving valiantly to make a silk purse out of a sow's ear, the Liberals' further net loss of seats made his position untenable.

Leadership 2023

Having regained his lost seat in 2022, John Pesutto was made leader of a diminished and unhappy party room by one vote over Battin. Pesutto had proved to be a hard-working ideological moderate and a genuine policy thinker, and his policy skills were much missed in the opposition's second term. Despite the close party room result, high hopes were held that Pesutto could lead the hard work to take the fight up to Labor in a post-Covid environment.

It has so far proved, however, not to be. In a rush of blood in March 2023, Pesutto dissipated much goodwill, split his party, and raised questions over his political judgment by moving to expel a first-term MP, Moira Deeming. A socially conservative women's rights campaigner and outspoken activist, she was highly popular with much of the rank-and-file Liberal membership.

In February 2023, Deeming co-organised a pro-women's rights rally featuring a controversial and polarising British speaker. The rally was bound to attract violent counter-protests from left-wing transgender activists, but it also, unexpectedly, attracted a band of neo-Nazis. Pesutto was appalled at the hostile media coverage, and reacted precipitately to expel Deeming.[13] In close party room votes, effectively on moderate-conservative lines, Deeming was first suspended for nine months, then finally expelled after further comments she made some weeks later. Relations between Pesutto and Deeming completely broke down, to the point that Deeming filed multiple defamation suits against him.

As an MP rather than as a single-issue activist, Deeming was naïve, even foolish, to have become involved with the "Let Women Speak" rally that promoted the expulsion. She was, however, entitled to a fair hearing, procedural fairness and natural justice before the leadership's sentence was passed: that this did not happen split the party room and widened the bitter gulf between moderates and social conservatives in the broader party membership and support base.

As a consequence of the Deeming affair, Pesutto's leadership is struggling, despite his good intentions, personal decency, and policy strengths. However, he has breathing space to rebuild and recover as there are no obvious immediate successors. The stronger than expected Liberal performance in the August 2023 Warrandyte by-election, in which Pesutto campaigned strongly on Labor's failings and cost-of-living pressures, temporarily eased the pressure on his leadership but this progress was contradicted by the Liberals going backwards in the late-2023 by-election in Andrews's former seat of Mulgrave.

The sudden resignation of Andrews in September 2023, and the messy accession of his anointed successor, Jacinta Allan, also gives Pesutto a chance to define himself positively. Allan is not a domineering political personality like Andrews, and will struggle in his long shadow, especially if a Labor caucus long cowed by Andrews rediscovers its voice. Moreover, as the minister responsible for the "big build blowouts" and Commonwealth Games non-delivery, Allan offers the hapless Opposition a real political target – if they can only take the opportunity.

Shallow talent pool

The 2014 election loss cost the Coalition no ministers, but the retirements of Napthine and long-serving frontbencher Terry Mulder in 2015 started an attrition in Coalition ranks, accelerated by MP retirements and defeated MPs in the elections of 2018 and 2002. As of early 2024, the composition of the Coalition joint party room, by year of election or appointment, is as follows:

Table 2: Victorian Coalition MLAs and MLCs – 2023[14]

Year elected	Liberal	National	Total
1992	1	0	1
1996	1	0	1
2002	1	1	2
2006	4	0	4
2010	4	2	6
2014[12]	2	1	3
2015[3]	2	2[4]	4
2018	4	0	4
2020[3]	1	0	1
2022	11	5	16
2023[3]	1	0	1
Total	**32**	**11**	**42**

NOTES

1	Includes Matthew Guy, first elected as an MLC in 2006
2	Includes John Pesutto, elected 2014-18 and 2022-
3	By-elections and appointments due to retirements
4	Includes Danny O'Brien, first elected as an MLC in 2014

These figures show the 2023 parliamentary Coalition overwhelmingly comprises MPs elected or appointed since the loss of government in 2014, who therefore have spent their entire parliamentary career in opposition. Only eight of 43 have experience as a minister or government parliamentary secretary: several of these, however, only held very junior portfolios, and only three Baillieu-Napthine ministers remain on the frontbench, while other former ministers and pre-2014 MPs have retired to the backbench, blocking talent renewal while clinging to their seats.

Arguably, too, those elected before 2014 have been in parliament so long that, for them, it has become a career rather than a vocation. That is a dangerous problem for a struggling opposition: when long-serving MPs get too comfortable with the wilderness, they are content to stay there.

Superficially, the sizeable 2022 intake, plus those entering from 2018, suggests significant renewal. However, the truth is that the depth of talent is shallow: they may mostly be solid and hard-working local members, but the Liberal Party room harbours too many mediocrities, serial networkers, and factional favourites. The party room, in particular, is a hot house of factional hatreds and petty jealousies. Worse, in terms of holding Labor to account and developing electorally-appealing policy, there are, to use Menzies's terminology, too many "leaners" and not enough "lifters". In a culture where MPs, not the party organisation and membership, determine policy, that is a danger to serious aspirations of returning to government,

For the Liberals, this talent problem is hardly surprising, given endorsing the best candidates on merit is seriously compromised by preselection plebiscites rewarding personal popularity, factional loyalties, and promoting gender and other diversity characteristics. Added to this is the problem of attracting top talent from business and the professions to join a long-term opposition. This is not helped when serving MPs of genuine talent, such as deputy upper house leader Matthew Bach, who in August 2023 suddenly resigned to return to his profession of teaching, do not persevere – however understandably – in such an unhappy environment with no foreseeable prospect of being in government.[15]

Given the political and structural woes of the Coalition parties, unless its electoral prospects improve it is likely that their talent pool will remain shallow after the 2026 election.

Organisational chaos and factional mayhem

Winning elections requires an efficient, and well-run, campaign organisation – and money. Since 2014, the Liberals have lacked both organisation quality and adequate funding.

In 2015 it emerged that then State Director, Damian Mantach, had defrauded the party of $1.5 million, most of which was never recovered. Besides the appalling breach of trust, the fraud highlighted that the party organisation was unfit for purpose.

A new Liberal president, grandee Michael Kroger, largely succeeded in enforcing a truce on this internal strife but, to fill the fraud-caused funding black hole, Kroger wasted much money and energy in a costly legal fight against the directors of the biggest source of the party's donor funding, the Cormack Foundation, which refused to release funds for the 2018 Victorian and 2019 federal campaigns without being satisfied the party's governance was reformed to avoid any future repetition of the 2015 fraud. Kroger won a Pyrrhic legal victory: a Federal Court judge ruled that the Liberal Party was a Cormack shareholder, but its shareholding did not entitle it to board representation.[16] Subsequent litigation changed nothing.

After the 2018 election disaster, Kroger was succeeded by a defeated former state minister, mild-mannered Robert Clark, who was left to pick up the pieces of both the electoral loss and the administrative shambles he inherited. Clark was in turn succeeded by a pugnacious former senator, Greg Mirabella.[17] At the same time, there was a succession of state directors, culminating in the importation of a Tasmanian state director, Sam McQuestin, who had run two winning election campaigns in that State. This experiment failed, however, and McQuestin became the undeserving scapegoat for 2022's heavy defeat.

The old cults of personality that once gathered around Kennett, on the one hand, and Peter Costello and Michael Kroger, on the other, have evolved into social moderates fighting ideological and religious conservatives for domination of the party's Administrative Committee and electorate conferences. In 2021, I wrote:

> While recent focus (of the progressive-dominated media) has been on hardline conservative powerbrokers cultivating the reli-

gious Right to get control of positions and agendas, some Liberal small-moderate figures, including MPs, use party and preselection games to promote their own. With their number-counting, cabals and conspiracies, they're as bad as each other.[18]

Since that was written, nothing has changed. Without the veneer of unity that government imposes, and the loss of the trappings of office, factional and personal power games are the only outlet for a constantly defeated parliamentary and organisational party.

Policy and values schizophrenia

Against an Andrews-dominated Government that, in its decade of office, has been mired in internal and labour movement scandals, enthusiastically pursued hard-Left identity and Indigenous politics, and over-committed to infrastructure projects to make Victoria by far, the most debt-laden state in the Commonwealth – all that before its conduct regarding the Covid pandemic – the ground should be fertile for an Opposition making a compelling policy case to Victorian voters.

What is needed is a comprehensive blueprint for the next Victorian Coalition government, just as the Kemp Report recommended in 2015. What so far has been delivered has been piecemeal: often constructive policy initiatives on specific problems, notably in bread-and-butter portfolios including health and education, and isolated "announceables" for State Council leader's speeches. But, even in the 2018 and 2022 election campaigns, there has been no coherent Coalition manifesto, or even, like John Howard's headland speeches of 1995, proof of an overarching values framework that told voters "this is the type of government we will be".

Fuelled by the vicious moderate-conservative conflicts in the Liberal camp, when the party itself could not itself agree on what it stands for – and, indeed, still does not – the post-2014 period has been a frustrating period of policy schizophrenia. This is illustrated by the Coalition's approaches to the 2018 and 2022 elections.

In 2018 the opposition tacked right, and largely staked its future on the conservative core issue of law-and-order, helped by the first-term Andrews government's various scandals. Much was made of supposed ethnic gang violence and crime rates in suburban Melbourne, and a main focus of the Opposition's election pitch was on more police, mandatory minimum gaol sentences, and a public registry for sex offenders. With a slogan borrowed from the successful 2016 Brexit campaign, "get back in control", and the major parties otherwise vying with each other on infrastructure and election giveaways, the law-and-order product differentiation failed.

In 2022, the opposite happened, again with Guy as leader. Having apparently concluded the Coalition could not beat Andrews from the Right, it tried doing so from the Left. Most notably, it promised to out-Labor Labor on green policy, carbon emissions reduction and Net Zero. It sought to purge an electable candidate from its ranks deemed by the leadership as too religiously conservative on progressive social issues.[19] Overall, the Coalition promised a big-government, socially-permissive and high-spending infrastructure alternative to Andrews, who himself was offering just that, assuming voters would turn on Andrews himself over his Covid and general record. But they didn't.

What 2018 and 2022 tells the opposition is that it needs to revisit Kennett's landslide victory in 1992. Kennett won not just because the then John Cain-Joan Kirner Government had virtually bankrupted the state. He won because he offered a comprehensive plan to deal with the mess and was frank with the electorate that there would need to be pain to attain eventual gain. In short, Kennett knew what he stood for and where he was going – not just for the next term, but for decades – and Victorian voters needed that reassurance to remove that discredited Labor government.

So far in the third Labor term, the Pesutto opposition has laid few markers on policy. The Deeming expulsion, however, and Pesutto's comments on it, indicate the current opposition supports predominant socially-progressive political and media elite agendas on gender, sexuality and

Indigenous issues, and resists the Howard "broad church" conception of the party. In doing so, it continues to risk confusing, and even losing, the confidence of its more socially conservative support base.

Social policy, however, does not win elections. The overall parlous state of the Victorian budget, with overwhelming public debt and a deteriorating fiscal position is ripe for an opposition that dares emulate Kennett's winning strategy in 1992. That requires thought and vision beyond the next opinion poll: discipline; teamwork; and a willingness to speak hard truths to the electorate.

Covid

Of all States and Territories, Covid hurt Victoria hardest in terms of the response. In the pandemic, Melbourne became the most locked down city in the Western world, at one stage surrounded by a ''ring of steel'' of roadblocks. Movement restrictions were draconian; Melburnians were placed under curfew for the first time in the city's history; schools, businesses and playgrounds were shut; mask and vaccine mandates were harsh.

Andrews had no interest in a unity approach and froze out the opposition. Attempts by then leader Michael O'Brien to offer cooperation to the government were ignored, and for an extended period parliament itself was shut down as a non-essential service. When O'Brien moved a motion of no-confidence in the Andrews Government in October 2020, citing the Government's lack of preparedness; the hotel quarantine fiasco, the Premier's failure to accept Australian Defence Force assistance; and excessive pain imposed on Victorians for no gain[20], the motion was not only voted down, but Andrews disdainfully refused to attend, dismissing the motion as "cheap politics".

The no-confidence failure sums up the Coalition's Covid experience. Ignored by the Government, ridiculed by the media, and succeeding only in highlighting the Opposition's impotence. Through Covid's height,

O'Brien sought to make constructive suggestions as well as attack the Government's performance, including a substantial policy statement on post-pandemic recovery, but he was mostly ignored by both Government and media.

Unfortunately for O'Brien's leadership, what the public and media *did* notice was attention-seeking undiscipline from Liberal MPs who took to social media, notably a frontbencher, Tim Smith, and a prominent backbencher, Bernie Finn, neither of whom held back with their abusive personal attacks on "Dictator Dan" or "the Despot" Andrews.[21] All they achieved was to persuade voters that while Andrews was trying to respond to the pandemic crisis, the Liberals had no answers except empty, "look-at-me" negativism. That impression helped overshadow and destroy O'Brien's leadership and persisted into the November 2022 election.

Conclusion – the permanent opposition?

It is an axiom of electoral politics that voters must not only need to want to vote a government out; they need a viable alternative to turn to. If they don't, enough will stick with the devil they know. In Victoria, voters do not yet have that viable alternative. Approaching the middle of its third consecutive four-year term in opposition, the prospects for the state Coalition returning to government seem more remote than ever, notwithstanding the sudden change of Premier.

Successive Victorian redistributions, reflecting population growth and distribution, have favoured Labor. The 2022 Australian Election Study illustrates how older, conservative-leaning, voter cohorts are dying off while Millennials and Generation Z voters look increasingly to the Green Left. To a great many younger voters, even Labor is seen as not progressive enough; the Liberals and Nationals, and the liberal-conservative values they embody, are about as relevant to them as a dinosaur fossil (see Cameron and McAllister et al 2022: 22-3). This contrasts with rank-and-file membership of the Coalition parties, which is older and on a different ideological wavelength to the young people whose votes their parties need to be competitive with the Left.

In sum, problems facing the Victorian Opposition are:

- A Liberal Party perpetually beset by factionalism and petty egos and a denuded parliamentary party populated by too many extinct volcanoes and under-contributors.
- No clear public policy agenda. The opposition enthusiastically criticises Andrews and now Allan, and their government's many scandals and shortcomings, but offers no comprehensive alternative vision.
- A near-moribund Liberal Party organisation, with an administrative committee riven by personality clashes and factional division, a secretariat that is a pale shadow of the powerful campaigning machine of the second half of last century, and an ageing and diminishing rank-and-file membership.
- A dearth of leadership talent. As of the time of writing, only two lower house MPs, Brad Rowswell (elected 2018) and Jess Wilson (elected 2022) show genuine leadership potential. Both are, however, still young and need more parliamentary and policy experience before the leadership next becomes vacant.

There are, however, some glimmers of hope for the Coalition in a post-Andrews Victoria.

First, the Nationals are holding up the Coalition, winning seats while the Liberals lose them. The Nationals are well-led, have a stable party room, and understand their regional constituents in a way the Liberals should emulate.

Second, the Teflon is finally wearing off the ageing Andrews-Allan Government. Andrews's out-of-the-blue July 2022 announcement repudiating his government's successful bid for the 2026 Commonwealth Games in regional Victoria – a pre-2002 election gimmick that Andrews subsequently claimed, without providing evidence, would cost thrice what his government first estimated, and required a $380 million compensation payout to the Games organisations – caused a fierce public and media backlash. The issue cut through to the electorate, even more than huge cost overruns on his overambitious infrastructure program, leading to post-election project cancellations and delays, broken election promises, eye-watering state public debt, and unpopular tax increases. That the Games fiasco was the portfolio responsibility of Andrews's handpicked successor, Allan, further punctured the Labor mythology of reliability and competent delivery.

Third, the "I stand with Dan" mantra of the Covid pandemic, when many Victorians rewarded Andrews for protecting them, is fading. As time lends perspective, more and more Victorians are seeing the lockdowns, vaccine mandates, curfews, public shamings, and loss of personal liberties of the Covid years as unnecessarily excessive, repressive, and reactive.

Lastly, by the 2026 election, Labor will have been in government continuously for twelve years, and for 33 of the previous 44 years. Despite its numerical superiority, it has failed adequately to renew its parliamentary and ministerial talent in the last decade: it has its own shallow talent pool when it comes to ministerial-level competence and, unlike the Liberals, the now-departed Andrews has so utterly dominated his party and caucus that post-Andrews Labor will itself be searching for a new direction, just as did the Liberals after the retirements of Sir Henry Bolte and Sir Rupert Hamer.

By 2026, the electorate may be far less forgiving of Labor, more so now Andrews has given way to Allan. Despite the leftwards shift of the electorate, there is still a market for a viable Coalition alternative to Labor that focuses, from the centre-right Burkean mainstream, on the traditional bread-and-butter issues of state government: budget repair and providing adequate services and infrastructure in a fiscally responsible and administratively competent manner.

Opportunities therefore exist for the Victorian Coalition, but they must bite bullets. A start would be paying more than lip service to David Kemp's 2015 post-election review and implementing his recommendations. Kemp provided a sensible blueprint for returning to government, yet his report still gathers dust while MPs and party bigwigs, who think they know better, dig bigger holes for themselves, and the Liberal Party.

It would mean ruthlessly retiring under-performers and time-servers from safe seats, replacing them with talented and enthusiastic MPs – regardless of gender or age. Furthermore, this talent search and talent nurturing – bringing electable new talent into both the Liberal and National parties – must also apply to finding strong candidates for winnable Labor seats.

Most importantly, it also would mean the Coalition developing a thematic and costed policy manifesto, consistent with mainstream, centre-right values and traditions, that is a strategic blueprint for the state into the middle of the century and beyond. Such a manifesto needs to be, like Kennett's in 1992, honest with voters: fiscally responsible and even austere, yet showing Victorians the opposition understands who they are as a community, and supports their values and aspirations; and offers a positive and constructive back-to-basics and budget repair program based on these insights. It means, as well, the Coalition and its MPs uniting around a shared consensus of what mainstream, centre-right values and traditions actually are, and then putting them into practice.

The opposition's challenge – especially for the Liberals – is to distinguish themselves from post-Andrews Labor and the Greens in what has become a permanently left-leaning State, where generational change is making the electorate largely dismissive of centre-right thought and tradition (that is, if Generation Z has ever heard of the likes of Locke, Burke, and Mill, let alone Menzies), yet avoiding taking themselves too far to the right.

With the possibility of election losses to Labor in 2026 and 2030, it is possible the next Liberal premier is not yet even in the parliament: indeed, I sometimes joke that my five-year-old daughter may be the next Liberal premier of Victoria. Based on the party's current performance in this former jewel of the Liberal crown, that joke may well be on me.

References

Cameron, S., and McAllister, I., Jackman S., and Sheppard, J., *The 2022 Australian Federal Election: Results from the Australian Election Study*, Canberra: ANU, 2022

Kemp, D., *Good Government for Victoria: Review of the 2014 State Election*, Liberal Party Victoria, 2015

Nutt, A., et al, *2018 State Election Review: Report to the Administrative Committee*, Liberal Party Victoria, 2019

O'Brien, M., MP, Victorian Legislative Assembly, *Hansard*, 13 October 2020, 2559-71

Endnotes

1   While the parties largely continued to cooperate with each other, the Nationals ended the formal Coalition agreement in 2002, and restored it in 2008.

2   Former Kennett minister and former Opposition leader, Denis Napthine.

3   As a former senior government adviser, the author was contracted as an interim chief-of-staff to two Baillieu ministers, to help them through the first Budget process, and observed the problems for himself.

4   The 2014 election review conducted by Dr David Kemp was especially critical of the party's lack of preparation for government in 2010-11. See Kemp, *Good Government for Victoria: Review of the 2014 State Election*, 2015, 46-47.

5   A scandal over police tapes and jobs-for-silence allegations.

6   Both policies were implemented by Andrews in government, and the level crossing policy became his government's signature measure – most removals have been finished on or ahead of schedule, if not on budget – when extolling its infrastructure-building credentials.

7   Seven seats lost (five Liberal, two Nationals), 3.5 per cent two-party preferred swing.

8   Source: Victorian Electoral Commission

9   Kemp, op cit.

10   Nutt el al, *2018 State Election Review: Report to the Administrative Committee*, Liberal Victoria, 2019, page 10.

11   McKenzie, Baker and Willingham, "Matthew and Madafferi: Opposition leader Matthew Guy dined with alleged mobster, *The Age*, 8 August 2017

12   Smethurst and Sakkal, "Liberal challenger quits frontbench after failing to topple O'Brien", *The Age*, 16 March 2021

13   Statement from the Leader of the Opposition, 19 March 2023: "This is not an issue about free speech but a member of the parliamentary party associating with people whose views are abhorrent to my values, the values of the Liberal Party and the wider community."

14   Source: Parliament of Victoria website: www.parliament.vic.gov.au

15   Bach's leaving was regretted by most of his colleagues. Commenting to the media, one MP said Bach was ''just a normal guy in a party full of nutters", and another said, "If we can't keep him in the party, then who are we left with?": Kovlos, "Where now for the Liberals after 'massive loss' of Matthew Bach?", *The Guardian*, 1 September 2023.

16   *Alston v Cormack Foundation Pty Ltd*, [2018] FCA 895, per Beach J. The judgment is a surprisingly readable detailed history of the history of the Cormack Foundation, the funds it administers, and the relationship between the Foundation and the Liberal Party.

17   Mirabella gained his Senate seat from a casual vacancy in early 2022, and lost it at the May 2022 federal election, making him one of the shortest-serving senators ever, if not the shortest.

18   Barnes, How the Liberal Party can step up its game, *Herald-Sun*, 15 January 2021

19   Legislative Council candidate for Eastern Victoria, Renee Heath, who was subsequently elected and admitted into the Liberal party room.

20   Michael O'Brien's no-confidence speech, 13 October 2020: Legislative Assembly *Hansard*, pages 2559-2571.

21   Smith left Parliament in 2022 after a drink-driving car accident destroyed his political career; Finn was expelled in 2022 largely relating to his caustic social media commentary, and failed to be re-elected as a Democratic Labor Party candidate.

15

The Effect of Opposition on the Composition of the Liberal-National Parties in Victoria, 1999-2010

Kate Jones

This chapter examines the changing composition of Liberal and National members in the Victorian Parliament in 1999, when the Liberal-National coalition lost government, and in 2010, when it was re-elected.

The Liberal-National Coalition in Victoria 1999-2010

The Victorian Parliament has generally had what Costar and Curtin (2004) described as a two-party dominant system. It appears that in recent years this has been eroded by the rise of independents and the Greens, but this is not completely new. There are precedents for minority government in Australian politics such as the minority governments in Victoria in 1999 and between the 1920s and the 1950s (Rodrigues and Brenton 2020). It is still possible, and indeed realistic, to see the Victorian Parliament as adhering to the Westminster-style system that Helms has summarised as a "parliament-centred opposition with no veto and/or cogoverning powers for the minority parties" (Helms 2004).

The Victorian Opposition in 1999 consisted of a coalition of the Liberal and National Parties. A Liberal-National Coalition Government had been elected in 1992 and unexpectedly lost office in 1999 when the Australian Labor Party (ALP) was able to govern with the support of three independents in the Legislative Assembly. The National Party terminated the coalition in 2000 and ran a separate campaign in the 2002 election (Costar and Campbell 2003). The two parties did not reunite in a coalition until 2008 (Best 2008). However, given the community of interests and historical relationship of the Liberal and National parties they will be regarded as the opposition for the purposes of this analysis. The independents and the smaller parties, the Greens and the Democratic Labor Party, are not considered as part of the opposition. The difference is that summed up by Kaiser as being between "small opposition parties that may exploit favourable constellations of executive–legislative relations, and large opposition parties, the 'official' opposition, which can only criticise the government and hope for the next general election" (Kaiser 2008). Thus, the Liberal and National parties comprised the opposition in the Victorian Parliament from 1999 until their unexpected win in 2010.

1999 and 2010

As Table 1 indicates the 2010 Opposition was less experienced than the 1999 Opposition. Thirty per cent of members were in their first term compared to 17 per cent in 1999. Even more striking was the difference in those who had served between six and nine years; this group constituted 34 per cent of the parliamentarians elected in 1999 and 9 per cent of those elected in 2010. Thus, the opposition had lost a large number of members who had enough experience to be good parliamentary operators and who could be expected to hold ambitions for future promotion. In contrast, the percentage of those who had been members of parliament for more than 20 years was the same in both 1999 and 2010 at 7 per cent of the total. Of the five in 1999 one (Robert Maclellan) had been a minister between 1976 and 1982 and became one again between 1992 and 1996. By contrast, three of the 2010 four (Robert Clark, Peter Hall and Denis Napthine) became ministers in the 2010 parliament; Clark and Napthine had also held ministerial positions during the 1990s.

Table 1: Length of service of Liberal and National Party members, 1999 and 2010

	1999 Number			Percent	2010 Number			Percent
	Liberal	National	Total		Liberal	National	Total	
Less than 3 years	11	1	12	17%	17	3	20	30%
3-6 years	13	1	14	20%	15	3	19	29%
6 - 9 years	21	3	24	34%	3	3	6	9%
10 - 12 years	4	3	7	10%	7	1	8	12%
13 - 15 years	5	1	6	8%	2	1	3	5%
16 - 18 years	2	1	3	4%	6	1	6	9%
19 - 21 years	0	0	0	0%	0	0	0	0%
22 - 25 years	1	1	2	3%	0	3	1	2%
More than 25 years	2	1	3	4%	3	0	3	5%
Total	59	12	71	100%	53	13	66	100%

It is also interesting to consider the previous occupations of the 1999 and 2010 cohorts. There has been substantial concern expressed in Australia and elsewhere about the rise of the professional politician. Much less has been made of the increasing lack of representation of most occupational groups. As the Table 2 below indicates the previous occupations of both the 1999 and 2010 cohorts were predominantly as managers and administrators and professionals. A significant pattern is the increase in the "Other" category. In 2010 this included military officers, police, real estate agents, small business proprietors, sport coaches and tradesmen. The time in opposition seems to have produced greater diversity.

Table 2: Previous occupations of Liberal and National Party members, 1999 and 2010

		1999			Percent	2010			Percent
		Number				Number			
		Liberal	National	Total		Liberal	National	Total	
Previous occupation									
	Managers and administrators	37	11	48	67%	29	5	34	52%
	Professional	18	1	19	26%	16	4	20	30%
	Other	4	1	5	7%	8	4	12	18%
Total		59	13	72	100%	53	13	66	100%

But what was the political background to the election or defeat of candidates between 1999 and 2010? In 1999 the election result was a shock to both sides and the ALP was only able to form a government with the support of the independents. Relatively few Liberal and National members lost their seats. In 2002, however, the ALP won a decisive victory with 62 members in the Legislative Assembly and 25 in the Legislative Council. The opposition was left with only 24 members (17 Liberals and seven Nationals) in the Legislative Assembly and 19 (15 Liberals and four Nationals) in the Legislative Council. Thirty-five (21 Liberals and 14 Nationals) had departed. Twenty-one of them stood for their own or another seat and were defeated. Some were exceptionally unlucky. Ronald Wilson had worked for Liberal members of parliament since 1984 and was chief of staff to the minister for health between 1996 and 1999 before entering parliament as the member for Bennettswood. His seemed the perfect trajectory for a successful political career but his electorate was abolished in the 2001 redistribution and he stood unsuccessfully for Mount Waverley. Fourteen did not stand, but four of these had seen their seat abolished or substantially changed in the 2001 redistribution. Twenty-one of them (60 per cent) had served for between six and twelve years, while three had been members of parliament for at least 25 years. Two were re-elected to parliament in 2006, one for the same seat and the other swapping a Legislative Assembly electorate for a Legislative Council one. Of the fourteen who did not stand, at least two experienced parliamentarians did not depart voluntarily. Robert Dean, who had been first elected in 1992, and Robert Maclellan, elected in 1970, had seen their electorates abolished in the re-distribution. Both contested the pre-selection for the new electorate of Gembrook; Dean won but was then disqualified when he was removed from the electoral roll because he did not live at the address in the electorate of Gembrook for which he was enrolled. The seat was won by the ALP

The ALP's victory in 2006 was not a landslide, although it won by a substantial margin (Economou 2006). The Labor Government had 55 members in the Legislative Assembly compared to the Coalition Opposition's 32 (23 Liberal and nine National) and one independent. The situation in the Legislative Council was rather more complex due to the 2003 reforms to the Legislative Council (Gardiner and Costar 2003). The 22 electoral provinces, each represented by two members, were replaced by eight electoral provinces, each represented by five members. The number of its members was thus reduced from 44 to 40. The old Legislative Council had been elected by preferential voting, with half its members being elected at each election. The new one was elected by proportional representation with all members coming up for election simultaneously. As a result, substantial changes in the Legislative Council included the election of three Greens and one member of the Democratic Labor Party. The government now had 19 members and the opposition 17 (15 Liberals and two Nationals). This time 14 opposition members departed parliament, six from the Legislative Assembly and eight from the Legislative Council. Thirteen of the 14 did not stand for election.

The electoral losses were significant in terms of occupational background and experience. The managers and administrators group had constituted 63 per cent of the opposition after the 2002 election and 56 per cent after the 2006 election, and the professionals group respectively 26 per cent and 24 per cent, so it can be argued that there was a disproportionate exodus of the first group.

Who stayed and who left?

In 2010 only 21 of the 1999 opposition members remained in parliament. There were 15 members of the Legislative Assembly and six members of the Legislative Council. Seventeen were Liberals, twelve in the Legislative Assembly and five in the Legislative Council. One of the six Nationals was a Legislative Councillor. Four had been first elected in 1988, five in 1992, three in 1996, eight in 1999 and one in 2006. Nine of the 21 had no experience of government, including Ted Baillieu, the leader of the Liberal Party and new premier, who had first been elected in 1999. Peter Ryan, the leader of the National Party and deputy premier, had been elected in 1992 but had not previously been a minister.

Table 3 below shows the length of service for members of parliament departing in 2002 and 2006. In 2002 66 per cent of departing members had been in parliament for twelve or less years; in 2006 only 14 per cent were in this category. By contrast, in 2006 85% had been in parliament for twelve years or more. In 2006 50 per cent of those who departed had served between twelve and 15 years. At least one lost as a result of the dissolution of the coalition arrangement between the two parties: the National Party's Bill Baxter, a member of parliament since 1973, who stood for the Legislative Assembly seat of Benambra but lost to the Liberal candidate. In 2002 eight had been ministers or parliamentary secretaries and sixteen had been in the shadow ministry. In 2006 four had been ministers or parliamentary secretaries and seven had been in the shadow ministry. In 2010 only one left; Ken Jasper who had first been elected in 1976 retired and was replaced by another member of the National Party.

Table 3: Length of service of opposition members departing in 2002 and 2006

	2002		2006	
Length of service	No	Percent	No	Per cent
3-6 years	12	6%	0	0%
7-9 years	0	29%	2	14%
10-12 years	11	31%	0	0%
13-15 years	3	9%	7	50%
16-18 years	2	6%	3	21%
19-21 years	4	11%	1	7%
22-25 years	0	0%	0	0%
Greater than 25 years	3	9%	1	7%
	35	100%	14	100%

Conclusion

Between 1999 and 2010 the Coalition Opposition had lost most of its experience in government and had acquired more diversity in the occupational background of its members. Its victory in the 2010 election was possibly related to this, in that it presented the electorate with a slightly more diverse set of candidates and an image less tarnished by the political realities of being in government. It should be remembered, however, that the members of the Victorian Liberal and National parties in 1999 and 2010 were no more representative of the Australian population than were members of parliament in general. In 1999, 2002 and 2006 more than 50 per cent of members of the opposition fell into the group of managers and administrators, yet that category comprised only 10 per cent of the Victorian population in both the 2001 and 2006 censuses. Similarly, in 1999, 2002 and 2006 respectively 35 per cent, 37 per cent and 34 per cent of members of the opposition were classified as professional, compared to 19 per cent and 20 per cent in the 2001 and 2006 censuses. The majority of occupational groups were not represented in parliament.

Members of parliament leave for many reasons, at the basic level because they fail to win election. For those who retire, or decide not to stand again, the situation is often more complex. Weller and Fraser (1987) observed in 1987 that Australian politicians are now entering politics, reaching the ministry and retiring at earlier ages; one of the implications of this is that being a member of parliament is now more likely to be just one part of a career or one of several careers. This explanation may be a key to understanding why a number of members of any opposition decide to leave. It is also tempting to conclude that the difference in years of service between the group that departed in 2002 and 2006 indicates that by 2006 many of those who had served 12 or more years had had enough of opposition and were ready to move on to something else.

Some of them did. Robert Doyle, former leader of the opposition, became Lord Mayor of Melbourne and Victor Perton, once a parliamentary secretary and then the opposition spokesperson on education, became Commissioner to the Americas for the State of Victoria. There may, however, be other reasons for their decision to leave. Doyle was blamed for the disastrous 2002 defeat and ceased to be the leader of the Opposition in May 2006. Andrew Olexander had in fact been expelled from the Liberal Party and was sitting as an independent by the time of the 2006 election.

The reform of the Legislative Council had led to major changes in members of that house. It may be that they had lost pre-selection, or even been expelled from the party, or increasingly that they wanted another career after their stint in parliament, or that they feel they are wasting their time in opposition. This last is a particularly likely explanation for those who departed in 2006. They had served two terms in opposition and knew the frustrations that it could bring. Many of them were able to start a new career or resume an old one, and for members of the Legislative Council the reform of that body might provide a good point to leave. Like the rest of the workforce, they have their time in a workplace and then move on. The corollary of this in all workplaces is that the workplace acquires new and enthusiastic workers, with new talents.

The difference between 2002 and 2006 was not that many more wanted to leave in 2002, but that many more had to. In both government and opposition members of parliament differ from the rest of the workforce in that they are subject to election rather than job selection. The profession of "politician" at any level of government contains inherent instabilities and uncertainties (Jones 2008). Parties frequently have as little choice about who they lose and who they keep as the individual members of parliament have about whether they win or lose. Elections can bring about substantial changes in the membership and capacity of government and opposition parties in parliament, as well as a change (or not) of government. Changes in the membership of the opposition could result in a decreased ability to make policy and be ready to take office (see Prasser 2010). Oppositions need to address the question of how they can maintain capacity during their periods out of government, but also to recognise the limitations on what they can do and focus on how they can do it better.

References

Best, C., "Coalition reunites in Victoria", *Sydney Morning Herald*, 11 February 2008

Costar, B., "Reformed bicameralism? The Victorian Legislative Council in the twenty-first century", in Aroney, N., Prasser, S., and Nethercote, J.R., (eds), *Restraining Elective Dictatorship: The Upper House Solution?* Crawley: University of Western Australia Press, 2008, 196-211

Costar, B., and Campbell, J., "Realigning Victoria: the state election of 30 November 2002", *Australian Journal of Political Science*, 38(2), July 2003, 313-23

Costar, B., and Curtin, J., *Rebels with a Cause: Independents in Australian Politics*, Sydney: UNSW Press, 2004

Donovan, B., *Re-connecting Labor*, Melbourne: Scribe, 2006

Economou, N., "The landslide revisited? The 2006 Victorian Election", *Democratic Audit of Australia, Discussion Paper*, 38/06, December 2006

Gardiner, G., and Costar, B., "A bicameral watershed: parliamentary reform in Victoria", *The Parliamentarian*, 84(4), 2003, 389-92

Helms, L., "Five ways of institutionalizing political opposition: lessons from the advanced democracies", *Government and Opposition*, 39(1), Winter 2004, 23-54

Hollander, R., "Who sits in Parliament? An analysis of state and federal members of parliament", Australasian Political Studies Association Conference, Hobart, 29 September-1 October 2003

Jones, K., "Professional politicians as the subjects of moral panic", *Australian Journal of Political Science*, 43(2), June 2008, 243-58

Kaiser, A., "Parliamentary opposition in Westminster democracies: Britain, Canada, Australia and New Zealand", *Journal of Legislative Studies*, 14(1/2), March-June 2008, 20-45

Miragliotta, N., and Errington, W., "Occupational profile of ALP, LP and National MHRs 1949–2007: from divergence to convergence", Australasian Political Studies Association Conference, Brisbane, 6-9 July 2008

Miskin, S., and Lumb, M., "The 41st Parliament: middle-aged, well-educated and (mostly) male", *Research Note*, no 24, 24 February 2006

Page, J.H., *The Education of a Young Liberal*, Carlton: Melbourne University Press, 2006

Parliament of Victoria, Remember <http://www.parliament.vic.gov.au/re-member>, viewed 23 November 2010

Parliamentary Handbook of the Commonwealth of Australia, 29th edition, Canberra: Commonwealth Parliamentary Library, 2006

Prasser, S., "Opposition one day, government the next: Can Oppositions make policy and be ready for office?" *Australasian Parliamentary Review*, 25(1), Autumn 2010, 151-61

Ray, R., "Are Factions Killing the Labor Party?" Address to the Fabian Society, Sydney, 20 September 2006

Rodrigues, M., and Brenton, S., "The age of independence? Independents in Australian parliaments", Parliamentary Library Research Paper, No. 4, Canberra> Commonwealth Parliamentary Library, 2010-11

Serle, G., "The Victorian Legislative Council, 1856-1890", *Historical Studies*, 6(22), May 1954, 186-203

Strangio, P., "Victorian Labor and the reform of the Legislative Council", *Labour History*, No 86, May 2004, 33-52

Strangio, P., and Costar, B., *The Victorian Premiers 1856-2006*, Sydney: Federation Press, 2006

Weller, P., and Fraser, S., "The younging of Australian politics or politics as a first career", *Politics*, 22(2), November 1987, 76-83

Wright, R., *A People's Counsel: A History of the Parliament of Victoria 1856-1990*, Melbourne: Oxford University Press, 1992

16

Opposition in Western Australia

Narelle Miragliotta and Finley Watson

Introduction

This chapter examines the evolution of opposition in Western Australia (WA)[1] since the grant of responsible government in 1890. We explore the patterns of opposition in WA since then. Three broad phases of opposition development are identified. The first phase includes the years between 1890 and 1943 and is described as non-party institutionalised opposition. The second period, which we term party institutionalised opposition, covers the period between 1947 and 1993. The third and present period is designated as the shrinking opposition, marked by the decline in the numerical presence of the official opposition in the Assembly relative to the government.

Theory and practice of opposition in the Western Australian Parliament

Like its federation counterparts, the theory and practice of opposition in WA is informed by Westminster principles.[2] This is reflected in the privileges and resources conferred on the leader of the second largest party in parliament.[3] The opposition leader, like the premier, is by convention a member of the Legislative Assembly. The opposition leader sits directly opposite the premier in the Assembly. The opposition leader is granted preferential rights and special recognition within parliamentary procedure, as set out within the *Legislative Assembly's Standing Orders*. Only one party is given the title of "Opposition", with all others designated as a "non-government party." The official or main opposition is distinguished by the higher remuneration allowance its leader receives compared to leaders of other parties. The WA Parliament describes the opposition as a unified and competitive entity that "coordinates the scrutiny of government policy and administration; formulates alternative policies that are responsible and practical to provide the electorate with an alternative government; and can force an election - provided a successful vote of no confidence against the government can be carried in the Legislative Assembly" (WA Parliament Factsheet).

As is the norm of Westminster opposition, there is a "power differential between the government and opposition," with the latter consigned to "an *alternative* government, or government-in-waiting." (Stone 2014: 20). This dynamic is assisted by an electoral system[4] that often over-represents the government in the Assembly, while party discipline ensures that the government is generally able to complete a full term without being subject to a successful vote of no confidence. Of the 41 elections that have been held between 1890 and 2021, only nine have yielded minority governments, with five such governments arising in the first five elections following the grant of responsible government, and before the consolidation of the WA party system (UWA Elections Database).

However, WA is not a faithful replica of the Westminster system. Two characteristics temper the operation of British Westminster principles of opposition. First, there are a greater number of "significant parliamentary actors than envisaged by the Westminster model" (Stone 2014: 21). The Westminster model is constructed around a two-party system in which the parties alternate between government and opposition. While Labor and the Liberals are the dominant parties, the National Party (formerly the Country Party) constitutes a third numerically smaller, albeit permanent presence in the Assembly. Consistent with their counterparts in other Australian settings, the WA Nationals have, for much of their existence, "adopt[ed] executive brokerage as its primary strategy" and opted for coalition with the Liberals (Stone 2014: 24). Yet, the Nationals' separate legal and organisational identity disperses the concentration of opposition, especially when Labor is in office.[5]

The second feature that modifies Westminster style opposition is near symmetrical bicameralism. WA has a constitutionally powerful Legislative Council (Council) that can oppose a government's legislative agenda if the majority so acts. The power of the Council intersects with a long history of electoral malapportionment which, prior to the 2000s, served as a powerful extension of the coalition opposition in the Assembly.[6] The introduction of proportional representation using the single transferable vote (PR-STV) for Council elections in 2005 attenuated the conservative dominance over the Council by admitting new parties to the chamber. This offered Labor governments opportunities to negotiate with one or more non-government Councillors when the major opposition grouping refused.[7]

Three phases of opposition development in Western Australia

Non-party institutionalised opposition 1890 - 1946

The first period is defined by weak party-based opposition. In the parliament's earliest years, there was "nothing which could be called an organised opposition" (de Garis and Stannage 1968: 56). There was initial reluctance by any grouping to assume the Opposition mantle, even if Members were willing to occupy seats opposite the government in the Assembly (de Garis and Stannage: 56), as this exchange demonstrates:

> THE PREMIER (The Hon. John Forrest) ... I am sure his chief object this evening has been to oppose the Government; he considers he is the leader of the Opposition, and that, therefore, it is

his duty to the Opposition to oppose everything.

MR. PARKER: Pardon me. Let me correct the hon. member. Firstly, it is not right to attribute motives, and, secondly, I do not consider myself the leader of the Opposition, nor am I leader of the Opposition.

MR. COOKWORTHY: The Hon. Member was the leader of this discussion at any rate; and, whether he is the leader of the Opposition or not, he has taken the position of leader of the Opposition this evening (WA Assembly 21 January 1891: 41-42).

Some tentativeness about the office remained following the announcement of George Randell as the first official Leader of the Opposition in 1894.[8] Randell was careful to strike a solicitous tone, articulating a vision for opposition that prioritised "honest criticism not factious opposition" (Randell quoted in de Garis 1991: 316).[9]

As a result, for the first decade of the new parliament, the Forrest (Ministerialist) Government avoided significant legislative strife even as more MPs identified as oppositionists (de Garis 1969: 318), and more of the government's proposed legislation was defeated (de Garis 1969: 326-7). The solicitousness of opposition reflected the absence of a party system, a Premier (John Forrest) who was attentive to parliamentary opinion (de Garis 1991: 63) and adept at incorporating his "abler critics" into his ministry (de Garis and Stannage 1968: 59), and a parliament composed of WA born elected members ("ancient colonialists") who coalesced around the shared interests of established settlers in the state (Stannage 1965: 7-8).

The onset of the gold rushes in the 1890s provided new impetus for the development of opposition. The discovery of gold, and the influx of people into the state, brought "recent arrivals" into the parliament, breaking the monopoly of the "ancient colonialists" and thereby introducing a new faultline into parliamentary politics (Stannage 1965:7-8). With Premier Forrest's exit to federal politics in 1900, a period of parliamentary flux ensued, and a view emerged (expressed by the then

Premier) that parliamentary politics required the certainty of two parties (not groupings) to occupy the government and opposition roles (de Garis 1991: 85; Stannage 1965: 15). Growth in Labor's parliamentary strength[10] (1991: 22) would provide this catalyst, prompting the previous opposition to collapse into a grouping around the government ("Ministerialists"). Fluid opposition gave way to organised opposition that increasingly coalesced around a Labor and anti-Labor divide, thereby heralding a two-party mode of politics (de Garis 1969: 344; Stannage 1965: 16).

While a two-party dynamic was firmly established by 1911, institutionalisation of the non-Labor groupings especially remained weak. The period between 1911 and 1924 was chaotic, with parliament and the parties marred by factionalism (Black 1991: 99). While Labor continued to consolidate, the institutionalisation of the non-Labor grouping was interrupted by the formation of the Country party (1914), along with various iterations of the Liberals before 1944 (Black 1979: 191-211). The high incidence of cross-party voting (Black 1991: 141), and the changing nomenclature among parties on the right suggested a party system that was only partially institutionalised. Moreover, alternation between government and opposition was semi-frequent, dominated by the anti-Labor groupings, although Labor did win four consecutive elections in the closing years of this period.

Consolidation of party centred opposition 1947-1993

The second era is inclusive of 1947 and 1993 and is marked by the institutionalisation of opposition in the Assembly. Three related developments define this period. The first is that opposition is consolidated under consistent party labels. The party system stabilises, with the number of parties in the Assembly distilled under three recurring, institutionalised, party groupings, a process completed with the establishment of the (modern) Liberal Party in 1944[11] (Black 1979: 211; Black 1991).

The second development was the increase in the seat share gained by the opposition (see, also Stone 2014:28). Previously, the size of the government in the Assembly significantly eclipsed that of the opposition, with the seat share of the main opposition averaging 34.4 per cent (median 36). However, the stabilisation of the three establishment parties, the enhanced cohesiveness of the Liberals, and the thinning in the ranks of electable independents created the conditions for the expansion of opposition. The average size of the main opposition grew to 44.3 per cent in the Assembly, and on three occasions rose as high as 48 per cent (median 48). Both enlargement and consistency in the average size of the opposition in the Assembly heralded what Bruce Stone has described as the "prominence and stability of opposition as a feature of Western Australia's political system" (2014:28).

The third development was a deepening in the institutionalisation of opposition more generally. In 1955, official recognition was given to the position of Leader of the Opposition in the Council (Black 1991: 134). Beginning in the 1960s, more frequent references by government members to "shadow ministers" were uttered in the Assembly[12], and by the 1970s the first shadow ministry was formalised when Labor appointed a shadow cabinet ministry[13] (Phillips 1991:210). The institutionalisation of the shadow ministry facilitated "an extra-parliamentary dimension to the contest between government and opposition" (Stone 2014:27).

While formal opposition consolidates, this era is also defined by sustained periods of government for the main anti-Labor grouping in the context of strong electoral competition. Of the 16 elections that were conducted during this period, Labor won government on six occasions, while coalitions composed of the Liberal Party and Country Democratic League won four consecutive elections, and a coalition of the Liberal Party and National Alliance won three consecutive elections.

The shrinking opposition

The third phase of opposition we identify commenced in the mid 1990s. We have labelled this as the era of the *shrinking opposition*, marked by the contraction in the numerical size of the main opposition in the Assembly relative to the government. The *shrinking opposition* is exemplified by decline in the average size of the opposition in the Assembly to 32.5 per cent. Only two oppositions since 1996 have managed to occupy 40 percent of seats in the Assembly (2005 and 2008).

Several developments have contributed to this phenomenon. In part it reflects a change in the concentration of the opposition on the centre right of parliamentary politics. For much of its existence, the Nationals chose "not to support any Labor government nor play a crossbench role," supporting the Liberals in an *almost* permanent coalition (Layman 1979:73). However, in 2006 the Nationals dissolved the coalition with the Liberals and declared the party open to "alliance arrangements"[14] with either governing party (Phillimore and McMahon 2015: 41). A measure of political pluralism also returned to the Assembly (UWA elections database). While no new parties overcame the high electoral thresholds to win seats in the Assembly, several independents were elected to the chamber between 1996 and 2008. Finally, contraction in the average size of the main opposition's seat share in the Assembly has occurred in parallel with growth in the government's presence. Governments, have on average, occupied 63 percent (median 61) of the Assembly in the third period.[15] This compares to the second period, where governments occupied on average 55 percent of Assembly seats.

While the seat share of the official opposition has declined over this period, shadow ministries have increased in size. This trend began gradually. In the 1970s, the average size of the shadow ministry was 12 but by the 1980s it had risen to 16. By the early 2000s, however, the average size of shadow ministries increased significantly, averaging 25 members.[16] In 2004, the Coalition Opposition innovated further by bifurcating the shadow ministry into an inner and outer ministry, with the outer ministry consisting of "spokespersons". When Labor returned to opposition in 2008, it maintained a unified shadow ministry. However, in 2013, the Labor shadow ministry was expanded and an inner and outer shadow ministry established following the appointment of opposition parliamentary secretaries.

While opposition contracted in this third phase, steady alternation in office between the parties of government and opposition has remained. Across the seven elections held in this period, Labor served in opposition in three parliaments, while the Liberals were in opposition in four, with each government securing at least one second consecutive term.

In summary, since the consolidation of the WA party system, there has been strong electoral competition with frequent government alternation. Of the 23 elections held since 1947, Labor has held office in ten instances, and the Coalition on 13 occasions. On average, State governments served 2.25 terms, suggesting that WA oppositions are perceived by voters as credible alternative governments. The more recent period suggests, however, that the numerical strength of the official opposition is shrinking over time.

Depleted opposition and the 41st parliament

The 2021 state election yielded the smallest opposition in the Assembly since 1911. The incumbent Labor Government won 53 of the 59 seats (90 percent) in the Assembly, while the Liberals retained only two seats (3 percent), and the Nationals, four (7 percent). The near annihilation of the opposition in the Assembly is a problem both in democratic theory and practice. Opposition strength is a definitional characteristic of liberal democratic practice (Blondel 1997), and it is encapsulated in Dahl's (1971) conceptualisation of "contestation", which has proven to be a robust measure of democratic health (Coppedge et al 2008).

Many factors affect the behaviour of opposition (Dahl 1966;

Garritzmann 2017), with institutional opportunity structures among the most important of them (Kaiser 2008). In Westminster systems, the concentration of opposition (how many parties and their internal unity) and its competitiveness are critical to how the opposition manoeuvres within these sites (Dahl 1966: 338). Pickles (1970:159) summarises the importance of these two conditions thus: "The essential requirement for an effective opposition is to have enough cohesion both to defeat a government and to replace it."

The qualities of concentration and competitiveness serve particular functions. Concentration is related to the cohesiveness of the opposition group or grouping, while competitiveness is related to (even if not strictly defined by) legislative strength.[17] In combination, they determine the ability of the opposition to constitute an alternative government (Tuttenauer 2018; Eggers and Spirling 2016) and for the incumbent government to perceive them as a credible existential threat (Stone 2014: 28). Competitiveness is also linked to perceptions of the opposition's democratic legitimacy among voters (Neumann 1969: 72), and practically to its ability to offer a sustained critique of the government.

Westminster democracies accept that the opposition will be, and should be, an inferior numerical lower house presence compared to the government, and generally powerless to prevent the government from implementing its agenda (Johnson 1997). Yet it does expect that the opposition can discharge critical roles of *control* (monitoring government actions), *critique* (emphasising government shortcomings) and *alternative* (capacity to propose policy goals, and personnel) (Garritzmann 2017: 7). While the Assembly is typically not the "site of genuine encounters", parliamentary debate is intended to "influence" the public (Dahl 1966:339). The 41st WA Parliament provides a window into how an opposition with a drastically reduced legislative presence strives to remain competitive and visible.

Opposition under strain

The opening of the 41st WA Parliament was like any other in many respects. The Opposition Leader, Mia Davies, in her Address-in-Reply, congratulated the Premier and the Labor Government on its victory, and acknowledged the Coalition's electoral defeat. After dispensing with the pleasantries, Davies reminded the government that the opposition was there "to ask questions on behalf of the Western Australian Public" (Davies, *Assembly*, 5 May 2021: 200) and launched into a critique of the Labor Government over its perceived lack of integrity, for its failure to declare its intentions regarding electoral reform and lack of transparency regarding infrastructure projects.

While Davies' speech was conventional in both spirit and in substance, the context in which it was delivered was not. First, it was the leader of the small conservative party, the Nationals that was delivering the opposition's Address-in-Reply speech, the first time a National MP had led opposition since 1947. Second, the opposition was constituted by an alliance between the National and the Liberals, the first since 2005 (Shine 2021) forged, according to Davies, by "a mix of circumstance, numbers, personality and political will"[18] (Davies, *Assembly*, 5 May 2021: 197). Moreover, Davies regarded the alliance as a moral obligation, explaining that the two parties have a "common purpose and duty to provide effective opposition" (Davies, *Assembly*, 5 May 2021: 197).

A combination of convention, duty and pragmatism informed the decision by the Nationals and Liberals to work together. The alliance was the only feasible solution to constituting a viable shadow ministry. By pooling their combined personnel of six Members in the Assembly, and ten Members in the Council (seven Liberals and three Nationals), the Nationals and Liberals were able to assemble a 15-member shadow ministry, albeit five members fewer than the Mike Nahan Liberal Shadow Ministry of the preceding parliament (Wildie 2017).[19]

While the alliance facilitated the formation of a shadow ministry, it did little to ameliorate other deficits arising from the opposition's meagre parliamentary contingent. One of the consequences was fewer personnel to amplify the opposition's profile, visibility and message in the electorate, namely MPs and electorate support staff attached to members' offices. More directly, perhaps, it affected funding for the office of the opposition, the leader of the alternative party in waiting. The amount awarded is determined by the premier commensurate with the numerical strength of the parliamentary opposition. The consequent reduction in allocated funding to the Leader of the Opposition's office caused Davies to publicly criticise the Labor government over their funding. Davies argued that the $1.92 million awarded to the opposition (Law 2021; Shine 2021) was insufficient compared to the average allocation of $3 million per ministerial office across the previous three parliaments.

The opposition's diminutive parliamentary contingent has had other consequences for its functional capacity. As Kaiser notes, parliamentary opposition depends on indirect opportunities to affect parliamentary decisions, of which committee participation is important (2008: 26). Committees constitute an important arena for the opposition to scrutinise and input into government policies in what is often a more collegiate inter-party context. However, parliamentary committees are generally strong mechanisms for review when there is ample opposition membership, when members can specialise in a particular area of policy expertise (Oñate and Ortega 2019) and when there is opposition chairmanship (Konig et al 2023), particularly of the all-important finance and auditing committees (Strøm 1998: 41).

Resourcing parliamentary committees with only seven opposition members is challenging. Of the seven Standing Assembly committees as of 2023, which have between four and five members, the opposition holds membership on six committees, although it did claim chairmanship of the Development and Justice Standing Committee, which oversees departments relating to socio-economic development and justice, including disability services and the police (Parliament of Western Australia 2023). The quantum of opposition committee membership is meagre compared to previous parliaments. Though working independently in the 40th parliament, Liberal and National members occupied 14 positions, including one chairmanship, while Labor held 15 positions and two chairmanships when in opposition during the 39th parliament. Moreover, the opposition has no representation on the Education and Health Standing Committee, even though this is a particular policy focus for the opposition.

The opposition's sparse representation also undercuts the ability of serving opposition members to specialise in portfolios and issues. For instance, the two Liberal MPs – Libby Mettam and David Honey – are members of multiple committees but also different committees from those that they served on in the 39th parliament. The situation for the Nationals is similar. Mia Davies joined the Crime and Corruption Standing Committee in 2023, while also serving as leader of the opposition. Davies had not been a member of a standing committee since 2012. Merome Beard was appointed as deputy chair of the Economics and Industry Standing Committee as a first term member of parliament. James Rundle is the only National who has committee experience.

Of course, this is not to suggest that opposition members are without influence on the committees that they serve. Libby Mettam, for example, who chaired the Development and Justice Standing Committee which produced the 2022 *"Enough is Enough": Sexual harassment against women in the FIFO mining industry* report, managed to convince the parliament to support most of the 24 recommendations tabled by the Committee (Government of WA 2022). Yet opportunities for the opposition to influence the government via committee membership are constrained when their levels of representation on committees is marginal.

The second arena in which the opposition can exert influence over the government is in relation to plenary debates (Kaiser 2008: 26) and more particularly parliamentary questions. Parliamentary questions allow for the opposition to scrutinise and critique government policy, to attempt to control legislation and to signal to voters their fitness as a government in waiting (Kaiser 2008: 28). Within Westminster parliaments, oral questions can help the opposition to boost its visibility (Garritzmann: 14) and increase public engagement (Salmond 2004). The opposition's performance at parliamentary questions provides voters with a means to assess the opposition's ability to compete with the government over the issues which define the agenda and the extent to which either party represents the public interest (Green-Pederson 2010).

In the WA Parliament, oral questions are asked without notice during Question Time each sitting day for a period of approximately 30 minutes and can be asked by the opposition, government as well as independents, although the opposition poses most questions. Questions on notice are only asked by the opposition, supplied in writing directly to the relevant minister and generally require more detailed responses than those asked during question time. If a response is not received within 30 days, the requesting member may raise the non-response during question time (Parliament of Western Australia 2021). Written questions are used by members to obtain detailed information from ministers about government activities and administration.

In this respect, the Opposition in the 41st parliament is performing at a similar level of activity as previous oppositions when assessed based on the number of oral questions it has asked. Across the five parliaments between 2001 and 2021, there has been an average ratio of 18 questions per day in the Assembly, whilst in the 41st parliament there have been 22, with 69 per cent asked by the opposition. Indeed, if the number of oral questions continues at the current rate it would represent the second highest rate in the history of the parliament.

While the opposition has maintained momentum in relation to oral questions, it has flagged on questions on notice. The data shows that there has been a noticeable decline in questions asked on notice over the same period. Using data collated from the five parliaments convened between 2001 and 2021, the opposition or independent members have asked questions on notice at a rate of 23 per day, while the Davies/Love opposition has only asked 10 per day, the lowest number since the 29th

Parliament of 1977. This decrease in questions on notice has occurred at a time when the Government's legislative agenda has expanded. The Labor Government has introduced 0.77 bills per day as of March 2023, the highest rate for nine years. The depleted size of the opposition, and the consequent loss of personnel and financial resources, might be affecting their capacity to prepare questions on notice.

Conclusion

Opposition in WA has evolved over time, from tentative and unorganised, to highly institutionalised. While Opposition is central to parliamentary politics in the state, the average size of the opposition is shrinking, with governments eclipsing the opposition to a much greater extent in recent times. While this is not ideal, regular alternation in office between the main parties continues and so the systemic benefits of opposition are generally realised (Stone 2014:29). The significantly reduced size of the opposition affects its access to the resources needed to influence public opinion and debate. Across a range of different dimensions, the opposition's depleted legislative strength constrains its competitiveness in ways that are not beneficial for them, the government or ultimately voters.

References

Australian Politics and Elections Archive 1856-2018 (UWA Election database), University of Western Australia (https://elections.uwa.edu.au/)

Black, D., *The Western Australian Parliamentary Handbook*, Perth: WA Parliament, 2014. url: https://web.archive.org/web/20160303183010/http://www.parliament.wa.gov.au/ParliamentaryHandbook/23rd%20Edition%20of%20the%20Parliament%20Handbook%20-%20Final%20Version.pdf

Black, D., "Factionalism and Stability," in Black, D., (ed), *The House on the Hill: A History of the Parliament of Western Australia, 1832-1990*, Perth: Western Australian Parliamentary History Project: Parliament of Western Australia, 1991, 97-51

Black, D., "The Liberal Party and its Predecessors" in Pervan, R., and Sharman, C., (eds), *Essays on Western Australian Politics*, Nedland: University of Western Australia Press, 1979, 191-230

Blondel, J., "Political Opposition in the Contemporary World", *Government and Opposition*, 32(4), 1997, 462–86

Community Development and Justice Standing Committee, *Western Australian Government response to the Community Development and Justice Standing Committee Report 2: 'Enough is Enough' Sexual harassment against women in the FIFO mining industry 'Enough is Enough' Sexual harassment against women in the FIFO mining industry*, Government of Western Australia, 2022, retrieved from https://www.dmirs.wa.gov.au/sites/default/files/atoms/files/enough_is_enough_response.pdf.

Community Development and Justice Standing Committee, *Terms of Reference*, Parliament of Western Australia, 2023. url: https://www.parliament.wa.gov.au/Parliament/commit.nsf/

Coppedge, M., Alvarez, A., and Maldonado, C., "Two persistent dimensions of democracy: Contestation and inclusiveness", *Journal of Politics*, 70(3), 2008, 632-47. https://doi.org/10.1017/S0022381608080663

Dahl, R., "Patterns of Opposition", in Dahl, R., (ed), *Political Oppositions in Western Democracies*, New Haven and London: Yale University Press, 1966, 332–47

Dahl, R., *Polyarchy: Participation and Opposition*, New Haven: Yale University Press, 1971

Davies, M., *Address in Reply*, Western Australian Legislative Assembly, 5 May 2021, 1-6

de Garis, B., "Western Australia", in Loveday, J., Martin, A., and Parker, S., (eds), *The Emergence of the Australian Party System*, Sydney: Hale and Iremonger, 1969, 298-354

de Garis, B., "Constitutional and Political Development: 1870-1890", in Black, *The House on the Hill*, 1991, 41-62

de Garis, B., and Stannage, T., "From responsible government to party politics in Western Australia," *Australian Economic History Review*, 8(1), 1968, 54-61

de Kruijff, P., "WA Nationals, Liberals form alliance for opposition - just don't call it a coalition," *WA Today*, 20 April 2021

Eggers, A. C., and Spirling, A., "The shadow cabinet in Westminster systems: Modelling opposition agenda setting in the house of commons, 1832-1915" *British Journal of Political Science*, 48(4), 2018, 343–67

Garritzmann, J., "How much power do oppositions have? comparing the opportunity structures of parliamentary oppositions in 21 democracies" *Journal of Legislative Studies,* 23(1), 2017, 1–30

Green-Pedersen, C., "Bringing parties into parliament: The development of parliamentary activities in Western Europe", *Party Politics,* 16(3), 2010, 347–69.

Hastie, H., "A guide to the political headaches ringing as WA parliament returns for 2023", *WA Today* 13 February 2023 (online NewsBank)

Hayward, A., "WA Election decided: Liberals to form alliance with Nationals," *The Age,* 14 September, 2008

Johnson, N., "Opposition in the British Political System," *Government and Opposition,* 32, 1997, 487–510

Kaiser, A., "Parliamentary Opposition in Westminster Democracies: Britain, Canada, Australia and New Zealand", *Journal of Legislative Studies,* 14(1/2), 2008, 20–45

König, T., Lin, N. and Silva, T., "Government dominance and the role of opposition in parliamentary democracies, *European Journal of Political Research,* 62, 2002, 594-611

Layman, L., "The Country Party: Rise and Decline", in Pervan, R., and Sharman, C., (eds), *Essays on Western Australian Politics,* Nedlands: UWA Press, 1979, 159-90

Layman, L., "Continuity and Change, 1947-1965", in Black, D., (ed), *The House on the Hill: A History of the Parliament of Western Australia, 1832-1990,* Perth: Western Australian, Parliamentary History Project: Parliament of Western Australia, 1991, 153-84

Loton, W., W*estern Australian Legislative Assembly,* 25 July 1897, 7

Miragliotta, N., Murray, S., and Harbord J., "Western Australia," in Barry, N., Chen, P., Haigh, Y., Motta, S., and Perche, D., (eds), *Australian Politics and Policy: Senior Edition.* Sydney, Sydney University Press, 2023, 683-718

Neumann, S., "Toward A Comparative Study of Political Parties", in Blondel, J., (ed), *Comparative Government: A Reader,* London: Macmillan, 1969, 69-76

Phillimore, J, and McMahon, L., "Moving Beyond 100 Years: The 'WA Approach' to National Party Survival," The Australian Journal of Politics and History, 6(1), 2015, 37-52

Phillips, H., "The modern parliament", in Black, D., (ed), *The House on the Hill: A History of the Parliament of Western Australia, 1832-1990,* Perth: Western Australian Parliamentary History Project: Parliament of Western Australia, 1991, 185-264

Pickles, D., *Democracy,* London: Batsford, 1970

Reid, G.S., and Forrest, M., *Australia's Commonwealth Parliament, 1901-1988: Ten Perspectives*. Carlton: Melbourne University Press, 1989

Salaries and Allowances Tribunal, Members of Parliament Tribunal Determination No. 1 of 2022. WA Government.url:https://www.wa.gov.au/government/publications/members-of-parliament-tribunal-determination-no-1-of-2022

Salaries and Allowances Tribunal, Report on the allowances provided to Members of Parliament. WA Government, 2020

Salmond, R., "Grabbing Governments by the Throat: Question Time and Leadership in New Zealand's Parliamentary Opposition", *Political Science*, 56(2), 2004, 75-90

Parliament of Western Australia, 2021, Standing Orders of the Legislative Assembly of the Parliament of Western Australia Parliament of Western Australia

Shine, R., "WA Liberals and Nationals enter alliance instead of formal coalition following electoral wipeout," *ABC News*, 19 April, 2021

Stannage, C., "The Composition of the Western Australian Parliament 1890-1911," *University Studies in History,* 4(3), 1965, 1-40

Stone, B., "Opposition in parliamentary democracies: a framework for comparison," *Australasian Parliamentary Review.* 29, 1, 2014, 19-31

Stone, B., "State legislative councils: designing for accountability", in Aroney, N., Prasser, S., and Nethercote, J.R., (ed.), *Restraining Elective Dictatorship: The Upper House Solution?*, Nedland: UWA Publishing, 2008, 175-95

Strøm, K., "Parliamentary committees in European democracies", *Journal of Legislative Studies,* 4(1), 1998, 21–59

Tuttnauer, O., "If you can beat them, confront them: Party-level analysis of opposition behavior in European national parliaments", *European Union Politics,* 19(2), 2018, 278–98

UWA Elections Database

Western Australian Parliamentary Library., Leader of the Opposition and Shadow Ministry, Factsheet No. 12, n.d..url: https://www.parliament.wa.gov.au/WebCMS/webcms.nsf/resources/file-12-opposition-leader-and-shadow-ministers/$file/Leader%20of%20the%20Opposition%202021.pdf

Wildie, T., "WA Liberal Leader Mike Nahan unveils shadow cabinet with 'extensive experience", *ABC News,* 25 March 2017. url: https://www.abc.net.au/news/2017-03-25/mike-nahan-unveils-wa-shadow-cabinet/8386498

Endnotes

1   Western Australia attained self-government several decades behind the other original colonies. Self-government of the colony became effective from 21 October 1890, with the UK parliament's enactment of the *Western Australian Constitution Act 1890* (UK), to which was scheduled the *Constitution Act 1889* (WA) (CA).

2   For overview of these principles as they pertain to oppositions, see Reid and Forrest 1989: 48-50 (Commonwealth); Potter 1966 (Britain) and Johnson 1997 (Britain).

3   Since 1911, the Leader of the Opposition has been paid a salary equivalent to government ministers and afforded special entitlements above those received by a backbench member. For example, the official leader of the opposition received $AUS285,881 compared to the $AUS 231626 received by the leader of a recognised non-government party in 2023. (Salary and Allowances Tribunal, 2022). There are other courtesies extended to the Leader of the Opposition, such as the requirement to consult with the Leader of the Opposition in relation to debate adjournments, seating allocations in the Assembly and longer speaking entitlements for various types of speeches (Standing Orders of the Assembly 2021:11-41)

4   Elections for the WA Assembly are conducted based on single member electoral districts, using the alternative vote.

5   The relationship within the coalition has been fractious over the years. In the 1970s, the Nationals wrestled with the question about the value of coalition, which led to a major split within the party and a brief break down in the coalition arrangement as the party battled between a "conservative majority who supported close and continuing coalition and the militant minority who wanted a more independent position either on the cross benches or within a coalition" (Layman 1979:79).

6   See Black (1991) and Phillips (1991:137) for an overview of Council refusals. The dominance of the conservatives in the Council disproportionately constrained Labor Governments in the Assembly especially.

7   The last vestiges of malapportionment in the Council were eliminated with the passage of the *Constitutional and Electoral Legislation Amendment (Electoral Equality) Act 2021* which provides, among other reforms, for a single state-wide electorate. (Miragliotta *et al* 2023).

8   While Randell is officially recorded as the first opposition leader, Sir James Steere was considered by some of his peers as the first recognised unofficial leader of the opposition under the old constitution. As William Loton recounted: "We know that under the old regime he was not able to do more than that, for, although he might have had a majority at his back, and might have been able to carry measures in opposition to the government of the day, the opposition party at that time were not able to go any further. They could not turn out the government in those days, and put another government in" (Loton, *Assembly* , 25 July 1897: 7)

9   In his Address in Reply, Randell declared: "I myself personally, in the position in which I am placed, am desirous of only exercising an honest and, so far as I am able, an intelligent criticism of all the measures they place before us; and that it will be the endeavour of all members-I think I am giving expression to their feelings-to give the Government a cordial and hearty support in all measures which they think may conduce to the progress and prosperity of the colony. I think I can promise them there will be no factious opposition on this side of the House, but a diligent and searching scrutiny into all the measures which they may bring before us (Randell, *Assembly*, 31 July 1894: 59).

10   de Garis and Stannage (1968) note that the first Trades and Labour Congress in 1899 created the "political Labour Party, which two years later won eight seats in the Legislative Assembly." (de Garis and Stannage 1968: 59).

11   Labor and the Liberals dominated government and opposition. However, other parties were occasionally invited to participate. In 1974, for example, the Opposition was composed of the Liberals and National Alliance, with the latter the result of a merger between the Democratic Labor Party and the Country Party. Similarly, in 1980, the then National Country Party split into two parties - the National Country Party which formed a coalition government with the Liberals, with the Nationals sitting on the crossbench (UWA Election Database).

12   See, for example, *Assembly* 8 August 1963: 172.

13   Although the shadow ministry has no official status or is eligible for additional resources - other than the Opposition Leader, Deputy Opposition Leader and Opposition Whip – the list of the names of the shadow ministry, and their shadow portfolio allocations, is published on the WA parliament website.

14   This strategy was developed under the then leader of the WA Nationals, Brendon Grylls. Under the terms of the alliance arrangement, the Nationals only accept ministries on condition that they retain their independence, and their right to vote against the government. The Nationals also refused the office of the Deputy Premier (Hayward 2008).

15   While the 2021 state election, discussed in the next section, has skewed the data, even if we exclude this election, the average size of the government in the third period was still higher than in the previous period at 59 percent.

16   Data on shadow ministries sourced from Black (2014: 317-46).

17   Bruce Stone proposes that the Opposition should, ideally, occupy at least 40 percent of the seats in the Assembly.

18   Under the agreement, both parties retain their ability to speak out on issues when they disagree but will create some joint policies and strategise how to approach by-elections and elections (de Kruijff 2021).

19   As of July 2023, the Love Shadow Ministry was reduced to 14 members when the incoming leader of the Liberals, Libby Mettam, managed to orchestrate the removal of Nick Goiran, a powerbroker, from the shadow cabinet (Hastie 2023).

17

The Opposition at Westminster

Nigel Fletcher

The foundations of "Loyal Opposition"

When seeking to understand the special position of the Official Opposition in the United Kingdom's constitution, a good place to start is its formal title: "His Majesty's Loyal Opposition". The name connotes an institution which combines insurgency with responsibility, dissent with respect. A body of people whose sole objective is to tear down and replace the government of the day is given official sanction for its endeavours, on the tacit understanding that it remains loyal to the Crown as the embodiment of the constitution. It is a curious and seemingly contradictory idea, but one which lies at the heart of the Westminster system, and on which the democratic settlement of the United Kingdom (UK) now rests.

Opposition as a political phenomenon is present wherever power is exercised, and it need not have official sanction to be tolerated. Many protest movements and campaign groups oppose government policy, and there are smaller opposition parties both inside and outside parliament. But the Official Opposition is a special case, enjoying a number of privileges within the parliamentary system and being seen as the legitimate alternative government of the country. It has evolved over the centuries, alongside the development of parliamentary democracy and the idea of a limited constitutional monarchy.

The notion of "Loyal" opposition emerged as a response to a very real dilemma within the British political system: how to oppose the actions of the King's government without being accused of treason. At a time when the monarch was a direct executive figure, any criticism of their actions was potentially dangerous. This is what gave rise to the frequently used device of politicians instead criticising the sovereign's "evil counsellors" for serving them badly. This began as a convenient fiction, allowing the sovereign to be absolved of blame for actions taken in their name by their chosen ministers, but gradually became formalised as royal involvement in day-to-day governance declined. With Ministers of the Crown taking over full executive responsibility, it became possible to criticise their performance without directly attacking the monarch. This was a necessary condition for the development of "Loyal Opposition."

By the eighteenth century, the opposition at Westminster was acknowledged as an integral part of the constitution. Henry Mackenzie, a Scottish Tory at the time of Pitt the Younger, wrote in 1784:

> The Opposition in Britain is a sort of public body, which, in the practice at least of our government, is perfectly known and established. The province of this ex-official body, when it acts in a manner salutary to the state, is to watch with jealousy over the conduct of administration; to correct the abuses, and to resist the corruptions of its power; to restrain whatever may be excessive, to moderate what may be inconsiderate, and to supply what may be defective in its measures (Mackenzie 1808: 396).

This would serve as a workable definition of the institution we see today, with the addition of the fact that it now also presents itself as an alternative government, capable and prepared to take office if required. This adds a harder edge to its criticism, with those in office knowing that ultimately there are others ready to replace them should they fail. In past centuries, this was a matter of Royal prerogative, with governments falling from office if they lost the confidence of the House of Commons or of the sovereign. But as time went on, the role of the Crown in determining the composition of the government waned, and the widening of the electoral franchise made the voters the decision-makers.

Now, it is the outcome of a General Election that determines which of the potential governments the King calls upon to rule in his name. The fact that a real choice is available to the people and to their sovereign is vital. As Ivor Jennings put it: "If there be no Opposition, there is no democracy. "His Majesty's Opposition" is no idle phrase. His Majesty needs an Opposition as well as a Government" (Jennings 1951: 15-16).

The Official Opposition in the United Kingdom therefore falls squarely into the category of being a "constitutional opposition" (Norton 2008; Sartori 1966), whose existence is officially recognised and whose legitimacy is not questioned by those in power. This categorisation has a number of implications, not least of which is the expectation that the opposition should itself respect the fundamentals of the constitution and the rule of law. Its members are not seeking to overthrow the state by violent or undemocratic means, and it is this commitment which leaves them at liberty to campaign vigorously to turn out the present government at the ballot box, or occasionally through a vote in parliament.

This inherent requirement to act constitutionally brings with it a number of assumptions about how the opposition and its leaders should conduct themselves. These, combined with the features of the official support and recognition given to the opposition as an institution, shape how it functions and its ability to fulfil its role.

Official recognition – Parliament

The constitutional nature of the opposition is apparent from the most cursory of glances at the way the House of Commons operates (and to some extent the House of Lords, but my focus here will be on the pre-eminent House). As a debating chamber, the Commons has a distinctively adversarial style, with its benches facing each other: government MPs to one side and opposition MPs to the other. The Official Opposition is afforded the privilege of occupying the front opposition bench opposite the government – a convention that is laid down in the parliamentary handbook Erskine May, whose 2019 edition states: "The front bench on the opposite side, though other Members occasionally sit there, is reserved by convention for the leading members of the opposition" (Natzler 2019).

This convention has from time to time been challenged by other opposition parties, such as when in 1997 the third party, the Liberal Democrats, sought to occupy the bench. They were swiftly evicted by the Speaker, Betty Boothroyd, who delivered an emphatic ruling that the existing convention would be maintained and sent the recalcitrant Liberal Democrat MPs scurrying back to their places below the gangway.

Much parliamentary procedure assumes the existence of an opposition, a fact that can be demonstrated by looking at occasions in history when it has temporarily been absent. The most notable of these was in the years 1940-45, when the Labour Party entered the wartime coalition of Winston Churchill as did the Liberals. With all the main parliamentary parties in government, the role of the Official Opposition looked to have fallen into abeyance. The next largest party in the House was the four-strong group of Independent Labour MPs led by James Maxton, who duly staked his claim to be considered as the Leader of the Opposition. Despite being technically correct, his bid was dismissed by the Speaker, who ruled that there "was no opposition in the hitherto accepted meaning in the House at the present moment" (HC Deb 21 May 1940).

This presented a number of procedural questions: who would occupy the Opposition Front Bench,? Who would respond first to government statements? Who would select the topics for "Supply Day" debates, traditionally allocated to the opposition? Maxton continued to press such issues in the early days of the new government and registered his concern that the new coalition had effectively led to all parliamentary opposition being abolished.

In some respects he was correct: instead of an opposition being formed from a distinct parliamentary party, the solution arrived at by agreement between the two main parties was for a senior Labour MP who was not in the government to fulfil the procedural duties of the Leader of the Opposition. This role went first to Hastings Lees-Smith (who was elected as acting Chairman of the Parliamentary Labour Party), and then to Frederick Pethick-Lawrence and Arthur Greenwood in turn until the end of the coalition in May 1945, when Labour left government and resumed its status as the Official Opposition under Clement Attlee.

The exceptional circumstances of the Second World War served to demonstrate that the Westminster model is based on a house divided, and also to some extent, balanced. With equal numbers of benches on either side of the chamber, there is even a physical assumption that supporters of the government will not hugely outnumber its opponents. Indeed, during those war years, the bulk of Labour MPs continued to sit on the opposition benches, which would otherwise have remained empty. But the most significant lesson from this interlude was that if a recognised Official Opposition did not exist, it was procedurally necessary to invent one.

From this, we can see that the opposition is afforded a special position in the procedures of the House. The most obvious of these is what we might call that of being the "first responder" – that is to say, being called upon to speak immediately after a minister has made a statement or introduced a bill. This convention provides many of the set piece occasions for the Leader of the Opposition, who responds to the Prime Minister in the debate on the Loyal Address at the beginning of the parliamentary session, and by tradition also responds to the Chancellor of the Exchequer's annual Budget speech. But on a day-to-day basis, other shadow ministers play a prominent role in responding from the opposition front bench.

The fact that the opposition is expected to reply in this way has led to the convention that shadow ministers are provided with an advance copy of the government's statement before it is made, to allow them some time to prepare. This expectation has been written into the *Ministerial Code*, and nowadays if a minister fails to give the required notice, they can expect to receive a public rebuke from their opponent and perhaps also the Speaker. This practice developed as a courtesy, but it also reflects a mutual understanding on the part of the two sides of the House of the role each has to play.

Useful though it is to get at least some advance sight of the statement about to be made, Shadow Ministers nevertheless face an uphill struggle as they prepare their response. The minister will have been working on the detail of the policy for a considerable time and has the backing of thousands of civil servants to brief them on every possible nuance. By contrast, a shadow minster when they stand up to reply will have had perhaps a few hours' notice of the statement, and the assistance of only a handful of political staff to put together their response. A useful skill for them to develop is to anticipate what statements are likely to occur well in advance (often helped by copious leaks and briefing to the media) and to prepare accordingly.

Aside from statements and speeches on the various stages of Bills, the other set-piece parliamentary occasion for an opposition spokesperson is the regular Oral Questions session. This has existed in something like its current form since the second half of the nineteenth century, becoming more formalised with the introduction of "starred" questions in 1902, distinguishing questions for oral answer from those for written answer. It takes place at the start of the day's sitting, and the time allocated rose from 40 minutes to 55 minutes in 1906, along with a requirement for at least two days' notice to be given. A formal rota for answering departments was introduced in the 1920s, creating the system which has existed, with some procedural changes, ever since.

Generally, it is only backbench MPs who table questions to the government for oral answer, with shadow ministers then asking a few supplementary questions on whichever topic they judge to be most important or topical. In this they are granted privileges by the Speaker, who will give priority to an opposition spokesperson who wishes to intervene on a particular question. The most famous (or infamous) example of this session is the weekly Prime Minister's Questions (PMQs), when the Leader of the Opposition is granted up to six supplementary questions to the Prime Minister, and seeks to score political points or raise a particular political issue of the moment. Whole books have been written on the art of PMQs (for example, Hazarika and Hamilton 2019), and a great deal of thought goes into how to use the opportunity, which is perhaps the most visible demonstration of the opposition's role in holding the government of the day to account in the House.

Another significant opportunity the opposition has to hold the government to account on the floor of the House is the choice of subject for a number of "Opposition Days" throughout the year. The Standing Orders of the House have now formalised this practice, specifying that twenty days in total shall be allocated to opposition business. Of these, 17 are "at the disposal of the Leader of the Opposition", with the remaining three being allocated by the leader of the second largest opposition party. Just as with oral questions, the opposition will seek to use these opportunities to highlight issues on which the government is perceived to be weak, or where they are most open to attack. The debate takes place on a substantive motion that is usually critical of the government's policies.

In the past, the government usually sought to amend or vote down such motions, but from the beginning of the 2017 parliament, after the Conservative government lost its majority, ministers declared that they considered motions passed on Opposition Days non-binding and adopted the practice of abstaining on them to allow them to pass without division. This was in response to what the then Leader of the House described as "political point-scoring" in the motions, with Labour framing them to demand the government do something, such as increase public sector wages, with the intention of forcing government MPs to vote against so they could then be condemned in the media for doing so. As the Commons' Public Administration Committee noted, this tactic was by no means unique to the current Labour Opposition, and is, in fact, a legitimate and rather effective use of a parliamentary device to raise issues of concern.

The government attracted understandable criticism for its decision to simply ignore Opposition Day motions, and its stance also prompted the opposition to devise new methods to hold them to account. One of these was to use Opposition Days to table "Motions for a return", otherwise known as a "Humble Address", calling for the government to produce certain papers relating to areas of policy. These motions have an effect, requiring the government to respond with the requested material, unless they vote the motion down. The device was used on a number of occasions in the succeeding years to require the government to produce material in relation to Brexit negotiations and was also used in March 2022 to require papers from the government relating to the appointment of Evgeny Lebedev to the House of Lords.

With the increased use of such devices, Opposition Days have remained an important tool for the Opposition to hold the government to account and highlight particular issues. Along with the precedence opposition spokespersons are given in procedure for questions and debates, the position of the Official Opposition in now firmly embedded in the UK's parliamentary arrangements.

Official Recognition – Crown and Government

I have already noted how the opposition is conventionally afforded some degree of consideration by the incumbent government in matters such as statements to parliament. But the recognition of the Opposition by the state goes further than such courtesies. The most immediate, which can become apparent early on in the tenure of a new Leader of the Opposition, is the fact that they are now routinely made a member of the Privy Council, as is the case for new members of the Cabinet. This is an overt demonstration of the reality of "Loyal Opposition", with the Leader being sworn in as a member of this ancient body in the presence of the Sovereign.

This convention is not always without controversy. When the republican left-winger Jeremy Corbyn became Leader of the Opposition in 2015 there was initially some doubt as to whether he would accept membership of the Privy Council, and if he did, whether he would kneel before Queen Elizabeth II to be sworn in. The issue became a topic of considerable speculation in the media, with Corbyn declining to attend the meeting at which he was due to be sworn, but he eventually attended and made the required affirmation to join the Council.

The Monarch has also officially recognised the Leader of the Opposition in other ways over time. A number of leaders in the 20th Century were received in audience by Elizabeth II on taking up the position, and also on relinquishing it. It has also become customary for the Leader of the Opposition and their partner to be invited to state banquets for visiting heads of state at the Palace, and some have also been invited to the more select "dine and sleep" events at Windsor Castle. The death of Elizabeth II and the accession of Charles III in 2022 also provided a demonstration of the status afforded to the Opposition, with Sir Keir Starmer being received in audience by The King immediately after the Cabinet. He was joined for this meeting by the Westminster leaders of the Liberal Democrats and the Scottish National Party, but unlike them Sir Keir was referred to in the Court Circular not as leader of his party but as "Leader of His Majesty's Opposition".

The practical effect of being sworn into the Privy Council is that it makes the Leader eligible to receive confidential briefings on security and other matters from the government on what is known as "Privy Council Terms", with their oath requiring them to keep such information secret. The extent to which this convention is exercised is a matter for the government of the day, and is often influenced by the state of the personal relationship between the prime minster and their opposite number. Some have got on much better than others, with a constructive relationship of trust developing between them, whilst others have barely been on speaking terms. But even with the most cordial of relationships, these contacts are usually restricted to occasional briefings on particularly sensitive security or defence matters, rather than implying any wider degree of political collaboration. Nevertheless, it is an important constitutional point that the incumbent prime minister and their leading opponent can set aside their public enmity and co-operate when required to in the national interest.

The other formalised process by which the opposition is officially recognised by the government comes in the run-up to a General Election, when the civil service is authorised to begin discussions with the opposition about their plans for government should they take office.

The current system of contacts goes back to the 1960s, when Harold Wilson formalised the practice followed by Alec Douglas Home in the run-up to the 1964 election, when he acquiesced in civil servants meeting Wilson and his colleagues to discuss proposed changes to the machinery of government were Labour to win, which it did. For this reason, the convention is sometimes referred to as the "Douglas Home rules", and it remains largely restricted to providing shadow ministers with an opportunity to be briefed by civil servants on factual matters around the organisation of government. The meetings are co-ordinated by the Cabinet Secretary, and the details are not reported back to incumbent ministers. There have been criticisms that the system as it stands is too limited to be truly useful for either side, with what might be useful discussion of policy options remaining outside their scope (Riddell and Haddon, 2009).

Financial and logistical support

The recognition of the opposition's official status has led to the provision over the years of a variety of forms of material support to assist its members in fulfilling their accepted role. These have predominantly focused on supporting its required duties in Parliament, with the question of state funding for political parties' broader activity in the country having proved too contentious over the years to have been pursued.

The first major element of financial support came in 1937 with the award for the first time of an official salary for the Leader of the Opposition. The initiative for this move came from Stanley Baldwin, the Conservative Prime Minister, who claimed he had been in favour of the idea for over a decade, and that he had been persuaded of its merits by friends in Canada, where the Leader of the Opposition had received an official salary as early as 1905. The argument he put forward in the House was that the job of leading the opposition was now effectively a full-time one, and that it was not reasonable to expect the Leader to take on outside work whilst doing it. The context for this was also important: with the Labour

Party having displaced the Liberals as the main party of opposition, it was clear that in the modern age it could not be assumed that political leaders would have independent financial means.

As an innovation it was a notable one – the first time that the position of Leader of the Opposition had been recognised and defined in statute, with the relevant clause of the Act stating that it "means that member of the House of Commons who is for the time being the Leader in that House of the party in opposition to His Majesty's Government having the greatest numerical strength in that House." It further determined that "If any doubt arises" about who that should be, the Speaker of the House of Commons would decide the matter (*Ministers of the Crown Act 1937*).

During debates on the provision before it was passed, a number of MPs expressed misgivings, including some who considered it illogical for the state to pay someone to oppose and turn out the government. On the Labour side, there was nervousness about accepting the salary, with some believing it was wrong to do so before the salaries of backbench MPs were also raised, whilst others feared it would be seen to compromise the party. In the end, however, they concluded that on principle it was right that full-time public service should be paid.

Some MPs during the passage of the legislation had questioned whether, once the principle of paying the Leader of the Opposition was accepted, it would lead to calls for other members of the opposition to be paid. This "thin end of the wedge" argument had some merit, but expansion of public funding was slow in coming. Whilst the Leader's salary was uprated periodically alongside ministers' salaries, there were no additional funds paid to the opposition until the 1960s, when Harold Wilson's government introduced additional salaries for the Opposition Chief Whip in the Commons, as well as for the Opposition Leader and Chief Whip in the House of Lords.

The next significant innovation in official support for the opposition was also introduced by Harold Wilson, after he returned to office in 1974. The Labour Government's programme outlined in the Queen's Speech in

March 1974 included a proposal for "the provision of financial assistance to enable Opposition parties more effectively to fulfil their Parliamentary functions" (HC Debs 12 March 1974). It is perhaps notable that Wilson decided on this initiative having just spent four years back in opposition, during which he was keenly aware of the severe limitations in resources compared to those available when he was in government. As he put it: "No government have anything to gain, and certainly the country has nothing to gain, from opposition parties lacking the necessary facilities, financial and otherwise, for doing their job in the House" (HC Debs 12 March 1974).

It was a further year before the Commons debated the final proposals, with the October 1974 General Election intervening to delay progress. But in March 1975 the Leader of the House of Commons, Ted Short, rose in the Commons to introduce the motion on introducing financial assistance to opposition parties. The scheme he proposed was not restricted to the Official Opposition, and it used a formula related to the number of seats and votes won by each opposition party in the House, up to a limit of £150,000. In the debate that followed, similar points were made about the justification for paying the Opposition as had been raised in 1937, with some MPs arguing that it was an unwelcome innovation to be effectively introducing state funding of political parties. Despite such objections, the motion was approved.

The scheme, which has become known as "Short Money" has endured, with some modifications, until the present day. The amounts parties were entitled to claim were uprated periodically to keep pace with inflation until 1999, when a much bigger increase was proposed. This came about following a recommendation of the Committee on Standards in Public Life, which had been asked by the incoming Labour government to examine the question of state funding of political parties. Whilst they concluded the time was not right for this to be introduced wholesale, it did recommend that the level of Short Money be significantly raised, after hearing evidence that the existing level was inadequate to allow the opposition to do its job effectively.

The backdrop to this had been the controversy caused by the operation of a "blind trust" funded by private donors to pay for the running of Tony Blair's office in opposition. This specific issue led to a modification of the original Short Money scheme, with the introduction for the first time of a new extra allowance for the running of the Leader of the Opposition's office. This, combined with the increased overall rates, meant that the amount available to the Conservative Opposition trebled from £1.1 million to £3.3 million. By 2022-23, the sum available to the Labour Party as the opposition was nearly £7 million. Whilst this is clearly a significant sum, set against the huge resources available to ministers, it is comparatively modest. Even the cost of government special advisers was much higher, at £15.9 million in 2022-23.

From its Short Money allocation, the opposition is able to fund staff to assist with its official duties. The spending has to be certified to the Commons authorities as being legitimately parliamentary in nature, but there has always been some ambiguity about the distinction between what is purely party political and what is "official" opposition business. Occasional political rows have been stoked over the years when the government party has accused its opponents of misusing taxpayers' money to fund party-political staff. A controversy broke out in 2015 when the Conservative government proposed to cut the overall level of Short Money, and the idea was soon dropped. They did however introduce a requirement for greater accountability for the sums spent, with the opposition now required to publish an annual breakdown of its spending and details of the salaries of senior staff.

Short Money remains the main form of assistance available to the Official Opposition in parliament, but there are a number of other elements of state support to which it has access. Perhaps the most visible of these has been the provision of an official car and driver from the government car service, a perk of the job which has been in place since the early 1970s, when Edward Heath granted it to Harold Wilson after agreeing with senior Labour MPs that it was unseemly for the former Prime Minister to be left to queue for a taxi outside the House of Commons. The official car, in line with the rules for ministers, is only supposed to be used for "Official business", but as with Short Money, the distinction between this and political activity in opposition has proved rather difficult to draw at times.

A shadow government?

As can be seen, the opposition has over the years acquired increased levels of formal recognition and official support. This greater institutionalisation has taken place in tandem with a more formalised approach to its duties under successive leaders. In the early part of the 20th century, the opposition's activity was loosely co-ordinated by the leader, with senior party figures who had held ministerial office assisting with duties in the House and leading on particular issues. But these arrangements were somewhat ad hoc, with any notion of a "Shadow Cabinet" being a much more informal grouping of former ministers chosen by the Leader to provide advice.

The ascent of the Labour Party to become the Official Opposition provided more structure to the Opposition front bench, with their system of electing a Parliamentary Executive Committee providing for the first time a clearly identifiable basis for a Shadow Cabinet. The Conservative version remained less democratic, with members of the "Leader's consultative committee" invited to join, and portfolios being less rigidly defined. After 1945, however, both parties formalised the organisation of their Shadow Cabinets and the wider opposition frontbench, with leaders increasingly seeking to present a full team of shadow ministers that could be seen as a full "government in waiting."

This trend is now well developed, to the extent that shadow ministers now have very clearly defined portfolios that directly mirror those of particular ministers in government. This mindset might help them in keeping their eyes on the prize of power, but it can also be somewhat limiting. One of the few benefits of being in opposition is having the space to refresh ideas and rethink policy, whilst not having the responsibilities of government. At the same time, there are those who believe that the role of the opposition is, in words attributed to George Tierney, "To oppose everything and propose nothing... and to turn out the government" (HC Debates, 4 June 1841). Adopting a rigid "minister-in-waiting" mindset too early arguably thwarts both these advantages, with shadow ministers subjecting themselves to all the constraints of being in government, but with none of the advantages.

Getting the balance right between kneejerk opposition and deep thinking about policy is one of the perennial challenges of strategy for any opposition seeking power. On the one hand they wish to score political points and be seen to hold the government to account, whilst on the other they need to develop a clear and coherent agenda of their own that will appeal to the electorate. The two are by no means mutually exclusive, but they are frequently in tension. Particularly in the modern era, shadow ministers are expected to have a view on everything, and the temptation to denounce everything the government is doing is very strong. But they also face persistent questions about what they would do differently in office, how their alternative policy would work, and how they would pay for it. Opposing a policy in itself implies that the opposition would reverse it when they take power, yet there have been many examples where an opposition has had to clarify that this might not necessarily be the case.

Conclusion

The opposition at Westminster remains, as was said at the time of Pitt, "a sort of public body", and the evolution of state recognition and support has made that even more true today. It performs a vital democratic role in holding the government to account and providing a credible alternative government to give the electorate a meaningful choice at elections. But despite the increases in official support, it still has nothing like the resources that are truly required to fulfil its fundamental roles of scrutiny and policy development. Meanwhile, pressures from a more intensive media and well-informed public have led to a much greater expectation that the opposition will behave as a disciplined and well-prepared shadow government. When they fall short of this ideal, they face severe criticism and even ridicule.

The mismatch between what the opposition is today expected to deliver and the resources it has to undertake the task has become increasingly glaring. At the same time, there have been other challenges to the model, with the assumption of two-party dominance breaking down, and the impact of other opposition parties inside and outside parliament being felt. The idea that only one party has the right to be considered the legitimate challenger to the government is looking increasingly unsustainable, and in order to accommodate the changing political landscape there may well need to be changes to how "His Majesty's Loyal Opposition" is defined in future.

References

Hazarika, A., and Hamilton, T., *Punch and Judy Politics – An insider's guide to Prime Minister's Questions*, London: Biteback, 2019

House of Commons Debates (Hansard), United Kingdom, Parliament

Jennings, I., *Cabinet Government*, Cambridge: Cambridge University Press, 1951

Mackenzie, H., *The Works of Henry Mackenzie, Esq. in Eight Volumes: Volume VII*, Edinburgh: 1808

Natzler, D., (ed), *Erskine May: Parliamentary Practice 25th Edition*, London: LexisNexis UK, 2019

Norton, P., "Making Sense of Opposition", *Journal of Legislative Studies*, 14(1-20), March 2008, 236-50

Riddell, P., and Haddon, C., *Transitions: Preparing for changes of government*, London: Institute for Government, 2009

Sartori, G., "Opposition and Control: Problems and Prospects", *Government and Opposition*, 1(2), January 1966, 150-51

18

Minority Parties and Opposition Roles in the United Kingdom

Louise Thompson

Introduction

Two party dominance is heavily entrenched throughout British politics and this extends into the House of Commons chamber where the layout as well as the procedural rules and customs create a hostile environment within which minor parties must operate. This chapter focuses on the nine political parties who sit outside the Government – Official Opposition dynamic in the 2019 Parliament, exploring the procedural, political and resource-based challenges which inhibit their opposition roles. It maps the unfavourable political and procedural environment within which small 'o' opposition parties at Westminster must work and how these difficulties are amplified by huge resource differences with the largest opposition party. Finally, it explores the ways in which these parties try to amplify opposition voices and scrutinise government by utilising Commons procedures to their advantage, negotiating additional rights with key figures and making the most of any opportunities which fall their way.

Background

The UK is the archetypal "Westminster model" system, characterised by two-party dominance. With the exception of the 2010 Coalition Government between the Conservative Party and the Liberal Democrats, only the two largest political parties (Labour and Conservative) have formed a government in the last 75 years of British politics. This alternation in power is underpinned by an overt adversarialism in parliamentary politics at Westminster, particularly within the House of Commons. However, this two party system is being increasingly challenged by the electoral and parliamentary presence of smaller political parties. Together these smaller parties received 33 per cent of the vote at the 2015 General Election, 18 per cent in the 2017 General Election and 25 per cent at the 2019 General Election. The 21st century has brought the first ever elected representatives of the Green Party, Respect, UK Independence Party, Change UK, Alba and the Reclaim Party[1] and seen the resurgence of other parties, particularly the Scottish National Party (SNP). At the 2015 General Election five small parties were given a platform during the televised leaders' debates for the very first time (Curtice et al 2016: 408). These smaller opposition parties have "fluctuating fortunes but [a] permanent presence" in British politics (Copus et al 2009) and must find a way to operate within the confines of a parliamentary system which privileges the two largest parties and constrains the rest.

Entrenched two (or three) partyism in Commons politics and procedures

Opposition rights are important in democratic parliamentary systems. Yet in the UK House of Commons these rights are applied unequally. The Official Opposition finds itself in an overtly privileged position. The second opposition party, currently the SNP, receives some privileges, while the smaller parties sit completely outside the formal system of opposition rights. One only needs to walk into the House of Commons chamber to see firsthand the emphasis placed on confrontation between two political parties – a governing party and an Official Opposition. The rows of green benches face each other and at the centre there are two despatch boxes with microphones, in which the Prime Minister faces the Leader of the Opposition in the well-known televised weekly confrontation of Prime Minister's Question Time, with their party colleagues filling the benches behind them. Television news broadcasts these clashes between the two party leaders. Beyond these two large political parties, nine other opposition parties were elected to the House of Commons at the 2019 General Election. Eight of these parties took their seats in the chamber. This later rose to nine following the defection of Andrew Bridgen to the Reclaim Party after his suspension as a Conservative MP. While the Official Opposition faces the Government across the Despatch Box, these nine smaller opposition parties must fill the benches to one side of the chamber. Although still facing government MPs, they must speak from their place on the green benches, with no despatch box or dedicated microphone for their frontbench spokespersons to speak from. Observers of House of Commons debates, either on television or in the visitors' gallery above the chamber, may struggle to see these opposition MPs speaking. They are quite literally out of the picture – either cropped out of the shot on television screens or seated below the gallery seating which has been designed to showcase the confrontation between Government and Official Opposition.

This binary division of parliamentary life into Government and Opposition dominated the procedures of the House through the twentieth century and continues to do so today. Although some rights for the third largest political party were introduced in the 1990s, Erskine May, the book of parliamentary procedure, continues to describe the conduct of business as being "arranged on the basis of a clear cut division between Government and Opposition". While the presence of additional opposition parties "may complicate" arrangements, it "does not destroy the broad principle" of them (Erskine May 2019: para 4.5). A look at the Standing Orders of the House of Commons further underscores this dominance of the two large parties in terms of participation in scrutiny tools. Standing Order 86 for instance sets out how committee allocations should "have regard" for the composition of the House, while Standing Order 122B states that this proportionate division will also include the chairs of investigative select committees. As of July 2023, this meant that the two largest parties held 205 of the

236 places available across all departmental select committees. A total of 29 seats are held by smaller parties, but this is predominantly the SNP who, as third party, hold one seat on almost all select committees.[3] The select committee with the broadest representation is the Northern Ireland Affairs Committee, which has places for Alliance, Democratic Unionist Party (DUP) and Social Democratic and Labour Party (SDLP) MPs alongside the two main parties. The position of Chair is taken by a Labour or Conservative Party MP in almost every instance, with just two Chairs (Scottish Affairs and Energy Security and Net Zero in the 2019 Parliament) taken by the SNP.[4] No other opposition party representatives act as committee chair. In some areas this division of membership by party is even more exclusionary for opposition parties. Key committees such as the Backbench Business Committee, the Committee of Selection and the powerful Liaison Committee which brings the prime minister before it on a regular basis, have no small party places available whatsoever. Here, all opposition parties are represented by a single SNP (third party) representative.

Similarly, while Standing Order 14 states that government business has "precedence at every sitting", it designates 20 days each session as opposition days. Here, opposition parties have control of the agenda. They can select a topic for debate, followed by a (non-binding) vote. Opposition day debates are regularly used to embarrass or influence government and therefore often focus on ministerial misdemeanours and popular policy changes. The Labour Party's debate on extensions to free school meals in June 2020 came on the back of a popular campaign by footballer Marcus Rashford and forced a government U-turn before the division (HC Debates 16 June 2020: c715). Labour's decision to use an opposition day debate in October 2022 to focus on 'fracking' brought chaos and confusion to the government benches and saw the collapse of the Liz Truss Government (see HC Debates 19 October 2022: cc 748-804). The Official Opposition party receives an allocation of 17 opposition days, with three left over for the second largest opposition party. As with committee places, the remaining opposition parties receive nothing.

Outside these specific scrutiny mechanisms, participation in House of Commons debates is limited. Business on the floor of the House of Commons chamber also privileges the Official Opposition and the second opposition party, given them guaranteed time which does not exist for other parties. At departmental question times and during Prime Minister's Questions the Official Opposition asks six questions and can choose how and when to deploy them. The SNP as third party receives two questions which are taken together. The remaining slots are filled by balloted questions available to all backbench MPs, or by MPs who "catch" the Speaker's eye during the question time session. This system of guarantees extends to all other debates where the Official Opposition party spokesperson and the second opposition party spokesperson are called to speak immediately after the government minister. Smaller parties are typically called much later on in debates alongside other backbench MPs. This can mean that their speeches have less impact, something which is exacerbated further by the time limits usually applied to backbench speeches which do not exist for the guaranteed opposition party slots at the start.

Small parties such as Plaid Cymru, the Democratic Unionist Party (DUP) or the Greens, sit mostly outside this structure. Although at times they may be given a short opposition day debate, this is not consistent or guaranteed. It is no wonder then that some say that discussions of the House of Commons usually proceed as though there are only two political parties in existence (Kaiser 2008: 1) or that minority party members describe feeling like "second class" representatives (Procedure Committee 2014) who are 'locked out' of scrutiny (Thompson 2018: 449) as a result of their exclusion from parliamentary mechanisms which are taken for granted by members of the Official Opposition.

Resource based constraints

Given the important position of the Official Opposition as the alternative party of government, the role of Leader of the Opposition is designated in legislation and comes with an individual salary and funds for an official office. Public funding known as "Short Money" is available to all opposition parties, providing they have either i) two or more MPs in the House of Commons or ii) one MP and over 150,000 votes at the last General Election (see Chapter 17 for more background on this). Party members must also be active in the Commons; those who have not taken the Oath following a General Election are ineligible. This therefore excludes Sinn Fein MPs. The funding formula is complex and differentiated by party size. In the 2023-24 session it totalled over £7.5 million for the Labour Party and £1.3m for the SNP. Figures for the smaller parties are less substantial. The Liberal Democrats received £1 million, the DUP £229,000, while Plaid Cymru and the SDLP both received £121,000. Although the Green Party had only one MP at this time, it received £211,000 during the same period, thanks to its greater vote share across the UK at the General Election (Kelly 2023: 6). The Alliance Party, with just one MP and 134,000 votes at the General Election, received no public funding at all. Small parties gaining representation through defections (eg The Alba Party) also receive no funding. These figures are limits; parties must submit expenses and provide annual returns showing the numbers of staff who were funded through Short Money allocations.

Given that small parties typically have smaller party memberships and fewer private donors, Short Money funding is a critical component of their parliamentary offices. The annual Short Money returns show that this public funding supported three members of staff for the DUP in the 2021-22 session, seven staff for the Green Party, 13 for the Liberal Democrats and four staff for the SDLP (UK Parliament 2023).[1] Green Party MP Caroline Lucas has described how it helps her to "skewer ministers with parliamentary questions" and "scour government files looking for wrongdoing" (Green Party 2017). Yet, public funding is not consistent and the way in which the funding formula is applied can have a drastic impact on small party resources from one parliament to the next. When the 2017 General Election result saw the Greens lose votes following an electoral pact with other left-wing parties, Lucas resorted to a Crowdfunding campaign to recoup the cut to the party's

Short Money funding which amounted to £8,000 a month and to ensure the salaries of 3.5 staff members in the party's parliamentary office could be paid (Green Party 2017). For many small opposition parties, this public funded parliamentary office is the largest professional and salaried wing of the national party.

The provision of public funding is a necessary part of increasing the capacity of minority opposition parties to fulfil their parliamentary work and to maximise their scrutiny of government. It is not sufficient, however, for them to act in the same manner as the Official Opposition because of the numbers of frontline representatives who are able to carry out the visible scrutiny role. The Official Opposition divides its organisation between frontbench MPs, who will hold one departmental policy portfolio, shadowing a single government department, and backbench MPs. By contrast, a minority party has far fewer MPs and there is unlikely to be any separation between frontbench and backbench MPs. MPs here straddle the distinction between front and backbench. Given their position in the chamber, they will never sit on the front benches. Yet all parties with more than one MP will try hard to cover all government departments. Their members therefore hold multiple policy portfolios, shadowing a wide range of government departments. In the 2022-23 session, Liberal Democrat MP Alistair Carmichael was the party's spokesperson for three policy areas; Home Affairs, Northern Ireland and Justice. At the same time, Plaid Cymru MP Hywel Williams acted as the party's spokesperson for no fewer than six policy areas: Work and Pensions, Cabinet Office, International Trade, Defence, International Development and Foreign Affairs. He also acted as the party's Shadow Chief Whip. As a result, Williams must be present for all statements, debates and question times relating to these six government departments.

This gives the party necessary coverage as it scrutinises government, but it adds considerable time pressures for its MPs. Not only will they have more compulsory time in the chamber, but they will also need additional preparation time. Given the way in which participation rights are restricted for smaller parties in the chamber, they will typically need to wait for much longer in order to contribute to a debate. With the lack of guaranteed speaking slots, they may not even be called by the Speaker. In this way, minority parties can be back room "heavy", with ample scrutiny and research support, but lacking in bodies and participation rights to make the fruits of this research visible on the floor of the Commons.

How do small parties perform their role as opposition parties?

All opposition political parties have a set of policy priorities that are important to them. Small parties are no different in this respect. While the Green Party seeks to create "a safer, fairer future for all" by tackling the Climate Emergency (Green Party 2019), Plaid Cymru campaigns for "policies that will directly improve the lives of Welsh families" (Plaid Cymru 2019). Unlike the Official Opposition party however, these small parties are not typically seen as an alternative government. For many like the DUP, Alliance or Plaid Cymru, the barrier is geographical; their regional party base means that they will never have the numbers of MPs required to form a government. Others, like the Greens and the Liberal Democrats, are more nationally focused but their small representation at Westminster means that at best they seek to be potential coalition partners. For the most part, these small parties focus on scrutiny of government and policy influence as their primary role and focus less on being seen to be a potential party of government. Nevertheless, there is a tension between their physical existence as a small party and their desire to behave in the same way as much larger parties. As already documented above, procedure and resource-based constraints hinder this. So how do small opposition parties carve out a role for themselves in the House of Commons?

Firstly, they *negotiate additional opposition privileges for themselves.* This requires cooperation with other opposition parties as well as with the government and key players such as the Speaker of the House of Commons. Cooperation with other opposition parties brings some occasional participation privileges. For example, the SNP may allow another small party to take one of its opposition day debates, either in its entirety or as a motion for debate sponsored by both parties on a topic which is of concern to both. The party may also give one of its places on a legislative committee to another small party, especially if it is a bill which is not one of its policy priorities. Negotiation can also bring additional resources, particularly in terms of information about parliamentary business. Green Party MP, Caroline Lucas, for example regularly sends a representative to the SNP and to Plaid Cymru party group meetings. The SNP whip is usually generous in sharing information on an *ad hoc* basis with other small parties. Before their elevation to official third party after the 2015 General Election, the SNP tried hard to negotiate a place for minority parties on the Backbench Business Committee – a group of MPs responsible for giving opportunities to individual backbench MPs to hold debates of their choosing. Although unsuccessful in persuading the government of the merits of this case, one of its MPs (Pete Wishart) served on the committee in an unofficial role for a period of time (Procedure Committee 2014).

Discussions with the Commons Speaker Lindsay Hoyle have brought about an informal arrangement whereby an unofficial rota basis exists for small party questions at Prime Minister's Question Time. One party each Wednesday will normally be called by the Speaker to ask an un-balloted supplementary question. This can be interrupted at times if small parties have been successful in the ballot, but it ensures some degree of consistency to opposition voices in the chamber, providing one opportunity every six weeks or so for small parties to ask the Prime Minister a question directly. During the four PMQs sessions in June 2023 for example, the Liberal Democrats, Alba, Alliance and Plaid Cymru were all called by the Speaker to ask un-balloted questions in the first half of PMQs. More recently, the Speaker has extended this inclusion of opposition parties into other high profile debates, ensuring that a representative of every opposition party is called to speak. Such privileges cannot be considered to be 'rights' as they are not formalised anywhere. They are informal and there is no guarantee that the privileges won in one Parliament will carry over to the next. At times this negotiation leads to privileges outside the chamber and its committees. Green MP Caroline Lucas has talked of how she "muscled" her way into the Conservative Government's Bullying and Harassment Commission, following pleas to the then Prime Minister Theresa May (Lucas 2018).

The need for negotiation means that small parties additionally *work on a cross party basis* by necessity to a much greater extent than the Official Opposition does. There is something of a camaraderie between small party groups, particularly those with similar ideological leanings. Plaid Cymru, the Greens and at times, the Liberal Democrats, will work formally with the SNP and this can bring extra visibility, enabling them to tag on to existing SNP privileges. In 2015 for instance, the SNP shared one of their opposition day debates formally with Plaid Cymru. The motion for the debate, which focused on opposition to the renewal of the Trident nuclear deterrent, stood in the names of the SNP, Plaid Cymru and the Green Party (HC Debates 20 January 2015: c90). The UK's withdrawal from the EU across the 2015 and 2017 parliaments and the coronavirus pandemic of 2020-2021 saw this cross-party cooperation heightened. The Greens, SDLP and SNP all supported Plaid Cymru's amendment to stop the EU (Notification of Withdrawal) Bill from receiving a second reading (HC Debates 1 February 2017: Division 134). All opposition party groups came together in 2020 to ask the government to form a cross party Coronavirus Select Committee. Although unsuccessful, a cross party All Party Parliamentary Group containing representatives from all opposition parties[5], would later take evidence from members of the public into the government's pandemic response (Proctor 2020). We can additionally see this cooperation between opposition parties in the seating arrangements within the chamber. Given the location of the small party benches, opposition MPs who wish to speak prefer to position themselves towards the centre of the chamber, at the very edge of the small party benches. Observers of the chamber may notice that opposition MPs regularly shuffle their seats on the benches, allowing different party spokespeople to occupy these prime seats over the course of a debate or question time session.

It is uncoordinated, informal but regular behaviour between opposition parties and it aids their visibility within debates.

Secondly, small opposition parties *use parliamentary procedures to their advantage*. The most frequent example of this is the use of interventions during debates in the chamber. This is a short comment, question or contribution which occurs during another front or backbench MP's speech. While the choice of who can make a formal speech lies with the Speaker of the Commons, interventions are governed by the MP making the speech. This means that anyone can rise from their seat and ask another MP to "give way". If small parties are worried that they may not be called during a debate, or if they wish to influence the topics being discussed early on, they will use interventions as a means to gain visibility and to put their concerns on the parliamentary record. During a Commons debate on the behaviour of Boris Johnson during the pandemic Plaid Cymru's group leader Liz Saville-Roberts made an intervention during government minister Penny Mordaunt's opening speech, putting on the record that 'my party has consistently advocated for a law against the peddling of political falsehoods in public life' (HC Debates 19 June 2023: c585). This made her the first non-government MP to contribute at all to the debate, it ensured that Plaid Cymru's position was clear to anyone watching. Green MP Caroline Lucas became the second backbench MP to speak, intervening during the speech of the Shadow Leader of the House to criticise any Conservative MPs who might choose to abstain from voting on the issue (HC Debates, 19 June 2023: c586). Over the course of five hours, the only small parties called formally to give a speech were the SNP, the Liberal Democrats and the Greens. Caroline Lucas had to wait over four hours to make her speech (Ibid: c651), while Plaid Cymru was not called. The intervention by Liz Saville-Roberts was thus significant, ensuring that the voice of her party was heard.

The SNP proved themselves to be incredibly adept at using interventions during the committee stage of the *European Union (Notification of Withdrawal) Bill* in 2017. Frustrated by their lack of contributions during the first day of scrutiny in the chamber despite having tabled fifty amendments to the bill, the first SNP member to be called to speak on the second day of debate (Patrick Grady) allowed every SNP member sitting behind him on the green benches to intervene during his speech. After holding the floor for an hour, Grady managed to bring in the voices of 19 of his party colleagues through interventions. He was later praised by the government minister for "the ingenuity with which he made sure that the Committee heard so many Scottish voices" (HC Debates 7 February 2017: no col). Another very useful piece of procedure to be deployed by opposition parties is the humble address; a motion which can be used on opposition days to call for particular documents to be released by the government. The Liberal Democrats used a "humble address" in June 2023 to put pressure on the government to release unredacted WhatsApp messages from government ministers during the pandemic (Liberal Democrats 2023). Although unsuccessful, it aimed to stop the government from trying to 'duck scrutiny' and ensure that MPs from all parties were equipped with the information they need to hold government ministers to account.

Thirdly, they *maximise parliamentary opportunities which come their way and do not turn anything down.* The Green Party's Caroline Lucas is not often appointed to legislative scrutiny committees. When she is though, she is by far the most active MP there. While serving on the Energy Bill Committee in 2011 she put forward 42 amendments to the bill and was commended by the government at the Bill's Third Reading debate for working so "tirelessly" on its scrutiny (HC Debates14 September 2011: c1140). This reluctance to turn down opportunities can mean taking on too much at times. Following a guest appearance at the Public Accounts Committee, Plaid Cymru MP Ben Lake was asked to become a full committee member in July 2023 (Davies 2023). Being the first small party member since 1997 is a special privilege, but this meant juggling two demanding select committee roles as he was already a member of the Welsh Affairs Select Committee.

Finally, they *prioritise the party group as a whole and not individual MPs*, acting as one core unit. There is an extremely strong sense of cohesion and collegiality across most small opposition parties. This is perhaps most associated with the SNP (see Thompson 2018: 453), but also applies to other groups such as Plaid Cymru, the DUP and the Liberal Democrats also. Plaid Cyrmu MPs for instance share the same corridor of offices in the Norman Shaw Building of the parliamentary estate and this means that not only their MPs, but the staff members, will spend a lot of time together, aiding intra-group working. Policy issues which are already on the news or parliamentary agenda are prioritised and if an MP has a high profile issue in their constituency, the whole party's resources will become focused on that one issue, highlighting it through as many different parliamentary tools as possible. In July 2023 for instance, Plaid Cymru MP Hywel Williams asked a question at Prime Minister's Question Time, referencing an earlier question already asked by his party colleague Ben Lake directly in order to follow up on his work on HS2, the high-speed railway infrastructure project (HC Debates 12 July 2023: c349). This can also help ensure that limited research staff resources are not overstretched (Thompson 2018: 452). In this way the success of one MP becomes the success of the whole party. We also saw evidence of this during the coronavirus pandemic where one small party MP often became the face of the party group in the House of Commons, enabling the rest of the group's MPs to remain in their constituencies (Thompson and Meakin 2021).

Conclusion

Small opposition parties find themselves in a tricky position in the House of Commons, straddling the divide between backbench and frontbench MPs. They are in essence a group of frontbenchers who are forced to act from the backbenches, but who on paper receive no additional rights or privileges than any other backbench MPs. Whilst all small parties appreciate that their limited numbers mean they do not deserve any additional guarantees of participation where pure parliamentary arithmetic is concerned (see Procedure Committee 2014), they require some additional privileges if they are to be visible opposition party groups. The negotiation of these extra privileges is the foundation of small opposition work in the House of Commons, facilitating greater access to key decision-making spaces on an informal and temporary basis. As small party electoral fortunes often fluctuate, there is much less consistency in their work from one Parliament to the next. This is offset however, by the strong collegiality and cross-party work on the small opposition benches, which ensures some uniformity of information resources and which aids visibility on the parliamentary stage. If the numbers of small party MPs increase further, the House of Commons may have to consider how best to integrate other opposition parties into its current two (or three) party procedures to accommodate them as more 'official' opposition parties.

References

Copus, C., Clark, A., Reynaert, H., and Steyvers, K., "Minor Party and Independent Politics beyond the Mainstream: Fluctuating Fortunes but a Permanent Presence", *Parliamentary Affairs,* 62(1), 2009, 4-18

Curtice, J., Fisher, S, D., and Ford, R., "The Results Analysed", in Cowley, P., and Kavanagh, D., (eds), *The British General Election of 2015,* Basingstoke: Palgrave, 2016, 387-431

Davies, D., "Ceredigion MP 'thrilled' to be appointed onto influential committee", *Cambrian News,* 3 July 2023

Green Party, "Help Support Caroline Lucas in Parliament", Crowdfunder, June 2017. Online at: https://www.crowdfunder.co.uk/p/help-fund-caroline-lucas-in-parliament (accessed 18 July 2023)

Green Party, *If Not Now, When? Manifesto 2019,* London: The Green Party, 2019

Kaiser, A., "Parliamentary Opposition in Westminster Democracies: Britain, Canada, Australia and New Zealand", *The Journal of Legislative Studies* 14(1), 2008, 20-45

Kelly, R., *Short Money,* Briefing No 1663, London: House of Commons Library, 2023

Liberal Democrats., "Covid inquiry: Lib Dems to table humble address forcing Government to hand over pandemic messages to the Covid inquiry", 5 June 2023. Online at: https://www.libdems.org.uk/press/release/covid-inquiry-lib-dems-to-table-humble-address-forcing-government-to-hand-over-pandemic-messages-to-the-covid-inquiry [accessed 18 July 2023]

Lucas, C., Comments made at fringe meeting, Green Party Autumn Conference, Bristol, 5 October 2018

Natzler, D., Hutton, M., Hamlyn, M., Lee, C., Mawson, C., Lawrence, K., Poyser, C., Samson, E. *Erskine May's treatise on the law, privileges, proceedings and usage of Parliament*, 25th Edition, London: Lexis Nexis Butterworths, 2019

Plaid Cymru., *Wales. It's Us: General Election Manifesto 2019*, Cardiff: Plaid Cymru, 2019

Procedure Committee (2014) Minority party participation in the Backbench Business Committee, *Oral Evidence*, London: House of Commons, HC 1288, 14 May

Thompson, L., "Understanding third parties at Westminster: The SNP in the 2015 parliament", *Politics* 38(4), 2018, 443-57

Thompson, L., *The End of the Small Party? Change UK and the Challenges of Parliamentary Politics*, Manchester: Manchester University Press, 2020

Thompson, L., and Meakin, A., *Written evidence to House of Commons Procedure Committee*, TTC 08, 10 March 2021. Online at: https://committees.parliament.uk/writtenevidence/22504/pdf/

UK Parliament, *Breakdown of Short Money Expenditure 1 April 2021 – 31 March 2022*, London: House of Commons, 2023. Online at: https://www.parliament.uk/globalassets/documents/commons-finance-office/short-representative-money/short-money-representative-money-breakdown-2021-22-v2.pdf [accessed 19 July 2023]

Endnotes

1   Some of these parties (Green, Alliance, Respect) have entered the House of Commons through General Elections. Others (Alba, Reclaim, Change UK) have entered the House of Commons through MP defections.

2   The remainder are held by Independents, though all of these are MPs who have been suspended from one of the three largest parties.

3   The suspension of Angus MacNeil from the SNP in July 2023 and his later decision not to rejoin the group means that at present the position of Energy Security and Net Zero select committee chair is held by an Independent MP.

4   Parties have to declare the total number of people employed where 50 per cent of their salary is, or has been, funded by Short Money. These figures are therefore not completely comparable between parties as the proportions are not declared.

5   The APPG was chaired by Liberal Democrat MP Layla Moran alongside eight Vice Chairs from five political parties.

19

The Loyal Opposition in Canada

David C. Docherty[1]

Introduction

Opposition parties are an intrinsic part of Westminster democracies and this is nowhere more true than in the Canadian case. His Majesty's Official Loyal Opposition is more than just a colloquial title. It signifies that the largest party in opposition understands the role and nature of parliamentary government and is loyal not just to the citizens of the state, but to the institutions that provide responsible government. Opposition parties that fail to realise this (and there have been some in Canadian history) are not only threatening their own success, but also the very legitimacy of the parliamentary system.[2] Small wonder that their own success is short lived, but the damage to the reputation of parliament lives on much longer.

This chapter examines the role and functions of opposition parties in Canadian legislatures. It argues that despite resources, rules and opportunities available to them, opposition parties often fail to fully perform the functions required of them by Westminster parliaments. As a result, opposition parties often assist in lowering levels of respect for parliament among citizens. In this sense, they are seldom better than governments at engaging citizens in political dialogue and participation.

There are three primary functions of parliament: scrutiny and accountability, legislation, and representation (Docherty 2005). In addition, legislatures also provide a training ground for future leaders and the opportunity for alternative governments (and the policies that they would produce and implement) to be presented to the public (Franks 1987). Turnbull breaks these duties down between those that take place within the legislature and those that focus on the constituency (Turnbull 2020). Opposition parties engage in each of these functions, though their success in doing so varies both by jurisdiction and by party. The rules of legislatures, both formal and informal, can often be a key determinant of the success of opposition parties and for the differing behaviour of parties across jurisdictions.

This chapter begins by describing the primary functions of modern Canadian legislatures and then more closely analyses how opposition parties fare in carrying out these tasks. The chapter argues that despite the obstacles facing them, opposition parties have managed to effectively challenge the government and force cabinets to be accountable for their actions. At the same time, the lack of resources and institutional rules that favour government has meant that the level of critical analysis offered by opposition parties is often reduced to negative attacks and attempts to embarrass the government. As a result, opposition parties rarely spend time developing and explaining their own policies and squander their chances to present voters with a viable positive alternative to the party in power. In this way, when a party in opposition eventually unseats a government, they come into power with a greater capacity to oppose than a capacity to govern.[3]

Functions of modern legislatures

Westminster legislatures are representative bodies. At the most basic level members are elected to represent the interests of their constituency, whether that role be one of a sage voice who might go against the short term or narrow interests of constituents for a longer or broader view, or someone who sees himself or herself as simply the voice of the majority of voters back home (see Birch 1964). But representation can be far more complicated. First, members get nominated by an ideologically distinctive constituency association, win an election typically with a plurality of voters, and then must represent every citizen in the district.

This alone often results in members re-evaluating the more strident ideological platform that saw them first nominated (Docherty 1997).

Second, given Canada's single member plurality electoral system coupled with parties whose primary distinctive features are ideological as opposed to demographic, means that elected members often represent interests and demographics that transcend politically created constituency boundaries.[4] Thus a women or a racialized MP elected from one riding might reasonably be expected (and indeed might seek) to represent gender or other interests from a broader region of the province or country (Black 1997). When successful, such representation evolves from symbolic to substantive. The same is true for politically defined segments of society, such as environmental supporters, labour groups or the anti-gun registry lobby, to name a few.

Representation is a critical part of an opposition party's role. Effective representation for an opposition party begins at the boundaries of one's riding. Re-election and responsive constituency work is a constant with all politicians, no matter where they sit in relation to the Speaker's dais. For opposition parties, the stake of future elections rests on reaching beyond a single riding and speaking to individuals who can help topple government incumbents.

Legislation is an equally important function of Westminster democracies. At some level all policies have a legislative origin, be they new statutes, revisions to existing laws or programs that are part of a budgetary package. With the exception of motions of no-confidence mandated by Standing Orders, the fate of governments rests with their ability to successfully navigate legislation through the parliamentary seas. This is particularly the case in the Canadian context where governments have an extraordinarily broad conception of what constitutes confidence (Desserud 2006). Unlike the mother of Westminster legislatures in London, the Canadian House of Commons and the sub-national assemblies have had very little experience with a three-line whip and traditionally consider every piece of government sponsored legislation to be a matter of utmost confidence in the government.

Of course, within a set of institutional rules that limits the role of initiating meaningful legislation to members of the executive, the power to become legislative entrepreneurs is more limited than in legislative bodies with greater freedoms. The fact that only the Crown can introduce legislation that impacts public revenues limits the ability of opposition parties (and government private members) to enjoy equal footing when it comes to legislation.

Instead, opposition members have the greatest influence in legislation during the committee stage and clause by clause voting on Bills. The fine-tuning stage of legislation provides opposition parties some greater impact for legislative influence. However, meaningful impact is limited, particularly in the case of majority governments where numbers favour the government. Opportunities are greater in minority governments but even under these circumstances governments control the legislative calendar and can often delay passage of Bills that they do not support. In the case of the federal parliament, the appointed Senate has not been above (or below) thwarting the will of the house to help a minority government that has been forced to accept opposition dominated legislation.[5]

There have been instances where opposition parties support a minority government in exchange for introducing legislation or policies that were part of their campaign pledges. However, in these circumstances it is not the Official Opposition that supports the government but a third or fourth opposition party. After the 2021 federal election, the fourth place New Democratic Party indicated that they would support the Liberal minority government in exchange for the introduction of a national dental program and a national day care subsidy.

Scrutiny is the third critical function of parliaments and it is here that opposition parties typically fare best. While accountability and scrutiny are functions that should be performed by both opposition parties and government private members, the latter's role is typically confined to the more secretive caucus and the success of this role is thus difficult to properly measure. Opposition parties have both a number of formal and informal opportunities for scrutiny including the regularly scheduled Question Period, debate on the budget and Speech from the Throne, Opposition Days and votes of confidence. Informal opportunities include regular press releases, opposition investigations and the uniquely Canadian scrum that follows Question Period. Officers of Parliament can assist in the scrutiny function though some critics have suggested that these officers actually can usurp the power of the Commons.

While accountability includes the role of government backbench members, high levels of party discipline in Canada, both nationally and in the provinces, renders much of the internal scrutiny function more theoretical than real. As a result, opposition parties perform the most critical part of the accountability and scrutiny function of legislatures. In many ways, opposition parties are well suited to this task and have at their disposal many resources to allow them to perform this role.

Two other roles, less central to the formal functioning of parliament but no less critical, also exist and in some ways are more specifically focused on opposition parties (Franks 1987). First, parliament is seen as a recruitment tool and training ground for new leaders. This is accomplished in two ways. First, whether in Question Period, committee work, relations with the press, private members business or scrums, members have the opportunity to build up their reputation beyond that of their own constituency. Second, once accomplished, members who have successfully managed to build up their reputation – and managed to remain steadfastly loyal to their leader – are well positioned for promotion to cabinet. Cabinet selection in Canada – both nationally and provincially – remains the undisputable choice of the prime minister (or premier). As a result, opportunities to recruit future cabinet ministers are not simply a matter of talent and respect in caucus. Demographic considerations and closeness to the leader are also important factors.

Finally, parliaments are supposed to provide citizens with an alternative government. One fundamental rule of Westminster democracies often lost on Canadian voters is as valid today as it was in 1867, namely that Canadians elect a parliament and parliament determines the government. Traditionally, this has meant that the party with the most seats forms the government, be it a majority or hung parliament. Yet, there exists no constitutional rule or convention that suggests that a party with fewer seats cannot govern (Russell 2009). The duty of the Queen's representative is to ensure a stable government. If that is best accomplished with the party with the second or third most seats forming the government, there is nothing preventing such an occurrence. However, if this is going to be politically successful, opposition parties must have a set of well-defined policies that the public can either get behind or oppose. Failure to do so would not provide the type of stability vice-regal representatives require to avoid an early election.[6]

The most recent example of a failed attempt to provide an alternative government between elections occurred shortly after the hung parliament of 2008. Conservative Prime Minister Harper had won a plurality of seats in the House of Commons, but the combined forces of the Liberals and New Democrats fell short of a majority, requiring support from the Quebec nationalist party, the Bloc Quebecois (BQ). In meeting the House after the election, and facing a severe economic crisis, Prime Minister Harper chose to present an economic update that penalised opposition parties more than it addressed the economy.[7]

The opposition parties rallied to face the "game of chicken" that the prime minister laid before them. The three parties indicated that they would defeat the government in a vote of non-confidence and form a coalition. The Liberals and New Democrats would govern with the support of the BQ. This would have been the first federal coalition government since the First World War. Political pundits and the public were left to debate the merits of a coalition consisting of the unpopular Liberals and fourth party New Democrats versus a prime minister who appeared to maximise economic stress by disadvantaging a financially strapped political opposition.

The Prime Minister Harper managed to avoid defeat by having the Governor General prorogue Parliament[8] (Malloy, 2023:136). One lesson from this experience was that the minority government was able to convince the public that an alternate government can only take power via an election. Political rhetoric won out over constitutional fact. The Liberal Party (with the most opposition seats) had an unpopular leader, which did not help their cause.

If there is a silver lining to this experience it was that the government opened a new session of parliament with an economic recovery package that at least partially reflected opposition concerns. Nonetheless, the notion that a prime minister can use the power of prorogation to avoid a united opposition has now been established in Canada.

How do opposition parties fare when performing these functions? Obviously for opposition parties, the only measure of success is to no longer be in opposition. Negotiating their way through these parliamentary functions is no guarantee of electoral victory, but it will position an opposition party well should they have the opportunity to form the government. Further, successfully performing these functions should build support for parliamentary democracy. Yet if this is the case, why do some many opposition parties fail at these tasks?

Legislatures in Canada are professional bodies where all members treat office as a full-time occupation. Most assemblies provide opposition parties with staff resources, assembly rules allow members access to question the government both formally and through committee work and legislative debates, and parties have ample opportunity to bring no-confidence votes to the floor of assembles. Further, Standing Orders in most assemblies favour party over individual legislators, thus providing opposition parties pride of place over individual private members (Thomas 1985). Indeed, the most significant number in legislatures across the country is not necessarily the number of seats, but rather the number of recognized political parties.

While the classical conception of a Commons (or provincial assembly) as a legislature that is elected to form a government is as true today as it was in 1867, the reality for most Canadians is that politics is dominated by parties. Marleau and Montpetit (2009 2nd ed), in their wonderful compendium of Canadian parliamentary procedure and practice, acknowledge the strong role played by opposition parties throughout their analysis of the Commons. From the ability of opposition party leaders to choose where they sit (based on the number of seats their party has) to the role of opposition parties in the legislative process and their right to have Opposition Days during supply, the role of opposition parties has been institutionalized in rule and in practice.

In addition, Canada has traditionally recognized the primacy of the Official Opposition over other political parties. Until recently the prime minister resided in well-appointed premises at 24 Sussex Drive Ottawa.[9] The leader of the official opposition is provided with an official residence, Stornoway. While some opposition leaders have decried the expense of an official residence, all have come to see the value in the leader of the opposition, who at some point may well become prime minister, having an official residence to host foreign and domestic delegations. The Leader of the Official Opposition has further perks of office including a salary similar to that of the Speaker and Cabinet Ministers, sits directly across from the Prime Minister in the House of Commons and in the Official Order of Precedence ranks ahead of provincial lieutenant governors (see www.parl.gc).

Further, as indicated above, leaders themselves hold a great deal of control over their respective caucuses, whether in government or opposition. Party discipline in Canada is extraordinarily high, particularly when compared to Great Britain (Kam 2009). Within Canadian assemblies, the notion of a one or two line whip is all but absent and party leaders are inclined to treat all matters as a three line whip.[10] While members in opposition have more freedom to criticise their leader than members in government, there remains a strong incentive to take direction from above. After all, a potential cabinet career is more likely to be gained by supporters of the party leader rather than by detractors or self-titled mavericks.

Opposition size and parliamentary functions

At the same time there are many obstacles facing opposition parties as they attempt to properly scrutinise the government of the day. Resources to cabinet far outweigh those provided to parties in opposition. The same party discipline that allows government backbenchers to be described as "trained seals" helps to solidify the leadership of opposition party leaders over private members. Rules of assemblies still benefit government over opposition. In many provincial jurisdictions, the tendency to maintain smaller assemblies has negatively impacted opposition parties while concentrating even more authority with the government executive. Finally, a disturbing trend of assemblies sitting less often means that opposition parties face even greater institutional challenges in holding the government to account (Docherty 2005).

Opposition parties require a combination of rules and a critical mass of members and talent to be effective. Rules set by the legislature provide only one part of the equation for successful opposition parties. The other variable on the independent side of the equation requires that there be a sufficient number of talented members who both have the opportunity and the knowledge to use the rules to perform the scrutiny functions of opposition parties.

Before having a critical mass of talented members an opposition party must first have a critical mass of members, period. Provincially, the small size of many assemblies, combined with the single member plurality system has meant that many opposition parties are simply outgunned by the government. This is particularly true in the Atlantic provinces, where assemblies are as small as twenty-seven (in Prince Edward Island) and only as large as fifty-five (New Brunswick).

Distortions created by the electoral system only exacerbate this problem. In the two-party PEI legislature, it is not unusual for a ten percent swing in vote share to reverse completely election results. In 2003, the Liberals won only four of the 27 seats in the legislature, the Progressive Conservatives captured the other 23 seats. Four years later this was completely reversed.

Even in larger assemblies electoral swings can decimate opposition parties. In 1987 in New Brunswick, the Liberals swept all fifty-seven seats. There was no opposition in the Assembly. In British Columbia, the New Democratic Party was reduced to just two seats after the 2001 vote, with the governing Liberal Party winning the remaining seventy-seven (Elections BC: 2001). While these are extreme examples, there are many other instances where opposition numbers severely compromise the ability of opposition parties to perform their functions.

Arbitrary rules do not help parties in this regard. In the aftermath of the 1993 election two of the traditionally strong parties, the Progressive Conservatives (PC) and the New Democrats (ND) fell below the twelve-seat minimum for Official Party status. This has also occurred at the provincial level, where parties have fallen short of recognised status. Failure to meet the required number of seats[11] often shuts a party out of many of the primary functions of political parties.

Seats on committees are distributed based on party standings in the assembly. Failure to meet the minimum seat totals effectively shuts a party out of the committee system, the one place where opposition parties can have an impact. Members can attend committees and question witnesses but are not allowed to vote. Further, as suggested above, Assembly Standing Orders tend to reflect parties not members. As such, parties that fail to achieve official status are technically prevented from asking questions in Question Period, arguably the most critically strategic part of the scrutiny function. Instead, members must rely on the good graces of the Speaker to recognize them. The same is true for participation in debates.

Interestingly, the critical mass necessary for Official Party status is entirely arbitrary. Federally, the number twelve originated with the professionalisation of parliament in the 1960s and the amount of additional salary deemed appropriate for opposition Whips and House Leaders (Blaikie 1994). It was not based on any sense of the real number of members required to adequately represent interests beyond single constituencies, or to properly engage in legislative or scrutiny functions. Yet premiers and prime ministers have been loath to revisit these numbers, content in the understanding that by doing so they are effectively neutering opposition.

Even when parties meet the minimum criteria for Official Party status, their numbers may not be enough to engage in effective representation. As Table One demonstrates the Official Opposition parties can be smaller than the cabinet. As a result, opposition members often have to double up on critical portfolios. With fewer resources than cabinet ministers, and fewer staff to assist in research, the scrutiny function can be compromised. This is true even in some of the larger assemblies such as Alberta, where opposition leaders have often not had a seat in the assembly. The same is true for committee work, where members of the Opposition find themselves serving on several committees. As a result, they can be less prepared for dealing with the details of legislation and questioning government motives than desired.

Table One:

Legislature, Cabinet size in Federal and Provincial Chambers

Jurisdiction	Assembly Size	Govt size	Size of Cabinet	Official Opp
House of Commons	338	160	39	119
British Columbia	87	57	28	28
Alberta	87	49	25	38
Saskatchewan	61	48	18	13
Manitoba	57	36	19	18
Ontario	112	76	29	38
Quebec	125	90	31	21
New Brunswick	49	27	19	17

Nova Scotia	54	31	19	17
Prince Edward Island	27	13	12	8
Newfoundland and Labrador	40	22	17	13
Yukon	19	8	7	8
Northwest Territories	19			7
Nunavut	22			8

Note: all figures derived from assembly Web sites.

Finally, the size of an opposition party can also hinder their ability to both train and recruit leaders and to provide an alternative to the government in power. Realistically, it is difficult for small opposition parties to have a cohort of experienced members ready to manage large and difficult ministries. It is far better for opposition parties to have spent some time as the Official Opposition and have a large talent pool for their leader to draw upon for cabinet. On occasions where opposition parties have skipped from third to first place without the benefit of being a larger opposition, they have been less than successful. The experience of the one term New Democratic Party in Ontario in 1990 is but one example.

Even when an opposition party wins power they are often at a disadvantage in the legislature. This was the case in Alberta in 2015. The New Democratic Party (NDP) went into that election holding only four of the available 87 seats. A combination of the dynamic leadership of NDP head, Rachel Notley, and a faltering Progressive Conservative (PC) campaign meant the NDP went from third party to government. However, with 54 seats, they still lacked any cabinet experience. The Conservatives were reduced to ten seats. Among those ten were individuals with extensive cabinet experience. It took time for the NDP to switch from an opposition mindset to a government one.

It is interesting to note that at the time these data were collected, all Speakers of the Assembly were members of the governing party. In Yukon and Prince Edward Island, not one member was left out of cabinet. There were no government backbenchers.

In sum, size matters in legislatures and it is particularly important for opposition parties. Smaller legislatures and large cabinets combine to make representation, scrutiny and legislation difficult. The advantage in such circumstances goes to the government, and the ability of opposition members to be fully engaged in their elected duties.

Scrutiny – Opposition's favourite function

If there is one task the opposition loves more than any other, it is the scrutiny function. Victories may be elusive but occur often enough to serve as a tantalising glimpse of the possible. The simplicity of responsible government thrusts much of the job of scrutiny on the opposition parties and cabinet. Cabinet is responsible for the activities of the bureaucracy, and opposition members must hold cabinet accountable for their activities, management of their departments and any political deeds gone awry.

Question Period is the most obvious forum for accountability. The amount of time allocated to daily questions varies by jurisdiction, but all have at least three days a week during the parliamentary calendar dedicated to question time. Particularly in Ottawa, but also in most other jurisdictions, Question Period is the most watched and least enjoyable part of the Orders of the Day. The tenor of debate is low – it is hardly a stretch to paraphrase the old joke that a citizen went to Question Period and a hockey game broke out.

Question Period does not necessarily perform the function it was designed to. Rarely do opposition members receive new information from the government. There is too much grandstanding and too little sharing of information (Malloy: 124-6). The fact that questions are not presented to the government in advance means that the Opposition can catch Ministers unaware, but they cannot expect fulsome answers.

Yet at the same time, Question Period does provide a focal point for opposition parties. It is the one place where opposition members can bring to light inappropriate behaviour of ministers knowing they will have the attention of the media. Opposition members have few venues to bring shame to the government for their actions or inactions. It is small wonder members in opposition enjoy Question Period far more than members of the government.

Question Period also provides a good training opportunity for would be cabinet ministers or at the very least a stage where opposition members can either build a national profile or alternatively short circuit any chances of an eventual cabinet career (Malloy 125). The development of shadow cabinets by opposition parties followed the development of the "modern parliament" where members were full time representatives of their constituents. The professionalisation of parliament (albeit incremental) meant that opposition members had more time to be better briefed on the activities of the executive and bureaucracy.[12]

The notion of a shadow cabinet or critic role serves two purposes. First, it allows leaders to place their most talented members in the critical shadow roles, thereby providing the opposition parties with some level of policy expertise. Second, it suggests to the public that an opposition party could be an alternative government as it have members with similar policy skills to the cabinet.

Leaders have not been shy about "shuffling" their shadow cabinets and this can occur just as often (if not more) than cabinet reshuffles. There have been only a few attempts at moving away from this model in past decades. The most notable was that of the Reform Party following the 1993 election. A populist right-of-centre party, the Reform Party burst onto the parliamentary scene in 1993, having elected only one member prior to that (in a by-election). Promising to do things differently, Reform Leader Preston Manning created "discussion groups" of Reform caucus members, hoping to create a more egalitarian approach to scrutiny. Unfortunately, with an entirely rookie caucus facing a Liberal cabinet with years of experience, the experiment was doomed to fail. Opposition Reform Party members did not concentrate on one or two ministries, they were unprepared to ask questions and were often embarrassed by the more experienced cabinet members. It was not long before the Reform Party reverted to the known standard shadow cabinet approach to scrutiny (Docherty 1997).

Other mechanisms of accountability include debates on the Speech from the Throne, budget bills and committee work. The opportunities for success here are more limited, though not so in minority government cases. Under hung parliaments, there is less certainty about the ability of government to survive these matters of confidence.

If opposition parties enjoy the scrutiny function it is largely because they see the function as the one duty that is likely to reap electoral rewards. Legislation may build support through the parliamentary process - though it is most likely to be very limited in scope and largely reactionary against government-initiated Bills. Representation is critical but takes place as much outside the chamber, and across the province or country. But scrutiny is fundamentally a legislative function and as such works best when the House meets.

In Canada, Officers of Parliament have begun to play an increasingly important role in the scrutiny function. But it is a role that is not without controversy. Originally Officers of Parliament were created to serve important non-partisan functions of governance and report to all members of the assembly. The primary officers were Chief Election Officers and the Auditor General. The creation of the Chief Election Officer coincided with the depoliticization of redistribution and redistricting at the turn of the Twentieth Century. The Auditor General was seen as an independent assessor of the state finances (Office of the Auditor General Canada, 2006).

Over time, the number of officers of parliament increased incrementally, but typically regarding policy areas that can be seen as requiring a degree of non-partisan oversight. These offices - both federally and sub-nationally – included Freedom of Information, Protection of Privacy, Official Languages, Ethics and Election Spending, and Ombudspersons.

While on the one hand such offices might be seen as an asset to Opposition parties - the annual report of the Auditor General is often fodder for Question Period attacks on the government - there is another view. In some cases, the Auditor General might be seen to move from a more technical assessment of spending – "how much did the government pay per hammer?" – to tread into the political realm – "should the government be in the business of buying hammers?" In this case, the opposition is as likely as the government to take issue with the Officer of Parliament.

Ultimate Success - forming the government

How successful are opposition parties? Clearly the goal of any opposition party is to form the government. Of course, parties that have few seats in a legislature may see this as a long term rather than short term goal. For parties that form the Official Opposition, the goal of defeating the government (either in the legislature or on the hustings) should be a more realistic target. Thus, we can argue that the first and perhaps truest measure of success for opposition parties is electoral success. Yet on this measure opposition parties do not score well. Table Two illustrates the fate of opposition parties on the straight up question of electoral success.

Table Two: Success Rate of Second Parties

Period	Rate of Forming Government	N
2011-2023	48.1%	27
2000-2010	30.3%	33
1990's	33.3%	30
1980"s	24.2%	33
1970's	37.5%	24

All figures from Chief Election Officer web sites for each jurisdiction studied.

The results are somewhat mixed. On one hand, a success rate of a little over one third is hardly an inspiration for opposition parties. Realistically it means that the Official Opposition will lose two out of every three elections it fights. Not surprisingly, opposition parties have a better net outcome when they increase their seat total. During the more tumultuous 1970s, governments were not only defeated more often, but opposition parties claimed more seats.

There are no significant differences across the country, though interestingly opposition parties tend to fare worse in the Western Canadian provinces, the birthplace of political populism, and are slightly more successful in the Atlantic Canadian provinces that are dominated by the more traditional Liberal and Conservative parties. Western Canada is more likely to see one party dominating for longer periods of time. For example, Alberta has seen only three changes of government since 1971. That year the Progressive Conservatives defeated the Social Credit Party and governed until 2015, when they were defeated by the New Democratic Party, who lasted one term before losing to the new United Conservative Party.

In the Atlantic provinces, it is rare to have a strong three-party legislature (Nova Scotia is the exception to this trend) and thus battles are fought between two parties. In these instances, a ten percent seat swing may be enough to turn defeat into victory. A stronger Green Party has emerged in Prince Edward Island and presently serves as the Official Opposition.

The one standout in Table Two is the large number of turnovers in government since 2011. Official Opposition parties have a far higher success rate than at any other point in the years examined. This may be reflective of the declining partisan identification of voters in Canada.

In his classic examination of the historical success of the federal Liberal Party, political scientist Reg Whitaker dubbed the Liberals, "the Government Party" (Whitaker 1977). While that might be true nationally, when it comes to provincial politics, the Liberals might better be labelled "the Opposition Party." Of the three major parties in Canada, the Liberals are the least successful at moving from opposition to government, winning power only 20 per cent of the time when they have been the Official Opposition. The Liberal Party has a weak track record west of the Ontario/Manitoba border. They have been successful in British Columbia, though they are "liberal" in name only, and are closer ideological cousins to the federal Conservative Party in Ottawa.

By contrast, the New Democrats managed to transition from opposition to government one third of the time they were the Official Opposition. The Progressive Conservatives had a success rate of 37 per cent, the best of the three parties. The greatest success rate for Opposition parties rests with Quebec's Parti Quebecois, who have moved from Official Opposition to the government in half of all attempts. This rate is more indicative of the essential two-party state of Quebec, with the PQ and Liberal party effectively alternating in the role of Official Opposition.[13]

The table only reflects opposition victories when it is the Official Opposition. Thus, for example, the New Democratic Party's victory in Alberta in 2015 is not included in this table as it went from third to first. While this does not happen often, there have been a number of occasions where parties that held the third most seats in the legislature formed the government after a general vote. However, the advantage for forming governments rests clearly with the Official Opposition.

The larger picture shows some interesting results within specific jurisdictions, as the aforementioned example of Alberta illustrates. During that time, Official Opposition duties have been held by three different political parties, none of them successful in winning government until 2015. In Ontario, the Progressive Conservatives governed uninterrupted for forty-three years, from 1942 to 1985. Official Opposition duties were held primarily by the Liberals with a brief two-year exception when the left wing NDP held the second most seats. In these cases, governments and the victorious political party almost merge into a single, undividable creature, and the opposition role also becomes a near permanent role.

By contrast in two of the four Atlantic provinces, only the two traditional Conservative and Liberal parties have held office or formed the Official Opposition, and they often alternate in and out of power on a fairly regular basis. As a result, success rates for Official Opposition are much higher in the smaller Eastern provinces than they are in other regions of the country.

Opposition styles and impacts

Opposition parties in Canada are generally well resourced. Opposition party leaders receive an additional salary as do many opposition members who hold parliamentary positions. In most assemblies, Standing Orders provide opposition members with some leadership roles in legislative committees - even in majority governments. The ability of opposition parties to hold governments to account has increased dramatically in the modern Canadian Parliament – and certainly has increased since the advent of politics as a full-time profession.

At the same time, opposition parties still face a number of barriers to success. Standing Orders favour political parties over individual members and party discipline further concentrates power within the Leader's Office, be that leader the head of government or the leader of the opposition. The increasing democratizing of the leadership of parties, providing every party member with a vote - has allowed unpopular opposition leaders to stay on longer than many caucus members would like.

It is also unwise to categorize all opposition parties as those intent on achieving power. Certainly, His Majesty's Official Opposition, no matter how large or small, sees power as within its grasp. But minor parties, relegated to a few seats in a legislature, may be more likely to see their role as a voice of conscience or moral legitimacy, more concerned with influencing the government than replacing it. Such parties necessarily see their role in the functions of parliament very differently to larger opposition parties. Representation here is to reach out to groups and individuals across the country, which may or may not result in greater political support. Scrutiny may be targeted at changing government policy, not embarrassing government personnel. During times of minority government, this also provides minor parties with a much more significant role in legislation.

Opposition parties that run against the institution, typically populist parties of the right, tend to criticize not just the government, but the functions of parliament as presently practiced. Parliament and its practices are seen as corrupt. Members from such parties run for office by running against the institution, existing parties and existing practices. When marginally successful - such as the Progressives of the 1920s – the party may just implode. When successful – notably in Ontario in the 1990s – such parties can do damage to the role of Opposition. Power can be further centralized by the leader and the role of Opposition is even further weakened. This is typified by smaller legislatures and fewer sitting days. In other cases, such as the Reform Party nationally in the 1990s, the end result is to bring all politicians and parties into disrepute. By holding the functions of parliament in contempt, it is then difficult for others to build support for any participation in the parliamentary process.

Finally, at the end of the day, the success of opposition parties largely rests with governments. In those instances where government leaders believe in the mechanisms of accountability and representation, Opposition parties have the pre-conditions of success. Parliaments meet regularly, resources are provided to opposition parties, and members in all parties have the ability to participate fully in the workings of the legislature. When this occurs and opposition parties fail, they have no one to blame but themselves. Sadly, modern governments tend too quickly to forget their days in opposition. As a result, governments spend more effort in avoiding opposition than embracing its important role in democratic governance.

References

Black, J., "Minority Women in the 35th Parliament, *Canadian Parliamentary Review,* 20(1), 1997, 17-22

Blaikie, B., "The Status of Small Parties in the Canadian House of Commons", *Canadian Parliamentary Review,* 17(3), 1994, 29-32

Desserud, D., *The Confidence Convention under the Canadian Parliamentary System,* The Canadian Study of Parliament Group, 2006

Docherty, D., *Mr. Smith Goes to Ottawa, Life in the House of Commons,* Vancouver: University of British Columbia Press, 1997

Docherty, D., *Legislatures,* Vancouver: University of British Columbia Press, 2005

Franks, C., *The Parliament of Canada,* Toronto: University of Toronto Press, 1987

Hyson, S., "A One Party Legislature: Where's 'Her Majesty's Loyal Opposition' in the Loyalist Province?", *Canadian Parliamentary Review,* 111(2), 1988, 22-5

Kam, C., *Party Discipline and Parliamentary Politics,* Cambridge: Cambridge University Press, 2009

Malloy, J., *The Paradox of Parliament,* Toronto: University of Toronto Press, 2023

Office of the Auditor General, "A Brief History" http:www.oag-bvg.gc.ca

Russell, P., "Learning to Live with Minority Governments" in Sossin, P., Toronto: University of Toronto Press, 2009

Thomas, P., "Parliamentary Reform Through Political Parties" in Courtney J., *The Canadian House of Commons: Essays in Honour of Norman Ward,* Calgary: University of Calgary Press, 1985

Turnbull, L., "The House of Commons and Responsible Government" in Bickerton J., and Gagnon A., *Canadian Politics,* Toronto: University of Toronto Press, 2020

Whitaker, R., *The Government Party: Organizing and Financing the Liberal Party of Canada, 1930-58,* Toronto: University of Toronto Press, 1977

https://elections.ab.ca
https://www.elections.bc.ca
https://www.elections.ca
https://www.elections.gov.nl.ca
https://www.learn.parl.ca
https://www.elections.mb.ca
https://www.elections.nb.ca
https://www.elections.ns.ca
https://www.elections.nu.ca

https://www.elections.on.ca.
https://www.electionspei.ca
https://www.electionsquebec.qc.ca
https://www.elections.sk.ca
https://www.electionsyukon.ca
https://www.electionsnwt.ca
https://www.sfu.ca/~aheard/elections/1867-present.html

Endnotes

1   The author thanks Miranda Anderson and Madalyn Pryke for their assistance on this chapter.

2   In the 1921 election, the populist Progressive Party won the right to form the Official Opposition in a hung parliament with the Liberal Party forming the government. One of the principle axioms of the Progressive Party was to disfavour party discipline and formal hierarchy. As such they refused to form the Official Opposition.

3   I wish to thank B. Guy Peters for the comments he made on a much earlier version of this chapter. Understanding the transition from an opposition mentality and capacity to a governance mentality and capacity is an excellent way to track the evolution of a political party in power.

4   Canada has a number of non-ideologically based parties, such as the Green Party. However, while the three major parties, the Conservatives, Liberals and New Democrat Party, can be placed on a respective right to left platform, parties such as the sovereigntist Parti Quebecois and Saskatchewan Party are locally identified with a particular ideological pre-disposition.

5   The most recent, and perhaps ironic, example of this occurred when the Conservative dominated Senate defeated a piece of Opposition sponsored legislation on climate change in November 2010. The three opposition parties managed to pass the Bill through the lower, democratically elected chamber. The Prime Minister had long been an advocate for substantial Senate reform and had a long history of publicly decrying both the appointment process of Senators and their ability to over-ride the will of the popularly elected House of Commons. The irony was not lost on the opposition who watched their legislation be defeated before it could reach committee by the very Senators the Prime Minister appointed. See CBC News 2010.

6   The reality of appointing governments is a little more complicated than indicated above. The Governor General or Lieutenant Governor must balance several considerations, primarily the time served by the outgoing government, time between elections and the stability of the incoming government. As will be discussed below, such opportunities occur rarely in Canada.

7   The most contentious part of the Conservative update was to eliminate public financing of all political parties.

8   The move by the Prime Minister to visit the Governor General with the request was awkward to say the least. The Governor General could either refuse the request, something no Governor General had previously done in Canada, or she could agree and therefore deny the opposition an opportunity to defeat the government in the House, also unprecedented.

9   While well appointed, 24 Sussex Drive has been closed for repair for some time. The National Capital Commission is now exploring a new residence for Canada's head of government. (https://www.cbc.ca/news/politics/24-sussex-prime-minister-trudeau-ottawa-1.6949710).

10   Paul Martin was more open than other prime ministers to experimenting with democratic reform. He lost more votes on division during his short-lived minority government (2004-06) than many prime ministers did during a full four-year term. However, his willingness to embrace a three line whip system did not survive his tenure in office.

11   The actual number varies by jurisdiction.

12   There is no fixed agreement on when the Canadian Parliament become "professional" though many point to either the election of Lester Pearson as Prime Minister in 1963 or Pierre Trudeau in 1968 as the critical points of professionalisation. Some argue it began occurring well prior to that. See for example Charles Gavin Power 1957.

13   The third party, the Action Democratique, formed the Official Opposition once, but never formed the government.

20

Opposition Politics in the USA

Kenneth Kitts

Introduction

As in most of the world's democracies, there is general agreement in the United States of America that differences of opinion are healthy and that it is important to protect the right to dissent. Freedom of speech, freedom of the press, and freedom of assembly count among the most cherished guarantees set forth by the Bill of Rights in the US Constitution. Similarly, elections, legislative deliberations, and judicial remedies are seen as important and appropriate mechanisms for making sure all voices are heard in the political process.

Despite the consensus on these points, the US system has not institutionalized political opposition to the same extent as the parliamentary democracies with which the country otherwise has much in common. There is no real equivalent to the loyal opposition tradition in the US – no shadow government, opposition days, or fixed opportunities to question the head of government. This analysis will explore the reasons why the US has evolved differently with regard to this political function.

The lack of an opposition tradition does not reflect reluctance by citizens to confront one another over public issues. Indeed, Americans are an outspoken, and sometimes even belligerent, lot when it comes to politics. The republic owes its very existence to a violent, late 18th century uprising against British rule. A popular military flag from the period carried the image of a coiled rattlesnake along with the slogan

"Don't Tread on Me," used then as a warning to King George III and the British Army.[1] Conservative groups continue to wave the flag today as a reminder that the US government is equally capable of intruding on individual rights. As motifs go, "Don't Tread on Me" remains popular enough to qualify as an official design option on automobile license plates in a dozen states (Henderson 2023).

The most famous manifestation of political violence in the US occurred in the nineteenth century. The American Civil War of 1861-65 remains the bloodiest conflict in the nation's history. The 750,000 deaths in that struggle were shocking for that historical era and continue to be so today, outpacing combined US losses in the two World Wars by a substantial margin (Gugliota 2012).

But one need not go back over a century to find evidence of deep political cleavages in the US. The Capitol riots of 6 January 2021 stunned the country and the world, as did related efforts to overturn the results of the 2020 presidential election. Although responsibility for those acts is not in dispute – the official report on the uprising notes that "the central cause of January 6th was one man, former President Donald Trump" – the country nonetheless remains divided over what the episode meant and what to do about it (*Final Report of the Select Committee* 2022).

As evidenced by this summary, distrust of government and a willingness to confront those in power remain part of the American political ethos today. The question, then, becomes all the more intriguing as to why this general level of discordance has not given rise to opposition politics as practiced and experienced elsewhere. In fact, the very concept of opposition in the US is quite slippery and can present analytical challenges for students of American politics.

Explaining the lack of a loyal opposition tradition in the US

The story of how and why the US has evolved differently on this question of opposition politics is rooted in history, governmental structure, and political development as shaped by time and events. From this mix it is possible to identify five factors that warrant special consideration.

An early aversion to political factions: A recurring theme in early American political thought was a strong preference for national unity and a related concern about the deleterious effects of "factions". The unrest in the colonies that eventually led to the revolution against British rule was only a century removed from the English Civil Wars of the mid-seventeenth century. Many of the leaders in the fight for American independence came from families who had emigrated to the New World to escape that unrest. They brought with them a distaste for political squabbles and internecine conflict (Randall 2022).

But history is nothing if not multi-layered, and the Founding Fathers stumbled badly in their first attempt to establish a new constitutional order for the emerging republic. The Articles of Confederation, intended as a constitution for the ages, collapsed instead after only twelve years in operation (1777-89). The Articles produced a system that was decentralized to the point of being chaotic. Citizens were scared and ready for change. They demanded law and order, even if it meant giving additional powers to a reconstituted national government. The virtues of dissent and opposition, so highly prized just a decade earlier in the fight against British rule, suddenly seemed less urgent.

This was the background that led to the calling of the Federal Convention of 1787, a meeting convened in Philadelphia for the express purpose of amending the Articles of Confederation. But a majority of the delegates agreed at the outset that the Articles were too structurally flawed to be fixable. Thus began the move to draft a new Constitution, a process that necessarily unfolded in secrecy as the delegates were by then operating well outside the charge given them by the Congress of the Confederation.

Behind closed doors, Founding Father and future US President James Madison emerged as the convention's power broker. His later writings in support of ratification of the new Constitution, grouped with other like-minded commentaries as *The Federalist Papers,* stand as staples of American political thought. In Federalist 10, Madison famously laments the "effects of unsteadiness and injustice with which a factious spirit has tainted our public administrations" (Hamilton et al 2006: 54). "A zeal for different opinions," he argues, has "… divided mankind into parties, inflamed them with mutual animosity, and rendered them much more disposed to vex and oppress each other than to co-operate for their common good" (Hamilton et al: 56).

Madison and his fellow Federalists prevailed in the fight over the new Constitution. By the spring of 1789, the new document had been ratified and a new president had been elected. George Washington gave divine thanks for the country's "opportunities for deliberating in perfect tranquility" as well as the "unparalleled unanimity" that had allowed the formation of the new political order in the US (First Inaugural Speech 1789).

Washington's ardour for national unity did not wane during his two terms as president. In 1796, he used the occasion of his farewell address to warn once again about the danger of political schisms. He counselled a "unity of government" as the "main pillar in the edifice of your real independence…(and) of that very liberty which you so highly prize." Washington also encouraged "fraternal affection" among the people and cautioned against "irregular oppositions to its [the government's] acknowledged authority" (Farewell Address 1796).

Looking back at that early era, it is easy to dismiss the Founding Fathers and Framers of the Constitution as naive. But theirs was a naivete born of idealism. They believed that the newly independent country for which they had paid a price in blood could be qualitatively different from its peers. They believed the US could and should become a "City Upon a Hill" or an "Empire of Liberty" – the common thread in these ideas being the country would represent a morally upright example that would rise above the corruption, cleavages, and aristocratic entitlement of the Old World.[2]

How much these late 18th century views continue to resonate today is debatable. Still, if there is anything to the notion that history carries a weight of its own, then surely some importance must attach to these pronouncements. The warnings about factions were clear and repeated frequently. And, they came from men who were at the very top of the early American social and political order.

The Madisonian Separation of Powers: More than most of his contemporaries, Madison understood the key challenge before the Philadelphia Convention was one of balancing the creation of a national authority with sufficient power to make policy and enforce rules while at the same time not being so powerful as to nullify the freedoms of a newly independent people.

In drafting the Constitution, Madison's solution to this dilemma was to borrow heavily from the Enlightenment thinker Baron de Montesquieu and disperse governmental power along the lines of executive, legislative, and judicial authority (Sheehan 2015). Each "department" would have the means to "resist encroachments of the others." "Ambition," he wrote, "must be made to counteract ambition" (Hamilton et al: 337). In so doing he created a government that was at once both fragmented but also very powerful.

The Madisonian separation of powers emerged as the defining hallmark of the new constitutional order. Madison's "departments" became the three distinct branches of government. Notably, the new system would feature a president (none existed under the Articles of Confederation) who would preside over an executive branch that would rival the Congress in power. Madison had less to say about an independent federal judiciary – Article III is the shortest of the first three instalments of the Constitution – but there was discernible intent to have appointed judges with lifetime tenure who themselves could act as a counterweight to the elected branches of government.

This horizontal separation of powers between branches of the federal government was further fragmented by the constitutionally-mandated sharing of powers between the national government and the states.

The new Constitution guaranteed state sovereignty and stipulated that each state would have a republican form of government. It also gave the states a starring role in the process of deciding future amendments to the Constitution. Even today, it remains a simple and powerful truth that the US Constitution cannot be changed without action by a supermajority of the states.

The process of balancing the relationship between the federal government and the states adds a vertical separation of powers to the mix of political dynamics that has proven every bit as meaningful as the more commonly understood separation of powers between the branches of government (Peabody and Nugent 2003). The resulting fragmentation of powers was profound in the late 18th century and remains so today. As will be discussed, these structural attributes continue to shape the way that opposition manifests in the US.

The American Two-Party System: A third reason for the lack of an opposition tradition in the US has to do with the number and nature of American political parties. President Washington had little good to say about the political parties which were just beginning to emerge in the American body politic. "There is an opinion that parties in free countries are useful checks upon the administration of the government," he observed. But however well those checks might work in "governments of a monarchical cast," Washington did not see similar value for parties in a republican system. "It is a spirit," he warned, "not to be encouraged" (Farewell Address 1796).

Washington's hopes would soon be dashed. In truth, the factionalisation of American politics was already well underway by the time of Washington's presidency courtesy of the recent row between Federalists and Anti-Federalists over ratification of the new Constitution. That important early clash set a precedent for the division of American politics into two camps.

By the end of Washington's time in office, the Federalist and Anti-Federalist camps had evolved into something more akin to political parties, complete with caucuses and nominating processes. Still, the number of blocs stayed at two, with the Federalists winning the presidency in 1796 over the newly retitled Democratic-Republicans. The Democratic-Republicans returned the favour by winning the next election in 1800. Three decades later, the competition on the national level had evolved into a contest between Whigs and Democrats (forebears of the modern party that continues by that name). The Whigs would eventually die out and reemerge alongside others as the Republican Party in 1856, and notably would win the presidency four years later behind the candidacy of Abraham Lincoln. Since the time of Lincoln and the Civil War, the US has been dominated by the Republican and Democratic parties.

This brief overview omits details on the periodic third-party surges that add richness to the story of American politics. But the stories of Teddy Roosevelt and his Bull Moose Party of 1912 or Strom Thurmond and the "Dixiecrats" of 1948 are novelties. They represent temporary exceptions to the rule of two-party dominance.

The hegemony of the large parties in the US is best underscored by the fact that, between them, Democrats and Republicans currently account for over 99 per cent of the seats in the US House of Representatives and Senate (Party Divisions... 2023). Contrast that degree of influence to other countries that are nominally two-party in structure. In Great Britain, the two largest parties currently control 85 per cent of the seats in the House of Commons (State of the Parties 2023). In Canada, the two largest parties account for just over 80 per cent of seats in the House of Commons (Party Standings 2023). In Australia, the two largest parties account for 75 per cent of seats in the House of Representatives and Senate (Political Parties 2023).

This bipolar dominance means that interparty coalitions are rare as the two-way split of legislative seats all but guarantees a clear majority within each chamber of Congress. More importantly for this analysis, the two-party system undermines party discipline. The sheer size of the two American parties means that each has to hold and defend a large swath of territory on the ideological spectrum. In order to do so, both parties have become sprawling, decentralized bodies with little agreement on issues or policy solutions beyond the general placement of the Democrats on the left of the political spectrum and the Republicans on the right. Internal fights are common and have become as important as interparty competition in determining policy outcomes.

When separation of powers meets large parties with little discipline or ideological coherence, the results are uneven at best. As noted by Mann and Ornstein, the Madisonian system "requires an unusual degree of consensus to act" and cannot function without compromise occurring across branches of government and across party lines (2012: 132). This leads to a very dynamic environment in which alliances are temporary and deals are brokered on an issue-specific basis. These forces also lead the government to alter its plans frequently, which in turn creates a moving target for those attempting to mount an aggressive and sustained opposition.

The Challenge of Divided Government: A fourth reason for the lack of a defined opposition tradition in the US is divided government. Because of differences in representation, it is common for a party to exercise majority control in one chamber of Congress while being a minority in the other. The same is true of the party that controls the White House, which may or may not enjoy a controlling interest in Congress. The tension between the executive and legislative branches of government is exacerbated during periods of divided government, when the normal contest of wills between the branches is heightened by an overlay of partisan pressures.

A look at party fortunes from the beginning of the twentieth century to the present is illuminating. As shown in Table 1, one party control of both houses of Congress was very common from 1900 to 1980. Each of the two parties had periods of sustained success during that era.

Table 1	
Party Control of the US Government, 1900-2024: A Tale of Two Eras	
1900-1980	1980-2024
• One party controlled both Chambers of Congress for 76 of 80 Years (95 per cent)	• One party has controlled both Chambers of Congress for 28 of 44 Years (64 per cent)
• Democratic Majority for 48 Years; Republican Majority for 32 Years	• Democratic majority for 14 Years; Republican Majority for 14 Years
• The Majority Party averaged control of 59 per cent of seats in Congress	• The Majority Party has averaged Control of 55 per cent of seats in Congress
• The President's Party held trifecta control of both Chambers of Congress for 40 of 80 Years (50 per cent)	• The President's Party has held trifecta control of both Chambers of Congress for 12 of 44 Years (27 per cent)
• 8 of 15 presidents held trifecta control for entire time in office	• None of 7 presidents have held trifecta control for entire time in office

Beginning in 1980 and continuing to the present, one party dominance of Congress has become much less common (Schaeffer 2021). The picture becomes murkier still when the president's party is added to the analytical mix. Presidents in the early and mid-twentieth century had a reasonable expectation of party support in Congress. That expectation has long since evaporated. Today, trifecta control – defined as the President's party simultaneously controlling both chambers of Congress -- has become an increasingly rare phenomenon.[3] As a case in point, Jimmy Carter, elected in 1976, was the last US president to enjoy the advantage of trifecta control during his entire time in office.[4]

The reality of divided government in the US makes it difficult to know which party is in opposition since it's not even clear much of the time who or what is in power. Most observers would agree that the president and his administration constitute "the government" as defined in the narrow sense of exercising control over the executive machinery of the state. However, it seems odd to argue that point too forcefully during times when Congress is controlled by the other party. Simply put, the concept of opposition politics makes greatest sense when there is a party that is demonstrably out of power – and that assumes there is another party no less demonstrably in power. These assumptions do not work, or at least work less well, in the US given the unique structure of the Madisonian system.

A Winner-Takes-All System: A final reason for the lack of an opposition tradition rests in the winner-takes-all provisions of the US political system. Much of the reason for the success of the two large parties is rooted in the use of the Single Member District (SMD) system of election for the House of Representatives. Elections for the Senate, while occurring at the state level and not being tied to representation based on population, are nonetheless very similar to House races in that each election in the Senate is geared toward filling one single, specified seat (the two Senate seats in each state operate on staggered terms). That prize goes to the top vote-getter.

Though not mandated by the Constitution, the SMD system of voting has gained statutory endorsement over the years and is today the most common method of election used across the country for both federal and state legislative contests (Ross and Anderson 2018). As with its "first-past-the-post" cousins in parliamentary systems, SMD is based on a winner-takes-all philosophy that gives a significant advantage to large, established political parties and conversely makes it difficult for minor parties to take root and grow.

This winner-takes-all emphasis is not confined to legislative races. The election of American presidents is accomplished by and through the Electoral College. As a method of choosing a national leader, the Electoral College is as byzantine as it is anachronistic. In operation, it distorts election outcomes by awarding, in 48 of 50 jurisdictions, all of a state's electoral votes to the candidate who wins a plurality of the state's popular votes.

The most visible of these distortions occurs when a candidate loses the national popular vote but goes on to be elected president by dint of cobbling together enough close victories at the state level. Such was the case with the Electoral College victories of George W. Bush in 2000 and Donald Trump in 2016. Because of those two elections, the Republicans have held the White House for 12 of the last 24 years despite winning the popular vote in only one of six contests during that same period. These outcomes have implications that go beyond the executive branch. A majority of current Supreme Court justices (5 of 9) were appointed to the Court by presidents who lost the popular vote in the election that first brought them to power.

The curiosities and shortcomings of the Electoral College are deserving of more attention than is warranted here. The most important point for the analysis at hand is that this mechanism is built on and around the philosophy of winner-takes-all. The Electoral College, likes its Single Member District counterpart in congressional races, is geared toward rewarding winners. Neither system is kind to new movements, small parties, or losing candidates. These attributes do little to encourage respect for minority views or create an appreciation of how loyal opposition can be a force for good.

A different view of opposition politics in the US

These factors help explain why the US has not developed a loyal opposition in the parliamentary tradition. But, having established what opposition doesn't mean in the US, the question remains about how opposition *as a function* plays out in the context of the Madisonian system that features two large, if somewhat amorphous, political parties.

As a point of definitional clarity, it is unusual to hear reference to "the opposition" in the US. The use of "the" as a definite article in this configuration suggests a degree of party unity that is rare. The party out of power is simply understood to be "in the minority." As such, the task of organizing what opposition exists typically falls to the leaders of the minority party in Congress (Congressional Research Service 2019). Noting the lack of literature on this topic, political scientist Matthew Green (2010) has declared minority parties to be the "neglected stepchild of congressional studies."

The tools at the disposal of minority party leaders are limited. They can use existing rules of Congress to force the temporary reconsideration of bills or to garner attention for policy alternatives. They can make appointments to standing and special committees. They can use their own visibility to critique the government's program through a steady stream of media engagements and social media activity. Along these lines, one of the country's more established opposition traditions is for the minority leadership to choose a spokesperson to deliver the party's official response to the President's annual State of the Union message. Since 1966, those responses have been televised and have served as a platform for both the party and for the individual so honoured (Senate Historical Office 2023).

The overarching goal for the minority party is, of course, to engineer a return to majority party status. But getting there requires discretion and finesse. Remembering that the US system cannot function without some degree of interparty and interbranch cooperation, minority leaders know they must be seen as something other than inveterate obstructionists. Wolfensberger (2010) calls this the "special challenge" of opposition leadership in the US – ie, knowing when to confront and when to collaborate.

Taken together, these elements of opposition in the US system still fall well short of the parliamentary ideal. Therein lies the heart of the matter. *The Madisonian and Westminster systems are organized so differently that it is problematic to judge one by the standards of the other.* This proposition becomes all the more intriguing when opposition is understood as a means to an end rather than being an end in itself. Loyal opposition adds value in Westminster systems because it enhances governmental accountability, provides a platform for alternative positions, and encourages dissent.

The fragmented Madisonian system checks these same boxes, albeit in different ways. Aggrieved parties in the US have multiple points of access to the political process. Those who take issue with a decision in the House of Representatives can attempt to block it in the Senate (which might be held by a different party). Those who don't like what Congress as a whole is doing can hope for a more sympathetic hearing, and a timely veto or two, from the president (whose party might be different from the majority in Congress). Those who are frustrated by inaction at the national level can lobby state governments, which feature their own separation of powers and party cleavages, to take up their cause. Finally, those who are unhappy with laws at the national and/or state levels of government can turn to the courts for judicial review of enactments on constitutional grounds.

The lack of party discipline presents other opportunities for dissenting voices to be heard. Internal disagreements are common in the fluid ranks of the Republican and Democratic Parties. With elections in the United States occurring on a constitutionally fixed and immutable schedule – recall that Franklin Roosevelt had to run for re-election at the height of the Second World War – a charismatic candidate or upstart movement with motivated followers can plan well in advance and wreak havoc in low-turnout primary elections and party conventions. Moreover, even when intraparty challenges fail, they often succeed in moving the needle on policy discussions as nervous incumbents shift positions to guard their ideological flanks against future attacks.

This, then, is the more holistic view of opposition politics in the United States of America. The governmental system, characterised as it is by a strong separation of powers and two-party dominance, lacks the clear accountability and logic of its parliamentary counterparts. Similarly, the concept of loyal opposition remains largely alien to most Americans and difficult to effect in practice. Yet the fact remains that the system has worked well for over two hundred years. It has generated stable government and delivered enough good policy outcomes to keep the citizenry satisfied. It has also managed to capture the spirit of opposition politics, even if that term is rarely invoked. Ironically, the same Madisonian structure that has discouraged the rise of a defined loyal opposition tradition in the US has also made it possible for the system to vent political steam and allow for minority interests to be heard.

References

Brodie, L., "The Disgraced Confederate History of the Don't Tread on Me Flag", *Washington Post*, 14 June 2023, A2

Brownstein, R., "Why One-Party Government Doesn't Last", *CNN Politics (online)*, 11 July 2017. Available at: https://www.cnn.com/2017/07/11/politics/why-one-party-government-doesnt-last/index.html

Congressional Research Service. 25 January 2019, "The Role of the House Minority Leader: An Overview", CRS Report No. L30666. Available at: https://crsreports.congress.gov/product/pdf/RL/RL30666

Ettenheim, R., and Yeip, R,. "Midterm Elections Produce More States Controlled by One Party", *Wall Street Journal (online)*, 30 November 2022. Available at: https://www.wsj.com/articles/midterm-elections-produce-more-states-controlled-by-one-party-11669785444

"Farewell Address, 19 September 1796," President George Washington, Founders Online, National Archives, https://founders.archives.gov/documents/Washington/05-20-02-0440-0002

Final Report of the Select Committee to Investigate the January 6th Attack on the US Capitol, US House of Representatives (H. Rept. 117-663), 22 December 2022. Available at: https://www.govinfo.gov/content/pkg/GPO-J6-REPORT/html-submitted/index.html

First Inaugural Address, George Washington, 30 April 1789, (SEN 1A-E1), Presidential Messages, 1789 – 1875. Records of the US Senate, Record Group 46, National Archives Building, Washington, DC.

Fisher, M., "Senate, House Control is Split. Can a Divided Government Make Progress?", *Washington Post*, 17 November 2022, A1

Green, M., "Influence Without Power: The Motives, Strategies, and Tactics of the Minority Party in the House of Representatives," prepared for panel discussion on the Role of Minority Parties in Congress. Woodrow Wilson International Center for Scholars, 15 November 2010. Available at: https://www.wilsoncenter.org/event/the-role-minority-parties-congress

Gugliota, G., "New Estimate Raises Civil War Death Toll", *New York Times*, 2 April 2012, D1

Hamilton, A., Jay, J., and Madison, J., *The Federalist Papers*, New York: Cosimo, 2006

Henderson, O., "Iowa Senate Subcommittee Advances Gadsden Flag License Plate Proposal", *RadioIowa*, 26 January 2023. Available at: https://www.radioiowa.com/2023/01/26/iowa-senate-subcommittee-advances-gadsden-flag-license-plate-proposal/

Kilgore, E., "History Suggests Democratic Trifecta Could Be Short-Lived", *Intelligencer – New York Magazine*, 20 January 2021. Available at: https://nymag.com/intelligencer/2021/01/history-suggests-democrats-trifecta-could-be-short-lived.html

Mann, T., and Ornstein N., *It's Even Worse Than It Looks: How the American Constitutional System Collided with the New Politics of Extremism*, New York: Basic Books, 2012

Opposition Responses to the State of the Union Address, 1966-Present. 2023. Senate Historical Office, US Senate. Available at: https://www.senate.gov/about/traditions-symbols/state-of-the-union-response-list.htm

Party Divisions of the House of Representatives, 1789-Present. History, Art, and Archives Division of the US House of Representatives. Available at: https://history.house.gov/Institution/Party-Divisions/Party-Divisions/. Party Divisions of the Senate. Senate Historical Office, US Senate. Available at: https://www.senate.gov/history/partydiv.htm

Party Standings in the House of Commons, Parliament of Canada. 2023. Available at: https://www.ourcommons.ca/members/en/party-standings

Peabody, B., and Nugent, J., "Toward a Unifying Theory of the Separation of Powers", *American University Law Review*, 53(1), 2003, 1-64

Political Parties, Infosheet 22. September 2022. Parliament of Australia. Available at: https://www.aph.gov.au/About_Parliament/House_of_Representatives/Powers_practice_and_procedure/00_-_Infosheets/Infosheet_22_-_Political_parties

Randall, W., *The Founders' Fortunes: How Money Shaped the Birth of America*, New York: Dutton, 2022

Ross, R., and Anderson, B., "Single-Member Districts are Not Constitutionally Required", *Constitutional Commentary*, 33(2), Summer 2018, 261-90

Schaeffer, K., "Single-Party Control in Washington is Common at the Beginning of a New Presidency, But Tends Not to Last Long," Pew Research Center, 3 February 2021. Available at: https://pewrsr.ch/39IxCxm

Sheehan, C., *The Mind of James Madison: The Legacy of Classical Republicanism,* Cambridge: Cambridge University Press, 2015

State of the Parties, UK Parliament: MPs and Lords. 2023. Available at: https://members.parliament.uk/parties/commons

Van Engen, A., *City on a Hill: A History of American Exceptionalism*, New Haven: Yale University Press, 2020

Washington, G., (1793) *George Washington Papers, Series 2, Letterbook 24, April 3, 1793 - March 3, 1797.* Library of Congress Manuscript Division. Available at: https://www.loc.gov/item/mgw2.024/

Wolfensberger, D., "Majority Rule & Minority Rights: An Introductory Essay," Congress Project Seminar: The Role of Minority Parties in Congress, The Wilson Center, 15 November 2010. Available at: https://www.wilsoncenter.org/sites/default/files/media/documents/event/minorityparties-intro.pdf

Endnotes

1   The Gadsden Flag was also used by Southern secessionists whose break with the Union precipitated the Civil War. See Brodie, "The Disgraced Confederate History of the Don't Tread on Me Flag" (2023).

2   Both terms are linked to the theme of American exceptionalism. "City Upon a Hill" is attributed to a sermon by Gov. John Winthrop in 1630, while Thomas Jefferson is credited with the first use of "Empire of Liberty" in a 1780 letter to an associate. For a modern interpretation of these concepts, see Van Engen's *City on a Hill* (2020).

3   As a political term, "trifecta" has been used most frequently to describe complete party control of the legislative and executive branches of government at the state level in the US. However, some observers also use it to analyze party support at the federal level as well. See Ettenheim and Yeip (2022), and Kilgore (2021).

4   Schaeffer (2021) and Fisher (2022) caution that periods of one-party control have not always resulted in greater legislative efficiency or presidential success. Brownstein (2017) makes the argument that voter backlash is greatest when one party is perceived to have too much power.

21

The Power of Opposition:
A Comparative Perspective

Simone Wegmann

Introduction

Oppositions are an inherent part of every democratic regime. However, how much power oppositions have varies significantly between democracies. For example, legislative organization – including the power granted to opposition actors – varies considerably between legislative chambers (see eg Garritzmann 2017; Wegmann 2022; Zubek 2021). One possible explanation of this variation is the fact that parliamentary time is scarce. Therefore, legislative chambers have resorted to constraining rules to make themselves efficient (Cox 1987). These constraining rules not only touch on governments, but also determine the power granted to opposition players. But, as these constraining rules are chosen and can be modified by legislative chambers themselves, we can observe considerable variation in legislative rules and procedures around the globe (see eg Wegmann 2022; Wegmann 2023; Zubek 2021; Garritzmann 2017; Sieberer et al. 2016; Diermeier, Prato and Vlaicu 2015; Müller and Sieberer 2014; Döring 1995a).

Despite the crucial role of oppositions for the functioning of democracy, the opposition has not been among the most prominently researched areas in political science generally, and in legislative studies in particular. Only recently have legislative scholars started to pay more attention to oppositions in democracies.[1] In this chapter, I focus on the power granted to opposition players during the policy-making process. This is not to say that granting power to opposition players during the policy-making process is the only way to increase opposition power. As Garritzmann (2017) has noted, oppositions might have other possible ways to exert influence, for example, through specific rights granting access to tools such as parliamentary questions. In this chapter, however, I will focus on the degree of power granted to opposition actors during the policy-making process.

In the following section, I first discuss the policy-making power granted to opposition players in Australia, Canada, Denmark, Finland, Germany, New Zealand, Norway, Sweden and the United Kingdom. These cases are not a completely representative sample and do not allow for conclusions regarding opposition power in democratic countries around the globe. However, they do allow for a comparison of Westminster style systems with other European parliamentary democracies. The focus here lies on a comparison with Nordic countries as well as Germany as, according to the literature, they tend to grant more power to opposition players (see eg Garritzmann 2017). In a second step, I turn to a discussion of initiation, debate, and veto power during the policy-making process in the selected countries more specifically. This more detailed description allows for a better understanding of how legislative rules and procedures are designed to grant more or less opposition power during these different stages of policy-making and how countries with similar overall power can grant strong power at different stages of policy-making. The chapter ends with a discussion about the variance in power granted to opposition players and possible implications and benefits for the functioning of parliamentary democracy.

Policy-making power of opposition players

The measure of *policy-making power of opposition players*[2] (Wegmann 2022) presented here is based on Strøm´s (1990: 42) logic of a *policy influence differential*. Accordingly, legislative rules and procedures result in a policy influence differential that indicates the relationship between power granted to the government party/parties and the power granted to opposition parties. A lower policy influence differential indicates more power for the opposition as compared with the government. Hence, from the perspective of the opposition, a low policy influence differential is desirable. Importantly, however, a low policy influence differential does not necessarily mean that the government only exerts weak power, but, that the difference between the power granted to government and opposition actors is small (i.e. the opposition enjoys very similar rights to the rights granted to government actors). Accordingly, more opposition rights and fewer government rights both might lead to a lower policy influence differential (Wegmann 2022: 3).

Most literature on legislative rules and procedures determining the policy-making process has focused on the role of the government. Nevertheless, much of this literature allows the identification of the policy influence differential and therefore assessment of the degree of power granted to opposition players (Wegmann 2022: 4). The resulting index of policy-making power of opposition players follows the three stages of policy-making – initiation, debate and veto – and includes a total of seven variables: bill introduction, agenda setting, amendments, committee structure, committee procedures, executive veto, and referendum (Wegmann 2022: 4).[3] For each of these areas, "[f]ew opportunities to take action and/or be included in the decision-making process indicates exclusionary parliamentary procedures (from the point of view of the opposition). On the contrary, many such opportunities for the opposition point to inclusive parliamentary procedures meaning more power of opposition players" (Wegmann 2022: 3). The seven variables are framed such as higher scores indicate more power granted to opposition players.

The overall index ranges from 0 (weakest power) to 1 (strongest power) and is the result of a weighted additive index based on the seven variables (Wegmann 2022: 11).

Before moving to a more detailed discussion of the power granted to opposition players during the three different stages, Figure 1 shows an overview of policy-making power of opposition players among 54 legislative lower chambers (in grey). The countries selected for further consideration are highlighted in black. Most importantly, Figure 1 shows considerable and significant variation in the power granted to opposition players during the policy-making process.[4] With a mean score of 0.59 the overall picture of policy-making power of opposition players points to intermediate power. Figure 1 also shows the majority of countries clustering around a level of policy-making power of opposition players above 0.4 and below 0.8 (see as well Wegmann 2022: 13).

Figure 1: Policy-Making Power of Opposition Players

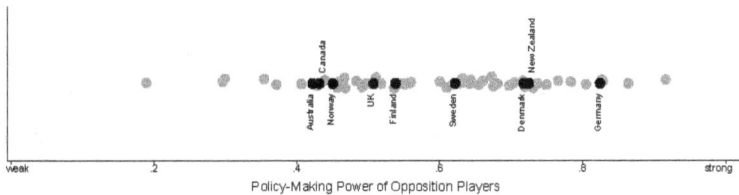

Policy-Making Power of Opposition Players

Also, Figure 1 shows a tendency of the Nordic countries to show strong opposition power and Westminster democracies scoring on the weaker end of the scale. Two exceptions here are Norway (with a score of 0.45) and New Zealand (with a score of 0.72). Importantly, however, Westminster democracies show scores below the mean, but not very weak scores. On the one hand, with the exception of New Zealand, all Westminster democracies score below 0.52 on the policy-making power of opposition players.[5] On the other hand, all Nordic countries and Germany, with the exception of Norway, score above 0.52 on the policy-making power of opposition players.[6] Overall, these results are in line with the existing literature on legislative rules and the role of oppositions in legislative chambers. For example, Garritzmann's (2017) measure of opposition power also shows stronger power for the Nordic countries and weaker (but not very weak) scores for Westminster democracies.

Other than the overall score, however, a closer look at the different dimensions of policy-making (i.e. initiation, debate, and veto power) allows for a more detailed understanding of the specific rights granted to opposition players. Therefore, in the following sections, I present each of the three dimensions separately.

Initiation power

The first dimension of the overall measure of policy-making power of opposition players considers rights to introduce bills and agenda setting. Bill introduction is captured by identifying the actors that have the right to introduce a bill (Wegmann 2022: 6). In representative democracies, this right is usually granted to individual MPs. Furthermore, especially in parliamentary democracies, the executive often dominates the right to initiate legislation (Mattson 1995: 455). At the same time, restrictions and possible veto players that might considerably reduce the right to introduce bills to opposition actors exist in many legislative chambers. The variable *bill introduction* combines both of these aspects. Consequently, strongest opposition power exists in legislative chambers in which at least one other actor than individual MPs and the executive can introduce bills without facing veto players or other numerical restrictions[7] (Wegmann 2022: 7). However, opposition players may face another potential obstacle during this first stage of policy-making. Even if parliamentary rules might grant strong power to opposition players to introduce bills, "[o]pposition bills may be stopped ... by simply keeping them off the agenda fixed by the government" (Döring 1995b: 224). Hence, *agenda setting* looks at two additional elements. First, it considers whether the government alone can decide on the plenary timetable or whether other actors, including opposition players, can decide on the plenary agenda. Second, it looks at the degree to which the government is granted priority access to the legislative agenda (Wegmann 2022: 7). Opposition actors are granted strongest power in legislatures in which the government is not granted priority access to the legislative agenda and the government does not alone decide on the plenary agenda.

Figure 2 shows the distribution of *initiation power* (ranging from 0 to 1, combining bill introduction and agenda setting power) among the 54 legislative chambers (in grey). The countries selected for this chapter are again highlighted in black. Results point towards considerable and significant variation in the degree of power granted to opposition players during this first stage of policy-making. In some legislative chambers, opposition players enjoy very strong initiation power meaning they are granted the right to introduce bills without restrictions and the government does not dominate the legislative agenda. In other chambers, however, these opposition rights are restricted considerably and the government dominates the initiation stage of policy-making.

Figure 2: Initiation Power of Opposition Players

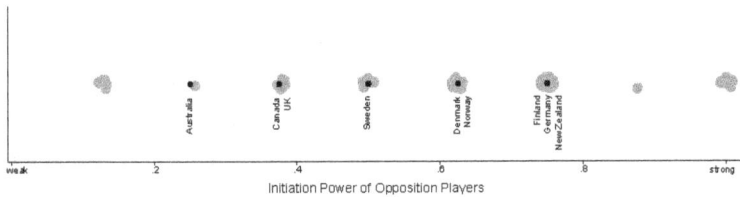

Initiation Power of Opposition Players

Taking a closer look at the selected countries shows interesting patterns. Similar to the results based on the overall index (Figure 1), Westminster democracies are located at the weaker end of the scale. However, similar to the overall index in Figure 1, they are not among the countries granting weakest power. Australia, Canada and the UK all show scores below 0.4. Again, New Zealand is the exception granting rather strong power to opposition players (a score of 0.75). In Germany and Finland, equally strong power is granted to opposition players during the initiation phase of policy-making. The result for Finland is worth mentioning here as the overall policy-making power of opposition players is at the intermediate level (with a score of 0.54). Nevertheless, as shown in Figure 2, opposition players benefit from strong initiation power in the Finnish legislature.

Debate power

The second dimension of the measure of policy-making power of opposition players considers the rights to introduce amendments as well as the committee structure and committee procedures. First, amendment power is captured similarly to bill introduction power presented above. Hence, *amendment power* is stronger the more actors including opposition players are entitled to propose amendments and the fewer numerical restrictions and potential veto players to do so exist (Wegmann 2022: 8). Second, the literature on policy-making in the legislature has largely focused on the important role of legislative committees. For example, Mattson and Strøm (1995: 249) highlight that "…much of the real deliberation of legislators takes place away from the plenary arena in much smaller groups of legislators such as legislative committees".[8] To measure the degree of power granted to opposition players based on the *committee structure*, I follow Strøm's (1990: 71) five point index including the following characteristics: the number of standing committees (more than ten to be considered strong); fixed areas of specialization that correspond to ministerial departments; restrictions on the number of possible committee assignments per MP; and a proportional distribution of committee chairs according to parliamentary parties. Finally, I measure the degree of opposition power based on *committee procedures* including the rights to include minority reports to the committee report; whether committees themselves can set their agenda or whether the government can exert influence over the committee agenda; and the right to rewrite bills (Wegmann 2022: 9).

Figure 3 shows the distribution of *debate power* (ranging from 0 to 1, combining amendment power, committee structure and procedures) among the 54 first chambers (in grey). Again, the countries selected for more detailed consideration are highlighted in black. Similar to the overall index (Figure 1) and initiation power (Figure 2), debate power varies considerably among legislative chambers. Whereas none of the chambers in Figure 2 exhibit very weak opposition debate power, in many chambers opposition players enjoy considerable power during this stage of policy-making.

Figure 3: Debate Power of Opposition Players

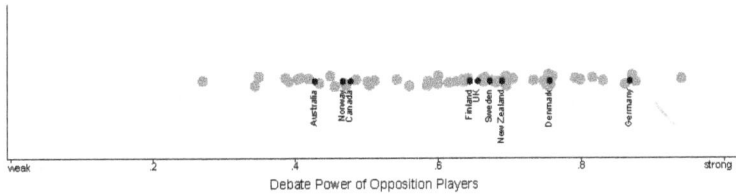

Debate Power of Opposition Players

Among the countries specifically considered here, Germany again shows the strongest power granted to opposition players and Australia the weakest. However, the clustering of Westminster democracies and the Nordic countries does not show the same pattern as with initiation power (Figure 2). Whereas Norway grants rather strong initiation power to opposition players, it grants considerably less power during the debate stage of policy-making with scores much closer to Australia and Canada than to the other Nordic countries. In the other Nordic countries (Denmark, Finland, and Sweden) opposition players are granted rather strong debate power. New Zealand and the UK show significantly stronger debate power of opposition players than the other Westminster democracies, Australia and Canada, and score much closer to Finland and Sweden.

Veto power

After successful adoption of a bill, many legislative rules specify rights of certain actors to veto such an adoption (Wegmann 2022: 10). Therefore, the final dimension of the policy-making power of opposition players considers veto power, more specifically the possibility of executive veto and decree power as well as referendum provisions. First, *executive power* considers veto and decree power, as both determine the degree to which the government is granted considerably more power than opposition players are. Regarding executive power, opposition power is considered strong if the executive has neither veto nor decree power.[9] Second, *referendums* considers whether the possibility exists to ask for a referendum and whether this right is restricted to government actors or extended to opposition players as well. The measure differentiates between no provision for referendums (constituting weak opposition power), mandatory referendums, and optional referendums. The latter is considered to grant strongest opposition power if opposition actors themselves can trigger the referendum (Wegmann 2022: 11).

Figure 4 shows the distribution of *veto power* (ranging from 0 to 1, combining executive veto and referendums) among the 54 legislative chambers (in grey). The countries selected for more detailed consideration are highlighted in black. Again, results point to considerable and significant variance of veto power granted to opposition players. But, other than the results presented above, in some legislative chambers very weak (score of 0) veto power exists whereas in some, opposition players enjoy very strong veto power (score of 1).

Figure 4: Veto Power of Opposition Players

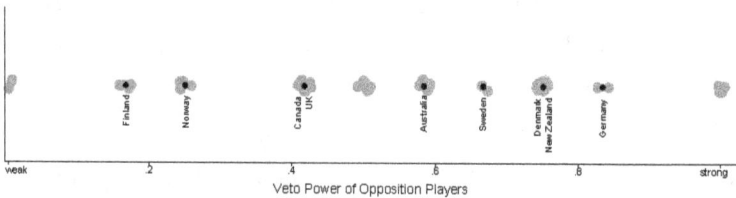

Veto Power of Opposition Players

Taking a closer look at the selected countries shows no clear pattern or clustering of countries. Germany again grants most power to opposition players during the veto stage of policy-making. However, it is not Westminster democracies that show the weakest veto power of opposition players, but two of the Nordic countries: Finland and Norway. Finland grants rather strong opposition power during the first two stages of policy-making (i.e. initiation and debate), but grants only very weak power during the last stage (i.e. veto), leading to an only intermediate overall score (see Figure 1). Norway shows a slightly different pattern: granting rather strong initiation, intermediate debate, and weak veto power (leading to an only intermediate overall score).

Extra-legislative consequences of strong opposition power

Results presented above clearly show a wide range of power granted to opposition players during the policy-making process. Policy-making power of opposition players not only differs on the overall scale (Figure 1), but countries show different degrees of power granted to opposition players during the three stages of policy-making (Figures 2 to 4). Most importantly, regime type does not seem to explain these differences. Even though, especially, parliamentary regimes are mostly represented as granting prerogatives to government, results show that the degree to which this is true varies significantly, not only among these regimes (see also Wegmann 2022, 2023), but also depending on the stage of policy-making. This is reflected among the countries specifically considered here as they show considerable variation in the degree of power granted to opposition players. Furthermore, a distinction between Westminster and other parliamentary democracies does not allow us to reliably infer the degree of power granted to opposition players.

Other than asking how to explain these differences in power granted to opposition players,[10] in this final section I address the question about potential consequences of weak and strong policy-making power of opposition players. In a first step, legislative rules and procedures determine the power granted to different actors. Hence, legislative organization significantly influences the behavior of MPs and legislative parties as it determines the room for manoeuvre of these actors (see eg Tuttnauer and Hazan 2023). This is not only true for government MPs and parties, but equally so for opposition players. The results here show that comparing the role of oppositions between different countries should also consider the specific environment (ie rules and procedures granting different degrees of power to the opposition) within which these opposition players operate.

In a second step, legislative behavior of government and opposition MPs and parties can have beneficial extra-legislative consequences. Even though the literature on oppositions in general is still young, recent research has pointed to consequences of legislative organization for the behavior of opposition players.

For example, opposition players can increase their sympathy and election results using tools such as bill introduction, parliamentary questions and legislative voting, or no-confidence motions (Däubler, Bräuninger and Brunner 2016; Williams and Indridason 2018; Marcinkiewicz and Stegmaier 2019 Williams 2011). Furthermore, research has shown that opposition behavior influences the evaluation of government parties (Seeberg 2020) and thereby also influences electoral success (Tuttnauer and Wegmann 2022).

In line with this literature, research also shows that the degree of policy-making power of opposition players can have important implications for the functioning of democracy more broadly. The way legislative chambers are organised not only influences the behavior of MPs and political parties, but also public support of the government and democracy more generally. For example, in countries granting strong policy-making power to opposition players, citizens are more likely to be satisfied with the way democracy works in their country. Most importantly, this is true for citizens that tend to be less satisfied with democracy (Wegmann 2023). However, this effect only unfolds after a certain period of democratic experience and is not present in very young democracies. Hence, strong policy-making power of opposition players might be of importance especially in more established democracies (Wegmann 2023: 160). But, to what extent it actually plays a significant role in relation to tendencies of democratic backsliding remains a question for further research.

Conclusion

In this chapter, I focused on the legislative rules and procedures that grant power to opposition players during the policy-making process. The results show descriptive evidence of considerable and significant variation in the degree of power granted to opposition players during the policy-making process. The selected countries show a wide range of powers granted to opposition players during the initiation (Figure 2) and veto (Figure 4) stage of policy-making. Several results are worth highlighting. First, with the exception of New Zealand, Westminster democracies grant weaker initiation power than the other parliamentary democracies considered in this chapter. Second, the pattern is less clear for veto power.

It is not necessarily Westminster democracies that grant the weakest veto power. Among the countries considered in this chapter, Finland and Norway show the weakest scores. Finally, the selected countries do cluster into two groups regarding debate power (Figure 3). However, this distinction does not follow the traditional one between Westminster and other parliamentary democracies for initiation power. On the one hand, New Zealand and the UK grant considerably stronger power to opposition actors than Australia and Canada. On the other hand, Norway shows considerably weaker scores than the other Nordic countries and Germany. In sum, these results clearly show that comparative studies should consider different legislative rules and procedures as they tend to vary considerably among countries. These rules and procedures grant opposition actors very different possibilities to influence the policy-making process and make it hard to compare actors without considering their specific environment within which they are embedded.

The political science literature has only recently started to explicitly focus on the role of oppositions and the consequences of their behavior for the functioning of democracy in comparative perspective. But, results of this growing research clearly show that opposition behavior in legislative chambers has both legislative and extra-legislative consequences. Implications for the functioning of democracy are significant. Even though the crucial role of the legislature for the consolidation of democracies has been highlighted in some contributions (see eg Barkan 2009; Fish 2006), the legislature – and especially the opposition – have not figured prominently in this research tradition. The influence of the strong policy-making power of opposition players on public opinion, especially in more established democracies, (Wegmann 2023) clearly shows that the opposition is not only vital during the first years of democratic consolidation, but legislative organization and the behavior of opposition players remains crucial for the stability of established democracies.

References

Barkan, J.D., "African Legislatures and the "Third Wave" of Democratization". In Barkan, J. D., (ed.), *Legislative Power in Emerging African Democracies*, CO: Lynne Rienner Publishers, 2009, 1-32

Cox, G.W., *The Efficient Secret: The Cabinet and the Development of Political Parties in Victorian England*, Cambridge: Cambridge University Press, 1987

Däubler, T., Bräuninger, T., and Brunner, M., "Is Personal Vote-Seeking Behavior Effective?", *Legislative Studies Quarterly,* 41(2), 2016, 419–444

Diermeier, D., Prato, C. and Vlaicu, R., "Procedural Choice in Majoritarian Organizations", *American Journal of Political Science* 59(4), 2015, 866–879

Döring, H., *Parliaments and Majority Rule in Western Europe*, Frankfurt: Campus Verlag, 1995a

Döring, H., "Time as a scarce resource: Government control of the agenda", in Döring, H., (ed.), *Parliaments and majority rule in Western Europe*, Frankfurt: Campus Verlag, 1995b, 223-246.

Fish, S. M., "Stronger Legislatures, Stronger Democracies", *Journal of Democracy*,1, 2006, 5-19

Garritzmann, J., "How much power do oppositions have? Comparing the opportunity structures of parliamentary oppositions in 21 democracies", *The Journal of Legislative* Studies,23(1), 2017, 1-30

Helms, L., "Political Opposition in Democratic and Authoritarian Regimes: A State-of-the-Field(s) Review", *Government and Opposition*. Online first, 2022, 1-24

Mattson, I., "Private members initiatives and amendments", in Döring, H., (ed), *Parliaments and majority rule in Western Europe*, St. Martins, 1995, 448-487.

Marcinkiewicz, K., and Stegmaier, M., "Speaking up to Stay in Parliament: The Electoral Importance of Speeches and Other Parliamentary Activities", *The Journal of Legislative Studies*, 25(4), 2019, 576–596

Müller, W. C., and Sieberer, U., "Procedures and Rules in Legislatures", in Martin, S., and Saalfeld, T., and Strøm, K. W., (eds), *The Oxford Handbook of Legislative Studies*, Oxford and New York: Oxford University Press, 2014, 312–331.

Sieberer, U., Meißner,P., Keh, J. F., and Müller, W. C., "Mapping and Explaining Parliamentary Rule Changes in Europe: A Research Program", *Legislative Studies Quarterly*, 41(1), 2016, 61–88

Siefken, S. T., and Rommetvedt, H., (eds), *Parliamentary Committees in the Policy Process*, London and New York: Routledge, 2022

Seeberg H.B., The Impact of Opposition Criticism on the Public's Evaluation of Government Competence. *Party Politics* 26 (4), 2020, 484–995.

Strøm, K., *Minority government and majority rule,* Cambridge: Cambridge University Press, 1990

Tuttnauer, O., and Wegmann, S., "Voting for Votes: Opposition Parties' Legislative Activity and Electoral Outcomes", *American Political Science Review* 116(4), 2022, 1357-1374

Tuttnauer, O., and Hazan, R.Y., "Government-Opposition Relations and the Vote of No-Confidence", *Political Studies.* Online first, 2023, 1-21

Wegmann, S., "Policy-Making Power of Oppositions Players. A Comparative Institutional Perspective", *The Journal of Legislative Studies* 28(1), 2022, 1-25

Wegmann, S., *The Power of Opposition. How Legislative Organization Influences Democratic Consolidation,* New York: Routledge, 2023

Williams, B.D., and Indridason, I.H., "Luck of the Draw? Private Members' Bills and the Electoral Connection", *Political Science Research and Methods* 6(02), 2018, 211–227

Williams, L.K., "Unsuccessful Success? Failed No-Confidence Motions, Competence Signals, and Electoral Support", *Comparative Political Studies* 44(11), 2011, 1474–1499

Zubek, R., "Committee strength in parliamentary democracies: A new index", *European Journal of Political Research* 60, 2021, 1018-1031

Endnotes

1   For an overview of this literature, see eg Helms (2022).

2   Opposition power as presented here is measured based on constitutions and rules of procedures of first chambers as of 2015 (see Wegmann 2022).

3   A more detailed discussion about how these seven areas are operationalised will follow in sections 2.1 to 2.3 and is also available in Wegmann (2022, 2023).

4   For a full list of countries and corresponding scores of policy-making power of opposition players, see Wegmann (2022).

5   Australia: 0.42; Canada: 0.43; UK: 0.51

6   Denmark: 0.72; Finland: 0.54; Germany: 0.82; Sweden: 0.62

7   Numerical restrictions exist for example if individual MPs can introduce bills but require a specific number of MPs to support the bill to do so.

8   However, more recent contributions question the central role of legislative committees for policy-making (see eg Siefken and Rommetvedt 2022).

9   In this sense, strong opposition power is not due to specific rights granted to opposition actors, but due to constraints of the executive (see Strøm, 1990: 42, on the *policy influence differential*).

10   For an analysis of the determinants of strong opposition power, see Wegmann (2022).

Contributors

Nicholas Aroney is Professor of Constitutional Law at the University of Queensland. He has published widely in constitutional law, comparative constitutional law and legal theory and has led several international research projects in these fields. His publications include *The Constitution of a Federal Commonwealth: The Making and Meaning of the Australian Constitution* (Cambridge, 2009); *The Future of Australian Federalism* (Cambridge 2012); *The Constitution of the Commonwealth of Australia: History, Principle and Interpretation* (Cambridge 2015); and *Christianity and Constitutionalism* (Oxford 2022). He is a Fellow of the Australian Academy of Law and the Academy of the Social Sciences and Co-Convenor of the Queensland Chapter of the Australian Association of Constitutional Law.

Terry Barnes has had an extensive career as a public servant, senior ministerial adviser, and consultant. He advised two Howard Government health ministers and was a chief-of-staff in the early stages of the Baillieu Government in Victoria. He is now a regular writer and media commentator on Australian politics and current affairs.

David Clune was Manager of the NSW Parliament's Research Service and the Parliament's Historian and is currently an Honorary Associate in the Department of Government and International Relations, University of Sydney. In addition to his many publications on NSW politics and history David has contributed to Connor Court's *Australian Biographical Series* writing on Jack Lang, William McKell and Neville Wran. He co-edited *The Whitlam Era* released in 2022 and was awarded the Centenary of Federation Medal in 2001 and the Order of Australia Medal in 2011.

David Docherty is President and Vice-Chancellor of Brandon University since his installation in 2019. An expert in parliamentary government in Canada, David is the author of two books, including *Mr. Smith Goes to Ottawa: Life in the House of Commons* and *Legislatures* and has written many articles and made numerous commentaries on Canadian legislatures and provincial and national politics. He holds a Bachelor of Arts in

Political Science (Honours) from Wilfrid Laurier University (1984), a Master of Arts in Political Science from McMaster University (1990) and a Doctorate in Political Science from the University of Toronto (1995).

Liz Dowd has extensive public policy and senior administrative experience, including senior leadership roles in several Commonwealth Government departments. She has worked for three Federal Ministers including serving as Chief of Staff to the Special Minister of State who is responsible for oversighting parliamentary resources. She was also involved in establishing the Commonwealth's Independent Parliamentary Expenses Authority. Liz has an MBA and a degree in Communications.

Nigel Fletcher is a Teaching Fellow in Politics and Contemporary History at King's College London and the Co-Founder of the Centre for Opposition Studies, an independent research group focussed on political opposition. His monograph on the development of the Official Opposition in the United Kingdom is due for publication by Routledge in early 2024.

Richard Herr teaches at the University of Tasmania where he manages the University's Parliamentary Internship program and, until recently, was the Academic Director of the ANZACATT Parliamentary Law, Practice and Procedure course which provides professional development for the ten Parliaments of Australasia as well as Samoa and Solomon Islands. For three decades, Richard was a television co-host for election night broadcasts and over this time also served as a media pollster.

John Howard, OM AC was Australia's second longest serving Prime Minister leading the Liberal-Country Party Coalition government (1996-2007). Howard entered the Commonwealth Parliament in 1974 and was quickly promoted in the new Fraser Coalition Government (1975-83) holding several ministerial posts before becoming Treasurer in 1977. In 1996 Howard led the Coalition to a landslide victory and went on to win three more elections before losing office in 2007. Since leaving politics John Howard completed his autobiography, *Lazurus Rising* which became a national bestseller. This was followed by his successful *The Menzies Era* which reviewed the achievements of Sir Robert Menzies, the founder of the Liberal Party and Australia's longest serving Prime Minister.

Kate Jones worked in Victorian and Commonwealth parliamentary libraries and universities as a researcher and librarian. She wrote extensively on parliamentary committees, Australian government and politics. Kate had qualifications in politics, economics and librarianship. In 2013 she published *Audit Commissions: Reviewing the Reviewers* (Connor Court). She passed away in 2015.

Kenneth Kitts is President of the University of North Alabama. Prior to taking up that role he served in various academic and administrative positions at universities in North Carolina and South Carolina. His academic interests cover the American presidency, national security and executive advisory systems. He is author of the award winning, *Presidential Commissions and National Security* and has recently contributed chapters on US presidential commissions of inquiry in recent publications covering royal commissions and public inquiries in Australia and internationally.

Graham Maddox FASSA is Emeritus Professor of Political Science at the University of New England, where he was Dean of the Faculty of Arts. He was President of the Australasian Political Studies Association in 1995-6. His books include *Political Parties in Australia* (1978) (joint author); *The Hawke Government and Labor Tradition* (1989); *Australian Democracy in Theory and Practice* (5th ed 2005); *Religion and the Rise of Democracy* (1996); *Political Writings of John Wesley* (1998); *Stepping Up to the Plate. America, and Australian Democracy* (MUP 2016). He has edited and co-edited other books on Australian republicanism, political legitimacy and cosmopolitanism.

Rob Manwaring is an Associate Professor at Flinders University in Adelaide, South Australia. Rob researches into democratic politics party politics, and public policy. He is the President of the Australian Political Science Association and is part of the editorial team for the Australian Journal of Political Science. Rob has written widely on various aspects of Australian and comparative politics, and in 2021, his book *The Politics of Social Democracy* was published with Routledge. Rob is also a regular commentator on national and South Australian politics and is a longstanding contributor on South Australian politics to the *Australian Australian Journal of Politics and History's* six-monthly Political Chronicles.

Kevin Martin has held senior positions in the Queensland Public Service in the justice area. He became Parliamentary Counsel in 1989, then was appointed Public Trustee, later Director-General, Department of Justice and Attorney General and subsequently became Adult Guardian, responsible for protecting the rights of children. Kevin served several stints as chief of staff to the leader of the Queensland Opposition. He holds Bachelor of Arts, Bachelor of Commerce and Master of Laws degrees from the University of Queensland and was admitted as a Barrister in the Supreme Court of Queensland.

Brendan McCaffrie is Senior Lecturer, School of Professional Studies UNSW Canberra, and Deputy Director of its new Public Partnerships and Impact Hub. He focuses on designing and teaching programs for the Australian Public Service, as part of the Public Partnerships and Impact Hub's mission to build capability in Australia's public sector, through meaningful, practical, bespoke academic and professional courses. His research covers political leadership, political participation and public policy and he is particularly interested in how political leadership can empower citizens at a time when trust in government is in decline. He recently co-edited *The Morrison Government: Governing through Crisis, 2019-2022* with Michelle Grattan and Chris Wallace.

Clement Mcintyre is Emeritus Professor in Politics at the University of Adelaide. He was educated at Murdoch University and the University of Cambridge and joined the University of Adelaide in 1991, where he taught European and Australian politics for 25 years and was a regular media commentator, especially on South Australian politics. From 2016 until 2018 he was the Political Officer at the Australian High Commission, where he provided analysis of British domestic politics with a special focus on Brexit.

Narelle Miragliotta is a Senior Lecturer in Australian politics in the Department of Politics and International Relations at Monash University. Before Monash, she taught at the University of Western Australia, where she obtained her PhD (politics). Narelle has broad teaching and research interests in many facets of Australian and liberal democratic political institutions, including constitutions, parliaments, political parties, and Australian elections and electoral systems.

Scott Prasser has worked in federal and state governments in senior policy and research roles and has held senior positions in academia. His recent publications include *Royal Commissions and Public Inquiries in Australia* (2nd ed 2021), *The Whitlam Era* (2022 co-edited with David Clune) and *New directions in royal commissions and public inquiries: Do we need them?* (2023). He is a graduate of the University of Queensland (BA and M Pub Admin) and Griffith University (PhD).

Benjamin Saunders is an Associate Professor at Deakin University Law School. His research interests are in constitutional law, the history of Australian federation, and law and religion. His most recent publication is *Responsible Government and the Australian Constitution: A Government for a Sovereign People* (Hart Studies in Comparative Public Law, 2023). He is a graduate of Melbourne, Deakin and Queensland universities.

Rodney Smith is Professor of Australian Politics at the University of Sydney. He has researched and written widely about NSW politics and public policy since the 1990s. His books include *Against the Machines: Minor Parties and Independents in New South Wales 1910-2006* (Federation Press, 2006) and *From Carr to Keneally: Labor in Office in NSW 1995-2011* (co-edited with David Clune, Allen and Unwin 2012).

Louise Thompson is Senior Lecturer in Politics at the University of Manchester. She specialises in the legislative process and political parties in the UK House of Commons. Louise is the author of *Making British Law* (Palgrave, 2015), *Exploring Parliament* (Oxford University Press, 2018) and *The End of the Small Party: Change UK and the Challenges of Parliamentary Politics* (Manchester University Press, 2020).

Rodney Tiffen is Emeritus Professor, Government and International Relations, University of Sydney. His publications include: *How America Compares* (2020, co-author); *Disposable Leaders. Media and Leadership Coups from Menzies to Abbott* (2017); *Rupert Murdoch. A Reassessment* (2014); *Scandals: Media, Politics and Corruption in Contemporary Australia* (1999); and *News and Power* (1989). He was Visiting Professor in Australian Studies at the University of Tokyo (1984-86); conducted three reviews of Radio Australia; was an observer of the media during South Africa's first democratic election in 1994; and worked on the Finkelstein Inquiry into Media and Media Regulation.

Finley Watson is a PhD candidate at La Trobe University and a Teaching Associate at Monash University. He is presently undertaking research on right-wing alternative media, parties and ideologies. Finley has worked as a teaching associate at La Trobe University and recently completed a Masters' degree that examined the role of interest groups in Australian politics.

Simone Wegmann is an Associate Professor of political science (especially democratic political systems) at Kiel University, Germany. In her research, she mainly focuses on the role of legislatures for democratic consolidation and the influence of legislative organization on public opinion and opposition behaviour. She is the author of *The Power of Opposition. How Legislative Organization Influences Democratic Consolidation* (Routledge 2023) in which she analysed the relationship between opposition power during the policy-making process and public support for democratic institutions.

John Williams AM is Provost at the University of Adelaide. Professor Williams holds the Dame Roma Mitchell Chair in Law. His research areas include Australian constitutional law, federalism, the High Court of Australia, Australian legal history and law reform. He is the Foundation Director of the South Australian Law Reform Institute.

Paul Williams is a political scientist and Associate Professor with the School of Humanities, Languages and Social Science at Griffith University in Brisbane. He has a special interest in Australian voter behaviour and Queensland political culture, is widely published in Australian scholarly journals, serves as the Queensland political chronicler for the *Australian Journal of Politics and History*, and is a regular commentator in the print and electronic media.

Index

216, 228, 243, 245–47, 273, 275,
277–81, 283, 294–97, 306, 322,
331, 337, 340, 361, 370, 375, 376,
378, 384, 389, 390, 395–402, 410,
413, 430, 441

legislature 8, 26, 51, 82, 88, 94,
295, 296, 302, 313, 424, 430–34,
438–43, 467, 468, 473

new zealand 138, 313, 372, 388,
421, 463, 465, 467, 469, 473

Norway 463, 465, 469, 470, 473

NSW 196–202, 204, 207, 208,
210–20, 222, 223, 225–30, 321,
476, 480

official recognition 394, 399

opposition 99, 100, 282

personnel 30, 55, 325, 381–83, 386,
442

preparation for government 104,
361

procedures 102, 209, 282, 283, 302,
324, 325, 396, 409, 410, 418, 421,
462–64, 468, 471–75

Queensland 231–68, 270–72, 274,
277–81, 283, 286–89

resources of 161, 169, 173, 174,
177, 269, 270, 282

role of 63, 73, 89, 197, 301, 337,
388, 430, 442

size of 23, 274, 378, 379, 386, 431,
434

South Australia 290–95, 297, 298,
300–303, 305, 308–12

success in winning office 311, 318,
319, 323, 324, 330, 340, 352, 353,

356, 358, 432

Sweden 25, 463, 469, 475

Tasmania 315, 316, 321, 322, 329,
335–38, 477

theory of opposition 66

united kingdom 394, 407–9, 411,
413, 415, 417, 421, 463, 477

USA 446

Victoria 339–43, 345–48, 350–52,
354–58, 360, 361, 363, 364, 366,
368–72

Western Australia 373–92

Palaszczuk, Annastacia 236, 239, 255,
256, 268, 281

Papua New Guinea 321, 336

Parkes,Henry 73, 74, 76, 77, 79–81,
84–86, 92–94

parliament
committee system 141, 209, 211,
214, 217, 329, 335, 432

executive dominance 98, 102, 330,
333

history of 372, 386, 388

legislative function 437

question time 16, 98, 170, 172, 174,
209, 212, 217, 240, 278, 286, 287,
302, 305, 325, 330, 333, 385, 389,
410, 412, 416, 418, 420, 435

scrutiny function 217, 329, 427,
432

size of 333

Pesutto, John 348–51, 355

Playford, Tom 83, 298, 305